Revising the Word and the World

Revising the Word
and the World

ESSAYS IN FEMINIST LITERARY CRITICISM

WITHDRAWI

EDITED BY

VèVè A. Clark, Ruth-Ellen B. Joeres, & Madelon Sprengnether

THE UNIVERSITY OF CHICAGO PRESS

Chicago and London

The essays in this volume originally appeared in various issues of SIGNS: JOURNAL OF WOMEN IN CULTURE AND SOCIETY. Acknowledgment of the original publication data can be found on the first page of each essay.

The University of Chicago Press, Chicago 60637
The University of Chicago Press, Ltd., London
© 1979, 1980, 1981, 1985, 1987, 1988, 1991, 1992, and 1993 by The University of Chicago
All rights reserved. Published 1993
Printed in the United States of America
97 96 95 94 93   5 4 3 2 1

Library of Congress Cataloging-in-Publication Data

Revising the word and the world : essays in feminist literary criticism / edited by VèVè Clark, Ruth-Ellen Boetcher Joeres, and Madelon Sprengnether.
    p.   cm.
    Collection of articles which appeared originally in Signs between 1979 and 1993.
    Includes bibliographical references and index.
    Contents: Audre Lorde interviewed by Adrienne Rich — Simone de Beauvoir interviewed by Alice Jardine — Carmen Naranjo interviewed by Lourdes Arizpe — Postmodernism and gender relations in feminist theory / by Jane Flax — African-American women's history and the metalanguage of race / by Evelyn Higginbotham — Critical clitoridectomy : female sexual imagery and feminist psychoanalytic theory / by Paula Bennett — No lost paradise : social gender and symbolic gender in the writings of Maxine Hong Kingston / by Leslie Rabine — The sultan and the slave : feminist orientalism and the structure of Jane Eyre / by Joyce Zonana — Dancing out the difference : cultural imperialism and Ruth St. Denis's "Radha" of 1906 / by Jane Desmond — Poetry as a strategy of power : the case of Riffian Berber women / by Terri Brint Joseph — Womanism : the dynamics of the contemporary black female novel in English / by Chikwenye Ogunyemi — Narrative of community : the identification of a genre / by Sandra Zagarell.
    ISBN 0-226-40063-8
    1. Feminist literary criticism. I. Clark, VèVè A. II. Joeres, Ruth-Ellen B., 1939– III. Sprengnether, Madelon.
PN98.W64R48   1993
809'.89287—dc20   93-10197
                                           CIP

CONTENTS

Acknowledgments

We are particularly grateful to Jeanne Barker-Nunn, the managing editor of *Signs,* who has coordinated the editing and production of this volume. We appreciate the many hours of effort that she has devoted to this project. Kim Surkan, one of our *Signs* student interns, provided a great deal of help on the initial research needed for the volume and on correspondence with the contributors. Melissa Rendler-Garcia, who was the *Signs* student assistant during 1992–93, was especially helpful in contacting the Spanish-speaking contributors to the volume.

The Editors

Revising the Word and the World

VèVè A. Clark, Ruth-Ellen B. Joeres, and Madelon Sprengnether

> At the moment of their emancipation, women have a need to write their own histories. [SIMONE DE BEAUVOIR]

WOMEN WHO TELL STORIES, women who write their own histories: these are women sounding the unspoken or the unspeakable. The personal narratives and the theoretical and critical pieces that we have assembled for this volume from issues of *Signs* that appeared between 1979 and 1993 reflect our engagement with the many ways in which women seek to represent their multiple social realities in words and thereby to change their world. In choosing to focus on women's words in various contexts of production, we have also chosen to expand what we mean by *literary criticism*. Feminist criticism of literature, which once borrowed heavily from New Criticism, has been made problematic by developments in poststructuralist, cultural-materialist, and psychoanalytic theories and has traversed the traditional boundaries of literature to include the "texts" of orature and performance. In addition, criticism may now embrace a wider range of voices, styles, and forms than the traditional academic article. We have sought to reflect these changing conditions by organizing our collection into three sections: interviews with significant feminist writers, theoretical articles, and essays that address women's words, all in a context of international and intercultural awareness. Implicit throughout is an assumption we draw from the very earliest stages of feminist criticism: that literature, broadly conceived, is a form of social action.

* * *

Expanding on Simone de Beauvoir's statement quoted above, we might say that women have a need not only to write but to tell their own histories. For that is what the personal narrative form of the oral history or the interview has enabled women to do: to provide testimony for an individual life that can thereby be emancipated and at the same time to share that testimony not only with a single other, the interviewer, but also with a larger reading audience.

For feminist literary critics, the interpretation of personal narratives (initially biographies and autobiographies, but more recently life histories and interviews as well) has offered a challenge to received ideas about what constitutes a legitimate genre for literary analysis. Autobiography has always been viewed as a boundary form, sliding between fact and fiction and hence not easily located in either; oral histories and interviews, for their part, provoked little interest among literary specialists until feminist critics, along with anthropologists, historians, and other social scientists, began the interdisciplinary investigation of personal narratives that has created a context for the field. Interest in these forms reflects the concern with self-identity that feminism tends to stress, including the need to know more about the lives of women who have been ignored or silenced, women for whom as writers such forms as biography and autobiography have been virtually inaccessible until the present century.

Ironically, feminist critical interest in personal narratives has emerged at a time when postmodernism, with its challenge to the idea of a unified self and its skepticism about the very effort to construct a self, autobiographically or otherwise, has been in sway. Yet the study of personal narratives, with its focus on the recovery of women's marginalized experiences and our wish to define our own lives, is central to feminist scholarship. We know the value of these texts not only as history, as sources of information and insights otherwise difficult to obtain, but also as evidence of the ways in which we struggle to create and to name ourselves. Social scientists who study personal narratives have taught us the importance of attending to the social, ideological, and cultural contexts revealed by these texts, to the ethical ramifications of conducting interviews, and to the personal investments of the interviewer or biographer. Those of us who are literary critics bring our own special expertise to this investigation through our concern with voice, form, style, and language. While necessarily problematic and complex, our reading of personal narratives is essential to contemporary feminist inquiry and to the expansion of the canon of feminist criticism.

The interviews with Audre Lorde, Simone de Beauvoir, and Carmen Naranjo with which we begin this volume give expression to the issues and concerns that unite the other essays we have chosen, namely an understanding of literature as a form of social action, a move away from structures of binary opposition, and an attention to cultural complexity and diversity in the feminist literary critical project. All of the interviews thematize social action and its connection to writing, but their very form suggests the sort of dialogue that removes literature from its lofty but solitary perch and subverts its claim to universal truth. Here there is an exchange: the interviewer plays an active role, as do the readers who are drawn, willy-nilly, into a conversation already begun. More effectively than any other text, perhaps, the interview draws the public into the field of its construction. The effect, first on the interviewer or compiler, then on the audience, is that of a dialogue or multilogue in which all are participants, all are involved. Furthermore, in its presentation of dialogue and the implied inclusion of others as readers, the interview as text can help to generate a desire for social change.

The very substance of the interviews presented here (despite the one-on-one nature of the interview situation) undermines structures of binary opposition. Ideas get generated and tossed about by both sides, get examined, discarded, built upon, improved, and in the excitement of this process there is a movement outward to include the audience of readers in an open and ongoing discussion. The feminist interview can also lend itself to the exploration of racial and ethnic differences and intercultural dialogue through the diversity of possible informants and the multileveled nature of the interaction between the interviewer and her subject. The interviewer begins by questioning but often finds herself unabashedly involved, revealing her connection to her informant by probing, arguing, and even, on occasion, adding her own views.

What we glean from the interviews with Lorde, Beauvoir, and Naranjo are not only the particulars of each conversation, although we learn a great deal on that level through Naranjo's exchange with Arizpe as they walk around the market square in Chichicastenango, through Lorde's talk with Rich about their mutually deep commitment to writing as survival, through Jardine's conversation with Beauvoir in the latter's apartment on a summer day in 1977. We also learn about the structure of narration, about the ways in which each woman seeks to make meaning out of the jumble of her life. We learn, in other words, as much about the process of writing and thinking and communicating as we do about what is written and communicated. We also receive a lesson in the nonlinear nature of this process in gaps, ambivalences, and contradictions. And finally we see that the interpretation of a life, whether by the literary critic, the interviewer, or the liver of the life herself, emerges through narrative strategies that hold interest for anyone engaged in textual analysis.

But it is the intimate dynamics of these texts that makes them so memorable. Audre Lorde sees herself, tells Adrienne Rich about that self, and thereby enlightens her readers. As she says, "The only thing I had to give was me. . . . That's the only thing I have to fight with, my whole life, preserving my perceptions of how things are, and later, learning to accept and correct both at the same time, and doing this in the face of tremendous opposition and cruel judgment." For Carmen Naranjo, who detects politics in everything, literature and the public dialogue implied in an interview are revolutionary activities. Unlike Lorde, she sees herself in a world in which she is clearly struggling for an identity that is, as she indicates, as bound up with issues of nationhood and politics as it is with her gender. Simone de Beauvoir sees her writing, indeed all of the activities of her life, as being "at the level of testimony." Like Naranjo, she makes the importance of concrete political action a leitmotif of her life, while Alice Jardine hears her, reacts to her, and provides a skeptical counterpoint throughout. Although two of these three interviewees are now dead, we can feel them as being alive and present through their words. These, then, are texts that teach us much about the dynamics of writing, speaking, and reading, texts that involve us, inform us, and make extremely real the nature and process of women's self-construction.

* * *

Feminist theorists reflect differently from creative writers, yet their aims are similar to those expressed by Lorde, Beauvoir, and Naranjo in their interviews. Like those writers, feminist theorists stress the need for the complexity of analysis undertaken from a variety of perspectives, including those of class and race as well as of sexual orientation. In this respect, they demonstrate some of the ways in which academic feminist criticism has changed since its founding by a group of predominantly white, middle-class women in the early 1970s. In the next sequence of essays, Jane Flax, Evelyn Brooks Higginbotham, and Paula Bennett address the areas of theory (postmodern philosophy, cultural materialism, and psychoanalysis) that have been most influential in recent feminist literary criticism. As each essay reveals, feminism introduces its own insights and goals into preexisting structures of analysis, hence altering the internal coherence of these systems as well as their effects. Feminist literary theory itself is more a process than a set of precepts. Its strategy of bringing multiple and conflicting viewpoints into conversation with one another makes it (like the interview process) inherently eclectic and dialogic.

Jane Flax situates postmodern philosophy in relation to the decline of a certain consensus among privileged white men in the West about human nature, society, and the environment that we understand today as the legacy of the Enlightenment. She defines Enlightenment philosophy less in terms of a specific set of beliefs than in its means of structuring analysis: through linear, teleological, hierarchical, holistic, or binary ways of thinking and perceiving. Such an approach to issues of social reality (including those of gender, race, and class) inevitably results in a system of dominance and subordination—a system that feminists seek to undermine.

While it offers a method of critiquing Enlightenment assumptions, postmodern philosophy does not highlight gender specifically as a concern. Nor does it focus on the material conditions of women's lives. For these reasons, Flax recommends that we maintain a critical and skeptical distance from postmodern theory itself. At the same time, postmodernism in its emphasis on the social construction of the categories of race, class, sexual orientation, and gender offers useful tools for feminist analysis. Postmodern insistence on the locatedness of every act of interpretation, on our embeddedness in a web of intellectual and social relations that we can only partially comprehend at any given moment, also reminds us of the necessity of keeping an open mind in regard to our own theoretical formulations. We must distrust the tendency within theory to suppress evidence of diversity in pursuit of neatness or coherence. "If we do our work well," Flax concludes, " 'reality' will appear even more unstable, complex, and disorderly than it does now."

Evelyn Brooks Higginbotham combines a postmodern awareness of the multiple variables in interpretation with a cultural-materialist emphasis on matters of race and class in her analysis of the social constructions of gender. She points to the solipsism in early feminist theory that assumed that gender oppression operates in the same way everywhere for everyone. While able to understand gender as a social rather than a biological category, white feminist theorists did not extend this comprehension to race. Yet race, as Higginbotham demonstrates, derives its meaning in a society from the way different groups of people are politically positioned in relation to one another within it. Only by deconstructing race as a natural and hence predetermined condition can we begin to see the myriad ways in which racialized assumptions inflect other forms of social classification. In the segregated South, as she points out, only a white woman of a certain class could aspire to the appellation *lady*. Under slavery a black woman's status as property even superseded her right to be considered a woman at all. "For black and white women," she observes, "gendered identity was reconstructed and represented in very different, indeed antagonistic, racialized contexts." Finally, the notion of race as a natural and homogeneous category suppresses the richness and heterogeneity within black experience itself. Only by understanding race as "an unstable, shifting, and strategic reconstruction" can we begin to discern the multiplicity of meanings that gender assumes in black (as well as white) women's lives.

Both Flax and Higginbotham stress the need for more flexible categories of feminist analysis along with a recognition of the situated, and hence dynamic, nature of interpretation. Paula Bennett's essay shows how this kind of critical awareness can transform the way we read classic literary and theoretical texts. Looking at Emily Dickinson's imagery through the lens of lesbian sexuality, Bennett perceives a symbolics of clitoral reference that reveals a powerful and hitherto unsuspected current of eroticism in her poetry. The tendency of earlier critics to trivialize Dickinson's fascination with small, self-contained objects (buds, seeds, berries, etc.) betrays a number of gendered assumptions regarding the importance of the domestic sphere, the sexual life of single women, and Dickinson's status as a poet. Perhaps most damaging of all is the repression of lesbianism per se in the failure to name the clitoris, women's primary organ of sexual pleasure. Bennett connects this type of literary interpretation with the construction of female sexuality in Freudian psychoanalytic theory. Feminist transformation of this construction, Bennett argues, must proceed, like her analysis of Dickinson's poetry, from a completely different base.

* * *

Feminist literary critics challenge our "memory of difference" when our readings are grounded in the specifics of culture.[1] The six essays, published between 1980 and 1993, that make up the concluding section of this volume revise the (always dubious) attraction to the Western male canon, establish dialogue across national borders with texts produced worldwide in English, and explicate gender contradictions within racial and ethnic oral and written traditions. These essays urge us to be literate beyond monocultural analyses, as we must (in social terms) move beyond monocrop production on plantations or the industrial piecework labor of women: beyond any monocultural conditions against which authors, theorists, and literary critics have struggled to have their multiple voices recorded as countermemory. In this new ideological territory, the U.S. women's movement of the seventies has had to reimagine and recommit itself—this time to global feminisms, to shared strategies for development, to different oppositional positions regarding patriarchy. Yet the

---

[1] Listeners or viewers who recognize variations in a concerto, jazz classic, popular song, or dance piece know that there is a quality of memory in our perceptions that has no name. VèVè Clark has coined the term "memory of difference" to describe this type of intertextual expertise in the performing arts and literary criticism. See VèVè A. Clark, "Performing the Memory of Difference in Afro-Caribbean Dance: Katherine Dunham's Choreography," in *History and Memory in African-American Culture*, ed. Robert O'Meally (Oxford and New York: Oxford University Press, in press); Susan Leigh Foster, *Reading Dancing: Bodies and Subjects in Contemporary American Dance* (Berkeley and Los Angeles: University of California Press, 1986), esp. 58.

consciousness underlying these international and interdisciplinary aware-
nesses has not come into being without struggle or conflict. In 1985,
13,000 Non-Governmental Organization (NGO) delegates to the United
Nations Conference for Women in Nairobi, Kenya, engaged in collaboration and contestation across nationalities, ideologies, socioeconomic
divisions, ethnicities, sexual orientations, and disciplines.[2] Through the
medium of cultural differences, that event helped to reshape feminism in
an atmosphere of exchange concerned primarily with social action, thus
helping to change the world through the word. Chikwenye Ogunyemi's
article on womanism that originally appeared in *Signs* that year reminds
us of the kinds of debates between peripheries and centers that occurred
then and that continue to circulate and evolve in a number of literature
departments today.

Creative writers, performers, and anonymous women all participate
in the progressive transformation of cultural topoi, as the essays in this
section demonstrate. Leslie Rabine points to the contradictory oral traditions among men and women upon which Maxine Hong Kingston drew
in her analysis of social and symbolic gender in *The Woman Warrior*
and *China Men*. Rabine does not confine her reading to the familiar
terms of male/female opposition but, rather, seeks to decipher the ways
that Kingston transformed the gender materials she worked with. In
Rabine's view, "Kingston violates the law of opposition, making gender
dichotomies proliferate into unresolvable gender differences," in this way
performing "a writerly liberation that also has social implications."

Such seemingly different "texts" as the novel *Jane Eyre*, the dance
"Radha" by the American choreographer and dancer Ruth St. Denis,
and the wedding songs performed by Riffian Berber women all have the
power to draw us into confrontations with cultural difference through
audience response. The orientalism represented in the narrative and choreographic structures of *Jane Eyre* and "Radha" for instance, draws on
similar strategies, as Joyce Zonana and Jane Desmond illustrate in their
respective essays. For Zonana, "Feminist orientalism is a rhetorical strategy (and a form of thought) by means of which the threat inherent in
feminist demands is neutralized and made palatable to an audience that
wishes to affirm its Occidental superiority." Similarly, Desmond ob-

---

[2] The NGO Forum in Nairobi (July 8–17, 1985) was co-convened by Dame Nita Bar-
row, Virginia Hazzard, and Alba Zazzamia as a prelude to the official United Nations
Conference for Women (July 15–26, 1985). Delegates from every region of the world,
including community activists, academics, and artists, came to celebrate the final international event of the United Nations Decade for Women and Development (1975–85),
held for the first time on the African continent. For an overview of the practical out-
comes of the decade and the forum, see Aruna Rao, ed., *Women's Studies International:
Nairobi and Beyond* (New York: Feminist Press, 1991).

serves, "We can see 'Radha' as a portrayal of Western desires and ambivalences displayed onto an orientalized, gendered body. The association between the cultural otherness of the Orient and the construction of gender in the West is the key to this linkage." Terri Joseph's investigation of the power of poetry among Riffian Berber unmarried girls demonstrates that the songs created for the marriage ceremonies of their elders master a form of public display rare in mixed-sex events, *de*form the mastery of that form through critiques of the father's control of mate selection, yet fail to *re*form the world in which these songs are set. As she concludes, "the songs may also be perceived as a mechanism which, while giving women the impression of gaining power, ultimately, supports the patriarchal system."

The construction of "narratives of community" in English beyond the boundaries of nationality and gender may be either conservative or liberatory, as demonstrated by Chikweyne Ogunyemi and Sandra Zagarell in the concluding essays. Ogunyemi examines the particulars of the writing self in African Diaspora literature, while Zagarell concentrates on nineteenth- and twentieth-century texts from the United States, Great Britain, and Ireland. Among other issues, Ogunyemi treats reader response to classics such as *Jane Eyre* from the perspective of African/ African American womanism, by which she means "a philosophy that celebrates black roots, the ideals of black life, while giving a balanced presentation of black womandom." This standpoint emerges clearly in her response to the trope of madness in *Jane Eyre* and to feminist criticism of the novel generally. "When Bronte allows Bertha, betrayed on all sides by white women—Adele's mother; her guard, Grace Poole; and her rivals for Rochester's love, especially Jane—to die as the patriarchy collapses, she creates a tragic vision of feminism for a black reader. . . . For black women who would be feminists the lesson is simple; in fighting the establishment, the black woman must not be so mad as to destroy herself with the patriarchy. The fact that this lesson has been learned by so many black women novelists partly explains their lack of enthusiasm for feminism's implied endorsement of total white control."

Sandra Zagarell's identification of a genre that she calls "the narrative of community" is expansive. Using Sarah Orne Jewett's *The Country of the Pointed Firs* and Flora Thompson's *Lark Rise* as exemplars, she defines the parameters of a literary tradition overlooked since the nineteenth century. "Narratives of community," she explains, "ignore linear development or chronological sequence and remain in one geographic place. Rather than being constructed around conflict and progress, as novels usually are, narratives of community are rooted in process. They tend to be episodic, built primarily around the continuous small-scale negotiations and daily procedures through which communities sustain themselves." Zagarell's multifaceted definition and choice of texts draw readers into writings by women (and men) whose participant/observer narrators, concerned with similar kinds of social repression, talk back. "Narrative community," according to Zagarell, "thus represents a coherent response to the social, economic, cultural, and demographic changes caused by industrialization, urbanization, and the spread of capitalism."

* * *

In their range and diversity, the interviews and essays in this collection demonstrate some of the ways in which feminist criticism has evolved through discussions on voice and subjectivity, through challenges to canonical thought, and through a bedrock of feminist concern, social action. They also show how contemporary feminist writers and theorists have moved beyond categories of binary opposition toward more differentiated views of women's multiple social realities. It is through our words, they tell us, and through our conversations with each other, that we have the power to re-create our worlds.

Interviews

Interviews

An Interview with Audre Lorde

Adrienne Rich

Audre Lorde has published seven books of poetry, most recently *Coal* (1976) and *The Black Unicorn* (1978), both published by W. W. Norton. Her *Cancer Journals*, a collection of prose, was published by Spinsters Ink in 1980. She was born in New York City, attended Hunter High School and Hunter College, received her degree as a librarian, and is a professor of English at the John Jay College of Criminal Justice in the City University of New York. She is now at work on a novel. This interview, held on August 30, 1979, was edited from three hours of tapes we made together. It was commissioned by Marilyn Hacker, the guest editor of *Woman Poet: The Northeast* (general editor, Elaine Dallman), where portions of it appear.

Montague, Massachusetts

* * *

ADRIENNE RICH: What do you mean when you say that those two

EDITORS' NOTE: *At one point in this conversation between poets, Audre Lorde says, "The only way you can head people off from using who you are against you is to be honest and open first, to talk about yourself before they talk about you." Her thought, lived out in many of the specific events she describes in this interview, fuses personal insight with political and social statement. It also brings another perspective to ideas suggested in this issue by Myra Jehlen and Martha Thompson: feminist answers can best be found by movement* toward *all points of stress and difficulty.*

[*Signs: Journal of Women in Culture and Society* 1981, vol. 6, no. 4]

essays—"Poems Are Not Luxuries"[1] and "Uses of the Erotic"[2]—are really progressions?

AUDRE LORDE: They're part of something that's not finished yet. I don't know what the rest of it is, but they're very clear progressions to me, in feeling out something that is connected also with the first piece of prose I ever wrote. The one thread I feel coming through over and over in my life is the battle to preserve my perceptions, the battle to win through and to keep them—pleasant or unpleasant, painful or whatever—

AR: And however much they were denied.

AL: And however much they were denied. And however painful some of them were. When I think of the way in which I courted punishment, the way in which I just swam into it: "If this is the only way you're going to deal with me, you're gonna have to deal with me this way."

AR: You're talking about as a young child?

AL: I'm talking about as an infant, as a very young child, over and over again throughout my life. I kept myself through feeling. I lived through it. And at such a subterranean level, I think, that I didn't know *how* to talk. I was really busy feeling out other ways of getting and giving information and whatever else I could, because talking wasn't where it was at. People were talking all around me all the time—and not either getting or giving much that was useful to them or to me, or that made sense to me at the time.

AR: And not listening to what you tried to say, if you did speak.

AL: When you asked how I began writing, I told you how poetry functioned specifically for me from the time I was very young, from nursery rhymes. When someone said to me, "How do you feel?" or "What do you think?" or asked another direct question, I would recite a poem, and somewhere in that poem would be the feeling, somewhere in it would be the piece of information. It might be a line. It might be an image. The poem was my response.

AR: Like a translation into this poem that already existed, of something you knew in a preverbal way. So the poem became your language?

AL: Yes. I remember reading in the children's room of the library, I couldn't have been past the second or third grade, but I remember the book. It was illustrated by Arthur Rackham, a book of poems. These were old books, the library in Harlem used to get the oldest books, in the

1. Audre Lorde, "Poems Are Not Luxuries," *Chrysalis: A Magazine of Female Culture*, no. 3 (1977), pp. 7–9.
2. Audre Lorde, "Uses of the Erotic: The Erotic as Power" (paper delivered at the Fourth Berkshire Conference on the History of Women, Mount Holyoke College, August 25, 1978). This piece has been published as a pamphlet by Out & Out Books, Brooklyn, N.Y., and in Laura Lederer, ed., *Take Back the Night: Women on Pornography* (New York: William Morrow & Co., 1980), pp. 295–301.

worst condition. Walter de la Mare's "The Listeners"—I will never forget that poem.

AR: Where the traveler rides up to the door of the empty house?

AL: That's right. He knocks at the door and nobody answers. " 'Is there anybody there?' he said." That poem imprinted itself on me. And finally, he's beating down the door and nobody answers, and he has a feeling that there really is somebody in there. And then he turns his horse and he says, " 'Tell them I came, and nobody answered. That I kept my word,' he said." I used to recite that poem to myself all the time. It was one of my favorites. And if you'd asked me, what is it about, I don't think I could have told you. But this was the first cause of my own writing, my need to say things I couldn't say otherwise, when I couldn't find other poems to serve.

AR: You had to make your own.

AL: There were so many complex emotions, it seemed, for which poems did not exist. I had to find a secret way to express my feelings. I used to memorize my poems. I would say them out, I didn't use to write them down. I had this long fund of poetry in my head. And I remember trying when I was in high school not to think in poems. I saw the way other people thought, and it was an amazement to me—step by step, not in bubbles up from chaos that you had to anchor with words. . . . I really do believe I learned this from my mother.

AR: Learned what from your mother?

AL: The important value of nonverbal communication, beneath language. My life depended on it. At the same time living in the world and using language. And I didn't want to have anything to do with the way she was using language. My mother had a strange way with words; if one didn't serve her or wasn't strong enough, she'd just make up another word, and then that word would enter our family language forever, and woe betide any of us who forgot it. But I think I got another message from her . . . that there was a whole powerful world of nonverbal communication and contact between people that was absolutely essential and that was what you had to learn to decipher and use. One of the reasons I had so much trouble growing up was that my parents, my mother in particular, always expected me to know what she was feeling and what she expected me to do without telling me. And I thought this was natural. But my mother would expect me to know things, whether or not she spoke them—

AR: Ignorance of the law was no excuse.

AL: That's right. It's very confusing. And eventually I learned how to acquire vital and protective information without words. My mother used to say to me, "Don't just listen like a ninny to what people say in their mouth." But then she'd proceed to say something that didn't feel right to me. You always learned from observing. You have to pick things up nonverbally because people will never tell you what you're supposed to know. You have to get it for yourself: whatever it is that you need in order to survive. And if you make a mistake you get punished for it, but that's no big thing. You become strong by doing the things you need to be strong for. This is the way genuine learning takes place. That's a very difficult way to live, but it also has served me. It's been an asset as well as a liability. When I went to high school, I found out that people really thought in different ways, perceived, puzzled out, acquired information, verbally. I had such a hard time; I never studied, I literally intuited all my teachers. That's why it was so important to get a teacher who I liked or could deal with, because I never studied, I never read my assignment, and I would get all of this stuff, what they felt, what they knew, but I missed a lot of other stuff, a lot of my own original workings.

AR: When you said you never read, you meant you never read the assignments, but you *were* reading?

AL: Yes, I was constantly reading, but not things that were assigned. And if I read things that were assigned I didn't read them the way we were supposed to. Everything was like a poem, with different curves, different levels. So I always felt that the ways I took things in were different from the ways other people took them in. I used to practice trying to think.

AR: That thing those other people presumably did. Do you remember what that was like?

AL: Yes. I had an image of trying to reach something around a corner, that it was just eluding me. The image was constantly vanishing around the corner. There was an experience I had in Mexico, when I moved to Cuernavaca . . .

AR: This was when you were about how old?

AL: I was nineteen. When I went to Mexico I felt myself just opening up, walking on the street, seeing all these dark people and the sunlight and the heat. I was in total ecstasy. And I was also terrified. I had never lived that far from New York before. I had gone to Stamford to work in the electronics factory, but that was a little trip. From Mexico City, I moved to Cuernavaca and I met Eudora and I was commuting to Mexico City for classes. In order to get to my early class I would catch a six o'clock *turismo* in the village plaza. I would come out of my house before dawn. You know, there are two volcanoes, Popocatepetl and Ixtacuhuatl. I thought they were clouds, the first time I saw them through my windows. It would be dark, and I would see the snow on top of the mountains, and the sun coming up. And when the sun crested, at a certain point, the birds would start. But because we were in the valley it would still look like night. But there would be the light of the snow. And then this incredible crescendo of birds. One morning I came over the hill and the green, wet smells came up. And then the birds, the sound of them I'd never really noticed, never *heard* birds before. I was walking down the hill and I was transfixed. It was very beautiful. I hadn't been writing all the time I was in Mexico. And the poetry was the thing I had with words, that was so important. . . . And on that hill, I had the first intimation that I could bring those two together. I could infuse words directly with what I was feeling. I didn't have to create the world I wrote about. I realized that words could tell. That there was such a thing as an emotional sentence. Until then, I would make these constructs and somewhere in there would be a nugget, like a Chinese bun, there would be a piece of nourishment, the thing I really needed, which I had to create. There on that hill, I was filled with the smell and feeling and the way it looked, filled with such beauty that I could not believe—I had always fantasized it before. I used to fantasize trees and dream forest. Until I got spectacles when I was four I thought trees were green clouds. When I read Shakespeare in high school I would get off on his gardens and Spanish moss and roses and trellises with beautiful women at rest and sun on red brick. When I was in Mexico I found out this could be a reality. And I learned that day on the mountain, that words can match that, *re*-create it.

AR: Do you think that in Mexico you were seeing a reality as extraordinary and vivid and sensual as you had been fantasizing it could be?

AL: I think so. I had always thought I had to do it in my head, make it up. I learned in Mexico that you can't even make it up unless it happens, or can happen. Where it happened first for me I don't know; I do remember stories my mother would tell us about Grenada in the West Indies, where she was born. . . . But that morning in Mexico I realized I did not have to make beauty up for the rest of my life. I remember trying to tell Eudora about this epiphany, and I didn't have the words for it. And I remember her saying, "Write a poem." When I tried to write a poem about the way I felt that morning, I could not do it, and all I had therefore was the memory that there must be a way. And that was incredibly important. I know that I came back from Mexico very very different, and much of it had to do with what I learned from Eudora and the ways in which I loved her, but more than that, it was a kind of releasing of my work, a real releasing of myself, a connection. I think probably also that I'd passed a very crucial adolescent point.

AR: Then you went back to the Lower East Side, right?

AL: Yes, I went back to living with my friend Ruth, and I began trying to get a job. I had had a year of college, but I could not function in those people's world. So I thought I could be a nurse. And I was having such a hard time getting any kind of work, I felt, well, a practical nursing license, and then I'll go back to Mexico—

AR: With my trade.

AL: Yes. But that wasn't possible either. I didn't have any money, and black women were not given practical nursing fellowships. I didn't realize it at the time, because what they said was that my eyes were too bad. But the first thing I did when I came back was to write a piece of prose about Mexico, called "La Llorona." La Llorona is a legend in that part of Mexico, around Cuernavaca. You know Cuernavaca? You know the big *barrancas*? When the rains come to the mountains, the boulders rush through the big ravines. The sound, the first rush, would start one or two days before the rains came. All the rocks tumbling down from the mountains made a voice, and the echoes would resound and it would be a sound of weeping, with the waters behind it. Modesta, a woman who lived in the house, told me the legend of La Llorona. A woman had three sons and found her husband lying in another woman's bed—it's the Medea story—and drowned her sons in the *barrancas*, drowned her children. And every year around this time she comes back to mourn the deaths. I took this story and out of a combination of ways I was feeling I wrote a story called "La Llorona." It's a story essentially of my mother and me, it was as if I had picked my mother up and put her in that place, here is this woman who kills, who wants something, the woman who consumes her children, who wants too much, but wants not because she's evil but because she wants her own life, but by now it is so distorted. . . . It was a very strange unfinished story, but the dynamic—

AR: It sounds like you were trying to pull those two pieces of your life together, your mother and what you'd learned in Mexico.

AL: Yes. You see, I didn't deal at all with how strong my mother was inside of me, but she was—nor with how involved I was. But this story is beautiful. Pieces of it are in my head where the poetry pool is—phrases and so on. I had never written prose before and I've never written any since until just now. I published it under the name "Rey Domini" in a magazine. . . .

AR: Why did you use a pseudonym?

AL: Because . . . I don't write stories. I write poetry. So I had to put it under another name.

AR: Because it was a different piece of you?

AL: That's right. I only write poetry and here is this story. But I used the name "Rey Domini," which is "Audre Lorde" in Latin.

AR: Did you really not write prose from the time of that story until a couple of years ago, when you wrote "Poems Are Not Luxuries"?

AL: I couldn't. For some reason, the more poetry I wrote, the less I felt I could write prose. Someone would ask for a book review, or, when I worked at the library, for a précis about books—it wasn't that I didn't have the skills. I knew about sentences by that time. I knew how to construct a paragraph. But communicating deep feeling in linear, solid blocks of print felt arcane, a method beyond me.

AR: But you'd been writing letters like wildfire, hadn't you?

AL: Well, I didn't write letters as such. I wrote stream of consciousness and for people who were close enough to me this would serve. My friends gave me back the letters I wrote them from Mexico—strange, those are the most formed. I remember feeling I could not focus on a thought long enough to have it from start to finish, but I could ponder a poem for days, camp out in its world.

AR: Do you think that was because you still had this idea that thinking was a mysterious process that other people did and that you had to sort of practice? That it wasn't something you just did?

AL: It was a very mysterious process for me. And it was one I had come to suspect, because I had seen so many errors committed in its name, and I had come not to respect it. On the other hand, I was also afraid of it, because there were inescapable conclusions or convictions I had come to about my own life, my own feelings that defied thought. And I wasn't going to let them go. I wasn't going to give them up. They were too precious to me. They were life to me. But I couldn't analyze or understand them, because they didn't make the kind of sense I had been taught to expect through understanding. There were things I knew and couldn't say, I couldn't talk about them, but I knew. And I couldn't understand them.

AR: In the sense of being able to take them out, analyze them, defend them?

AL: . . . write prose about them. Right. I wrote a lot of those poems you first knew me by, those poems in *The First Cities,* way back in high school. If you had asked me to talk about one of those poems, I'd have talked in the most banal ways. All I had was the sense that I had to hold on to these things and that I had to air them in some way.

AR: But they were also being transformed into language.

AL: That's right. When I wrote something that finally had it, I would say it aloud and it would come alive, become real. It would start repeating itself and I'd know, that's struck, that's true. Like a bell. Something struck true. And there the words would be.

* * *

AR: How do you feel writing connected for you with teaching?

AL: Adrienne, I know teaching is a survival technique. It is for me, and I think it is in general; and that's the only way real teaching, real learning, happens. Because I myself was learning something I needed, to continue living. And I was examining it and teaching it at the same time I was learning it. I was teaching it to myself *aloud.* And it started out at Tougaloo in a poetry workshop.

AR: You were ill when you were called to go down to Tougaloo?

AL: Yes, I felt—I had almost died.

AR: What was going on?

AL: Diane di Prima—that was 1967—she had started the Poets Press; and she said, "You know, it's time you had a book." And I said, "Well, who's going to print it?" I was going to put those poems away, because I had found I was revising too much instead of writing new poems, and that's how I found out, again through experience, that poetry is not Play-Doh. You can't take a poem and keep re-forming it. It is itself, and you have to know how to cut it, and if there's something else you want to say, that's fine. But I was repolishing and repolishing, and Diane said, "You have to print these. Put 'em out." And the Poets Press published *The First Cities.* Well, I worked on that book, getting it together, and it was going into press. . . . I had gotten the proofs back and I started repolishing again and realized, "This is going to be a book!" Putting myself on the line. People I don't even know are going to read these poems. What's going to happen? It felt very critical, and I was in an absolute blaze of activity, because things financially were so bad at home. And I went out and got a job, I was with the two kids in the daytime and worked at the library at night. Jonathan used to cry every night when I left, and I would hear his shrieks going down this long hall to the elevator. I was working nights, and I'd apprenticed myself to a stained-glass-window maker, and I was working in my mother's office, and making Christmas for my friends, and I became very ill—I had overdone it. I was too sick to get up, and Ed answered the phone. It was Galen Williams from the Poetry Center asking if I'd like to go as poet in residence to Tougaloo, a black college in Mississippi. I'd been recommended for a grant. It was Ed who said, "You have to do this." My energy was at such a low ebb that I couldn't see how—first of all, it was very frightening to me, the idea of someone responding to me as a poet. This book, by the way, hadn't even come out yet, you understand?

AR: And suddenly you were already being taken seriously by unseen people out there.

AL: That's right. In particular, I was asked to be public; to speak *as,* rather than *to.* But I felt as if I'd come back from the dead at that point, and so everything was up for grabs. I thought, hey, very good, let's see—not because I felt I could do it, I just knew it was new and different. I was terrified to go south. Then there were echoes of an old dream: I had wanted to go to Tougaloo years before. My friend Elaine and I were going to join the Freedom Riders in Jackson when we left California in 1961 to return to New York, and Elaine's mother got down on her knees in San Francisco and begged us please not to do this, that they would kill us, and we didn't do it. So going to Tougaloo in Jackson was part of the mythic—

AR: But it sounds as if earlier you had been more romantic about what going south would mean, and six years later, with two kids *and* everything that had happened in between in the south—

AL: I was scared. I thought: "I'm going." Really, it was the first thing that countered the fury and pain I felt at leaving that little boy screaming every night. It was like—all right, if I can walk out and hear that child screaming in order to go down to the library and work every night, then

I'm gonna be able at least to do something that I want to find out about. So I went.

AR: Were you scared at Tougaloo, in terms of teaching, meeting your first workshop?

AL: Yes, but it was a nurturing atmosphere. I'd lived there for two weeks. I went around really gathering people, and there were eight students who were already writing poetry. The ways in which I was on the line in Tougaloo. . . . I began to learn about courage, I began to learn to talk. But this was a small group and there was a dynamic between us. We became very close. I learned so much from listening to people. And all I knew was, the only thing I had was honesty and openness. And it was absolutely necessary for me to declare, as terrified as I was, from the very get-go as soon as we were opening to each other, to say, "The father of my children is white." And what that meant in Tougaloo to those young black people then, and to deal with it, to talk about myself openly, to deal with their hostility, their sense of disillusionment, to come past that, was very hard.

AR: It must have been particularly hard since you knew by then that the marriage was going nowhere. It's like having to defend something that was not in itself defensible.

AL: What I was defending was something that needs defense. And this almost moved it out of "I'm defending Ed because I want to live with him." It was "I'm defending this relationship because we have a right to examine it and try it." So there's Audre as the northern black poet, making contact with these young southern black people who are *not* saying, "This is what we need you for," but were telling me by who they were what they needed from me. In the poem "Black Studies"[3] a lot of that starts coming through. Tougaloo laid the foundation for that poem, that knowledge born five years later. My students needed my perception, yet my perception of their need was different from what they were saying. What they were saying aloud was, "We need strong black people"—but what they were also saying was that their ideas of what strong was had come from our oppressors and didn't jibe with their feelings at all.

It was through poetry that we began to deal with these things—formally, I knew nothing. Adrienne, I had never read a book *about* poetry! Never read a book about poetry. I picked up one day a book by Karl Shapiro—a little thin white book. I opened it and something he said made sense. It was, "Poetry doesn't make Cadillacs." That was a symbol for all the things I was—yes. So I would talk to the students, and I was learning. It was the first time I'd ever talked about writing, because always before I'd listened—part of my being inarticulate, inscrutable,

3. Audre Lorde, *New York Head Shop and Museum* (Detroit: Broadside Press, 1974), pp. 52–56.

because I didn't understand in terms of verbalization, and if I did I was too terrified to speak anyway. But at Tougaloo *we* talked about poetry. And I got the first copies of my book there at Tougaloo. I had never been in this relationship with black people before. Never. There had been a very uneasy dialogue between me and the Harlem Writers' Guild, where I felt I was tolerated but never really accepted—that I was both crazy and queer but would grow out of it all. Johnny Clarke adopted me because he really loved me, and he's a kind man, you know? And he taught me wonderful things about Africa. And he said to me, "You are a poet. You *are* a poet. I don't understand your poetry but you are a poet, you are." So I would get this underlining of me. "You're not doing what you're supposed to do, but, yes, you can do it and we totally expect you to. You are a bright and shining light. You're off on a lot of wrong turns, women, the Village, white people, all of this, but you're young yet. You'll find your way." So I would get these double messages. This kind of underlining and rejection at the same time—it reduplicated my family, you see. In my family it was: "You're a Lorde, so that makes you special and particular above anybody else in the world. But you're not our kind of Lorde, so when are you going to straighten up and act right?"

AR: And did you feel, there in the Harlem Writers' Guild, the same kind of unwritten laws that you had to figure out in order to do right?

AL: Yes, I would bring poems to read at the meetings. And hoping, well, they're gonna tell me actually what it is they want, but they never could, never did.

AR: Were there women in that group, older women?

AL: Rosa Guy was older than I, but she was still very young. I remember only one other woman, Gertrude McBride. But she came in and out of the workshop so quickly I never knew her. For the most part the men were the core. My friend Jeannie and I were members but in a slightly different position, we were in high school, you see.

AR: And so Tougaloo was an entirely different experience of working with other black writers.

AL: When I went to Tougaloo, I didn't know what to give or where it was going to come from. I knew I couldn't give what regular teachers of poetry give, nor did I want to, because they'd never served me. I couldn't give what English teachers give. The only thing I had to give was me. And I was so involved with these young people—I really loved them. I knew the emotional life of each of those students because we would have conferences, and that became inseparable from their poetry. And I would talk to them in the group about their poetry in terms of what I knew about their lives, and that there was a real connection between the two that was inseparable no matter what they'd been taught to the contrary.

I knew by the time I left Tougaloo that teaching was the work I needed to be doing, that library work—by this time I was head librarian at the Town School—being a librarian was not enough. It had been very satisfying to me. And I had a kind of stature I hadn't had before in terms of working. But from the time I went to Tougaloo and did that workshop, I knew: not only, yes, I am a poet, but also, this is the kind of work I'm going to do.

Practically all the poems in *Cables to Rage*[4] I wrote in Tougaloo. I was there for six weeks. I came back knowing that my relationship with Ed was not enough: either we were going to change it or end it. I didn't know how to end it, because there had never been any endings for me. But I had met Frances at Tougaloo, and I knew she was going to be a permanent person in my life. However, I didn't know how we were going to work it out. I'd left a piece of my heart in Tougaloo not just because of Frances but because of what my students there had taught me.

And I came back, and my students called me and said—they were all of them also in the Tougaloo choir—they were coming to New York to sing in Carnegie Hall with Duke Ellington on April 4, and I covered it for the *Clarion-Ledger,* in Jackson, so I was there, and while we were there Martin Luther King was killed.

AR: On that night?

AL: I was with the Tougaloo choir at Carnegie Hall when he was killed. They were singing "What the World Needs Now Is Love." And they interrupted it to tell us that Martin Luther King had been killed.

AR: What did people do?

AL: Duke Ellington started to cry. Honeywell, the head of the choir, said, "The only thing we can do here is finish this as a memorial." And they sang again, "What the World Needs Now Is Love." The kids were crying. The audience was crying. And then the choir stopped. They cut the rest of it short. But they sang that song and it kept reverberating. It was more than pain. The horror, the enormity of what was happening. Not just the death of King, but what it meant. I have always had the sense of Armageddon and it was much stronger in those days, the sense of living on the edge of chaos. Not just personally, but on the world level. That we were dying, that we were killing our world—that sense had always been with me. That whatever I was doing, whatever we were doing that was creative and right, functioned to hold us from going over the edge. That this was the most we could do, while we constructed some saner future. But that we were in that kind of peril. And here it was reality, in fact. Some of the poems—"Equinox" is one of them—come from then. I knew then that I had to leave the library. And it was just about this time that Yolanda took my book, *The First Cities,*[5] to Mina Shaughnessy[6] who had been her teacher, and I think she said to Mina,

4. Audre Lorde, *Cables to Rage* (London: Paul Breman, Heritage Series, 1970).

5. Audre Lorde, *The First Cities* (New York: Poets Press, 1968).

6. Mina Shaughnessy (1924–78), then director of the SEEK Writing Program at the City College, City University of New York.

"Why don't you have her teach?"—because that's the way, you know, Yolanda is.

AR: But also, Mina would have listened to that.

AL: So Yolanda came home and said, "Hey, the head of the SEEK[7] English program wants to meet you. Maybe you can get a job there." And I thought, I have to lay myself on the line. It's not going back south and being shot at, but when Mina said to me, "Teach," it was as threatening as that was. I felt at the time, I don't know how I'm gonna do it, but that's the front line for me. And I talked to Frances about this, because we'd had the Tougaloo experience, and I said, "If I could go to war, if I could pick up a gun to defend the things I believe, yes—but what am I gonna do in a classroom?" And Frances said, "You'll do just what you did at Tougaloo." And the first thing that I said to my SEEK students was, "I'm scared too."

AR: I know *I* went in there in terror. But I went in white terror: you know: now you're on the line, all your racism is going to show . . .

AL: I went in in Audre terror, black terror. I thought, I have responsibility to these students. How am I going to speak to them? How am I going to tell them what I want from them—literally, that kind of terror. I did not know how to open my mouth and be understood. And my *commadre*, Yolanda, who was also a student in the SEEK program, said, "I guess you're just going to have to talk to them the same way you talk to me because I'm one of them and you've gotten across to me." I learned every single thing in every classroom. Every single class I ever walked into was like doing it anew. Every day, every week; but that was the exciting thing.

AR: Did you teach English 1—that back-to-back course where you could be a poet—a writing teacher—and not teach grammar, and they had an English instructor to teach the grammar? That was the only way I could have started doing it either.

AL: I learned to teach grammar. And then I realized that we can't separate these two things. We have to do them together because they're integral. That's when I learned how important grammar is, that part of the understanding process is grammatical. That's how I taught myself to write prose. I kept learning and learning. I'd come into my class and say, "Guess what I found out last night. Tenses are a way of ordering the chaos around time." About grammar I learned that it was arbitrary, that it served a purpose, that it helped to form the ways we thought, that it could be freeing as well as restrictive. And I sensed again how as children we learn this, and why; it's like driving a car, once we know it we can choose to discard it or use it, but you can't know if it has useful or destructive power until you have a handle on it. It's like fear, once you

7. "Search for Education, Elevation, and Knowledge": A prebaccalaureate program in compensatory education in the City University of New York in which a number of writer-teachers participated in the 1960s and early 1970s.

put your hand on it you can use it or push i̇
things in class and dealing with what was b
me, what was going on with this insane m'
continue pretending life could be looked ᵃ
All this, every bit of it funneling into that cla̅
learning to read in school, and that was importaṅ
watch their processes. Then it got even heavier w̅
Lehmann College and was teaching a class on racism
teaching these white students how it was, the connections be̅
lives and the fury. . . .

AR: You taught a course on racism for white students at Lehmaṅ

AL: They were inaugurating a program in the education department, for these white kids going into teaching in the New York City
schools. Lehmann used to be 99 percent white, and it was these students
coming out of the education department who were going to teach black
children in the city schools. So the course was called "Race and the
Urban Situation." I had all these white students, wanting to know, "What
are we doing? Why are our kids hating us in the classroom?" I could not
believe that they did not know the most elementary level of interactions.
I would say, "When a white kid says $2 + 2 = 4$, you say 'right.' In the
same class, when a black kid stands up and says $2 + 2 = 4$, you pat him
on the back, you say, 'Hey, that's wonderful.' But what message are you
really giving? Or what happens when you walk down the street on your
way to teach? When you walk into class? Let's playact a little." And all the
fear and loathing of these young white college students would come
pouring out; it had never been addressed.

AR: They must have been mostly women, weren't they? In the education department?

AL: Yes, mostly women, and they felt like unwilling sacrifices. But I
began to feel by the end of two terms that there ought to be somebody
white doing this. It was terribly costly emotionally. I didn't have more
than one or two black students in my class. One of them dropped out
saying this wasn't right for him, and I thought, wait a minute, racism
doesn't just distort white people—what about us? What about the effects
of white racism upon the ways black people view each other? Racism
internalized? What about black teachers going into ghetto schools? And I
saw there were different problems, that were just as severe, for a black
teacher going into New York City schools after a racist, sexist education.

AR: You mean in terms of expectations?

AL: Not just in terms of expectations, but of self-image, in terms of
confusion about loyalties. In terms of identifying with the oppressor.
And I thought, who is going to start to deal with that? What do you do
about it, Audre? This was where I wanted to use my energies. Meanwhile, this is 1969, and I'm thinking, what is my place in all this? There
were two black women in the class, and I tried to talk to them about us, as

ɔmen, having to get together. The black organizations on the
ses were revving up for the spring actions. And the women said,
ɪre insane, our men need us. It was a total rejection. "No, we can't
ɪe together as women. We're black." But I had to keep trying to
ɔighten out the threads, because I knew the minute I stopped trying
ɔ straighten this shit out it was going to engulf me. So the only hope I
had was to work at it, work on all the threads. My love with Frances, Ed,
the children, teaching black students, the women.

And in '69 came the black and Puerto Rican occupation at City
College. I was dealing with the black students outside of class on the
barricades, Yolanda and I would bring over soup and blankets, and see
black women getting fucked on tables and under desks—see what went
down in those occupied buildings. And meanwhile we'd be trying to
speak to them as women, and all we'd hear is, "The revolution is here,
right?" Seeing how black women were being used and abused was
painful—putting those things together. I said, I want to teach black
students again. I went to John Jay College and discussed a course with
the dean on racism and the urban situation, and he said, Come teach it. I
taught two courses, that one and another new course I introduced to the
English department, remedial writing through creative writing. It was
confrontation teaching.

AR: John Jay was largely a police college, right?

AL: It had been a police college, but I began in 1970, after open
admissions started, and John Jay was now a four-year senior college with
a regular enrollment as well as an enrollment of City uniformed person-
nel. There were no black teachers in English or history. Most of our
incoming freshmen were black or Puerto Rican. And my demeanor was
very unthreatening.

AR:—I've seen your demeanor at John Jay and it was not unthreatening, but that was a bit later—

AL: —and also, I was a black *woman*. So then I came in and started
this course and really meant business. And it was very heavily attended.
A lot of black and white policemen registered for it. And literally, I used
to be terrified about the guns.

AR: They were wearing guns?

AL: Yes. And since open admissions made college accessible to all
high school graduates, we had cops and kids off the block in the same
class. In 1970, the Black Panthers were being murdered in Chicago.
Here we had black and white cops, and black and white kids off the
block. Most of the women were young, black, together women who had
come to college now because they'd not been able to get in before. Some
of them were SEEK students, but not all, and this was the one chance for
them. A lot of them were older; they were very street wise but they had
done very little work with themselves as black women, as black people.

They'd done it only in relation to, against, whitey. The enemy was always outside. I did that course in the same way I did all the others, which was learning as I went along, asking the hard questions, not knowing what was coming next. Very good things happened in the classes. I wish I had recorded some of it. Like the young white cop in the class saying, "Yeah, but everybody needs someone to look down on, don't they?" By then I'd learned how to talk. In my own fashion. Things weren't all concise or refined, but enough of it got through to them, their own processes would start. I came to realize that in one term that is the most you can do. There are people who can give chunks of information, perhaps, but that was not what I was about. The learning process is something you can incite, literally incite, like a riot. And then, just possibly, hopefully, it goes home, or on.

By that time the battle over the Black Studies Department had started at John Jay. And again I saw the use and abuse of women, of black people, saw how black studies was being used by the university in a really cynical fashion. A year later, I returned to the English Department. I had made a number of enemies. One of the attempts to discredit me among black students was to say I was a lesbian. Now by this time, I would have considered myself uncloseted, but I had never discussed my own poetry at John Jay, nor my sexuality. I knew, as I had always known, that the only way you can head people off from using who you are against you is to be honest and open first, to talk about yourself before they talk about you. It wasn't even courage. Speaking up was a protective mechanism for myself—like publishing "Love Poem" in *MS. Magazine* in 1971 and bringing it in and putting it up on the wall of the English department.

AR: I remember hearing you read "Love Poem" on the Upper West Side, a coffeehouse at 72d Street. It was the first time I'd heard you read it. And I think it was about that time, the early seventies. You read it. It was incredible. Like defiance. It was glorious.

AL: That's how I was feeling. I was always feeling my back against the wall, because, as bad as it is now, the idea of open lesbianism in the black community was—I mean, we've moved miles in a very short time. But in the early seventies it was totally horrible. My publisher called and literally said he didn't understand the words of "Love Poem." He said, "Now what is this all about, are you supposed to be a man?" And he was a poet! And I said, "No, I'm loving a woman."

AR: Well, don't tell me that your publisher had never heard of lesbians.

AL: I'm sure he had, but the idea that *I'd* write a poem—

AR: —That one of his poets in the Broadside Series—

AL: That's right. And he was a sensitive man. He was a poet.

AR: But he did print your work.

AL: Yes, he did. But he didn't print that poem, the first time around. "Love Poem" was supposed to have been in *From a Land Where Other People Live.*[8]

AR: And it wasn't published in that book? You took it out?

AL: Yes. He didn't want it. There was another—was it "American Cancer Society"?—that belonged in *From a Land.* But when you heard me read "Love Poem," I had already made up my mind that I wasn't going to be worrying any more over who knows and who doesn't know that I have always loved women. One thing has always kept me going— and it's not really courage or bravery, unless that's what courage or bravery is made up of—is a sense that there are so many ways in which I'm vulnerable and cannot help but be vulnerable, I'm not going to be vulnerable by putting weapons of silence in my enemies' hands. Being a lesbian in the black community, or even being woman-identified, is difficult and dangerous.

When a people share a common oppression, certain kinds of skills and joint defenses are developed. And if you survive you survive because those skills and defenses have worked. When you come into conflict over other existing differences, there already is an additional vulnerability to each other which is desperate and very deep. And that is, for example, what happens between black men and women, because we have certain weapons we have perfected together that white women and men have not shared. I said this to someone, and she said, very rightly, the same thing exists within the Jewish community between Jewish men and Jewish women. I think the oppression is different, therefore the need for connection is on a different level, but the same mechanism of vulnerability exists. When you share a common oppression you have certain additional weapons against each other, because you've forged them in secret together against a common enemy. It's a fear that I'm still not free of and that I remember all the time when I deal with other black women: the fear of the excomrade.

* * *

AR: In "Poems Are Not Luxuries," you wrote: "The white fathers told us, 'I think therefore I am,' and the black mothers in each of us—the poets—whisper in our dreams, 'I feel therefore I can be free.'" I've heard it remarked that here you are simply restating the old stereotype of the rational white male and the emotional dark female. I believe you were saying something very different, but could you talk a little about that?

AL: There are a couple of things. I have heard that accusation, that

8. Audre Lorde, *From a Land Where Other People Live* (Detroit: Broadside Press, 1973).

I'm contributing to the stereotype, that I'm saying the province of intelligence and rationality belongs to the white male. But that is like—if you're traveling a road that begins nowhere and ends nowhere, the ownership of that road is meaningless. If you have no land out of which the road comes, no place that road goes to, geographically, no goal, then the existence of that road is totally meaningless. So leaving rationality to the white man is like leaving to him a piece of that road that begins nowhere and ends nowhere. When I talk about the black mothers in each of us, the poets, I don't mean the black mothers in each of us who are called poets, I mean the black mother—

AR: Who *is* the poet?

AL: The black mother who is the poet in every one of us. Now when males, or patriarchal thinking whether it's male or female, reject that combination then we're truncated. Rationality is not unnecessary. It serves the chaos of knowledge. It serves feeling. It serves to get from some place to some place. If you don't honor those places then the road is meaningless. Too often, that's what happens with intellect and rationality and that circular, academic, analytic thinking. But ultimately, I don't see feel/think as a dichotomy. I see them as a choice of ways and combinations.

AR: Which we are constantly making. We don't make it once and for all. We constantly have to be making it, depending on where we are, over and over.

AL: But I do think that we have been taught to think, to codify information in certain old ways, to learn, to understand in certain ways. The possible shapes of what has not been before exist only in that back place, where we keep those unnamed, untamed longings for something different and beyond what is now called possible, to which our analysis and our understanding can only build roads. But we have been taught to deny those fruitful areas of ourselves which exist in every human being. I personally believe that those black mothers exist more in women; yet that is the name for a humanity that men are not without. But they have taken a position against that piece of themselves, and it is a world position, a position throughout time. And I've said this to you before, Adrienne, I feel that we're evolving. In terms of a species—

AR: That women are evolving—

AL: Yes, that the human race is evolving through women. That it's not by accident that there are more and more women, the—this sounds crazy, doesn't it—the production of women, women being born, women surviving. . . . And we've got to take that promise of new power seriously, or we'll make the same mistakes all over again. Unless we learn the lessons of the black mothers in each of us, whether we are black or not—I believe this exists in men also but they choose to eschew it, not to deal with it. Which is, as I learned, their right of choice. Hopefully this choice can be affected, but I don't know. I don't believe this shift from conquering problems to experiencing life is a one-generational shot or a single investment. I believe it's a whole signature which you try to set in motion and have some input into. But I'm not saying that women don't think or analyze. Or that white does not feel. I'm saying that we must amalgamate the two, never close our eyes to the terror, the chaos which is black which is creative which is female which is dark which is rejected which is messy which is—

AR: Sinister—

AL: Sinister, smelly, erotic, confused, upsetting—

AR: I think we have to keep using and affirming a vocabulary that has been used negatively and pejoratively. And I assume that's the statement you're making in that sentence, that you make over and over in your poetry. And it's nothing as simplistic as saying "black is beautiful," either.

AL: There's nothing beautiful about a black machine. You know, Adrienne, when I was in high school, I was trying to get a poem about love published in the school magazine. The editor of the magazine was named Reneé—she was very intelligent, very grown-up, very beautiful. And Renée said to me, softening her rejection of my poem, "After all, Audre, you don't want to be a sensualist poet." That, obviously, was something you're not supposed to be.

AR: I was told, as a poet, you're not supposed to be angry, you're not supposed to be personal.

AL: After I published "Uses of the Erotic," a number of women who read it said that this is antifeminist, that the use of the erotic as a guide is—

AR: Antifeminist?

AL: Is reducing us once again to the unseen, the unusable. That in writing it I am returning us to a place of total intuition without insight.

AR: And yet, in that essay you're talking about work and power—about two of the most political things that exist.

AL: Yes, but what they see is—and I address this at the very beginning: I try to say that the erotic has been used against us, even the word itself, so often, that we have been taught to suspect what is deepest in ourselves, and that is the way we learn to testify against ourselves, against our feelings. When we talk about racism or nationalism we can see it. When we're talking in terms of our lives and survival as women, we don't. The way you get people to testify against themselves is not constantly to have police tactics and oppressive techniques. What you do is to build it in, so people learn to distrust everything in themselves that has not been sanctioned, to reject what is most creative in themselves—to have *them* reject it to begin with, so you don't even need to stamp it out. A black woman devaluating another black woman's work. The black women buying that hot comb and putting it in my locker at the library. It wasn't even black men, it was black women testifying against ourselves.

This turning away from the erotic on the part of some of our best minds, our most creative and analytic women, is disturbing and destructive, and should be countered. Because we cannot fight old power in old power terms. The only way we can do it is by creating another whole structure that touches every aspect of our existence.

AR: And as you were saying about courses, black studies, women's studies: this is not just a question of being "allowed" to have our history or literature or theory in the old power framework. It is every minute of our lives, from our dreams to getting up and brushing our teeth to when we go to teach—

AL: There are different choices facing black and white women in life, certain specifically different pitfalls surrounding us because of our experiences, our color. Not only are some of the problems that face us dissimilar, but some of the entrapments and the weapons used to neutralize us are not the same. For instance, being used against another oppressed group is not something that exists for white women in the same way as it does for black women. It's very easy for black women to be used against black men, not because they're men but because they're black. And we have to be able to separate the oppressor's needs from our legitimate conflict of interests at any time. Another example, for white women, is the pitfall of being invited to join the oppressor in his oppressing.

AR: The invitation to inclusion . . .

AL: Yes. The apparent invitation to power. It's not something that exists on a real level for black women. The closest face is tokenism, but that is not an invitation to power. We are never invited to join the real power, that's understood, simply because we *are* black, and that would mean having to accommodate visible, constant difference. White women can be more easily ignored, assimilated, or explained away.

AR: I wish we could explore this more—about you and me, but also in general. I think it needs to be talked about, written about: the differences in alternatives or choices we are offered as black and white women. There is a danger of seeing it in an all-or-nothing way. I think it's a very complex thing. White women are constantly offered choices, or the appearance of choices. But also real choices that are undeniable. We don't always perceive the difference between the two.

AL: Adrienne, in my journals I have a lot of pieces of conversations that I'm having with you in my head. I'll be having a conversation with you and I'll put it in my journal because stereotypically or symbolically these conversations occur in a space of black woman/white woman, where it's beyond Adrienne and Audre, almost as if we're two voices.

AR: You mean the conversations you have in your head and your journal, or the conversations we're having on this earth?

AL: The conversations that exist in my head that I put in the journal. This piece, I think, is one of them—about the different pitfalls. I've never forgotten the impatience in your voice that time on the telephone—when you said, "It's not enough to say to me that you intuit it." Do you remember? I will never forget that. Even at the same time that I understood what you meant, I felt a total wipeout of my modus, my way of perceiving and formulating.

AR: Yes, but it's not a wipeout of your modus. Because I don't think my modus is unintuitive, right? And one of the crosses I've borne all my life is being told that I'm rational, logical, cool—I am not cool, and I'm not rational and logical in that icy sense. But there's a way in which, trying to translate from your experience to mine, I do need to hear chapter and verse from time to time. I'm afraid of it all slipping away into: "Ah, yes, I understand you." You remember, that telephone conversation was in connection with the essay I was writing on feminism and racism. I was trying to say to you, don't let's let this evolve into "You don't understand me" or "I can't understand you" or "Yes, of course we understand each other because we love each other." That's bullshit. So if I ask for documentation, it's because I take seriously the spaces between us that difference has created, that racism has created. There are times when I simply cannot assume that I know what you know, unless you show me what you mean.

AL: But I'm used to associating a *request* for documentation as a questioning of my perceptions, an attempt to devalue what I'm in the process of discovering.

AR: It's not. Help me to perceive what you perceive. That's what I'm trying to say to you.

AL: But documentation does not help one perceive, at best it only analyzes the perception. At worst, it provides a screen by which to avoid concentrating on the core revelation, following it down to how it feels. Again, knowledge and understanding. They can function in concert, but they don't replace each other. But I'm not rejecting your need for documentation.

AR: And in fact, I feel you've been giving it to me, in your poems always, and most recently in the long prose piece you've been writing, and in talks we've been having. I don't feel the absence of it now.

AL: Don't forget I'm a librarian. I became a librarian because I really believed I would gain tools for ordering and analyzing information. I couldn't know everything in the world, but I thought I would gain tools for learning it. But that was of limited value. I can document the road to Abomey for you, and true, you might not get there without that information. I can respect what you're saying. But once you get there, only you know why, what you came for, as you search for it and perhaps find it.

So at certain stages that request for documentation is a blinder, a questioning of my perceptions. Someone once said to me that I hadn't documented the goddess in Africa, the woman bond that moves throughout *The Black Unicorn*. I had to laugh. I told her, "I'm a poet, not a historian. I've shared my knowledge, I hope. Now you go document it, if you wish."

I don't know about you, Adrienne, but I have a difficult enough time making my perceptions verbal, tapping that deep place, forming that handle, and documentation at that point is often useless. Perceptions precede analysis just as visions precede action or accomplishments. It's like getting a poem—

That's the only thing I have to fight with, my whole life, preserving my perceptions of how things are, and later, learning to accept and correct both at the same time, and doing this in the face of tremendous opposition and cruel judgment. And I spent a long period of time questioning my perceptions and my first interior knowledge, not dealing with them, being tripped by them.

AR: Well, I think that there's another element in all this between us. Certainly in that particular conversation on the telephone where I said, you have to tell me chapter and verse. I've had great resistance to some of your perceptions. They can be very painful to me. Perceptions about what goes on between us, what goes on between black and white people, what goes on between black and white women. So, it's not that I can just accept your perceptions unblinkingly. Some of them are very hard for me. But I don't want to deny them. I know I can't afford to. I may have to take a long hard look and say, Is this something I can use? What do I do with this?—try to stand back and not become immersed in what you so forcefully are pronouncing. So there's a piece of me that wants to resist wholly, and a piece that wants to accept wholly, and there's some place in between where I have to find my own ground. What I can't afford is either to wipe out your perceptions, or to pretend I understand you when I don't. And then, if it's a question of racism—and I don't mean just the overt violence out there but also all the differences in our ways of seeing—there's always the question: How do I use this? What do I do about it?

AL: "How much of this truth can I bear to see / and still live / unblinded? How much of this pain / can I use?"[9] What holds us all back is being unable to ask that crucial question, that essential step deflected. You know the piece I wrote for *The Black Scholar*?[10] The piece was useful, but limitedly so because I didn't ask some essential question. And not having asked myself that question, not having realized that it *was* a question, I was deflecting a lot of energy in that piece. I kept reading it over, thinking, this isn't quite what it should be. I thought at the time I was holding back because it would be totally unacceptable in *The Black*

9. From "Need," in the special issue, "Third World Women: The Politics of Being Other," *Heresies: A Feminist Publication* 2, no. 4 (1979): 112–13.

10. Audre Lorde, "Scratching the Surface: Some Notes on Barriers to Women and Loving," *Black Scholar* 9, no. 7 (1978): 31–36.

Scholar. That wasn't it really. I was holding back because I had not asked *myself* the question: Why is women loving women so threatening to black men, unless they want to assume the white male position? It was a question of how much I could bear, and of not realizing I could bear more than I thought I could at the time. It was also a question of how could I use that perception other than just in rage or destruction.

AR: Speaking of rage and destruction, what do you really mean by the first five lines of "Power"?[11]

AL: "The difference between poetry / and rhetoric / is being / ready to kill yourself / instead of your children." What was I feeling? I was very involved in a case—

AR: The white policeman who shot the black child and was acquitted. We had lunch around the time you were writing that poem and you were full of it.

AL: I was driving in the car, and heard the news on the radio—that the cop had been acquitted. I was really sickening with fury, and I decided to pull over and just jot some things down in my notebook to enable me to cross town without an accident, to continue functioning because I felt so sick and so enraged. And I wrote those lines down—I was just writing, and that poem came out without craft, that's probably why I was talking to you about it, because I didn't feel it was really a poem. I was thinking that the killer had been a student at John Jay and that I might have seen him in the hall, that I might see him again. What was retribution? What could have been done? There was one black woman on the jury. It could have been me. Now I am here teaching in John Jay College. Do I kill him? What is my effective role? Would I kill her in the same way—the black woman on the jury. What kind of strength did she, would I, have at the point of deciding to take a position—

AR: Against eleven white men . . .

AL: . . . That archaic fear of the total reality of a power that is not on your terms. There is the jury, white male power, white male structures, how do you take a position against them? How do you reach down into threatening difference without being killed or killing? How do you deal with things you believe, live them not as theory, not even as emotion, but right on the line of action and effect and change? All of those things were riding in on that poem. But I had no sense, no understanding at the time, of the connections, just that I *was* that woman. And that to put myself on the line to do what had to be done at any place and time was so difficult, yet absolutely crucial, and not to do so was the most awful death. And putting yourself on the line is like killing a piece of yourself, in the sense that you have to kill, end, destroy something familiar and

11. In Audre Lorde, *The Black Unicorn* (New York: W. W. Norton & Co., 1978), pp. 108–10.

dependable, so that something new can come, in ourselves, in our world. And that sense of writing at the edge, out of urgency, not because you choose it but because you have to, that sense of survival—that's what the poem is out of, as well as the pain of my son's death over and over. Once you live any piece of your vision it opens you to a constant onslaught. Of necessities, of horrors, but of wonders too, of possibilities.

AR: I was going to say, tell it on the other side.

AL: Of wonders, absolute wonders, possibilities, like meteor showers all the time, bombardment, constant connections. And then, trying to separate what is useful for survival from what is distorted, destructive to self.

AR: There's so much with which that has to be done—rejecting the distortions, keeping what we can use. Even in work created by people we admire intensely.

AL: Yes, a commitment to being selectively open. I had to do that with my physical survival. How am I going to live with cancer and not succumb to it in the many ways that I could? What do I have to do? And coming up against: There's no one to tell you even possibilities. In the hospital I kept thinking, let's see, there's got to be someone somewhere, a black lesbian feminist with cancer, how'd she handle it? Then I realized, hey, honey, you are *it*, for now. I read all of those books and then I realized, no one can tell me how to do it. I have to pick and choose, see what feels right. Determination, poetry—well that's all in the work.

AR: I'm thinking about when you had just had the first biopsy, in 1977, and we were both supposed to speak on a panel in Chicago. On "The Transformation of Silence into Language and Action." And you said there was no way you were going to the MLA—remember? That you couldn't do it, you didn't need to do it, that doing it could not mean anything important to you. But in fact you went out there and said what you said, and it was for yourself but not only for yourself.[12]

AL: You said, why don't you tell them about what you've just been through? That's what you said. And I started saying, now that doesn't have anything to do with the panel. And as I said that I felt the words "silence." "Transformation." I hadn't spoken about this experience. . . . This is silence. . . . Can I transform this? Is there any connection? Most of all, how do I share it? And that's how a setting down became clear on paper, as if the connections became clear in the setting down. That paper and "A Litany for Survival"[13] came about at the same time. I had the feeling, probably a body sense, that life was never going to be the same. If not now, eventually, this was something I would have to face, if not cancer, then somehow, I would have to examine the terms and means as well as the whys of my survival—and in the face of alteration.

12. See "The Transformation of Silence into Language and Action," *Sinister Wisdom* 6 (1978): 11–15.

13. Lorde, *The Black Unicorn*, p. 31.

So much of the work I did, I did before I knew consciously that I had cancer. Questions of death and dying, dealing with power and strength, the sense of "What am I paying for?" that I wrote about in that paper, were crucial to me a year later. "Uses of the Erotic" was written four weeks before I found out I had breast cancer, in 1978.

AR: Again, it's like what you were saying before, about making the poems that didn't exist, that you needed to have exist.

AL: The existence of that paper enabled me to pick up and go to Houston and California, it enabled me to start working again. I don't know when I'd have been able to write again, if I hadn't had those words. Do you realize, we've come full circle, because that is where knowing and understanding mesh. What understanding begins to do is to make knowledge available for use, and that's the urgency, that's the push, that's the drive. I don't know how I wrote the long prose piece I have just finished, but I just knew that I had to do it.

AR: That you had to understand what you knew and also make it available to others?

AL: That's right. Inseparable process now. But for me, I had to know I knew it first—I had to feel.

An Interview with Simone de Beauvoir

Alice Jardine

We have begun to hear echoes of certain "new French feminisms" on this side of the Atlantic:[1] Translations and studies of the works of such theorists as Hélène Cixous, Luce Irigaray, and Julia Kristeva are appearing with increasing frequency. In the midst of these new, diverse, and complex voices, Simone de Beauvoir continues to speak out for an activist, Marxian feminism that opposes various "theories of the feminine" developed by French women in the wake of Lacanian and Derridian epistemologies.[2]

For the American feminist, *The Second Sex* (1949) remains one of the single most important studies on women. In spite of caveats concerning Beauvoir's affiliation with Sartre and her adherence to existentialism, for example, American feminists are in basic agreement with her analysis of the female condition, her emphasis on language as social communication, and her belief in the possibilities of a revolution in the existing order. In France, however, linguistic, psychoanalytic, and philosophical interrogations during the last two decades have placed the emphasis elsewhere: on the decentered subject, the unconscious, and on language as the essential force which orders our perceptions of "history" and "reality." "Woman" is no longer that biological being opposed to "man," but something else—"*she* is elsewhere." In a sense, "woman" has become a metaphor for everything that escapes and defies Western monological thought. These new emphases might well seem incompatible with

---

1. See Elaine Marks and Isabelle de Courtivron, eds., *New French Feminisms* (Amherst: University of Massachusetts Press, 1979).

2. Simone de Beauvoir and other feminists (including Christine Delphy and Monique Wittig) have started a journal, *Questions féministes,* designed to speak directly to these issues. An English language edition, *Feminist Issues,* will appear soon in the United States.

[*Signs: Journal of Women in Culture and Society* 1979, vol. 5, no. 2]

38   Jardine

feminism as defined by Beauvoir and other feminists in both France and
the United States.

As an American feminist working in contemporary French
theory—a problematic position further complicated by my personal admiration for Beauvoir—I felt it increasingly important to elicit her reactions to some of the issues which mark the new feminisms in France.
From our first conversation in 1973, it became clear that Beauvoir had
not essentially changed her position since *The Second Sex*. Although I
sensed a certain hesitation or ambivalence in her conception of women's
relationship to language and literature, her attitude to those who posit
woman as "elsewhere" remains strong and unflinching. The interview
which follows took place at Simone de Beauvoir's apartment on June 2,
1977.[3]

French Department
Columbia University

* * * *

A.J.: To begin with, what is your present relationship to the wom-
en's movement in France? Are there any groups which you consider
particularly important? How effective is the Mouvement de libération
des femmes [MLF] today?[4]

S.B.: That's a very difficult question, because there are major rifts,
great debates within the MLF. There is a group called Psychanalyse et
politique, which is involved at present in a libel suit against the women
whom they published, women who weren't happy with the conditions of
publication.[5] I am absolutely on the side of those women, the ones who
have been called revolutionary or radical, and most decidedly opposed
to Psych et po, which has turned out to be a very capitalist group. The
group uses its own money to do something which is useful—to publish
women's books and to try to have a women's newspaper. Nonetheless,
because it is rich, it is also exploitative. Unfortunately, the other side is
divided. But I would say that right now the most important groups are
those working on the issues of rape and battered wives. You know,
despite the enormous effort that was made for abortion, very little was
gained. So, given the everyday concrete resistance which always exists,
the attempt to get to women who have been raped, to help them not to
feel humiliated, to help them see that it's necessary to talk about it, and

3. This interview is part of a larger project funded by the National Endowment for
the Humanities. Ellen Evans translated from the French.
4. For two overviews of the women's movement(s) in France, see Elaine Marks,
"Women and Literature in France," *Signs: Journal of Women in Culture and Society* 4, no. 2
(Summer 1978): 832–42; Carolyn Burke, "Report from Paris: Women's Writing and the
Women's Movement," ibid., pp. 843–55.
5. See Burke for a discussion of the group, Psychoanalysis and Politics.

then to attack the rapists, and so forth . . . this is all extremely important. Perhaps the battered wives are even more important. We are trying to provide a shelter for them, but it's been very difficult because we still haven't found appropriate space. I work a great deal with these groups; I'm the director of the League for Women's Rights, which is essentially concerned with battered wives. There are a lot of committed militants who are working on this problem. I haven't done most of the work; my work is either at the level of testimony, a declaration, an article, or something like that, but I'm not associated with any particular group.

A.J.: And Choisir?[6]

S.B.: I left Choisir a long time ago, for a number of reasons. I think Choisir is in trouble. It may be breaking up, because of problems of authoritarianism. In any event, the last news I had was that there was major dissent at the heart of the group.

A.J.: And politically? Are you actively involved in protests against the government, for example?

S.B.: Not much, because not much is possible—of course, there are always petitions, signatures, conversations with people, with the opposition. Things like that. But, at the moment, there essentially is no left—I mean the extreme left, not the socialists or the communists. In any case, there's nothing very organized. I am in contact with them, but I don't have responsibilities there either, or any particular duties.

A.J.: To come back to the feminist movement. . . . As we said, there are great divisions. Proper strategy, marginality, Marxism—there's a whole gamut of controversies. And there is always a certain feminism which is quite easily co-opted, as your interview with Betty Friedan has shown.[7]

S.B.: Yes, that "we want to be just like men," that is, men as they are today, when in truth we need to change the society itself, men as well as women, to change everything. It is very striking in Betty Friedan: What she wants is for women to have as much power as men do. Obviously, if you are truly on the left, if you reject ideas of power and hierarchy, what you want is equality. Otherwise, it won't work at all.

A.J.: On the other hand, there are women who work on the margins of the society—as Marxists or not—who work toward a subversion, an explosion of the dominant ideology. How do you see the function of marginality in the movement?

S.B.: That again is a difficult point. But I wouldn't call it that. . . . I reject the word marginality. I would rather say revolutionary, radical, whatever.

A.J.: All right, then, do you believe that one must remain "radical" or that one must work with women who are, if you like, in the system?

6. The group Choisir grew out of the effort for an abortion law in France.

7. Betty Friedan, "A Dialogue with Simone de Beauvoir," *It Changed My Life: Writings on the Women's Movement* (New York: Random House, 1976), pp. 304–16.

S.B.: I wouldn't put the question exactly that way, but it's true that this is one of the problems which often arises among my radical, revolutionary feminist friends: Do you have to join the system or not? On the one hand, if you don't, you risk being ineffectual. But if you do, from that moment on, you place your feminism at the service of a system which you want to take apart; because for me and my friends at least, feminism is one way of attacking society as it now exists. Therefore, it's a revolutionary movement . . . which is different from the class struggle movement, the proletarian movement, but which is a movement which must be leftist. By that I mean at the extreme left, a movement working to overthrow the whole society. Besides, if women really did have complete equality with men, society would be completely overturned. For instance, there is the problem of unpaid labor, such as housework, which represents millions and millions of unsalaried work hours and on which masculine society is firmly based. To put an end to this would be to send the present-day capitalist system flying in a single blow. Only we can't do it by ourselves; there have to be other kinds of attacks on the system. So a certain alliance with revolutionary systems is necessary, even masculine ones. But this is very hard, because most feminists in France came to feminism after '68 as a result of the hypocrisy they experienced in leftist movements. In these movements, where everyone believed there was going to be true equality, fraternity between men and women, and that together they were going to struggle against this rotten society, even there they noticed that the leftists, the militants, kept them "in their place." Women made the coffee while the others did the talking; they were the ones who typed the letters. So this is certainly a very tricky point: How to ally yourself to other leftist forces without losing your feminist specificity. For example, there are women who work for leftist newspapers, like *Libération,* a newspaper for which I have a certain sympathy, despite some reservations. Anyway, these women felt crushed, as women, whatever other good work they were doing, so about two years ago they were successful in shifting the newspaper to a much more feminist perspective. And about accepting positions? Well, if you accept certain situations, you become a token. "Ah, you see there is a Miss So-and-so who was first in her class at the École polytechnique; Madam X has such and such a position; therefore, women are the equals of men." This is obviously completely false, because there are always some exceptions, some women who make it for one reason or another. That doesn't mean that, on the whole, women's position is equal to that of men. So it all depends on the particular case. Sometimes you can accept an important post, on condition that it really puts you in a position to help women. Unfortunately, women who have important posts very often adopt masculine standards—power, ambition, personal success—and cut themselves off from other women. On the other hand, to refuse everything, to say, even when there is something which really should be done, "Ah, that's no longer feminist," is a pessimistic, even masochistic tendency in women, the result of having been habituated to inertia, to pessimism. To be feminist doesn't mean simply to do nothing, to reduce yourself to total impotence under the pretext of refusing masculine values. There is a problematic, a very difficult dialectic between accepting power and refusing it, accepting certain masculine values, and wanting to transform them. I think it's worth a try.

A.J.: Does the same problem exist with systems of thought? For example, women who reject Marx or Freud because they were men?

S.B.: I think that Freud understood absolutely nothing about women—as he himself said. I admire Freud a great deal as a person and thinker. Despite everything, I find his work very, very rich, but I think that for women he has been absolutely disastrous. And even more so, everyone who came after him.

A.J.: Including Lacan?[8]

S.B.: Yes, Lacan. All of that stuff still minimizes women. I would certainly like to see some young women take up psychoanalysis seriously and reconstruct it from an absolutely new viewpoint. There is a woman in France named . . .

A.J.: Luce Irigaray?[9]

S.B.: That's it, Irigaray . . . she is trying to do something. She hasn't gone quite far enough, in my opinion. But she is trying to construct a psychoanalysis which would be feminist.

A.J.: What do you think of her book, *Speculum de l'autre femme?*

S.B.: I found it laborious to read because of the Lacanian style, which persists in spite of everything . . . but I read her second book with far greater pleasure, *Ce sexe qui n'en est pas un.* It's written in a much simpler style, much more direct, without a "scholastic" vocabulary—psychoanalysts have fallen into a kind of horrifying, almost Aristotelian, scholasticism. On the whole, however, I am interested in the kind of work she is doing and I found her book very interesting. Still, she seems to lack audacity, which is necessary to demolish the ideas of Freud on feminine psychoanalysis.

A.J.: Along the same line, what do you think of the people involved in the antipsychiatry movement? Deleuze, Guattari, R. D. Laing?[10]

S.B.: At bottom, antipsychiatry is still psychiatry. And it doesn't really address itself to women's problems. But then, there have been

8. Jacques Lacan—French psychoanalyst, interrogator of Freud, and founder of the Freudian School in Paris—is now a somewhat legendary figure whose work is fundamental to debates among French feminists. For a recent discussion of Lacanian theory and women see Jane Gallop, "Psychoanalysis in France," *Women and Literature* 7, no. 1 (Winter 1979): 57–63. For a survey of the contemporary French psychoanalytic movement, see Sherry Turkel, *Psychoanalytic Politics* (New York: Basic Books, 1976).

9. See Marks; Burke. Irigaray's two principal books on women have not yet been translated: Luce Irigaray, *Speculum de l'autre femme* (Paris: Editions de Minuit, 1974), and *Ce Sexe qui n'en est pas un* (Paris: Editions de Minuit, 1977).

10. Gilles Deleuze and Félix Guattari, *Anti-Oedipus* (New York: Viking Press, 1976).

some interesting books on women and madness, in America as well. Given masculine norms, it is clear that women are more likely to be considered crazy—I'm not saying to be crazy. As soon as a woman refuses to be perfectly happy doing housework eight hours a day, society has a tendency to want to do a lobotomy on her. I have seen such things, perfectly horrible things. The renewed use of lobotomy today is particularly applicable to women: Because they do routine things, it is possible to take away their spirit of revolt, of debate, of criticism, and still leave them perfectly capable of making stews or washing dishes. It's terrible, this tendency to consider women something dangerous to society . . . but, truthfully speaking, they are dangerous, even those who aren't feminists, because there has always been a women's revolt. Only it has usually translated itself into solitary, individualist, disagreeable manifestations—the whole history of the taming of the shrew, the woman-shrew. They weren't shrews without cause. But I think that feminism permits women to speak among themselves, instead of simply being resentful, having personal complaints, which get them nowhere and which make them sick and ill-tempered, depressive . . . and poison the lives of their husbands and children. It's much better to arrive at a collective consciousness of this problem, which is both a kind of therapy and the basis for a struggle.

A.J.: So, you have to work first of all in the world as it is, before dreaming up a scenario à la Deleuze or Guattari where there would no longer be a division between the sexes.

S.B.: Absolutely. In fact, that's utopian and useless. You have to start from where you are today and from what can be done.

A.J.: Do you know the work of Laing with Mary Barnes? What do you think of it?

S.B.: I find it an interesting revolt against classical psychiatry. And yet, the denouement has been bizarre, for Laing went to India and fell into Zen . . . but on the whole I agree with his position. I also like Cooper a great deal—I liked *Family Life*—I like everyone who tries to show that madness is, in large part, conditioned by society and particularly by the family, and therefore, strongly affects women.

A.J.: We've spoken a little of Irigaray, the antipsychiatrists, and so forth. Do you know the work of Hélène Cixous?[11]

S.B.: Yes, but I'm of an older generation; I can't read her, understand her. And I think it's wrong to write in a totally esoteric language when you want to talk about things which interest a multitude of women. You can't address yourself to women by speaking a language which no average woman will understand. In my opinion, it's wrong. There is something false in this search for a purely feminine writing style. Language, such as it is, is inherited from a masculine society, and it contains

---

11. See Marks; Burke; and Hélène Cixous, "The Laugh of the Medusa," *Signs: Journal of Women in Culture and Society* 1, no. 4 (Summer 1976): 875–94.

many male prejudices. We must rid language of all that. Still, a language is not something created artificially; the proletariat can't use a different language from the bourgeoisie, even if they use it differently, even if from time to time they invent something, technical words or even a kind of worker's slang, which can be very beautiful and very rich. Women can do that as well, enrich their language, clean it up. But to create a language all of a piece which would be a women's language, that I find quite insane. There does not exist a mathematics which is only a women's mathematics, or a feminine science. . . . We can reorient science—for example, a kind of medicine much more directed toward the enormous number of women's health problems which are neglected now. But the original givens of this science are the same for men and for women. Women simply have to steal the instrument;[12] they don't have to break it, or try, a priori, to make of it something totally different. Steal it and use it for their own good.

A.J.: Yes, but in *La Jeune née*, for example, the text that Hélène Cixous and Catherine Clément have written together, they insist on the notion of the "voice."[13] Do you see language only as a social practice, as communication, or is there possibly something else? For instance, how do you see the role of the unconscious in the production of language?

S.B.: Well, the writer can't stop her unconscious from showing up, that's certain. But it's not something you do . . . you do not deliberately try to rummage in your unconscious. It doesn't even make sense, since it is precisely unconscious. I believe that we must use language. If it is used in a feminist perspective, with a feminist sensibility, language will find itself changed in a feminist manner. It will nonetheless be *the* language. You can't not use this universal instrument; you can't create an artificial language, in my opinion. But naturally, each writer must use it in his/her own way. If the writer is a woman, feminist or not, it will give the language something that it would not have if it had been used by a man.

A.J.: Yes, but I wonder if women don't have a different relation to language than men do at the level of enunciation; is it simply a function of their social situation, or is it more complicated than that?

S.B.: For me, it comes from the social situation. I consider it almost antifeminist to say that there is a feminine nature which expresses itself differently, that a woman speaks her body more than a man, because after all, men also speak their bodies when they write. Everything is implicated in the work of a writer.

A.J.: Then, if we changed the social situation would everyone have an unconscious which would work in the same way?

S.B.: No, I don't believe that, because each person has his or her own very particular history . . . and after all, the unconscious is the most

12. In French, "to steal" is the verb *voler,* which also means "to fly." Ironically, this verb is used extensively in its double meaning by Hélène Cixous to designate the gesture of the woman writer.

13. Catherine Clément and Hélène Cixous, *La Jeune née* (Paris: 10/18, 1975).

secret part of ourselves. In any case, if the unconscious must express itself it will do so through the work that you do consciously . . . or subconsciously, with words, with what you have to say.

A.J.: So at our present historical moment there should be a difference between feminine and masculine discourse?

S.B.: That depends on what it's *about.* Because there are topics which are common to men and women. I think that if a woman speaks of oppression, of misery, she will speak of it in exactly the same way as a man. But if she speaks of her own personal problems as a woman, she will obviously speak in another way. It depends a great deal on what is being treated, because I think that a woman is at the same time universal and a woman, just as a man is universal and a male. There is a kind of universality in the human condition, masculine or feminine. That's one thing I continue to believe. I am not at all for a feminism which is entirely separatist, which would say, "this domain is purely for women." I don't believe that at all.

A.J.: Do you think that literature consists only of what has been defined as literature by the dominant ideology? Is this one of the reasons for the repression of women's writing?

S.B.: Obviously, everything has always been defined by the dominant ideology. But the dominant ideology has been able to accept women's literature as well as men's literature. I would say that women have been hindered from creating for a variety of reasons, as Virginia Woolf so admirably explained in *A Room of One's Own.* When they have created, on the whole they have been recognized. In literature it hasn't been nearly as oppressive as in, say, painting, where even the existence of so many women painters has always been denied. Of course, literature is always what the dominant ideology recognizes as literature. But as for what there is outside of that . . . what is very troubling is that people who have tried to write literature, even, for example, proletarian writers, seem to write within the norms of the dominant class. So, can one say that there is a way of crying out, of speaking, which is properly feminine? Personally, I don't think so. In the end, I find this is another way of putting women in a kind of . . . singularity, a ghetto, which is not what I want. I want them to be singular and universal at the same time.

A.J.: So that means that you don't agree with Cixous when she says . . .

S.B.: No, not at all.

A.J.: What is your position on the avant-garde? For example, the avant-garde has been defined as a way of speaking to the future.

S.B.: It's so easy to be mistaken about the future. Sometimes there are avant-gardes which believe themselves to be the avant-garde and which later find themselves to be absolutely dated . . . a bit Alexandrian, in fact. . . . you can't define the future. And in my opinion, you can't define the avant-garde.

A.J.: Twenty years ago, more than a few people would have placed *you* among the avant-garde.

S.B.: I never thought of myself as being in the avant-garde. I said what I had to say, as I was able to say it.

A.J.: But, isn't the idea of the avant-garde worth something in itself? Can't it signify the unexpected, the striking . . . whatever overthrows accepted ideas?

S.B.: Yes, but that's not necessarily avant-garde. That's being original, personal, having something to say. If you try consciously to be avant-garde, it's a little dangerous, like the present state of modern painting, where dealers try to be avant-garde, and under this pretext, painters take some old scraps and call it avant-garde. Picasso never thought of himself as avant-garde. I just find it a bad way to think of yourself. It's important that you think of your relationship with the world and the way you can express that world and that you not be stopped if it scandalizes or embarrasses; but you must not look for scandal or for the avant-garde as a thing in itself.

A.J.: What do you think of *Tel Quel's* work on the avant-garde, particularly, of Julia Kristeva, who focuses on women as she works on the avant-garde?[14]

S.B.: I don't approve of their notion of the avant-garde. Besides, the avant-garde is what led them to *Tel Quel,* from being Stalinist and then Maoist, and it finally pushed them, or let them fall, to the right. That's not authentic, that's no way to act. . . . But I should also say that I don't know Kristeva's work very well.

A.J.: Do you think that the work of women like Kristeva and Irigaray on the unconscious undermines the notion of existential choice?

S.B.: It doesn't inevitably eliminate the notion of choice, because choice springs from the totality of the person. Thus, to study, to analyze what a person is, does not eliminate the idea of freedom.

A.J.: Fascism has been defined as the institutionalization of the unconscious. Do you think that women are more easily swayed by fascism than men, because of this institutionalization?

S.B.: No. But in any case, I don't believe in a notion which leaves out historical and social circumstances, and these are so important in defining fascism. Women aren't more easily swayed than men, but I believe that their situation makes them in effect more slavish than men, as I said in the discussion of masculine ideology in *The Second Sex.* Men create their own gods and thus have some slight understanding that they are self-fabricated. Women are much more susceptible, because they are

14. The *Tel Quel* collective was founded in 1960 with the aim of constituting a general theory of writing. Its political, cultural, and theoretical history is integral to the Parisian intellectual environment in which the French feminisms were born. For an excellent introduction to Kristeva's own work, see Philip Lewis, "Revolutionary Semiotics," *Diacritics* 4, no. 3 (Fall 1974): 28–32. See also Julia Kristeva, "On the Women of China," *Signs: Journal of Women in Culture and Society* 1, no. 1 (Autumn 1975): 57–81, a translation of a chapter of *Des Chinoises;* Marks; Burke.

completely oppressed by men; they take men at their word and believe in the gods that men have made up. The situation of women, their culture, makes them kneel more often before the gods that have been created by men than men themselves do, who know what they've done. To this extent, women will be more fanatical, whether it is for fascism or for totalitarianism.

A.J.: To return for a moment to the question of women and writing: Virginia Woolf has said that it is fatal for anyone who writes to think of their sex.

S.B.: Nonetheless, Virginia Woolf thought a lot about her own sex when she wrote. In the best sense of the word, her writing is very feminine, and by that I mean that women are supposed to be very sensitive to . . . I don't know . . . to all the sensations of nature, much more so than men, much more contemplative. . . . It's this quality that marks her best works. Colette is another case in point. Even if they had not wanted to make their writing feminine, it is nonetheless very feminine. I think that you have to think of a whole being, in its entirety. It also depends somewhat on the subject being treated. There are moments when you have to write certain things and you don't have to think of your sex. If you are writing about the population of the thirteenth district in Paris, even if you are writing on the women in the thirteenth district, there's no need to consider your sex. I mean that there are jobs that can be done equally well by men or by women and that finally you can't see a difference. But from the moment that you involve yourself fully in writing a novel, for example, or an essay, then you are involved as a woman, in the same way that you can't deny your nationality—you are French, you are a man, you are a woman . . . all this passes into the writing. If you are writing something in which you are really involved, you don't even need to think about it any longer. The situation itself demands your total commitment as an individual, just as in your political commitments. A man of the right doesn't write in the same way as a man of the left . . . you can see that right away . . . or a woman of the right or a woman of the left.

A.J.: Do you think that your books could have been written by a man?

S.B.: No, certainly not.

A.J.: How are they marked?

S.B.: I'm not sure. Perhaps by the fact that the hero is a woman in whom I put a great deal of myself, as in *She Came to Stay* or in *The Mandarins.* A man couldn't invent that feminine sensibility, that feminine situation in the world. I have never read a really good novel written by a man where women are portrayed as they truly are. They can be portrayed externally very well—Stendhal's Madame de Rênal, for example—but only as seen from the *outside.* But from within . . . only a woman can write what it is to feel as a woman, to be a woman.

A.J.: Do you think autobiography is especially important for women?

S.B.: Yes, I think there is a great tendency toward autobiography among women today. It is perhaps facile—and I say that even though I have written one myself. I receive a large number of manuscripts which are only autobiographies. Of course, they can be remarkable. At the moment of their emancipation, women have a need to write their own histories. This certainly occured in China around 1936; there were a number of incredible Chinese biographies. And today I find Kate Millett's work, for example, very beautiful. Some autobiographies are as well written as novels. In fact, people seem to be tired of fiction now. There are so many other ways of exploring humanity—by ethnology, psychoanalysis, and so on. . . . It's a little boring to make up stories. So many people think that it's better to be very close to reality and to recount one's life as it is rather than . . . to fictionalize, as they say, that is to transpose, and therefore to cheat.

A.J.: Do you see a difference in autobiographies between "expression" and "content"? Between style and what is narrated?

S.B.: No, for me they are really the same thing.

A.J.: So the life must be interesting if the autobiography is to be good.

S.B.: There has to be a certain relationship between the life and the writing style, and that is really . . . a problem. For example, take the biography of Emma Goldman, the American anarchist. You can't say that she wrote in a striking manner, but it's so passionate; her life, the conferences, the meetings in the USSR and then with Lenin, the whole problem of anarchism at that particular moment—you read it very passionately even if it doesn't have a remarkable stylistic or literary value.

A.J.: Do you like the autobiography of Anaïs Nin?[15]

S.B.: No, I don't like it at all . . . naturally I recognize that she has some talent, and that from time to time she evokes some powerful things. She shows an occasional grace in writing, but her work is quite foreign to me, precisely because she wants so much to be feminine and not feminist. And then she is so gaga before so many men. She talks about men I know in France, men who were less than nothing, and she considers them kings, extraordinary people.

A.J.: Henry Miller?

S.B.: Henry Miller, well, at least he was someone; but I knew others whom she talks about with enormous respect and admiration, and who were really less than nothing. An absence of judgment, a terrible narcissism, on top of which I find her novels extremely bad.

A.J.: Do you think that there are certain themes—defined by the

15. Anaïs Nin, *The Diary of Anaïs Nin*, 6 vols. (1931–66) (New York: Swallow Press, 1966–74).

situation of the writer, of course—but which are particular to women? I've noticed, for example, that women writers seem to have a different relationship to property.

S.B.: Maybe, because this reflects the thematics of their situation. Obviously, there was a time, in the nineteenth century, for example, when women spoke mostly about the house, children, birth, and so forth, because it was their domain. That's changing a little, now.

A.J.: Are there any young women writers who interest you?

S.B.: Not too many, but there aren't too many men either. Literature in France seems to be undergoing a crisis now, and nothing comes immediately to mind.

A.J.: Do you find that there have been essential shifts in your thinking since 1949?

S.B.: Well, I already explained it in *All Said and Done,* and I don't have much to add. I discovered feminism around 1970–72—precisely the time when feminism began to exist in France. Before that, there was no feminism. In 1949, I believed that social progress, the triumph of the proletariat . . . socialism would lead to the emancipation of women. But I saw that nothing came of it: first of all, that socialism was not achieved anywhere, and that in certain countries which called themselves socialist, the situation of women was no better than it was in so-called capitalist countries. Thus, I finally understood that the emancipation of women must be the work of women themselves, independent of the class struggle. That is the major change in my position between 1949 and today.

A.J.: Do you think that women's emancipation must *precede* the social revolution?

S.B.: I don't know. But they should occur simultaneously.

A.J.: What goal should women work for today?

S.B.: Essentially, for the women's revolution. Because if it were accomplished, it would, at the same time, shake society. That said, women should continue to be involved in other questions, and sometimes, in collaboration with men. There are so many problems. Women can go to work on these as well without giving up their feminism. But I think that feminism can be very important, as we can see right now in Italy, where the movement is strong and revolutionary.[16]

A.J.: For example, should we strive to destroy the mythology of the family?

S.B.: Yes, certainly. But, of course, socialism has its own mythology of the family.

A.J.: Two last questions. Are you writing anything, right now?

16. At the time of this interview, the Italian women's movement was mobilizing large numbers of women to fight for an abortion law. Since the passage of that law in March 1978, there has been a lull in activity. See Domna C. Stanton, "Activism and the Academy: A Report from Europe," *Signs: Journal of Women in Culture and Society* 5, no. 1 (Autumn 1979): 179–86.

S.B.: No. I've been keeping pretty busy with the film and television adaptions of my works: They've just finished shooting *La Femme rompue*.[17]

A.J.: How do you envision the effect of your work on future generations?

S.B.: I don't envision it at all. It's something you can't see.

A.J.: Well, what do you hope for?

S.B.: I think that *The Second Sex* will seem an old, dated book, after a while. But nonetheless . . . a book which will have made its contribution. At least, I hope so.

17. *La Femme rompue* appeared on French television in 1978. The novel was translated into English as *The Woman Destroyed* (New York: G. P. Putnam's Sons, 1969).

An Interview with Carmen Naranjo

Lourdes Arizpe

Carmen Naranjo (1930–) has written six novels, seven books of poems, and two of essays when she ought to have been silent.[1] She has experimented in literary form and style when she ought to have followed the "feminine" literary tradition exemplified by Gabriela Mistral. In holding high political office in Costa Rica—among other posts, as ambassador to Israel during Golda Meier's regime and as minister of culture—she turned what was supposed to have been a glamorous and ineffectual performance into a forceful campaign for social reforms and for effective political action. In fact, she opposed such powerful interests when she strove to increase national control of the mass media that she was forced to resign. Her political opinions are highly influential in Central America, yet she has avoided the easy position of taking refuge in an empty revolutionary rhetoric. Naranjo is, as she herself puts it, a political and literary "problem" for Costa Rica and, for that matter, for conservative projects in Latin American societies.

The question for anyone familiar with Latin America is, How does such a woman survive? An answer lies in her tremendous inner strength. In affluent countries such force can be directed at mobilizing women, at organizing a movement, and at sophisticated intellectual debate; but in

1. Carmen Naranjo gave one of the opening speeches at the Symposium on Research on Women held in Mexico City in 1977. She also presented a paper on "The Cultural Myths on Women" in the session on women in literature and art. Her books: *Canción de la ternura* (1964), *Hacia tu isla* (1965), *Los perros no ladraron* (1966), *Misa a oscuras* (1967), *Camino al mediodía* (1968), *Memoria de un hombre palabra* (1968), *Los girasoles perdidos* (1968), *Responso para el niño Juan Manuel* (1971), *Idioma de invierno* (1972), *Hoy es un largo día* (1974), *Diario de una multitud* (1974), *Por las Páginas de la Biblia y los camino de Israel* (1976), *Mi guerrilla* (1977), *Cinco temas en busca de pensador* (1977). This interview took place in December 1978. Lourdes Arizpe translated the interview and all quotations from Naranjo's works.

[*Signs: Journal of Women in Culture and Society* 1979, vol. 5, no. 1]

poor, economically subjected countries it goes into resistance of destitu-
tion, violent death, brutality, and psychological pressures. In this sense,
the terms of discourse in Latin America are in themselves explanatory.
Why the obsession with politics in Latin America? American feminist
friends have asked me. Because, among other things, the oppression of
women is directly proportional to national oppression—which, in turn,
determines the degree and mode of development of a country.

In the sixties, in the Western hemisphere, we naively believed that
liberation was synonymous with consciousness raising, that liberation
was an act of will. In Latin America, *concientización* became the rallying
cry for radical movements. Now, the seventies have shown us, brutally,
that no amount of consciousness will erase the political margins of social
action. In this respect, the distance between social action and violence or
death is much shorter in dependent countries. Even if one can avoid
death or violence, because one is in a privileged position, too great a
feminist consciousness becomes a luxury, because it cannot always be
carried into action. Naranjo implies this, again and again, and refuses to
go beyond the realm of what is possible, given Latin American reality.
Her interview shows that the terms of reference for feminist militancy
cannot be the same for rich and for poor countries, because the interplay
between violent repression and social and ideological compensations for
women is totally different.

How is this conflict between consciousness and reality worked out in
Latin American literature? In her novels Naranjo moves her characters
deftly inside this movable space between individual thought and social
convention. In *Diario de una multitud* [Diary of a crowd], the individual
voices of women and men in the street slowly converge into open social
revolt. "Mother," a little girl asks, "what do men talk about?" "About
women, dear, they talk about women and about politics. And you know
why they talk about politics? Because politics [la política] is a feminine
word, and they think they can go to bed with her and become eternal
fathers" (p. 127). This novel won the National Book Award in Costa
Rica; two other of her novels have also won awards in Central America.
In *Memoria de un hombre palabra* [Diary of a word man], she follows the
main character, a petty bureaucrat, down the path of total degradation.
He is shoved about; he loses his friends and ultimately his job; he becomes an alcoholic. In the end a prostitute with whom he used to play as
a child takes him in. She alone has safeguarded a capacity for feeling, an
inner resistance which gives some sense to the despair and the vicious
social predation encircling them. Another of Naranjo's themes is death,
seen as an awakening, a turning back to understand one's own life and
those of others. In *Camino al mediodía* [Path toward midday], she indulges
in magical realism, as this trend has been called in Latin American literature, by having the main character walk alongside those attending his
own funeral. Of Aurora, his high-class wife, he says: "Aurora, faded

soul, wanted a nest of her own, to lock herself at a card-playing table where she could display her intelligence, where she could drown her orgasms, where her destiny could become reality, where she could punctiliously point out what morals are and what an honest life is" (p. 82).

Naranjo never stops her denunciation of the despair and of the useless lives into which people are locked, but she does not make a distinction between the plight of women and the plight of men. For her, salvation can be found only along two paths: in love, which she lyrically describes as a blending of companionship, sensuality, and the contemplation of nature in *Idioma de invierno* [Language of winter]; and in fighting against oppression, both social and political. In *Mi guerrilla* [My guerrilla], she builds a spiraling tension between the hidden rage of nature and the rage of people fighting against human oppression that bursts in the end with a cry for militancy.

Because of her concern for social issues, Naranjo accepted the difficult task of balancing political engagement and political office. Costa Rica, at least, is well known as one of the most democratic countries in Latin America and one of the few where the military have not been pushed into taking power. But the challenges for a woman in such a position are fierce, as they are elsehwere. Naranjo was a close witness to Golda Meier's political battles. She and Meier and Rosario Castellanos, the distinguished Mexican writer who was then Mexican ambassador to Israel, would meet occasionally: Golda Meier would cry remembering the Israeli women and men soldiers who had been killed in the war; Rosario would tell them about the brutality against the *tzotzil* Indians among whom she lived as a child; Naranjo would describe the maimed, inarticulate lives of people in the streets in San José.

At present, Naranjo is working for UNICEF in Guatemala. The setting of our interview said as much as the words we exchanged. We walked around the marketplace in Chichicastenango, an Indian village not our own and yet, so much our own, with a group of Cakchiquel women following us, trying to sell us their wares. At one point in the interview, we stopped in front of a Catholic church and the figure of the Holy Mother, a Virgin, stood out in the darkness of the aisles. That darkness, also reflected in the eyes of the women around us, is a world full of unknown words, caught in the web of a religious and scholastic culture, which we, as women, are only just beginning to explore.

Colegio de Mexico

* * *

CARMEN NARANJO: No, I don't believe men alone have taken over language. What has happened is that, as we have become more "civilized"—it is unbelievable—but because of this "civilization" and the cultural myths it has created about women, women have been left aside. Even now, when you think of it, much effort is going into incorporating women into production—a salaried, solitary, alienated production, mind you—but there's very little effort going into incorporating them into artistic creation.

LOURDES ARIZPE: Then you would not say that separate male and female cultures exist?

CN: No, there is only human culture, created for everyone.

LA: What about consciousness? Would you say that the female and male consciousness are . . . how to put it, . . . identical? From your books it seems to me you find it easy to reflect a man's mind. Why are so many of your main characters men?

CN: Look, I think it is totally possible for a woman to portray a man's mind. Yes, why do I always write about men in my books? Probably because I have always lived in a world of men, because in the world of public office or political affairs I am surrounded and have always been surrounded by men. What's more, when I attended the university in Costa Rica, there were many more men than women. So, being surrounded by men, I had a wide range for observation and, since they are allowed a wider field of experience in our society, a wider field for expression, I became interested in looking at them through novels. This does not mean that I don't have women characters and notes and texts on them. One of my novels is specifically on women.

LA: I agree with that in the sense that, by writing about men, you are encompassing the total culture. In fact, this is the way men have become culturally dominant, by dealing with everything and by asserting that they are speaking out for everyone, including women. Don't you think it is about time we women did the same?

CN: Yes, that has been one of my aims since I began to write. I did not want to write "feminine" literature because I do not believe in "feminine" or "feminist" culture as such. I believe women have a right to get out of the geography they have been assigned to, that is, the kitchen and the bed. Women have not even had the right to encompass the living room or the desk or the office in their geography. I did not want to write about those confined spaces, they are too poor in experience. A woman has the right to think about the macroworld, to give views on it and to get into men's minds, because, ultimately, she is helping shape men's minds but in not so visible ways.

LA: Yes, but women in Latin America have always claimed they have rights to this and to that, but making the claim and being able to get those rights are two different things. How were you able, personally, to make the break that allowed you to write, to publish, and to become a political leader, coming as you did from a traditional family in a traditional society?

CN: It began with the death of my father, who had great influence on me. He was a tyrannical figure, and I lived very shyly until 1962. I had lived only by studying, by reading endlessly, and I wrote small personal diaries which were kept in drawers at the bottom of the most enormous wardrobes—like all the women in the world, right? Like all of them, secretly looking for that which was being denied, all those years. After that, I found support from other women and also from men, and I began to write. First I wrote poems, intimate poems. By then I was working in the Social Security Institute, and by looking at what went on there I put together my first novel, and I wrote it breaking with the literary tradition in Costa Rica. This tradition was based on novels, some very beautiful, that depicted life in rural areas, in peasant villages. So then I decided to go into urban life and into the psychological density of a large institution, and I found that characters of fiction are walking all over, they are all around.

LA: Would you say there was a break in your writing or your view of life going from personal sentiment and illusion to a broader concern for social and artistic issues? Because women seem to have been trapped in the first, and circumstances do easily allow them to pass on to the latter.

CN: It would seem to me that there is room for both things. And I got interested in everyday people. But I still write poetry which reflects more of my feelings. My first novel was rejected by the editors. They said it had too many bad words in it, but what I had done was simply to reflect the language as it is spoken in offices. Then they were critical of the form of the novel, and finally they said it said nothing new, that it only showed what went on in a large institution. As you can see, all very absurd. Finally someone opposed that decision, and the novel was published. It is now in its fourth edition. It got a cool reception at first, though, because some women complained it had a foul vocabulary and that such and such a well-known family was being criticized.

LA: Do you think you had greater difficulty in publishing because you are a woman?

CN: No, Lourdes, I have found that because I protest, because I am critical of society, people respect me. In a sense being openly critical, revolutionary, for a woman is better. Because women who stay on in the traditional sphere and write or try to do things find greater obstacles. I have seen it with other women, but it has not happened to me. But I must tell you that people have sometimes said I have a man's brain, that I think like a man.

LA: They would. You have stepped out of all bounds.

CN: It is funny, actually, as in children's games, they try to capture a person who expresses herself in the same terms as they do. But I was too aware not to have known when something was meant as praise and what it meant to be told I thought like a man. Because they were in fact denying that women can think, that they can be intelligent.

LA: You are a well-known writer in Central America now. Have your books been well received?

CN: Yes, you could say that. I have always tried to break with the traditional style. And when you do that, you get what happens to a lot of people. Reviewers were very critical of my first book. Then, when I published the second novel, they said the first was marvelous and that now I was experimenting too much. And when I published the third novel, they said the first and second were works of art. So you learn the relativity of literary criticism, and you begin to assert whatever it is you want to say or do. In my case, undoubtedly because of my personality, what attracts me most is the search for new forms, new themes, and to delve into this character who is always my main character, the person who is a nobody, one belonging to an anonymous crowd.

LA: Why are you interested in nobodies?

CN: Well, Lourdes, I seem to be very sensitive to people whom nobody cares about, grey unknown faces. When I look at those queues at the cinema, at the women and men who walk in the streets as if they were abandoned, and I think of their total lack of ways of expressing themselves, I have to put up a protest. There is such an urgent need for real values. And we have to change this. So my protest is not only toward a certain regime but against society itself, as it is now, degraded, hollowed.

LA: Social protest has become one of the main literary currents in Latin America today. And in several of your books, in *Diario de una multitud* and especially in *Mi guerrilla,* you look for a revolution. . . .

CN: Yes, but you see, rather than think in terms of "-isms," I think more in terms of a real revolution, which is always someone's revolution, that is, inside you. Only by changing what is inside you can you change society in a way that will not produce a dominant elite again who will keep all the benefits to themselves. This happens in both capitalist and socialist countries. And to do this, it is people in the streets you have to look at. And it's people's attention and engagement that you have to get as readers. I try to write in such a way that readers participate in the reading.

LA: But this has produced very doctrinaire and bad literature in Latin America.

CN: That is the mistake of portraying a revolution or reflecting one's revolutionary feelings in literature instead of using literature as a revolutionary force and experience. Only in this way can you expand the scope of action going on. For example, in a society where injustice and corruption abound, what can I do? Exaggerate what is going on? Pull it though my subjectivity? Or show it nakedly, as it is, and let the reader bring in all her sense of indignation and protest, through her own reading? This is a reader who is used to having everything described for her, who has been told she must protest. This is a type of literature that demands conformity, that is, conformity to protest. But I believe the effort, the indignation, and the will to change must grow in the reader by herself. This sort of writing, of course, brings about strong reactions, many of them negative. So I cannot say I am a bestselling author; rather, I am a writer who is many times rejected. People are even afraid of me.

LA: Ah, yes, are you threatening?

CN: It seems so. I have discovered, little by little, that a woman who is not rejected—seen as being threatening as you say—is a woman who has accepted all possible limitations. But a woman who is considered intelligent because she has discovered key things, such a woman is treated in a special way. There is fear of having a dialogue with her, and when she is given a role to play she is given something like a monologue or a speech to give, but she will not be asked to be in a panel or a dialogue. Speaking of myself, people in my country—where there are few creative values—consider me very avant-garde. But this is an aberration because deep down I am very insecure and very conscious of the limitations of my intelligence, but that makes people afraid of my writings and at the same time it also makes people write me hundreds of letters about my books, which do not refer to anyone specifically, saying, with great emotion, without ever having met me, you have written out my life in this book.

LA: Would people in our countries be as afraid of an avant-garde man?

CN: No, because being progressive in a man is seen as a natural thing in our societies. Men are expected to be awake, progressive. But a progressive woman is considered dangerous. First, because she may be a subversive element for "our women"—as men say; she might make them think, she can bring a revolution into the home, she can actually show that a woman can attain fulfillment, whether she is married or has children or not. She blatantly shows that things must change in our traditions.

LA: So you blast away . . .

CN: Yes, I suppose I am a problem as a person for my society, for the political system, and for traditional literature.

LA: But you have been able to put up with the pressures very well, in fact, in an admirable way, if you think of all the women in Latin America, women in politics we do not know about, and women writers and poets who have been destroyed. How have you done it?

CN: You know how? Power is like a soft cushion: you begin to want to mold yourself to it, to want to change your ideals to suit this person or that person, and slowly you lose what you are or were. What has helped me is that I have a wide perspective and I have never let myself be diverted or changed. For example, I have never been to the hairdresser. I have been in political office, as an administrator, as a minister, and I stayed there if I could help change things, if not, I left. You know,

Lourdes, the day I take office, I know my resignation is in the first drawer to my right, and from the moment I accept, from the moment they are congratulating me, I know I will have to leave one day because I have that way out. . . .

LA: Do you think, and this is the big question for Latin America today—if there is no outside intervention, that is—do you think you can change things from within?

CN: If you want to fight inside the power structure, I think people like myself cannot do very much. I think what you are able to do is to make people aware, and they are the ones who keep you in check. But otherwise it is so easy for public officials to become corrupt, and women, too, in a specific way. I see them lose themselves in trying to achieve small things; you can no longer recognize what their ideology is, what they stand for; they allow things which in the end are worse than the results they hoped for . . .

LA: It is privilege, this blind striving for privilege in our hierarchical Latin American societies . . .

CN: I think you find it everywhere. People will blindly accept what others define as privilege. I was able not to fall into that because I have the ability of converting any public post into an infinite source of work. And the privileges for me are, for example, to walk in a forest, to be alone for awhile, to write two or three pages a day.

LA: Do you think women can be effective in governments in Latin America?

CN: That is difficult to answer. First of all, a woman in public office must work toward benefiting the whole of society. She cannot be sectarian. Her ideals must enforce policies that will reach the largest number of people. In this sense, women face the same options as men in office.

LA: And the present trend to have a few more women in governments in Latin America today . . . ?

CN: I am afraid it is now becoming fashionable to have women in office as political decor. They are expected to be sweet, feminine, to make lovely speeches, and to dutifully accept not getting anything done. But when a woman accepts a political post, she must decide whether she will be a passive or an active member of the government. If the latter, then she must lead for everyone. But what I cannot understand is how some women have accepted office in dictatorships that have trodden on every basic human right, as in Nicaragua. Those women just sit there and decorate.

LA: Now, let's talk about women poets and writers in Latin America. You are a problem, but you have found a way out—companionship, political work, writing. So many women have been unable to survive. Alfonsina Storni who wrote so beautifully about the sea and one day walked right into it, much like Virginia Woolf. And Alejandra Pizarnik, the young poet who also committed suicide. And Rosario Castellanos, so unhappy in her personal life. Would you say there is something specific of Latin American societies that they tear women artists apart?

CN: What I can say specifically of women's position in our societies is that, from the moment a woman is outstanding, she is expected to act as a circus performer. Acrobatics, clowning, everything is expected. Why? Because there are so few women who are able to stand out. That is, women's social participation is so sporadic, that out of these sporadic appearances they are forced to do wonders or to make fools of themselves. If you do things more or less well, you get a little applause, but if you do something wrong, you fall all the way to hell, and you come very near your death. You do not even have to commit suicide, you are socially and personally annihilated. The only thing that can save you from all this is being sustained by someone, by love. Because you are in the forefront, everything you do is criticized. Take Rosario Castellanos. Even though she already had several excellent novels and poems published, even though she accepted a political and social engagement toward people, she was greatly criticized for taking the post as ambassador to Israel. . . .

LA: She increasingly had the feeling everyone was attacking her. But, in fact, it was true . . .

CN: And if it had been a man, people would have found it natural that she should have taken a post as ambassador. Men get thousands of cultural opportunities, and no one thinks twice about their accepting them. But with women, we are not expected to advance. This is what women must be very conscious of. And now is a difficult period in Latin America for women who want to do things and to change them.

LA: Yes, that is ominous. The more you do, the more you are hated, it seems, so that walking forward becomes a path toward self-destruction. What is one supposed to do, be a bloody martyr?

CN: Nothing will happen to you if you walk inside your own path and you know it. You see, when a women starts doing things, just doing them changes the situation, and the conflict arises when you are made to expect recognition and prizes for what you have done. But this is a conflict men suffer as well. Men are bribed into complacency, too, and into relying on praise and privilege. So either you expect recompense and then there was nothing genuine there, or you go on believing you are a conscious worker like any nobody. I do not feel anyone is going to destroy me, and I am not waiting for any thanks, I do not need positions or anything. If I see little of the world, I see little of it; if I am given few cultural opportunities, I will have few cultural opportunities; but when I, or you, need a prize for whatever we are doing then we are caught.

Now, going back to women in Latin American literature, for me the towering figure here is Sor Juana Inés de la Cruz. A whole trend of reflective literature stems from her work, a literature that has often been termed "masculine." In fact, her writings are so critical and so deep that she clearly outlined the way in which women have been treated as objects in our societies. Really, going deeply into Sor Juana's work must be the first step for any Latin American women. Then, I am struck by the poetic beauty and the undertones of Gabriela Mistral's poetry. However, she represents the typical figure of feminine literature, which so many of us woman writers will be against. The fact that we are against it does not mean we do not recognize its values, we do . . .

LA: You mean she seemed to be obsessed with motherhood, precisely that which she never had. Rosario Castellanos has written a frightening story of a meeting of several women writers with Gabriela wherein she dramatically decried all her work because her "womb had never borne fruit." Would you say this is the feminine heritage we Latin American women get?

CN: No, this heritage I think all women of the world get, and I find it legitimate for women who have felt and been moved by these feelings to express them in art and in literature. But what has happened is that their example has been used to say this is the "eternal feminine spirit"— el eterno femenino—and this is your only field. Luckily for us, I would say Gabriela Mistral took on that role of a motherly woman and depleted it in her poetry. In this way, she opened up avenues to other fields. There is a new generation of women writers who have opposed this tradition. And I think Mistral would have understood this need to break with tradition. So there is a new, bolder women's literary movement now, of which Mexico has three excellent writers: Rosario Castellanos, Luisa Josefina Hernández, and Elena Poniatowska. Incidentally, Elena's biographical novel on la Jesusita (Hasta no verte Jesús mío) is astonishing. Then I would say there are three great creative writers in Central America, two from Costa Rica and one from San Salvador: Carmen Lira, who brings colloquial language into her novels; Yolanda Oreamuno, who brings new techniques into Latin literature, especially English ones; and Claudia Lars, who, without following Mistral's footsteps, brings in a Central American way of looking at things which is very valuable. Now, the most interesting things are going on in Venezuela and Argentina and several other countries of South America with women holding totally different positions in their thinking, in their way of fighting, and with a very clear concept of what a woman's role is in literature and art. Those that I know best are young women like Luisa Valenzuela from Argentina and Antonieta Madrid, a Venezuelan. I believe we are witnessing a renaissance in women's expression in the arts, in the sense that they are showing what they are capable of doing.

LA: Why do you think this is happening now?

CN: Well, you know I was very critical of International Women's Year because I think that was all blah-blah, but it certainly opened up an opportunity to think about women's problems. Official recognition always surfaces several years after such concerns are going on, and before IWY there was already an awareness among women writers that views were being debated on women and artistic creation.

LA: Who would you mention as women poets in Latin America?

CN: I would mention Sara de Ibañez, although she is a bit rigid; Alejandra Pizarnik; Alfonsina Storni; and I would add one more, Eunice Odio, who is part Mexican, part Costa Rican. Personally, because of my taste, the one whose poetry interests me most is Pizarnik, because she definitely goes beyond that which could be thought of as feminine into a wider human scope and she brings up things that men would say they alone discuss. She goes into the mysteries of memory and remembrances, how one's life is always bounded by memory. She was an outstanding poet.

LA: One who died young, too. Like Sylvia Plath and so many others. Pizarnik also wrote with great resentment about her life being more terrible than that of a man.

CN: I do not know very much about their personal lives, but, on the surface, I would say, Lourdes, that their thinking was really on individual, human life, because they could have been men and they could also have committed suicide. I am not denying the fact that they were women, but the problems they faced were problems of being alive. Of course, as you say, and as we all know, these are more difficult for women, but they are basically the same problems for humanity in our time.

LA: Then you do not think women poets face greater anguish in developing in our society than men do?

CN: Perhaps a bit more anguish, but the same thing happened to Pavese and to Modigliani and to Van Gogh. When you face the problems of creative work, you face universal problems, so immense, so terrifying, that being a woman or a man can be an attenuating force but not the final one.

LA: Writing in Latin America also brings one into conflict with the social conditions. Just sitting here, talking smoothly about literature while these Indian women are desperately trying to sell us their wares makes it so painful. And this pain you can find in the writing of most Latin Americans, and it is certainly present in your writing.

CN: Yes, it sometimes becomes so terrible that you think, "Is it worthwhile to take up a pen, or should I take up a rifle and go fight in the mountains to help the people?" And I don't have an answer to this question. You wonder if it is worth keeping up a continuous denunciation of the poverty and hunger in our countries, when it is never heeded by our governments and by the system and you have to protest in a more violent way. You ask yourself that every day, and every day you give yourself a different answer. Sometimes you convince yourself that only by writing, by exposing things—as far as they let you—can you help change things; at other times you think you are in a very comfortable position writing cozily inside a room while others are dying in the streets. Faced with this problem, all I have been able to do is to adopt a way of life that keeps me closely associated to struggles for liberation and to wait until a time when I can do more. . . . I have not found any other answer.

LA: And do you feel that the same type of conflict arises in working toward the liberation of women in societies where the basic political and economic liberation still has to be fought for?

CN: No, I have no problem there, because the fight to improve women's lives is identical with the fight to improve society. Now, you cannot begin the first if you find that Latin American women in general cannot even conceive of new liberties, if they have no perspective of the world outside the home. The first thing a Latin American woman needs is freedom of movement to have it. But I would not say that women themselves should do it, but that society itself must go through self-analysis and give women this freedom. Because our society cannot go on like this. I see a tremendous decline coming, even an unlivable and unbearable violence.

LA: When you say society, who do you mean?

CN: Men and women together, of course.

LA: You do not see women as outside society, having to push in to take what is their due?

CN: No. In fact, I do not see women as a single group. There are women who have had opportunities and who forget the poor women, those who are nobodies. An affluent woman easily forgets because of her privileges, her comfort; she forgets the misery of lower-class women; and the only way out of the present poverty of women is to put them back into a creative economic role, into small enterprises, banks, factories, cooperatives, and household industries. This to me is a valid way of fighting for women today.

LA: Would you consider this feminism? Is this a version of feminism for you?

CN: Yes. For me, the feminist struggle is one to improve the human condition. And dividing lots into men on one side and women on the other is a regression. To me, the women's question is not a household problem or a psychological one. Both women and men must search for new values and break the chains of consumer society. Writings that oppose men and women seem to me absurd, like those between Catholics and Protestants. It is not a question of who is good, who has suffered injustice. In a sense, everyone has suffered from injustice. Rather, it is a question of working for causes, leaving resentment aside.

LA: You don't think this will dilute women's struggles? Is protest unnecessary then?

CN: Oh, certainly not, Lourdes. Protest we must, because by protesting we raise consciousness. But we must not lose sight of what we are protesting against. We are against the enslavement of women and that means a new education is needed, because remember that women are themselves educating their children in the worst of cultural values: daughters in human servitude and sons in machismo. But new efforts at education are pushing us into homogenized middle-class values. These values push us toward being civilized in buying and barbarous in producing. We are expanding markets of expensive goods, based on cheap labor in order to maintain this middle class. So what we must ultimately struggle against is consumer society and the exploitation of human beings.

Theoretical Approaches

Postmodernism and Gender
Relations in Feminist Theory

Jane Flax

As the thought of the world, [philosophy] appears only when actuality is already there cut and dried after its process of formation has been completed. . . . When philosophy paints its grey in grey, then has a shape of life grown old. By philosophy's grey in grey it cannot be rejuvenated but only understood. The owl of Minerva spreads its wings only with the falling of the dusk. [G. W. F. HEGEL, preface to *Philosophy of Right*]

It seems increasingly probable that Western culture is in the middle of a fundamental transformation: a "shape of life" is growing old. In retrospect, this transformation may be as radical (but as gradual) as the shift from a medieval to a modern society. Accordingly, this moment in the history of the West is pervaded by profound yet little-comprehended change, uncertainty, and ambivalence. This transitional state makes certain forms of

This paper has been through many transformations. It was originally written for presentation at the annual meeting of the German Association for American Studies, June 1984, Berlin. Travel to Germany was made possible by a grant from the Volkswagen Foundation. An earlier version of this paper, entitled "Gender as a Problem: In and for Feminist Theory," will appear in the German journal, *Amerikastudien/American Studies*. I have been fortunate to have many attentive readers of this paper whose influences undoubtedly improved it, including Gisela Bock, Sandra Harding, Mervat Hatem, Phyllis Palmer, and Barrie Thorne.

[*Signs: Journal of Women in Culture and Society* 1987, vol. 12, no. 4]

thought possible and necessary, and it excludes others. It generates problems that some philosophies seem to acknowledge and confront better than others.

I think there are currently three kinds of thinking that best present (and represent) our own time "apprehended in thought": psychoanalysis, feminist theory, and postmodern philosophy. These ways of thinking reflect and are partially constituted by Enlightenment beliefs still prevalent in Western (especially American) culture. At the same time they offer ideas and insights that are only possible because of the breakdown of Enlightenment beliefs under the cumulative pressure of historical events such as the invention of the atomic bomb, the Holocaust, and the war in Vietnam.[1]

Each of these ways of thinking takes as its object of investigation at least one facet of what has become most problematic in our transitional state: how to understand and (re-)constitute the self, gender, knowledge, social relations, and culture without resorting to linear, teleological, hierarchical, holistic, or binary ways of thinking and being.

My focus here will be mainly on one of these modes of thinking: feminist theory. I will consider what it could be and reflect upon the goals, logics, and problematics of feminist theorizing as it has been practiced in the past fifteen years in the West. I will also place such theorizing within the social and philosophical contexts of which it is both a part and a critique.

I do not mean to claim that feminist theory is a unified or homogeneous discourse. Nonetheless, despite the lively and intense controversies among persons who identify themselves as practitioners concerning the subject matter, appropriate methodologies, and desirable outcome of feminist theorizing, it is possible to identify at least some of our underlying goals, purposes, and constituting objects.

A fundamental goal of feminist theory is (and ought to be) to analyze gender relations: how gender relations are constituted and experienced and how we think or, equally important, do not think about them.[2] The study of gender relations includes but is not limited to what are often

---

[1] For a more extended discussion of these claims, see my forthcoming work "Freud's Children? Psychoanalysis and Feminism in the Postmodern West."

[2] Representative examples of feminist theories include Barbara Smith, ed., *Home Girls: A Black Feminist Anthology* (New York: Kitchen Table: Women of Color Press, 1983); Cherríe Moraga and Gloria Anzaldúa, eds., *This Bridge Called My Back* (Watertown, Mass.: Persephone Press, 1981); Elizabeth Abel, Marianne Hirsch, and Elizabeth Langland, *The Voyage In: Fictions of Female Development* (Hanover, N.H., and London: University Press of New England, 1983); Zillah R. Eisenstein, ed., *Capitalist Patriarchy and the Case for Socialist Feminism* (New York: Monthly Review Press, 1979); Annette Kuhn and Ann Marie Wolpe, eds., *Feminism and Materialism* (Boston: Routledge & Kegan Paul, 1978); Hunter College Women's Studies Collective, *Women's Realities, Women's Choices* (New York: Oxford University Press, 1983); Elaine Marks and Isabelle de Courtivron, eds., *New French Feminisms* (New York: Schocken Books, 1981); Joyce Trebilcot, ed., *Mothering: Essays in Feminist Theory* (Totowa, N.J.: Rowman & Allanheld, 1984); Sherry B. Ortner and Harriet

considered the distinctively feminist issues: the situation of women and the analysis of male domination. Feminist theory includes an (at least implicit) prescriptive element as well. By studying gender we hope to gain a critical distance on existing gender arrangements. This critical distance can help clear a space in which reevaluating and altering our existing gender arrangements may become more possible.

Feminist theory by itself cannot clear such a space. Without feminist political actions theories remain inadequate and ineffectual. However, I have come to believe that the further development of feminist theory (and hence a better understanding of gender) also depends upon locating our theorizing within and drawing more self-consciously upon the wider philosophic contexts of which it is both a part and a critique. In other words, we need to think more about how we think about gender relations or any other social relations and about how other modes of thinking can help or hinder us in the development of our own discourses. In this paper, I will be moving back and forth between thinking about gender relations and thinking about how I am thinking—or could think—about them.

Metatheory: Thinking about thinking

Feminist theory seems to me to belong within two, more inclusive, categories with which it has special affinity: the analysis of social relations and postmodern philosophy.[3] Gender relations enter into and are constituent

---

Whitehead, eds., *Sexual Meanings: The Cultural Construction of Gender and Sexuality* (New York: Cambridge University Press, 1981); Nancy C. M. Hartsock, *Money, Sex, and Power* (New York: Longman, Inc., 1983); Ann Snitow, Christine Stansell and Sharon Thompson, eds., *The Powers of Desire: The Politics of Sexuality* (New York: Monthly Review Press, 1983); Sandra Harding and Merrill B. Hintikka, eds., *Discovering Reality: Feminist Perspectives on Epistemology, Metaphysics, Methodology, and Philosophy of Science* (Boston: D. Reidel Publishing Co., 1983); Carol C. Gould, *Beyond Domination: New Perspectives on Women and Philosophy* (Totowa, N.J.: Rowman & Allanheld, 1984); Alison M. Jaggar, *Feminist Politics and Human Nature* (Totowa, N.J.: Rowman & Allanheld, 1983); Isaac D. Balbus, *Marxism and Domination* (Princeton, N.J.: Princeton University Press, 1982).

[3] Sources for and practitioners of postmodernism include Friedrich Nietzsche, *On the Genealogy of Morals* (New York: Vintage, 1969) and *Beyond Good and Evil* (New York: Vintage, 1966); Jacques Derrida, *L'écriture et la différence* (Paris: Editions du Seuil, 1967); Michel Foucault, *Language, Counter-Memory, Practice* (Ithaca, N.Y.: Cornell University Press, 1977); Jacques Lacan, *Speech and Language in Psychoanalysis* (Baltimore: Johns Hopkins University Press, 1968), and *The Four Fundamental Concepts of Psychoanalysis* (New York: W. W. Norton & Co., 1973); Richard Rorty, *Philosophy and the Mirror of Nature* (Princeton, N.J.: Princeton University Press, 1979); Paul Feyerabend, *Against Method* (New York: Schocken Books, 1975); Ludwig Wittgenstein, *On Certainty* (New York: Harper & Row, 1972), and *Philosophical Investigations* (New York: Macmillan Publishing Co., 1970); Julia Kristeva, "Women's Time," *Signs: Journal of Women in Culture and Society* 7, no. 1 (Autumn 1981): 13–35; and Jean-François Lyotard, *The Postmodern Condition* (Minneapolis: University of Minnesota Press, 1984).

elements in every aspect of human experience. In turn, the experience of gender relations for any person and the structure of gender as a social category are shaped by the interactions of gender relations and other social relations such as class and race. Gender relations thus have no fixed essence; they vary both within and over time.

As a type of postmodern philosophy, feminist theory reveals and contributes to the growing uncertainty within Western intellectual circles about the appropriate grounding and methods for explaining and/or interpreting human experience. Contemporary feminists join other postmodern philosophers in raising important metatheoretical questions about the possible nature and status of theorizing itself. Given the increasingly fluid and confused status of Western self-understandings, it is not even clear what would constitute the basis for satisfactory answers to commonly agreed upon questions within feminist (or other forms of social) theory.

Postmodern discourses are all "deconstructive" in that they seek to distance us from and make us skeptical about beliefs concerning truth, knowledge, power, the self, and language that are often taken for granted within and serve as legitimation for contemporary Western culture.

Postmodern philosophers seek to throw into radical doubt beliefs still prevalent in (especially American) culture but derived from the Enlightenment, such as:

1. The existence of a stable, coherent self. Distinctive properties of this Enlightenment self include a form of reason capable of privileged insight into its own processes and into the "laws of nature."

2. Reason and its "science"—philosophy—can provide an objective, reliable, and universal foundation for knowledge.

3. The knowledge acquired from the right use of reason will be "True"—for example, such knowledge will represent something real and unchanging (universal) about our minds and/or the structure of the natural world.

4. Reason itself has transcendental and universal qualities. It exists independently of the self's contingent existence (e.g., bodily, historical, and social experiences do not affect reason's structure or its capacity to produce atemporal knowledge).

5. There are complex connections between reason, autonomy, and freedom. All claims to truth and rightful authority are to be submitted to the tribunal of reason. Freedom consists in obedience to laws that conform to the necessary results of the right use of reason. (The rules that are right for me as a rational being will necessarily be right for all other such beings.) In obeying such laws, I am obeying my own best transhistorical part (reason) and hence am exercising my own autonomy and ratifying my existence as a free being. In such acts, I escape a determined or merely contingent existence.

6. By grounding claims to authority in reason, the conflicts between

truth, knowledge, and power can be overcome. Truth can serve power without distortion; in turn, by utilizing knowledge in the service of power both freedom and progress will be assured. Knowledge can be both neutral (e.g., grounded in universal reason, not particular "interests") and also socially beneficial.

7. Science, as the exemplar of the right use of reason, is also the paradigm for all true knowledge. Science is neutral in its methods and contents but socially beneficial in its results. Through its process of discovery we can utilize the "laws of nature" for the benefit of society. However, in order for science to progress, scientists must be free to follow the rules of reason rather than pander to the "interests" arising from outside rational discourse.

8. Language is in some sense transparent. Just as the right use of reason can result in knowledge that represents the real, so, too, language is merely the medium in and through which such representation occurs. There is a correspondence between "word" and "thing" (as between a correct truth claim and the real). Objects are not linguistically (or socially) constructed, they are merely *made present* to consciousness by naming and the right use of language.

The relation of feminist theorizing to the postmodern project of deconstruction is necessarily ambivalent. Enlightenment philosophers such as Kant did not intend to include women within the population of those capable of attaining freedom from traditional forms of authority. Nonetheless, it is not unreasonable for persons who have been defined as incapable of self-emancipation to insist that concepts such as the autonomy of reason, objective truth, and beneficial progress through scientific discovery ought to include and be applicable to the capacities and experiences of women as well as men. It is also appealing, for those who have been excluded, to believe that reason will triumph—that those who proclaim such ideas as objectivity will respond to rational arguments. If there is no objective basis for distinguishing between true and false beliefs, then it seems that power alone will determine the outcome of competing truth claims. This is a frightening prospect to those who lack (or are oppressed by) the power of others.

Nevertheless, despite an understandable attraction to the (apparently) logical, orderly world of the Enlightenment, feminist theory more properly belongs in the terrain of postmodern philosophy. Feminist notions of the self, knowledge, and truth are too contradictory to those of the Enlightenment to be contained within its categories. The way(s) to feminist future(s) cannot lie in reviving or appropriating Enlightenment concepts of the person or knowledge.[4]

---

[4] In "The Instability of the Analytical Categories of Feminist Theory," *Signs* 11, no. 4 (Summer 1986): 645–64, Sandra Harding discusses the ambivalent attraction of feminist

Feminist theorists enter into and echo postmodernist discourses as we have begun to deconstruct notions of reason, knowledge, or the self and to reveal the effects of the gender arrangements that lay beneath their "neutral" and universalizing facades.[5] Some feminist theorists, for example, have begun to sense that the motto of Enlightenment, "*sapere aude*— 'Have courage to use your own reason,'"[6] rests in part upon a deeply gender-rooted sense of self and self-deception. The notion that reason is divorced from "merely contingent" existence still predominates in contemporary Western thought and now appears to mask the embeddedness and dependence of the self upon social relations, as well as the partiality and historical specificity of this self's existence. What Kant's self calls its "own" reason and the methods by which reason's contents become present or "self-evident," it now appears, are no freer from empirical contingency than is the so-called phenomenal self.[7]

In fact, feminists, like other postmodernists, have begun to suspect that all such transcendental claims reflect and reify the experience of a few persons—mostly white, Western males. These transhistoric claims seem plausible to us in part because they reflect important aspects of the experience of those who dominate our social world.

A feminist problematic

This excursus into metatheory has now returned us to the opening of my paper—that the fundamental purpose of feminist theory is to analyze how we think, or do not think, or avoid thinking about gender. Obviously, then,

---

theorizing to both sorts of discourse. She insists that feminist theorists should live with the ambivalence and retain both discourses for political and philosophical reasons. However, I think her argument rests in part on a too uncritical appropriation of a key Enlightenment equation of knowing, naming, and emancipation.

[5] Examples of such work include Alice A. Jardine, *Gynesis: Configurations of Woman and Modernity* (Ithaca, N.Y.: Cornell University Press, 1985); Donna Haraway, "A Manifesto for Cyborgs: Science, Technology, and Socialist Feminism in the 1980s," *Socialist Review* 80 (1983): 65–107; Kristeva; Kathy E. Ferguson, *The Feminist Case against Bureaucracy* (Philadelphia: Temple University Press, 1984); and Luce Irigaray, *Speculum of the Other Woman* (Ithaca, N.Y.: Cornell University Press, 1985).

[6] Immanuel Kant, "What Is Enlightenment?" in *Foundations of the Metaphysics of Morals* (Indianapolis: Bobbs-Merrill Co., 1959), 85.

[7] For critiques of the mind (reason)/body split, see Naomi Scheman, "Individualism and the Objects of Psychology," in Harding and Hintikka, eds.; Susan Bordo, "The Cartesian Masculinization of Thought," *Signs* 11, no. 3 (Spring 1986): 439–56; Nancy C. M. Hartsock, "The Feminist Standpoint: Developing the Ground for a Specifically Feminist Historical Materialism," in Harding and Hintikka, eds.; Caroline Whitbeck, "Afterword to the 'Maternal Instinct,'" in Trebilcot, ed.; and Dorothy Smith, "A Sociology for Women," in *The Prison of Sex: Essays in the Sociology of Knowledge*, ed. J. Sherman and E. T. Beck (Madison: University of Wisconsin Press, 1979).

to understand the goals of feminist theory we must consider its central subject—gender.

Here, however, we immediately plunge into a complicated and controversial morass. For among feminist theorists there is by no means consensus on such (apparently) elementary questions as: What is gender? How is it related to anatomical sexual differences? How are gender relations constituted and sustained (in one person's lifetime and more generally as a social experience over time)? How do gender relations relate to other sorts of social relations such as class or race? Do gender relations have a history (or many)? What causes gender relations to change over time? What are the relationships between gender relations, sexuality, and a sense of individual identity? What are the relationships between heterosexuality, homosexuality, and gender relations? Are there only two genders? What are the relationships between forms of male dominance and gender relations? Could/would gender relations wither away in egalitarian societies? Is there anything distinctively male or female in modes of thought and social relations? If there is, are these distinctions innate and/or socially constituted? Are gendered distinctions socially useful and/or necessary? If so, what are the consequences for the feminist goal of attaining gender justice?[8]

Confronted with such a bewildering set of questions, it is easy to overlook the fact that a fundamental transformation in social theory has occurred. The single most important advance in feminist theory is that the existence of gender relations has been problematized. Gender can no longer be treated as a simple, natural fact. The assumption that gender relations are natural, we can now see, arose from two coinciding circumstances: the unexamined identification and confusion of (anatomical) sexual differences with gender relations, and the absence of active feminist movements. I will return to a consideration of the connections between gender relations and biology later in the paper.

Contemporary feminist movements are in part rooted in transformations in social experience that challenge widely shared categories of social meaning and explanation. In the United States, such transformations include changes in the structure of the economy, the family, the place of the United States in the world system, the declining authority of previously powerful social institutions, and the emergence of political groups that have increasingly more divergent ideas and demands concerning justice, equality, social legislation, and the proper role of the state. In such a "decentered" and unstable universe it seems plausible to question one of the most natural facets of human existence—gender relations. On the other

[8] These questions are suggested by Judith Stacey, "The New Conservative Feminism," *Feminist Studies* 9, no. 3 (Fall 1983): 559–83; and Nancy Chodorow, "Gender, Relation, and Difference in Psychoanalytic Perspective," in *The Future of Difference*, ed. Hester Eisenstein and Alice Jardine (1980; reprint, New Brunswick, N.J.: Rutgers University Press, 1985).

74   *Flax*

hand, such instability also makes old modes of social relations more attractive. The new right and Ronald Reagan both call upon and reflect a desire to go back to a time when people and countries were in their "proper" place. The conflicts around gender arrangements become both the locus for and symbols of anxieties about all sorts of social-political ideas, only some of which are actually rooted primarily in gender relations.[9]

The coexistence of such social transformations and movements makes possible an increasingly radical and social, self-conscious questioning of previously unexamined "facts" and "explanations." Thus, feminist theory, like all other forms of theory (including gender-biased ones), is dependent upon and reflects a certain set of social experiences. Whether, to what extent, and why feminist theory can be "better" than the gender-biased theories it critiques are questions that vex many writers.[10] In considering such questions feminist theorists invariably enter the epistemological terrain shared in part with other postmodern philosophies. Hence, I wish to bracket these questions for now in order to consider more closely a fundamental category and object of investigation of feminist theory—gender relations.

Thinking in relations

"Gender relations" is a category meant to capture a complex set of social relations, to refer to a changing set of historically variable social processes. Gender, both as an analytic category and a social process, is relational. That is, gender relations are complex and unstable processes (or temporary "totalities" in the language of dialectics) constituted by and through interrelated parts. These parts are interdependent, that is, each part can have no meaning or existence without the others.

Gender relations are differentiated and (so far) asymmetric divisions and attributions of human traits and capacities. Through gender relations two types of persons are created: man and woman. Man and woman are posited as exclusionary categories. One can be only one gender, never the

[9] On the appeal of new right ideology to women, see Stacey.

[10] Harding discusses these problems in detail. See n. 4 above. See also Sandra Harding, "Is Gender a Variable in Conceptions of Rationality? A Survey of Issues," in Gould (n. 2 above), and "Why Has the Sex/Gender System Become Visible Only Now?" in Harding and Hintikka, eds.; and Jaggar (n. 2 above), 353–94. Since within modern Western cultures science is the model for knowledge and is simultaneously neutral/objective yet socially useful/powerful (or destructive), much epistemological inquiry has focused on the nature and structure of science. Compare Hilary Rose, "Hand, Brain, and Heart: A Feminist Epistemology for the Natural Sciences," *Signs* 9, no. 1 (Autumn 1983): 73–90; and Helen Longino and Ruth Doell, "Body, Bias, and Behavior: A Comparative Analysis of Reasoning in Two Areas of Biological Science," *Signs* 9, no. 2 (Winter 1983): 206–27.

other or both. The actual content of being a man or woman and the rigidity of the categories themselves are highly variable across cultures and time. Nevertheless, gender relations so far as we have been able to understand them have been (more or less) relations of domination. That is, gender relations have been (more) defined and (imperfectly) controlled by one of their interrelated aspects—the man.

These relations of domination and the existence of gender relations themselves have been concealed in a variety of ways, including defining women as a "question" or the "sex" or the "other"[11] and men as the universal (or at least without gender). In a wide variety of cultures and discourses, men tend to be seen as free from or as not determined by gender relations. Thus, for example, academics do not explicitly study the psychology of men or men's history. Male academics do not worry about how being men may distort their intellectual work, while women who study gender relations are considered suspect (of triviality, if not bias). Only recently have scholars begun to consider the possibility that there may be at least three histories in every culture—"his," "hers," and "ours." "His" and "ours" are generally assumed to be equivalents, although in contemporary work there might be some recognition of the existence of that deviant—woman (e.g., women's history).[12] However, it is still rare for scholars to search for the pervasive effects of gender relations on all aspects of a culture in the way that they feel obligated to investigate the impact of relations of power or the organization of production.

To the extent that feminist discourse defines its problematic as "woman," it, too, ironically privileges the man as unproblematic or exempted from determination by gender relations. From the perspective of social relations, men and women are both prisoners of gender, although in highly differentiated but interrelated ways. That men appear to be and (in many cases) are the wardens, or at least the trustees within a social whole, should not blind us to the extent to which they, too, are governed by the rules of gender. (This is not to deny that it matters a great deal—to individual men, to the women and children sometimes connected to them, and to those concerned about justice—where men as well as women are distributed within social hierarchies.)[13]

[11] For example, the Marxist treatments of the "woman question" from Engels onward, or existentialist, or Lacanian treatment of woman as the "other" to man.

[12] On this point, see Joan Kelly, "The Doubled Vision of Feminist Theory," *Feminist Studies* 6, no. 2 (Summer 1979): 216–27; and also Judith Stacey and Barrie Thorne, "The Missing Feminist Revolution in Sociology," *Social Problems* 32, no. 4 (April 1985): 301–16.

[13] Compare Phyllis Marynick Palmer, "White Women/Black Women: The Dualism of Female Identity and Experience in the United States," *Feminist Studies* 9, no. 1 (Spring 1983): 151–70.

76   Flax

Feminist theorizing and deconstruction

The study of gender relations entails at least two levels of analysis: of gender as a thought construct or category that helps us to make sense out of particular social worlds and histories; and of gender as a social relation that enters into and partially constitutes all other social relations and activities. As a practical social relation, gender can be understood only by close examination of the meanings of "male" and "female" and the consequences of being assigned to one or the other gender within concrete social practices.

Obviously, such meanings and practices will vary by culture, age, class, race, and time. We cannot presume a priori that in any particular culture there will be a single determinant or cause of gender relations, much less that we can tell beforehand what this cause (or these causes) might be. Feminist theorists have offered a variety of interesting causal explanations including the "sex/gender system," the organization of production or sexual division of labor, child-rearing practices, and processes of signification or language. These all provide useful hypotheses for the concrete study of gender relations in particular societies, but each explanatory scheme also seems to me to be deeply flawed, inadequate, and overly deterministic.

For example, Gayle Rubin locates the origin of gender systems in the "transformation of raw biological sex into gender."[14] However, Rubin's distinction between sex and gender rests in turn upon a series of oppositions that I find very problematic, including the opposition of "raw biological sexuality" and the social. This opposition reflects the idea predominant in the work of Freud, Lacan, and others that a person is driven by impulses and needs that are invariant and invariably asocial. This split between culture and "natural" sexuality may in fact be rooted in and reflect gender arrangements.

As I have argued elsewhere,[15] Freud's drive theory reflects in part an unconscious motive: to deny and repress aspects of infantile experience which are relational (e.g., the child's dependence upon and connectedness with its earliest caregiver, who is almost always a woman). Hence, in utilizing Freud's concepts we must pay attention to what they conceal as well as reveal, especially the unacknowledged influences of anxieties about gender on his supposedly gender-neutral concepts (such as drive theory).

Socialist feminists locate the fundamental cause of gender arrange-

---

[14] This is Gayle Rubin's claim in "The Traffic in Women: Notes on the 'Political Economy' of Sex," in *Toward an Anthropology of Women*, ed. Rayna Rapp Reiter (New York: Monthly Review Press, 1975).

[15] I develop this argument in "Psychoanalysis as Deconstruction and Myth: On Gender, Narcissism and Modernity's Discontents," in *The Crisis of Modernity: Recent Theories of Culture in the United States and West Germany*, ed. Kurt Shell (Boulder, Colo.: Westview Press, 1986).

ments in the organization of production or the sexual division of labor. However, this explanatory system also incorporates the historical and philosophical flaws of Marxist analysis. As Balbus convincingly argues,[16] Marxists (including socialist feminists) uncritically apply the categories Marx derived from his description of a particular form of the production of commodities to all areas of human life at all historical periods. Socialist feminists replicate this privileging of production and the division of labor with the concomitant assumptions concerning the centrality of labor itself. Labor is still seen as the essence of history and human being. Such conceptions distort life in capitalist society and surely are not appropriate to all other cultures.[17]

An example of the problems that follow from this uncritical appropriation of Marxist concepts can be found in the attempts by socialist feminists to "widen" the concept of production to include most forms of human activity. These arguments avoid an essential question: why "widen" the concept of production instead of dislodging it or any other singularly central concept from such authoritative power?

This question becomes more urgent when it appears that, despite the best efforts of socialist feminists, the Marxist concepts of labor and production invariably exclude or distort many kinds of activity, including those traditionally performed by women. Pregnancy and child rearing or relations between family members more generally cannot be comprehended merely as "property relations in action."[18] Sexuality cannot be understood as an "exchange" of physical energy, with a "surplus" (potentially) flowing to an "exploiter."[19] Such concepts also ignore or obscure the existence and activities of other persons as well—children—for whom at least a part of their formative experiences has nothing to do with production.

However, the structure of child-rearing practices also cannot serve as *the* root of gender relations. Among the many problems with this approach is that it cannot explain why women have the primary responsibility for

[16] See Balbus (n. 2 above), chap. 1, for a further development of these arguments. Despite Balbus's critique of Marx, he still seems to be under Marx's spell on a metatheoretical level when he tries to locate a root of all domination—child-rearing practices. I have also discussed the inadequacy of Marxist theories in "Do Feminists Need Marxism?" in *Building Feminist Theory*, ed. Quest Staff (New York: Longman, Inc., 1981), and "The Family in Contemporary Feminist Thought: A Critical Review," in Jean Bethke Elshtain, ed., *The Family in Political Thought* (Amherst: University of Massachusetts Press, 1982), 232–39.

[17] Marx may replicate rather than deconstruct the capitalist mentality in his emphasis on the centrality of production. Compare Albert O. Hirschman, *The Passions and the Interests* (Princeton, N.J.: Princeton University Press, 1977) for a very interesting discussion of the historical emergence and construction of specifically *capitalist* mentality.

[18] Annette Kuhn, "Structures of Patriarchy and Capital in the Family," in Kuhn and Wolpe, eds. (n. 2 above), 53.

[19] Ann Ferguson, "Conceiving Motherhood and Sexuality: A Feminist Materialist Approach," in Trebilcot (n. 2 above), 156–58.

child rearing; it can explain only some of the consequences of this fact. In other words, the child-rearing practices taken as causal already presuppose the very social relations we are trying to understand: a gender-based division of human activities and hence the existence of socially constructed sets of gender arrangements and the (peculiar and in need of explanation) salience of gender itself.

The emphasis that (especially) French feminists place on the centrality of language (e.g., chains of signification, signs, and symbols) to the construction of gender also seems problematic.[20] A problem with thinking about (or only in terms of) texts, signs, or signification is that they tend to take on a life of their own or become the world, as in the claim that nothing exists outside of a text; everything is a comment upon or a displacement of another text, as if the modal human activity is literary criticism (or writing).

Such an approach obscures the projection of its own activity onto the world and denies the existence of the variety of concrete social practices that enter into and are reflected in the constitution of language itself (e.g., ways of life constitute language and texts as much as language constitutes ways of life). This lack of attention to concrete social relations (including the distribution of power) results, as in Lacan's work, in the obscuring of relations of domination. Such relations (including gender arrangements) then tend to acquire an aura of inevitability and become equated with language or culture (the "law of the father") as such.

Much of French (including feminist) writing also seems to assume a radical (even ontological rather than socially constructed) disjunction between sign/mind/male/world and body/nature/female.[21] The prescription of some French feminists for the recovery (or reconstitution?) of female experience—"writing from the body"—seems incoherent given this sort of (Cartesian) disjunction. Since "the body" is presocial and prelinguistic, what could it say?

All of these social practices posited as explanations for gender arrangements may be more or less important, interrelated, or themselves partially constituted in and through gender relations depending upon context. As in any form of social analysis, the study of gender relations will necessarily reflect the social practices it attempts to understand. There cannot, nor should we expect there to be, a feminist equivalent to (a falsely universaliz-

---

[20] The theories of French feminists vary, of course. I am focusing on a predominant and influential approach within the variations. For further discussion of French feminisms, see the essays in *Signs*, vol. 7, no. 1 (Autumn 1981) and *Feminist Studies*, vol. 7, no. 2 (Summer 1981).

[21] Domna Stanton, in "Difference on Trial: A Critique of the Maternal Metaphor in Cixous, Irigaray, and Kristeva," in *The Poetics of Gender*, ed. Nancy Miller (New York: Columbia University Press, 1986), discusses the ontological and essentialist aspects of these writers' work.

ing) Marxism; indeed, the epistemologies of feminism undercut all such claims, including feminist ones.[22]

It is on the metatheoretical level that postmodern philosophies of knowledge can contribute to a more accurate self-understanding of the nature of our theorizing. We cannot simultaneously claim (1) that the mind, the self, and knowledge are socially constituted and that what we can know depends upon our social practices and contexts *and* (2) that feminist theory can uncover the Truth of the whole once and for all. Such an absolute truth (e.g., the explanation for all gender arrangements at all times is X . . .) would require the existence of an "Archimedes point" outside of the whole and beyond our embeddedness in it from which we could see (and represent) the whole. What we see and report would also have to be untransformed by the activities of perception and of reporting our vision in language. The object seen (social whole or gender arrangement) would have to be apprehended by an empty (ahistoric) mind and perfectly transcribed by/into a transparent language. The possibility of each of these conditions existing has been rendered extremely doubtful by the deconstructions of postmodern philosophers.

Furthermore, the work of Foucault (among others) should sensitize us to the interconnections between knowledge claims (especially to the claim of absolute or neutral knowledge) and power. Our own search for an "Archimedes point" may conceal and obscure our entanglement in an "episteme" in which truth claims may take only certain forms and not others.[23] Any episteme requires the suppression of discourses that threaten to differ with or undermine the authority of the dominant one. Hence within feminist theory a search for a defining theme of the whole or a feminist viewpoint may require the suppression of the important and discomforting voices of persons with experiences unlike our own. The suppression of these voices seems to be, a necessary condition for the (apparent) authority, coherence, and universality of our own.

Thus, the very search for a root or cause of gender relations (or more narrowly, male domination) may partially reflect a mode of thinking that is itself grounded in particular forms of gender (and/or other) relations in which domination is present. Perhaps reality can have "a" structure only

[22] Catherine MacKinnon, in "Feminism, Marxism, Method, and the State: An Agenda for Theory," *Signs* 7, no. 3 (Spring 1982): 515–44, seems to miss this basic point when she makes claims such as: "The defining theme of the whole is the male pursuit of control over women's sexuality—men not as individuals nor as biological beings, but as a gender group characterized by maleness as socially constructed, of which this pursuit is definitive" (532). On the problem of the "Archimedes point," see Myra Jehlen, "Archimedes and the Paradox of Feminist Criticism," *Signs* 6, no. 4 (Summer 1981): 575–601.

[23] Compare Michel Foucault, *Power/Knowledge*, ed. Colin Gordon (New York: Random House, 1981).

from the falsely universalizing perspective of the dominant group. That is, only to the extent that one person or group can dominate the whole, will reality appear to be governed by one set of rules or be constituted by one privileged set of social relations. Criteria of theory construction such as parsimony or simplicity may be attained only by the suppression or denial of the experiences of the "other(s)."

The natural barrier

Thus, in order for gender relations to be useful as a category of social analysis we must be as socially and self-critical as possible about the meanings usually attributed to those relations and the ways we think about them. Otherwise, we run the risk of replicating the very social relations we are attempting to understand. We have to be able to investigate both the social and philosophical barriers to our comprehension of gender relations.

One important barrier to our comprehension of gender relations has been the difficulty of understanding the relationship between gender and "sex." In this context, sex means the anatomical differences between male and female. Historically (at least since Aristotle), these anatomical differences have been assigned to the class of "natural facts" of biology. In turn, biology has been equated with the pre- or nonsocial. Gender relations then become conceptualized as if they are constituted by two opposite terms or distinct types of being—man and woman. Since man and woman seem to be opposites or fundamentally distinct types of being, gender cannot be relational. If gender is as natural and as intrinsically a part of us as the genitals we are born with, it follows that it would be foolish (or even harmful) to attempt either to change gender arrangements or not to take them into account as a delimitation on human activities.

Even though a major focus of feminist theory has been to "denaturalize" gender, feminists as well as nonfeminists seem to have trouble thinking through the meanings we assign to and the uses we make of the concept "natural."[24] What after all, is the "natural" in the context of the human world?[25] There are many aspects of our embodiedness or biology that we

[24] But see the work of Evelyn Fox Keller on the gendered character of our views of the "natural world," especially her essays "Gender and Science," in Harding and Hintikka, eds., and "Cognitive Repression in Physics," *American Journal of Physics* 47 (1979): 718–21.

[25] In *Public Man, Private Woman*, Jean Bethke Elshtain provides an instructive instance of how allegedly natural properties (of infants) can be used to limit what a "reflective feminist" ought to think. In Elshtain's recent writings it becomes (once again) the responsibility of *women* to rescue children from an otherwise instrumental and uncaring world. Elshtain evidently believes that psychoanalytical theory is exempt from the context-dependent hermeneutics she believes characterize all other kinds of knowledge about social relations. She utilizes psychoanalytic theory as a warrant for absolute or foundational claims about the nature

might see as given limits to human action which Western medicine and science do not hesitate to challenge. For example, few Westerners would refuse to be vaccinated against diseases that our bodies are naturally susceptible to, although in some cultures such actions would be seen as violating the natural order. The tendency of Western science is to "disenchant" the natural world.[26] More and more the "natural" ceases to exist as the opposite of the "cultural" or social. Nature becomes the object and product of human action; it loses its independent existence. Ironically, the more such disenchantment proceeds, the more humans seem to need something that remains outside our powers of transformation. Until recently one such exempt area seemed to be anatomical differences between males and females.[27] Thus in order to "save" nature (from ourselves) many people in the contemporary West equate sex/biology/nature/gender and oppose these to the cultural/social/human. Concepts of gender then become complex metaphors for ambivalences about human action in, on, and as part of the natural world.

But in turn the use of gender as a metaphor for such ambivalences blocks further investigation of them. For the social articulation of these equations is not really in the form I stated above but, rather, sex/biology/nature/woman:cultural/social/man. In the contemporary West, women become the last refuge from not only the "heartless" world but also an increasingly mechanized and fabricated one as well.[28] What remains masked in these modes of thought is the possibility that our concepts of biology/nature are rooted in social relations; they do not merely reflect the given structure of reality itself.

Thus, in order to understand gender as a social relation, feminist theorists need to deconstruct further the meanings we attach to biology/sex/gender/nature. This process of deconstruction is far from complete and certainly is not easy. Initially, some feminists thought we could merely separate the terms "sex" and "gender." As we became more sensitive to the social histories of concepts, it became clear that such an (apparent) disjunc-

of "real human needs" or "the most basic human relationships" and then bases political conclusions on these "natural" facts. See Jean Bethke Elshtain, *Public Man, Private Woman* (Princeton, N.J.: Princeton University Press, 1981), 314, 331.

[26] See Max Weber, "Science as a Vocation," in *From Max Weber*, ed. H. H. Gerth and C. Wright Mills (New York: Oxford University Press, 1958); and Max Horkheimer and Theodor W. Adorno, *Dialectic of Enlightenment* (New York: Herder & Herder, 1972).

[27] I say "until recently" because of developments in medicine such as "sex change" operations and new methods of conception and fertilization of embryos.

[28] As in the work of Christopher Lasch, *Haven in a Heartless World* (New York: Basic Books, 1977). Lasch's work is basically a repetition of the ideas stated earlier by members of the "Frankfurt School," especially Horkheimer and Adorno. See, e.g., the essay, "The Family," in *Aspects of Sociology*, Frankfurt Institute for Social Research (Boston: Beacon Press, 1972).

tion, while politically necessary, rested upon problematic and culture-specific oppositions, for example, the one between "nature" and "culture" or "body" and "mind." As some feminists began to rethink these "oppositions," new questions emerged: does anatomy (body) have no relation to mind? What difference does it make in the constitution of my social experiences that I have a specifically female body?

Despite the increasing complexity of our questions, most feminists would still insist that gender relations are not (or are not only) equivalent to or a consequence of anatomy. Everyone will agree that there are anatomical differences between men and women. These anatomical differences seem to be primarily located in or are the consequence of the differentiated contributions men and women make to a common biological necessity—the physical reproduction of our species.

However, the mere existence of such anatomical differentiation is a descriptive fact, one of many observations we might make about the physical characteristics of humans. Part of the problem in deconstruction of the meaning of biology/sex/gender/nature is that sex/gender has been one of the few areas in which (usually female) embodiment can be discussed at all in (nonscientific) Western discourses. There are many other aspects of our embodiedness that seem equally remarkable and interesting, for example, the incredible complexity of the structure and functioning of our brains, the extreme and relatively prolonged physical helplessness of the human neonate as compared to that of other (even related) species, or the fact that every one of us will die.

It is also the case that physically male and female humans resemble each other in many more ways than we differ. Our similarities are even more striking if we compare humans to (say) toads or trees. So why ought the anatomical differences between male and female humans assume such significance in our sense of our selves as persons? Why ought such complex human social meanings and structures be based on or justified by a relatively narrow range of anatomical differences?

One possible answer to these questions is that the anatomical differences between males and females are connected to and are partially a consequence of one of the most important functions of the species—its physical reproduction. Thus, we might argue, because reproduction is such an important aspect of our species life, characteristics associated with it will be much more salient to us than, say, hair color or height.

Another possible answer to these questions might be that in order for humans physically to reproduce the species, we have to have sexual intercourse. Our anatomical differences make possible (and necessary for physical reproduction) a certain fitting together of distinctively male and female organs. For some humans this "fitting together" is also highly desirable and pleasurable. Hence our anatomical differences seem to be inextricably connected to (and in some sense, even causative of) sexuality.

Thus, there seems to be a complex of relations that have associated, given meanings: penis or clitoris, vagina, and breasts (read distinctively male or female bodies), sexuality (read reproduction—birth and babies), sense of self as a distinct, differentiated gender—as either (and only) a male or female person (read gender relations as a "natural" exclusionary category). That is, we believe there are only two types of humans, and each of us can be only one of them.

A problem with all these apparently obvious associations is that they may assume precisely what requires explanation—that is, gender relations. We live in a world in which gender is a constituting social relation and in which gender is also a relation of domination. Therefore, both men's and women's understanding of anatomy, biology, embodiedness, sexuality, and reproduction is partially rooted in, reflects, and must justify (or challenge) preexisting gender relations. In turn, the existence of gender relations helps us to order and understand the facts of human existence. In other words, gender can become a metaphor for biology just as biology can become a metaphor for gender.

Prisoners of gender: Dilemmas in feminist theory

The apparent connections between gender relations and such important aspects of human existence as birth, reproduction, and sexuality make possible both a conflating of the natural and the social *and* an overly radical distinction between the two. In modern Western culture and sometimes even in feminist theories, "natural" and "social" become conflated in our understanding of "woman." In nonfeminist and some feminist writings about men a radical disjunction is frequently made between the "natural" and the "social." Women often stand for/symbolize the body, "difference," the concrete. These qualities are also said by some feminist as well as nonfeminist writers to suffuse/define the activities most associated with women: nurturing, mothering, taking care of and being in relation with others, "preserving."[29] Women's minds are also often seen as reflecting the qualities of our stereotypically female activities and bodies. Even feminists sometimes say women reason and/or write differently and have different interests and motives than men.[30] Men are said to have more interest in utilizing the power of abstract reason (mind), to want mastery over nature (including bodies), and to be aggressive and militaristic.

[29] Compare Sara Ruddick's essays, "Maternal Thinking," and "Preservative Love and Military Destruction: Some Reflections on Mothering and Peace," both in Trebilcot, ed. (n. 2 above).

[30] On women's "difference," see the essays in Eisenstein and Jardine, eds. (n. 8 above); and Marks and de Courtivron (n. 2 above); also Carol Gilligan, *In a Different Voice* (Cambridge, Mass.: Harvard University Press, 1982); and Stanton (n. 21 above).

The reemergence of such claims even among some feminists needs further analysis. Is this the beginning of a genuine transvaluation of values and/or a retreat into traditional gendered ways of understanding the world? In our attempts to correct arbitrary (and gendered) distinctions, feminists often end up reproducing them. Feminist discourse is full of contradictory and irreconcilable conceptions of the nature of our social relations, of men and women and the worth and character of stereotypically masculine and feminine activities. The positing of these conceptions such that only one perspective can be "correct" (or properly feminist) reveals, among other things, the embeddedness of feminist theory in the very social processes we are trying to critique and our need for more systematic and self-conscious theoretical practice.

As feminist theorizing is presently practiced, we seem to lose sight of the possibility that each of our conceptions of a practice (e.g., mothering) may capture an aspect of a very complex and contradictory set of social relations. Confronted with complex and changing relations, we try to reduce these to simple, unified, and undifferentiated wholes. We search for closure, or the right answer, or the "motor" of the history of male domination. The complexity of our questions and the variety of the approaches to them are taken by some feminists as well as nonfeminists as signs of weakness or failure to meet the strictures of preexisting theories rather than as symptoms of the permeability and pervasiveness of gender relations and the need for new sorts of theorizing.

Some of the reductive moves I have in mind include the constricting of "embodiedness" to a glorification of the distinctively female aspects of our anatomy.[31] This reduction precludes considering the many other ways in which we experience our embodiedness (e.g., nonsexual pleasures, or the processes of aging, or pain). It also replicates the equating of women with the body—as if men did not have bodies also! Alternatively, there is a tendency simply to deny or neglect the meaningfulness or significance of any bodily experience within both women's and men's lives or to reduce it to a subset of "relations of production" (or reproduction).

Within feminist discourse, women sometimes seem to become the sole "bearers" of both embodiedness and difference. Thus we see arguments for the necessity to preserve a gender-based division of labor as our last protection from a state power that is depersonalizing and atomizing.[32] In such arguments the family is posited as an intimate, affective realm of natural relations—of kinship ties, primarily between mothers, children, and female kin—and it is discussed in opposition to the impersonal realms of the state and work (the worlds of men). Alternatively, feminists some-

---

[31] As in, e.g., Hélène Cixous, "Sorties," in *The Newly Born Woman*, ed. Hélène Cixous and Catherine Clement (Ithaca, N.Y.: Cornell University Press, 1986).

[32] See for instance, Elshtain (n. 25 above), and Elshtain, ed. (n. 16 above), 7–30.

times simply deny that there are any significant differences between women and men and that insofar as such differences exist, women should become more like men (or engage in men's activities). Or, the family is understood only as the site of gender struggle and the "reproduction" of persons—a miniature political economy with its own division of labor, source of surplus (women's labor), and product (children and workers).[33] The complex fantasies and conflicting wishes and experiences women associate with family/home often remain unexpressed and unacknowledged. Lacking such self-analysis, feminists find it difficult to recognize some of the sources of our differences or to accept that we do not necessarily share the same past or share needs in the present.[34]

Female sexuality is sometimes reduced to an expression of male dominance, as when Catherine MacKinnon claims "gender socialization is the process through which women come to identify themselves as sexual beings, as beings that exist for men."[35] Among many other problems such a definition leaves unexplained how women could ever feel lust for other women and the wide variety of other sensual experiences women claim to have—for example, in masturbation, breast feeding, or playing with children. Alternatively, the "essence" of female sexuality is said to be rooted in the quasi-biological primal bonds between mother and daughter.[36]

For some theorists, our fantasy and internal worlds have expression only in symbols, not in actual social relations. For example, Iris Young claims that gender differentiation as a "category" refers only to "ideas, symbols and forms of consciousness."[37] In this view, fantasy, our inner worlds, and sexuality may structure intimate relations between women and men at home, but they are rarely seen as also entering into and shaping the structure of work and the state. Thus feminist theory recreates its own version of the public/private split. Alternatively, as in some radical feminist accounts, innate male drives, especially aggression and the need to domi-

[33] This seems to be the basic approach characteristic of socialist-feminist discussions of the family. See, e.g., the essays by A. Ferguson (n. 19 above); and Kuhn (n. 18 above).
[34] See, e.g., Barbara Smith's discussion of the meanings of "home" to her in the "Introduction" to *Home Girls* (n. 2 above). Smith's definition contrasts strongly with the confinement and exploitation some middle-class white women associate with "home." See, e.g., Michele Barrett and Mary McIntosh, *The Anti-social Family* (London: Verso, 1983); and Heidi I. Hartmann, "The Family as the Locus of Gender, Class, and Political Struggle: The Example of Housework," *Signs* 6, no. 3 (Spring 1981): 366–94.
[35] MacKinnon (n. 22 above), 531.
[36] This seems to be Adrienne Rich's argument in "Compulsory Heterosexuality and Lesbian Existence," *Signs* 5, no. 4 (Summer 1980): 631–60. See also Stanton (n. 21 above) on this point.
[37] Iris Young, "Is Male Gender Identity the Cause of Male Domination?" in Trebilcot, ed. (n. 2 above), 140. In this essay, Young replicates the split Juliet Mitchell posits in *Psychoanalysis and Feminism* (New York: Pantheon Books, 1974) between kinship/gender/superstructure and class/production/base.

nate others are posited as the motor that drives the substance and teleology of history.[38]

Feminist theorists have delineated many of the ways in which women's consciousness is shaped by mothering, but we often still see "fathering" as somehow extrinsic to men's and children's consciousness.[39] The importance of modes of child rearing to women's status and to women's and men's sense of self is emphasized in feminist theory; yet we still write social theory in which everyone is presumed to be an adult. For example, in two recent collections of feminist theory focusing on mothering and the family,[40] there is almost no discussion of children as human beings or mothering as a relation between persons. The modal "person" in feminist theory still appears to be a self-sufficient individual adult.

These difficulties in thinking have social as well as philosophical roots, including the existence of relations of domination and the psychological consequences of our current modes of child rearing. In order to sustain domination, the interrelation and interdependence of one group with another must be denied. Connections can be traced only so far before they begin to be politically dangerous. For example, few white feminists have explored how our understandings of gender relations, self, and theory are partially constituted in and through the experiences of living in a culture in which asymmetric race relations are a central organizing principle of society.[41]

Furthermore, just as our current gender arrangements create men who have difficulties in acknowledging relations between people and experiences, they produce women who have difficulties in acknowledging differences within relations. In either gender, these social relations produce a disposition to treat experience as all of one sort or another and to be intolerant of differences, ambiguity, and conflict.

The enterprise of feminist theory is fraught with temptations and pitfalls. Insofar as women have been part of all societies, our thinking cannot be free from culture-bound modes of self-understanding. We as well as men internalize the dominant gender's conceptions of masculinity

---

[38] As in Shulamith Firestone, *The Dialectic of Sex* (New York: Bantam Books, 1970); and MacKinnon (n. 22 above).

[39] On this point, see the essay by Nancy Chodorow and Susan Contratto, "The Fantasy of the Perfect Mother," in *Rethinking the Family*, ed. Barrie Thorne with Marilyn Yalom (New York: Longman, Inc., 1983).

[40] Trebilcot, ed. (n. 2 above); and Thorne and Yalom, eds.

[41] But see the dialogues between Gloria I. Joseph and Jill Lewis, *Common Differences: Conflicts in Black and White Feminist Perspectives* (New York: Doubleday & Co., 1981); and Marie L. Lugones and Elizabeth V. Spelman, "Have We Got a Theory for You," in *Women and Values*, ed. Marilyn Pearsall (Belmont, Calif.: Wadsworth Publishing Co., 1986); and Palmer (n. 13 above). Women of color have been insisting on this point for a long time. Compare the essays in B. Smith, ed. (n. 2 above); and Moraga and Anzaldúa, eds. (n. 2 above). See also Audre Lorde, *Sister Outsider* (Trumansburg, N.Y.: Crossing Press, 1984).

and femininity. Unless we see gender as a social relation, rather than as an opposition of inherently different beings, we will not be able to identify the varieties and limitations of different women's (or men's) powers and oppressions within particular societies. Feminist theorists are faced with a fourfold task. We need to (1) articulate feminist viewpoints of/within the social worlds in which we live; (2) think about how we are affected by these worlds; (3) consider the ways in which how we think about them may be implicated in existing power/knowledge relationships; and (4) imagine ways in which these worlds ought to/can be transformed.

Since within contemporary Western societies gender relations have been ones of domination, feminist theories should have a compensatory as well as a critical aspect. That is, we need to recover and explore the aspects of social relations that have been suppressed, unarticulated, or denied within dominant (male) viewpoints. We need to recover and write the histories of women and our activities into the accounts and stories that cultures tell about themselves. Yet, we also need to think about how so-called women's activities are partially constituted by and through their location within the web of social relations that make up any society. That is, we need to know how these activities are affected but also how they effect, or enable, or compensate for the consequences of men's activities, as well as their implication in class or race relations.

There should also be a transvaluation of values—a rethinking of our ideas about what is humanly excellent, worthy of praise, or moral. In such a transvaluation, we need to be careful not to assert merely the superiority of the opposite. For example, sometimes feminist theorists tend to oppose autonomy to being-in-relations. Such an opposition does not account for adult forms of being-in-relations that can be claustrophobic without auton-omy—an autonomy that, without being-in-relations, can easily degenerate into mastery. Our upbringing as women in this culture often encourages us to deny the many subtle forms of aggression that intimate relations with others can evoke and entail. For example, much of the discussion of mothering and the distinctively female tends to avoid discussing women's anger and aggression—how we internalize them and express them, for example, in relation to children or our own internal selves.[42] Perhaps women are not any less aggressive than men; we may just express our aggression in different, culturally sanctioned (and partially disguised or denied) ways.

Since we live in a society in which men have more power than women, it makes sense to assume that what is considered to be more worthy of praise may be those qualities associated with men. As feminists, we have the right to suspect that even "praise" of the female may be (at least in part)

[42] Compare the descriptions of mothering in Trebilcot, ed. (n. 2 above); especially the essays by Whitbeck and Ruddick.

motivated by a wish to keep women in a restricted (and restrictive) place. Indeed, we need to search into all aspects of a society (the feminist critique included) for the expressions and consequences of relations of domination. We should insist that all such relations are social, that is, they are not the result of the differentiated possession of natural and unequal properties among types of persons.

However, in insisting upon the existence and power of such relations of domination, we should avoid seeing women/ourselves as totally innocent, passive beings. Such a view prevents us from seeing the areas of life in which women have had an effect, in which we are less determined by the will of the other(s), and in which some of us have and do exert power over others (e.g., the differential privileges of race, class, sexual preference, age, or location in the world system).

Any feminist standpoint will necessarily be partial. Thinking about women may illuminate some aspects of a society that have been previously suppressed within the dominant view. But none of us can speak for "woman" because no such person exists except within a specific set of (already gendered) relations—to "man" and to many concrete and different women.

Indeed, the notion of *a* feminist standpoint that is truer than previous (male) ones seems to rest upon many problematic and unexamined assumptions. These include an optimistic belief that people act rationally in their own interests and that reality has a structure that perfect reason (once perfected) can discover. Both of these assumptions in turn depend upon an uncritical appropriation of the Enlightenment ideas discussed earlier. Furthermore, the notion of such a standpoint also assumes that the oppressed are not in fundamental ways damaged by their social experience. On the contrary, this position assumes that the oppressed have a privileged (and not just different) relation and ability to comprehend a reality that is "out there" waiting for our representation. It also presupposes gendered social relations in which there is a category of beings who are fundamentally like each other by virtue of their sex—that is, it assumes the otherness men assign to women. Such a standpoint also assumes that women, unlike men, can be free of determination from their own participation in relations of domination such as those rooted in the social relations of race, class, or homophobia.[43]

I believe, on the contrary, that there is no force or reality "outside" our social relations and activity (e.g., history, reason, progress, science, some transcendental essence) that will rescue us from partiality and differences. Our lives and alliances belong with those who seek to further decenter the world—although we should reserve the right to be suspicious of their

[43] For contrary arguments, see Jaggar (n. 10 above); and also Hartsock, "The Feminist Standpoint" (n. 7 above).

motives and visions as well.[44] Feminist theories, like other forms of post-modernism, should encourage us to tolerate and interpret ambivalence, ambiguity, and multiplicity as well as to expose the roots of our needs for imposing order and structure no matter how arbitrary and oppressive these needs may be.

If we do our work well, "reality" will appear even more unstable, complex, and disorderly than it does now. In this sense, perhaps Freud was right when he declared that women are the enemies of civilization.[45]

Department of Political Science
Howard University

[44] I discuss the gender biases and inadequacies of postmodern philosophy in "Freud's Children" (n. 1 above). See also Naomi Schor, "Dreaming Dissymmetry: Barthes, Foucault, and Sexual Difference" (paper delivered to the Boston Area Colloquium on Feminist Theory, Northeastern University, Fall 1986).

[45] Sigmund Freud, *Civilization and Its Discontents* (New York: W. W. Norton & Co., 1961), 50–51.

African-American Women's History
and the Metalanguage of Race

Evelyn   Brooks   Higginbotham

HEORETICAL DISCUSSION in African-American wom-
en's history begs for greater voice. I say this as a black woman
who is cognizant of the strengths and limitations of current
feminist theory. Feminist scholars have moved rapidly forward
in addressing theories of subjectivity, questions of difference, the construction of social relations as relations of power, the conceptual implications of binary oppositions such as male versus female or equality
versus difference—all issues defined with relevance to gender and with
potential for intellectual and social transformations.[1] Notwithstanding a
few notable exceptions, this new wave of feminist theorists finds little to
say about race. The general trend has been to mention black and Third
World feminists who first called attention to the glaring fallacies in essentialist analysis and to claims of a homogeneous "womanhood,"
"woman's culture," and "patriarchal oppression of women."[2] Beyond
this recognition, however, white feminist scholars pay hardly more than

A number of people read earlier versions of this article. I am especially grateful to
the insights, suggestions, and probing questions of Sharon Harley, Paul Hanson, Darlene
Clark-Hine, and Carroll Smith-Rosenberg.

[1] See, e.g., Teresa de Lauretis, *Alice Doesn't: Feminism, Semiotics, Cinema* (Bloom-
ington: Indiana University Press, 1984), and Teresa de Lauretis, ed., *Feminist Studies,
Feminist Criticism* (Bloomington: Indiana University Press, 1986); Toril Moi, *Sexual/
Textual Politics* (New York: Routledge, 1985); Joan W. Scott, *Gender and the Politics of
History* (New York: Columbia University Press, 1988); Judith Butler, *Gender Trouble:
Feminism and the Subversion of Identity* (New York: Routledge, 1990).

[2] By the early 1980s women of color from various disciplines had challenged the no-
tion of a homogeneous womanhood. A few include: Sharon Harley and Rosalyn
Terborg-Penn, eds., *The Afro-American Woman: Struggles and Images* (Port Washing-
ton, N.Y.: Kennikat, 1978); Gloria T. Hull, Patricia Bell Scott, and Barbara Smith, eds.,
But Some of Us Are Brave (Old Westbury, N.Y.: Feminist Press, 1982); Barbara Smith,
ed., *Home Girls: A Black Feminist Anthology* (New York: Kitchen Table: Women of
Color Press, 1983); Cherrie Moraga and Gloria Anzaldua, eds., *This Bridge Called My
Back: Writings by Radical Women of Color* (New York: Kitchen Table: Women of
Color Press, 1983); Bonnie Thornton Dill, "Race, Class, and Gender: Prospects for an
All-Inclusive Sisterhood," *Feminist Studies* 9 (Spring 1983): 131–50.

[*Signs: Journal of Women in Culture and Society* 1992, vol. 17, no. 2]
© 1992 by The University of Chicago. All rights reserved. 0097-9740/92/1702-0002$01.00

lip service to race as they continue to analyze their own experience in ever more sophisticated forms.

This narrowness of vision is particularly ironic in that these very issues of equality and difference, the constructive strategies of power, and subjectivity and consciousness have stood at the core of black scholarship for some half-century or more. Historian W. E. B. Du Bois, sociologist Oliver Cox, and scientist Charles R. Drew are only some of the more significant pre-1950s contributors to the discussion of race as a social category and to the refutation of essentialist biological and genetic explanations.[3] These issues continue to be salient in our own time, when racism in America grows with both verve and subtlety and when "enlightened" women's historians witness, as has been the case in recent years, recurrent racial tensions at our own professional and scholarly gatherings.

Feminist scholars, especially those of African-American women's history, must accept the challenge to bring race more prominently into their analyses of power. The explication of race entails three interrelated strategies, separated here merely for the sake of analysis. First of all, we must define the construction and "technologies" of race as well as those of gender and sexuality.[4] Second, we must expose the role of race as a metalanguage by calling attention to its powerful, all-encompassing effect on the construction and representation of other social and power relations, namely, gender, class, and sexuality. Third, we must recognize race as providing sites of dialogic exchange and contestation, since race has constituted a discursive tool for both oppression and liberation. As Michael Omi and Howard Winant argue, "the effort must be made to understand race as an unstable and 'decentered' complex of social meanings constantly being transformed by political struggle."[5] Such a three-

---

[3] Charles Drew, in developing a method of blood preservation and organizing blood banks, contributed to the explosion of the myth that blacks were physiologically different from whites. See Charles E. Wynes, *Charles Richard Drew: The Man and the Myth* (Urbana: University of Illinois Press, 1988), 65–71; and C. R. Drew and J. Scudder, "Studies in Blood Preservation: Fate of Cellular Elements and Prothrombin in Citrated Blood," *Journal of Laboratory and Clinical Medicine* 26 (June 1941): 1473–78. Also see W. E. B. Du Bois, "Races," *Crisis* (August 1911), 157–58, and *Dusk of Dawn: An Essay toward an Autobiography of a Race Concept* (New York: Harcourt Brace, 1940), 116–17, 137; Oliver C. Cox, *Caste, Class and Race* (1948; reprint, New York: Monthly Review Press, 1970), 317–20.

[4] Michel Foucault, *History of Sexuality*, vol. 1, *An Introduction*, trans. Robert Hurley (New York: Vintage, 1980), 127, 146. Teresa De Lauretis criticizes Foucault for presenting a male-centered class analysis that disregards gender (see *Technologies of Gender* [Bloomington: Indiana University Press, 1987], 3–30). In both cases "technology" is used to signify the elaboration and implementation of discourses (classificatory and evaluative) in order to maintain the survival and hegemony of one group over another. These discourses are implemented through pedagogy, medicine, mass media, etc.

[5] For discussion of race and signification, see Robert Miles, *Racism* (New York: Routledge, 1989), 69–98; also, Michael Omi and Howard Winant, *Racial Formation in*

pronged approach to the history of African-American women will require borrowing and blending work by black intellectuals, white feminist scholars, and other theorists such as white male philosophers and linguists. Indeed, the very process of borrowing and blending speaks to the tradition of syncretism that has characterized the Afro-American experience.

Defining race

When the U.S. Supreme Court had before it the task of defining obscenity, Justice Potter Stewart claimed that, while he could not intelligibly define it, "I know it when I see it."[6] When we talk about the concept of race, most people believe that they know it when they see it but arrive at nothing short of confusion when pressed to define it. Chromosome research reveals the fallacy of race as an accurate measure of genotypic or phenotypic difference between human beings. Cross-cultural and historical studies of miscegenation law reveal shifting, arbitrary, and contradictory definitions of race. Literary critics, as in the collection of essays "Race," Writing, and Difference, edited by Henry Louis Gates, compellingly present race as the "ultimate trope of difference"—as artificially and arbitrarily contrived to produce and maintain relations of power and subordination. Likewise, historian Barbara Fields argues that race is neither natural nor transhistorical, but must rather be analyzed with an eye to its functioning and maintenance within specific contexts.[7]

Like gender and class, then, race must be seen as a social construction predicated upon the recognition of difference and signifying the simultaneous distinguishing and positioning of groups vis-à-vis one another. More than this, race is a highly contested representation of relations of power between social categories by which individuals are identified and identify themselves. The recognition of racial distinctions emanates from and adapts to multiple uses of power in society. Perceived as "natural" and "appropriate," such racial categories are strategically necessary for the functioning of power in countless institutional and ideological forms,

---

the United States from the 1960s to the 1980s (New York: Routledge & Kegan Paul, 1986), 68.

[6] Jacobellis v. State of Ohio, 378 U.S. 184, 197 (1964).

[7] Although Fields does not use the term "trope," her discussion of race parallels that of Gates. Henry Louis Gates, Jr., ed., "Race," Writing, and Difference (Chicago: University of Chicago Press, 1986), esp. articles by Gates, Jr., "Introduction: Writing 'Race' and the Difference It Makes," 1–20; Anthony Appiah, "The Uncompleted Argument: Du Bois and the Illusion of Race," 21–37; and Tzvetan Todorov, " 'Race,' Writing, and Culture," 370–80. See also Barbara J. Fields, "Ideology and Race in American History," in Region, Race, and Reconstruction: Essays in Honor of C. Vann Woodward, ed. J. Morgan Kousser and James M. McPherson (New York: Oxford University Press, 1982), 143–47.

both explicit and subtle. As Michel Foucault has written, societies engage in "a perpetual process of strategic elaboration" or a constant shifting and reforming of the apparatus of power in response to their particular cultural or economic needs.[8]

Furthermore, in societies where racial demarcation is endemic to their sociocultural fabric and heritage—to their laws and economy, to their institutionalized structures and discourses, and to their epistemologies and everyday customs—gender identity is inextricably linked to and even determined by racial identity. In the Jim Crow South prior to the 1960s and in South Africa until very recently, for instance, little black girls learned at an early age to place themselves in the bathroom for "black women," not in that for "white ladies." As such a distinction suggests, in these societies the representation of both gender and class is colored by race. Their social construction becomes racialized as their concrete implications and normative meanings are continuously shaped by what Louis Althusser terms "ideological state apparatuses"—the school, family, welfare agency, hospital, television and cinema, the press.[9]

For example, the metaphoric and metonymic identification of welfare with the black population by the American public has resulted in tremendous generalization about the supposed unwillingness of many blacks to work. Welfare immediately conjures up images of black female-headed families, despite the fact that the aggregate number of poor persons who receive benefits in the form of aid to dependent children or medicare is predominantly white. Likewise, the drug problem too often is depicted in the mass media as a pathology of black lower-class life set in motion by drug dealers, youthful drug runners, and addicted victims of the ghetto. The drug problem is less often portrayed as an underground economy that mirrors and reproduces the exploitative relations of the dominant economy. The "supply-side" executives who make the "big" money are neither black nor residents of urban ghettos.

Race might also be viewed as myth, "not at all an abstract, purified essence" (to cite Roland Barthes on myth) but, rather, "a formless, unstable, nebulous condensation, whose unity and coherence are above all

[8] Michel Foucault describes the strategic function of the apparatus of power as a system of relations between diverse elements (e.g., discourses, laws, architecture, moral values, institutions) that are supported by types of knowledge: "I understand by the 'term' apparatus a sort of . . . formation which has its major function at a given historical moment that of responding to an *urgent need.* . . . This may have been, for example, the assimilation of a floating population found to be burdensome for an essentially mercantilist economy" (*Power/Knowledge: Selected Interviews and Other Writings, 1972–1977,* ed. Colin Gordon [New York: Pantheon, 1980], 194–95).
[9] Louis Althusser, "Ideology and Ideological State Apparatuses (Notes toward an Investigation)," in his *Lenin and Philosophy, and Other Essays,* trans. Ben Brewster (New York: Monthly Review Press, 1972), 165.

due to its function."[10] As a fluid set of overlapping discourses, race is perceived as arbitrary and illusionary, on the one hand, while natural and fixed on the other. To argue that race is myth and that it is an ideological rather than a biological fact does not deny that ideology has real effects on people's lives. Race serves as a "global sign," a "metalanguage," since it speaks about and lends meaning to a host of terms and expressions, to myriad aspects of life that would otherwise fall outside the referential domain of race.[11] By continually expressing overt and covert analogic relationships, race impregnates the simplest meanings we take for granted. It makes hair "good" or "bad," speech patterns "correct" or "incorrect." It is, in fact, the apparent overdeterminancy of race in Western culture, and particularly in the United States, that has permitted it to function as a metalanguage in its discursive representation and construction of social relations. Race not only tends to subsume other sets of social relations, namely, gender and class, but it blurs and disguises, suppresses and negates its own complex interplay with the very social relations it envelops. It precludes unity within the same gender group but often appears to solidify people of opposing economic classes. Whether race is textually omitted or textually privileged, its totalizing effect in obscuring class and gender remains.

This may well explain why women's studies for so long rested upon the unstated premise of racial (i.e., white) homogeneity and with this presumption proceeded to universalize "woman's" culture and oppression, while failing to see white women's own investment and complicity in the oppression of other groups of men and women. Elizabeth Spelman takes to task this idea of "homogeneous womanhood" in her exploration of race and gender in *Inessential Woman*. Examining thinkers such as Aristotle, Simone de Beauvoir, and Nancy Chodorow, among others, Spelman observes a double standard on the part of many feminists who fail to separate their whiteness from their womanness. White feminists, she argues, typically discern two separate identities for black women, the racial and the gender, and conclude that the gender identity of black women is the same as their own: "In other words, the womanness underneath the black woman's skin is a white woman's and deep down inside the Latina woman is an Anglo woman waiting to burst through."[12]

Afro-American history, on the other hand, has accentuated race by calling explicit attention to the cultural as well as socioeconomic implications of American racism but has failed to examine the differential class

---

[10] Roland Barthes, *Mythologies*, trans. Annette Lavers (New York: Hill & Wang, 1972), 118, 120.

[11] Ibid., 114–15.

[12] Elizabeth V. Spelman, *Inessential Woman: Problems of Exclusion in Feminist Thought* (Boston: Beacon, 1988), 13, 80–113.

and gender positions men and women occupy in black communities—
thus uncritically rendering a monolithic "black community," "black experience," and "voice of the Negro." Notwithstanding that this discursive
monolith most often resonates with a male voice and as the experience of
men, such a rendering precludes gender subordination by black men by
virtue of their own blackness and social subordination. Even black women's history, which has consciously sought to identify the importance of
gender relations and the interworkings of race, class, and gender, nonetheless reflects the totalizing impulse of race in such concepts as "black
womanhood" or the "black woman cross-culturally"—concepts that
mask real differences of class, status and color, regional culture, and a
host of other configurations of difference.

Racial constructions of gender

To understand race as a metalanguage, we must recognize its historical
and material grounding—what Russian linguist and critic M. M. Bakhtin
referred to as "the power of the word to mean."[13] This power evolves
from concrete situational and ideological contexts, that is, from a position of enunciation that reflects not only time and place but values as
well. The concept of race, in its verbal and extraverbal dimension, and
even more specifically, in its role in the representation as well as self-
representation of individuals in American society (what psychoanalytic
theorists call "subjectification"), is constituted in language in which (as
Bakhtin points out) there have never been " 'neutral' words and forms—
words and forms that can belong to 'no one'; language has been completely taken over, shot through with intentions and accents."[14]

The social context for the construction of race as a tool for black
oppression is historically rooted in the context of slavery. Barbara Fields
reminds us: "The idea one people has of another, even when the difference between them is embodied in the most striking physical characteristics, is always mediated by the social context within which the two
come in contact."[15] Race came to life primarily as the signifier of the
master/slave relation and thus emerged superimposed upon class and

[13] M. M. Bakhtin, *The Dialogic Imagination: Four Essays*, ed. Michael Holquist,
trans. Caryl Emerson and Michael Holquist (Austin: University of Texas Press, 1981),
352.
[14] Bakhtin argues: "Language is not an abstract system of normative forms but
rather a concrete heteroglot conception of the world." For my purposes of discussion,
"race," therefore, would convey multiple, even conflicting meanings (heteroglossia) when
expressed by different groups—the multiplicity of meanings and intentions not simply
rendered between blacks and whites, but within each of these two groups. See Bakhtin
on "heteroglossia" (293, 352).
[15] Fields, "Race and Ideology in American History," 148–49.

property relations. Defined by law as "animate chattel," slaves constituted property as well as a social class and were exploited under a system that sanctioned white ownership of black bodies and black labor.[16] Studies of black women in slavery, however, make poignantly clear the role of race not only in shaping the class relations of the South's "peculiar institution," but also in constructing gender's "power to mean." Sojourner Truth's famous and haunting question, "Ar'n't I a Woman?" laid bare the racialized configuration of gender under a system of class rule that compelled and expropriated women's physical labor and denied them legal right to their own bodies and sexuality, much less to the bodies to which they gave birth. While law and public opinion idealized motherhood and enforced the protection of white women's bodies, the opposite held true for black women's. Sojourner Truth's personal testimony demonstrated gender's racial meaning. She had "ploughed, and planted, and gathered into barns," and no male slave had outdone her. She had given birth to thirteen children, all of whom were sold away from her. When she cried out in grief from the depths of her motherhood, "none but Jesus heard."[17]

Wasn't Sojourner Truth a woman? The courts answered this question for slavewomen by ruling them outside the statutory rubric "woman."[18] In discussing the case of *State of Missouri v. Celia,* A. Leon Higginbotham, Jr., elucidates the racial signification of gender. Celia was fourteen years old when purchased by a successful farmer, Robert Newsome. During the five years of his ownership, Newsome habitually forced her into sexual intercourse. At age nineteen she had borne a child by him and was expecting another. In June 1855, while pregnant and ill, Celia defended herself against attempted rape by her master. Her testimony reveals that she warned him she would hurt him if he continued to abuse her while sick. When her threats would not deter his advances, she hit him over the head with a stick, immediately killing him. In an act presaging Richard Wright's *Native Son,* she then burned his body in the fireplace and the next morning spread his ashes on the pathway. Celia was apprehended and tried for first-degree murder. Her counsel sought to lower the charge of first degree to murder in self-defense, arguing that

---

[16] Eugene D. Genovese, *Roll Jordan Roll: The World the Slaves Made* (New York: Pantheon, 1974), 3–7, 28.

[17] Sojourner Truth's speech appears in Bert James Loewenberg and Ruth Bogin, *Black Women in Nineteenth Century American Life* (University Park: Pennsylvania State University Press, 1976), 235. For works on slave women, see Deborah Gray White, *Ar'n't I a Woman? Female Slaves in the Plantation South* (New York: Norton, 1985); Elizabeth Fox-Genovese, *Within the Plantation Household: Black and White Women of the Old South* (Chapel Hill: University of North Carolina Press, 1988), esp. chaps. 3 and 6.

[18] Fox-Genovese, 326.

Celia had a right to resist her master's sexual advances, especially because of the imminent danger to her health. A slave master's economic and property rights, the defense contended, did not include rape. The defense rested its case on Missouri statutes that protected women from attempts to ravish, rape, or defile. The language of these particular statutes explicitly used the term "any woman," while other unrelated Missouri statutes explicitly used terms such as "white female" and "slave" or "negro" in their criminal codes. The question centered on her womanhood. The court found Celia guilty: "If Newsome was in the habit of having intercourse with the defendant who was his slave, . . . it is murder in the first degree." Celia was sentenced to death, having been denied an appeal, and was hanged in December 1855 after the birth of her child.[19]

Since racially based justifications of slavery stood at the core of Southern law, race relations, and social etiquette in general, then proof of "womanhood" did not rest on a common female essence, shared culture, or mere physical appearance. (Sojourner Truth, on one occasion, was forced to bare her breasts to a doubting audience in order to vindicate her womanhood.) This is not to deny gender's role within the social and power relations of race. Black women experienced the vicissitudes of slavery through gendered lives and thus differently from slave men. They bore and nursed children and performed domestic duties—all on top of doing fieldwork. Unlike slave men, slave women fell victim to rape precisely because of their gender. Yet gender itself was both constructed and fragmented by race. Gender, so colored by race, remained from birth until death inextricably linked to one's personal identity and social status. For black and white women, gendered identity was reconstructed and represented in very different, indeed antagonistic, racialized contexts.

Racial constructions of class

Henry Louis Gates argues that "race has become a trope of ultimate, irreducible difference between cultures, linguistic groups, or adherents of specific belief systems which—more often than not—also have fundamentally opposed economic interest."[20] It is interesting that the power of race as a metalanguage that transcends and masks real differences lies in

[19] A. Leon Higginbotham, Jr., notes: "One of the ironies is that the master's estate was denied a profit from Celia's rape. Despite the court's 'mercy' in delaying execution until the birth of the child, the record reflects that a Doctor Carter delivered Celia's child, who was born dead" ("Race, Sex, Education and Missouri Jurisprudence: Shelley v. Kraemer in a Historical Perspective," *Washington University Law Quarterly* 67 [1989]: 684–85).
[20] Gates, Jr., "Introduction: Writing 'Race' and the Difference It Makes" (n. 7 above), 5.

the remarkable and longstanding success with which it unites whites of disparate economic positions against blacks. Until the Civil Rights era of the 1960s, race effectively served as a metaphor for class, albeit a metaphor rife with complications. For example, not all Southern whites were slave owners. Nor did they share the same economic and political interests. Upcountry yeomen protested the predominance of planters' interests over their own in state legislatures, and white artisans decried competition from the use of slave labor.[21] Yet, while Southern whites hardly constituted a homogeneous class, they united for radically different reasons around the banner of white supremacy, waged civil war, and for generations bemoaned the Lost Cause.

The metalanguage of race also transcended the voices of class and ethnic conflict among Northern whites in the great upheavals of labor during the late nineteenth and early twentieth centuries. Amid their opposition, capital and labor agreed sufficiently to exclude blacks from union membership and from more than a marginal place within the emerging industrial work force.[22] Job ceilings and hiring practices limited the overwhelming majority of black men and women to dead-end, low-paying employment—employment whites disdained or were in the process of abandoning.[23] The actual class positions of blacks did not matter, nor did the acknowledgment of differential statuses (such as by income, type of employment, morals and manners, education, or color) by blacks themselves. An entire system of cultural preconceptions disregarded these complexities and tensions by grouping all blacks into a normative well of inferiority and subserviency.[24]

The interplay of the race-class conflation with gender evoked very different social perceptions of black and white women's work roles. This is exhibited by the concern about "female loaferism," which arose in the

[21] Fields, "Ideology and Race in American History" (n. 7 above), 156.

[22] Abram Harris and Sterling Spero, *The Black Worker: A Study of the Negro in the Labor Movement* (1931; reprint, New York: Atheneum, 1968), 158–61, 167–81; Joe William Trotter, *Black Milwaukee: The Making of an Industrial Proletariat, 1915–45* (Urbana: University of Illinois Press, 1985), 13–14, 18, 39–79; Dolores Janiewski, *Sisterhood Denied: Race, Gender, and Class in a New South Community* (Philadelphia: Temple University Press, 1985), 152–78; Jacqueline Jones, *Labor of Love: Labor of Sorrow* (New York: Basic, 1985), 148, 168, 177–79.

[23] See Sharon Harley, "For the Good of Family and Race," *Signs: Journal of Women in Culture and Society* 15, no. 2 (Winter 1990): 340–41.

[24] Patricia Hill Collins argues persuasively for the continued role of race in explaining social class position in her analysis of studies of contemporary black low-income, female-headed families. In her critique of the Moynihan report and the televised Bill Moyers documentary on the "vanishing black family," Collins argues that social class is conceptualized in both these studies as "an outcome variable" of race and gender rather than the product of such structural factors as industrial flight, mechanization, inadequate schools, etc. ("A Comparison of Two Works on Black Family Life," *Signs* 14, no. 4 [Summer 1989]: 876–77, 882–84).

years immediately following Emancipation. Jacqueline Jones vividly exposes the ridicule and hostility meted out to black families who attempted to remove their wives and mothers from the work force to attend to their own households. In contrast to the domestic ideal for white women of all classes, the larger society deemed it "unnatural," in fact an "evil," for black married women "to play the lady" while their husbands supported them. In the immediate postwar South, the role of menial worker outside their homes was demanded of black women, even at the cost of physical coercion.[25]

Dolores Janiewski calls attention to the racialized meaning of class in her study of women's employment in a North Carolina tobacco factory during the twentieth century. She shows that race fractured the division of labor by gender. Southern etiquette demanded protection of white women's "racial honor" and required that they work under conditions described as "suitable for ladies" in contradistinction to the drudgery and dirty working conditions considered acceptable for black women. Janiewski notes that at least one employer felt no inhibition against publicly admitting his "brute treatment" of black female employees.[26]

The most effective tool in the discursive welding of race and class proved to be segregation in its myriad institutional and customary forms. Jim Crow railroad cars, for instance, became strategic sites of contestation over the conflated meaning of class and race: blacks who could afford "first class" accommodations vehemently protested the racial basis for being denied access to them. This is dramatically evident in the case of Arthur Mitchell, Democratic congressman to the U.S. House of Representatives from Illinois during the 1930s. Mitchell was evicted from first-class railroad accommodations while traveling through Hot Springs, Arkansas. Despite his protests, he was forced to join his social "inferiors" in a Jim Crow coach with no flush toilet, washbasin, running water, or soap. The transcript of the trial reveals the following testimony:

> When I offered my ticket, the train conductor took my ticket and tore off a piece of it, but told me at that time that I couldn't ride in that car. We had quite a little controversy about it, and when he said I couldn't ride there I thought it might do some good for me to tell him who I was. I said . . . : "I am Mr. Mitchell, serving in the Congress of the United States." He said it didn't make a damn bit

[25] For discussion of "female loaferism," see Jacqueline Jones, 45, 58–60.

[26] Dolores Janiewski, "Seeking 'a New Day and a New Way': Black Women and Unions in the Southern Tobacco Industry," in *"To Toil the Livelong Day": America's Women at Work, 1780–1980*, ed. Carol Groneman and Mary Beth Norton (Ithaca, N.Y.: Cornell University Press, 1987), 163.

of difference who I was, that as long as I was a nigger I couldn't ride in that car.[27]

Neither the imprimatur of the U.S. House of Representatives nor the ability to purchase a first-class ticket afforded Mitchell the more privileged accommodations. The collective image of race represented Mitchell, the individual, just as he singularly represented the entire black race. Despite the complicating factor of his representing the federal government itself, Mitchell, like his socially constructed race, was unambiguously assigned to the second-class car, ergo lower-class space.

A long tradition of black protest focused on such treatment of women. During the late nineteenth century, segregated railroad trains were emblematic of racial configurations of both class and gender; the first-class railroad car also was called the "ladies car." Indeed, segregation's meaning for gender was exemplified in the trope of "lady." Ladies were not merely women; they represented a class, a differentiated status within the generic category of "women." Nor did society confer such status on all white women. White prostitutes, along with many working-class white women, fell outside its rubric. But no black woman, regardless of income, education, refinement, or character, enjoyed the status of lady. John R. Lynch, black congressman from Mississippi during Reconstruction, denounced the practice of forcing black women of means and refinement out of first-class accommodations and into smoking cars. He characterized the latter accommodations as "filthy . . . with drunkards, gamblers, and criminals." Arguing in support of the Civil Rights Bill of 1875, Lynch used the trope of "lady" in calling attention to race's inscription upon class distinctions:

Under our present system of race distinctions a *white woman* of a questionable social standing, yea, I may say, of an admitted immoral character, can go to any public place or upon any public conveyance and be the recipient of the same treatment, the same courtesy, and the same respect that is usually accorded to the most refined and virtuous; but let an intelligent, modest, refined *colored lady* present herself and ask that the same privileges be accorded to her that have just been accorded to her social inferior of the white race, and in nine cases out of ten, except in certain portions of the country, she will not only be refused, but insulted for making the request. [Emphasis added][28]

[27] Mitchell v. United States, 313 U.S. 80 (1941), app.; also see Catherine A. Barnes, *Journey from Jim Crow: The Desegregation of Southern Transit* (New York: Columbia University Press, 1983), 1–2.
[28] See John R. Lynch's speech on the Civil Rights Bill of 1875 in U.S. Congress, *Congressional Record* (February 3, 1875), 944–45.

Early court cases involving discrimination in public transportation reveal that railroad companies seldom if ever looked upon black women as "ladies." The case of Catherine Brown, a black woman, was the first racial public transportation case to come before the U.S. Supreme Court. In February 1868, Brown was denied passage in the "ladies car" on a train traveling from Alexandria, Virginia, to Washington, D.C. Brown disregarded the demand that she sit in the "colored car" instead. Her persistence in entering the ladies car was met with violence and verbal insults.[29] The resultant court case, decided in her favor in 1873, indicated not an end to such practices but merely the federal government's short-lived support of black civil rights during the era of radical Reconstruction. The outcome of Brown's case proved to be an exception to those that would follow.

Within a decade, Ida B. Wells sued the Chesapeake, Ohio, and Southwestern Railroad for physically ejecting her out of the "ladies" car. When the conductor grabbed her arm, she bit him and held firmly to her seat. It took two men finally to dislodge her. They dragged her into the smoking car and (as she recalled in her autobiography) "the white ladies and gentlemen in the car even stood on the seats so that they could get a good view and continued applauding the conductor for his brave stand." Although her lawsuit was successful at the lower court level, the state Supreme Court of Tennessee reversed the earlier decision, sustaining both the discrimination and the bodily harm against her.[30] The racist decision, like others of the courts, led to *Plessy v. Ferguson* in 1896 and the euphemistic doctrine of "separate but equal."

Racial constructions of sexuality

The exclusion of black women from the dominant society's definition of "lady" said as much about sexuality as it did about class. The metalanguage of race signifies, too, the imbrication of race within the representation of sexuality. Historians of women and of science, largely influenced by Michel Foucault, now attest to the variable quality of changing conceptions of sexuality over time—conceptions informed as much by

---

[29] Railroad Co. v. Brown, 84 U.S. 445 (Wall) 445 (1873).

[30] See Ida B. Wells-Barnett, *Crusade for Justice: The Autobiography of Ida B. Wells*, ed. Alfreda M. Duster (Chicago: University of Chicago Press, 1970), 18–20; for full discussion of this case and those of other black women on buses and streetcars, see Willie Mae Coleman, "Black Women and Segregated Public Transportation: Ninety Years of Resistance," *Truth: Newsletter of the Association of Black Women Historians* (1986), reprinted in Darlene Clark Hine, ed., *Black Women in United States History* (Brooklyn: Carlson, 1990), 5:296–98.

race and class as by gender.[31] Sexuality has come to be defined not in terms of biological essentials or as a universal truth detached and transcendent from other aspects of human life and society. Rather, it is an evolving conception applied to the body but given meaning and identity by economic, cultural, and historical context.[32]

In the centuries between the Renaissance and the Victorian era, Western culture constructed and represented changing and conflicting images of woman's sexuality, which shifted diametrically from images of lasciviousness to moral purity. Yet Western conceptions of black women's sexuality resisted change during this same time.[33] Winthrop Jordan's now classic study of racial attitudes toward blacks between the sixteenth and nineteenth centuries argues that black women's bodies epitomized centuries-long European perceptions of Africans as primitive, animallike, and savage. In America, no less distinguished and learned a figure than Thomas Jefferson conjectured that black women mated with orangutans.[34] While such thinking rationalized slavery and the sexual exploitation of slave women by white masters, it also perpetuated an enormous division between black people and white people on the "scale of humanity": carnality as opposed to intellect and/or spirit; savagery as opposed to civilization; deviance as opposed to normality; promiscuity as opposed to purity; passion as opposed to passionlessness. The black woman came to symbolize, according to Sander Gilman, an "icon for black sexuality in general."[35] This discursive gap between the races was if anything greater between white and black women than between white and black men.

Violence figured preeminently in racialized constructions of sexuality. From the days of slavery, the social construction and representation of black sexuality reinforced violence, rhetorical and real, against black

[31] For work by historians on sexuality's relation to class and race, see the essays in Kathy Peiss and Christina Simmons, with Robert Padgug, eds., *Passion and Power: Sexuality in History* (Philadelphia: Temple University Press, 1989).

[32] Foucault, *History of Sexuality*, 1:14, 140, 143, 145–146, and *Power/Knowledge* (n. 8 above), 210–11.

[33] Nancy Cott calls attention to the role of evangelical Protestantism and, later, science in contributing to the image of "passionlessness" for American northern women ("Passionlessness: An Interpretation of Victorian Sexual Ideology, 1790–1850," *Signs* 4, no. 2 (Winter 1978): 219–36); for changing Western representations, see Thomas Laqueur, *Making Sex: Body and Gender from the Greeks to Freud* (Cambridge, Mass.: Harvard University Press, 1990).

[34] See discussion of Jefferson and larger discussion of Western views toward blacks in Winthrop D. Jordan, *White over Black: American Attitudes toward the Negro, 1550–1812* (New York: Norton, 1977), 24–40, 151, 154–59, 458–59.

[35] See Sander L. Gilman, "Black Bodies, White Bodies: Toward an Iconography of Female Sexuality in Late Nineteenth-Century Art, Medicine, and Literature," in Gates, ed. (n. 7 above), 223–40.

women and men.[36] That the rape of black women could continue to go on with impunity long after slavery's demise underscores the pervasive belief in black female promiscuity. This belief found expression in the statement of one Southern white woman in 1904: "I cannot imagine such a creation as a virtuous black woman."[37]

The lynching of black men, with its often attendant castration, reeked of sexualized representations of race.[38] The work of black feminists of the late nineteenth century makes clear that lynching, while often rationalized by whites as a punishment for the rape of white women, more often was perpetrated to maintain racial etiquette and the socioeconomic and political hegemony of whites. Ida Wells-Barnett, Anna J. Cooper, Mary Church Terrell, and Pauline Hopkins exposed and contrasted the specter of the white woman's rape in the case of lynching and the sanctioned rape of black women by white men. Hazel Carby, in discussing these black feminist writers, established their understanding of the intersection of strategies of power with lynching and rape:

Their legacy to us is theories that expose the colonization of the black female body by white male power and the destruction of black males who attempted to exercise any oppositional patriarchal control. When accused of threatening the white female body, the repository of heirs to property and power, the black male, and his economic, political, and social advancement, is lynched out of existence. Cooper, Wells, and Hopkins assert the necessity of seeing the relation between histories: the rape of black women in the

[36] Jacquelyn Dowd Hall, *Revolt against Chivalry: Jessie Daniel Ames and the Women's Campaign against Lynching* (New York: Columbia University Press, 1979), 129–57, 220; Ida Wells-Barnett, *On Lynching,* reprint ed. (New York: Arno Press, 1969); Joel Williamson, *A Rage for Order* (New York: Oxford University Press, 1986), 117–51; Howard Smead, *Blood Justice: The Lynching of Mack Charles Parker* (New York: Oxford University Press, 1986).

[37] "Experiences of the Race Problem: By a Southern White Woman," *Independent,* vol. 56 (March 17, 1904), as quoted in Anne Firor Scott, "Most Invisible of All: Black Women's Voluntary Associations," *Journal of Southern History* 56 (February 1990): 10. Neil R. McMillen observes for the early twentieth century that courts did not usually convict white men for the rape of black women, "because whites generally agreed that no black female above the age of puberty was chaste" (*Dark Journey: Black Mississippians in the Age of Jim Crow* [Urbana: University of Illinois Press, 1989], 205–6).

[38] A number of writers have dealt with the issue of castration. For historical studies of the early slave era, see Jordan, 154–58, 463, 473; also discussing castration statutes as part of the slave codes in colonial Virginia, South Carolina, and Pennsylvania is A. Leon Higginbotham, Jr., *In the Matter of Color: Race and the American Legal Process* (New York: Oxford University Press, 1978), 58, 168, 177, 282, 413, n. 107. For discussion of castration during the twentieth century, see Richard Wright, "The Ethics of Living Jim Crow: An Autobiographical Sketch," in his *Uncle Tom's Children* (1938; reprint, New York: Harper & Row, 1965); and Trudier Harris, *Exorcising Blackness: Historical and Literary Lynching and Burning Rituals* (Bloomington: Indiana University Press, 1984), 29–68.

nineties is directly linked to the rape of the female slave. Their analyses are dynamic and not limited to a parochial understanding of "women's issues"; they have firmly established the dialectical relation between economic/political power and economic/sexual power in the battle for control of women's bodies.[39]

Through a variety of mediums—theater, art, the press, and literature— discourses of racism developed and reified stereotypes of sexuality. Such representations grew out of and facilitated the larger subjugation and control of the black population. The categorization of class and racial groups according to culturally constituted sexual identities facilitated blacks' subordination within a stratified society and rendered them powerless against the intrusion of the state into their innermost private lives. This intrusion went hand in hand with the role of the state in legislating and enforcing racial segregation, disfranchisement, and economic discrimination.

James Jones's *Bad Blood: The Tuskegee Syphilis Experiment* provides us with a profoundly disturbing example of such intrusion into blacks' private lives. Jones recounts how a federal agency, the Public Health Service, embarked in 1932 upon decades of tests on black men with syphilis, denying them access to its cure in order to assess the disease's debilitating effects on the body.[40] The federal agency felt at liberty to make the study because of its unquestioning acceptance of stereotypes that conflated race, gender, and class. By defining this health problem in racial terms, "objective scientific researchers" could be absolved of all responsibility. Some even posited that blacks had "earned their illness as just recompense for wicked life-styles."[41]

The Public Health Service's willingness to prolong syphilis despite the discovery of penicillin discloses not only the federal government's lack of concern for the health of the men in its study, but its even lesser concern for black women in relationships with these men. Black women failed to receive so much as a pretense of protection, so widely accepted was the belief that the spread of the disease was inevitable because black women were promiscuous by nature. This emphasis on black immorality pre-

[39] Bettina Aptheker, *Woman's Legacy: Essays on Race, Sex and Class in American History* (Amherst: University of Massachusetts Press, 1982), 53–77; Hazel V. Carby, " 'On the Threshold of Woman's Era': Lynching, Empire, and Sexuality in Black Feminist Theory," in Gates, ed., 314–15.

[40] James H. Jones, *Bad Blood: The Tuskegee Syphilis Experiment* (New York: Free Press, 1981), 11–29.

[41] Ibid., 22. Elizabeth Fee argues that in the 1920s and 1930s, before a cure was found for syphilis, physicians did not speak in the dispassionate tone of germ theory but, rather, reinforced the image of syphilis as a "black problem" (see her study of Baltimore, "Venereal Disease: The Wages of Sin?" in Peiss and Simmons, eds. [n. 31 above], 182–84).

cluded any sensitivity to congenital syphilis; thus innocent black babies born with the disease went unnoticed and equally unprotected. Certainly the officials of the Public Health Service realized that blacks lived amid staggering poverty, amid a socioeconomic environment conducive to disease. Yet these public servants encoded hegemonic articulations of race into the language of medicine and scientific theory. Their perceptions of sexually transmitted disease, like those of the larger society, were affected by race.[42] Jones concludes:

> The effect of these views was to isolate blacks even further within American society—to remove them from the world of health and to lock them within a prison of sickness. Whether by accident or design, physicians had come dangerously close to depicting the syphilitic black as the representative black. As sickness replaced health as the normal condition of the race, something was lost from the sense of horror and urgency with which physicians had defined disease. The result was a powerful rationale for inactivity in the face of disease, which by their own estimates, physicians believed to be epidemic.[43]

In response to assaults upon black sexuality, according to Darlene Clark Hine, there arose among black women a politics of silence, a "culture of dissemblance." In order to "protect the sanctity of inner aspects of their lives," black women, especially those of the middle class, reconstructed and represented their sexuality through its absence— through silence, secrecy, and invisibility. In so doing, they sought to combat the pervasive negative images and stereotypes. Black clubwomen's adherence to Victorian ideology, as well as their self-representation as "super moral," according to Hine, was perceived as crucial not only to the protection and upward mobility of black women but also to the attainment of respect, justice, and opportunity for all black Americans.[44]

Race as a double-voiced discourse

As this culture of dissemblance illustrates, black people endeavored not only to silence and conceal but also to dismantle and deconstruct the

---

[42] For a study of the social construction of venereal disease, from the late nineteenth century through the AIDS crisis of our own time, see Allan M. Brandt, *No Magic Bullet: A Social History of Venereal Disease in the United States since 1880* (New York: Oxford University Press, 1987); also see Doris Y. Wilkinson and Gary King, "Conceptual and Methodological Issues in the Use of Race as a Variable: Policy Implications," *Milbank Quarterly* 65 (1987): 68.

[43] James H. Jones, 25, 28.

[44] Darlene Clark Hine, "Rape and the Inner Lives of Black Women in the Middle West: Preliminary Thoughts on the Culture of Dissemblance," *Signs* 14, no. 4 (Summer 1989): 915.

dominant society's deployment of race. Racial meanings were never internalized by blacks and whites in an identical way. The language of race has historically been what Bakhtin calls a double-voiced discourse — serving the voice of black oppression and the voice of black liberation. Bakhtin observes: "The word in language is half someone else's. It becomes 'one's own' only when the speaker populates it with his [or her] own intention, his [or her] own accent, when he [or she] appropriates the word, adapting it to his [or her] own semantic and expressive intention."[45] Blacks took "race" and empowered its language with their own meaning and intent, just as the slaves and freedpeople had appropriated white surnames, even those of their masters, and made them their own.[46]

For African-Americans, race signified a cultural identity that defined and connected them as a people, even as a nation. To be called a "race leader," "race man," or "race woman" by the black community was not a sign of insult or disapproval, nor did such titles refer to any and every black person. Quite to the contrary, they were conferred on Carter G. Woodson, W. E. B. Du Bois, Ida Wells-Barnett, Mary McLeod Bethune, and the other men and women who devoted their lives to the advancement of their people. When the National Association of Colored Women referred to its activities as "race work," it expressed both allegiance and commitment to the concerns of black people. Through a range of shifting, even contradictory meanings and accentuations expressed at the level of individual and group consciousness, blacks fashioned race into a cultural identity that resisted white hegemonic discourses.

The "two-ness" of being both American and Negro, which Du Bois so eloquently captured in 1903, resonates across time. If blacks as individuals referred to a divided subjectivity — "two warring ideals in one dark body" — they also spoke of a collective identity in the colonial terms of a "nation within a nation."[47] The many and varied voices of black nationalism have resounded again and again from the earliest days of the American republic. Black nationalism found advocates in Paul Cuffee, John Russwurm, and Martin Delany in the nineteenth century, and Marcus

[45] Bakhtin (n. 13 above), 293, 324.

[46] On slave surnames, see Herbert G. Gutman, *The Black Family in Slavery and Freedom, 1750–1925* (New York: Pantheon, 1976), 230–56; also George P. Cunningham, " 'Called into Existence': Desire, Gender, and Voice in Frederick Douglass's Narrative of 1845," *Differences* 1, no. 3 (1989): 112–13, 117, 129–31.

[47] Martin Robison Delany wrote in the 1850s of blacks in the United States: "We are a nation within a nation; — as the Poles in Russia, the Hungarians in Austria, the Welsh, Irish, and Scotch in the British Dominions" (see his *The Condition, Elevation, Emigration and Destiny of the Colored People of the United States,* reprint ed. [New York: Arno, 1969], 209; also W. E. Burghardt Du Bois, *The Souls of Black Folks* [New York: Washington Square Press, 1970], 3).

Garvey, Malcolm X, and Stokely Carmichael in the twentieth.[48] We know far too little about women's perceptions of nationalism, but Pauline Hopkins's serialized novel *Of One Blood* (1903) counterposes black and Anglo-Saxon races: "The dawn of the Twentieth century finds the Black race fighting for existence in every quarter of the globe. From over the sea Africa stretches her hands to the American Negro and cries aloud for sympathy in her hour of trial. . . . In America, caste prejudice has received fresh impetus as the 'Southern brother' of the Anglo-Saxon family has arisen from the ashes of secession, and like the prodigal of old, has been gorged with fatted calf and 'fixin's.' "[49]

Likewise Hannah Nelson, an elementary school graduate employed most of her life in domestic service, told anthropologist John Langston Gwaltney in the 1970s: "We are a nation. The best of us have said it and everybody feels it. I know that will probably bother your white readers, but it is nonetheless true that black people think of themselves as an entity."[50] Thus, when historian Barbara Fields observes that "Afro-Americans invented themselves, not as a race, but as a nation," she alludes to race as a double-voiced discourse.[51] For blacks, race signified cultural identity and heritage, not biological inferiority. However, Fields's discussion understates the power of race to mean nation—specifically, race as the sign of perceived kinship ties between blacks in Africa and throughout the diaspora. In the crucible of the Middle Passage and American slavery, the multiple linguistic, tribal, and ethnic divisions among Africans came to be forged into a single, common ancestry. While not

[48] See, devoted to the subject of nationalism, John H. Bracey, Jr., August Meier, and Elliott Rudwick, eds., *Black Nationalism in America* (New York: Bobbs-Merrill, 1970); Sterling Stuckey, *Slave Culture: Nationalist Theory and the Foundations of Black America* (New York: Oxford University Press, 1987), and *The Ideological Origins of Black Nationalism* (Boston: Beacon, 1972); Wilson Jeremiah Moses, *The Golden Age of Black Nationalism, 1850–1925* (Hamden, Conn.: Archon, 1978).

[49] Pauline Hopkins, "Heroes and Heroines in Black," *Colored American Magazine* 6 (January 1903): 211. The original publication of *Of One Blood* was serialized in issues of the *Colored American Magazine* between November 1902 and November 1903. See the novel in its entirety, along with Hazel Carby's introduction to the Oxford edition, in Pauline Hopkins, *Magazine Novels of Pauline Hopkins* (New York: Oxford University Press, 1988); also Hazel V. Carby, *Reconstructing Womanhood: The Emergence of the Afro-American Woman Novelist* (New York: Oxford University Press, 1987), 155–62.

[50] See John Langston Gwaltney, "A Nation within a Nation," in *Drylongso: A Self-Portrait of Black America*, ed. John Langston Gwaltney (New York: Random House, 1980), 3–23; and Patricia Hill Collins, "The Social Construction of Black Feminist Thought," *Signs* 14, no. 4 (Summer 1989): 765–70. For a critique of race and essentialism, see Diana Fuss, *Essentially Speaking: Feminism, Nature, and Difference* (New York: Routledge, 1989), 73–96.

[51] Robert Miles (n. 5 above) argues that both race and nation are "supra-class and supra-gender forms of categorisation with considerable potential for articulation" (89–90). Also, see Barbara Jeanne Fields, "Slavery, Race, and Ideology in the United States of America," *New Left Review*, no. 181 (May/June 1990), 115.

adhering to "scientific" explanations of superior and inferior races, African-Americans inscribed the black nation with racially laden meanings of blood ties that bespoke a lineage and culture more imagined than real.

Such imaginings were not unique to African-Americans.[52] As nation states emerged in Europe during the fifteenth and sixteenth centuries, the concept of "race" came increasingly to articulate a nationalist ideology. Racial representations of nation included, on the one hand, "cosmopolitan" views that characterized each national grouping as contributing its own "special gift" to the complementarity of humankind, and, on the other hand, views of hierarchical difference that justified the existence of nation states and the historical dominance of certain groupings over others. Hence, Thomas Arnold could speak of the Anglo-Saxon's lineage in an 1841 lecture at Oxford: "Our English race is the German race; for though our Norman forefathers had learnt to speak a stranger's language, yet in blood, as we know, they were the Saxons' brethren: both alike belonged to the Teutonic or German stock."[53] Such cultural conceptions surely informed nineteenth-century African-American perceptions of the black nation as a site of group uniqueness.

Throughout the nineteenth century, blacks and whites alike subscribed to what George Fredrickson terms "romantic racialism."[54] Blacks constructed and valorized a self-representation essentially antithetical to that of whites. In his article "The Conservation of Races," published in 1897, Harvard-trained W. E. B. Du Bois disclosed his admiration for what he believed to be the "spiritual, psychical" uniqueness of his people—their "special gift" to humanity.[55] Twentieth-century essentialist concepts

[52] See Benedict R. Anderson's discussion of nation as "imagined" in the sense of its being limited (not inclusive of all mankind), sovereign, and a community, in his *Imagined Communities: Reflections on the Origin and Spread of Nationalism* (New York and London: Verso, 1983), 14–16.

[53] Arthur Penryhn Stanley, *The Life and Correspondence of Thomas Arnold, D.D.*, 12th ed. (London 1881), 2:324, quoted and cited in Reginald Horsman, *Race and Manifest Destiny: The Origins of American Racial Anglo-Saxonism* (Cambridge, Mass.: Harvard University Press, 1981), 66.

[54] George Fredrickson discusses "romantic racialism" within the context of "benign" views of black distinctiveness. This view was upheld by romanticism, abolitionism, and evangelical religion and should be distinguished from "scientific" explanations or cultural interpretations that vilified blacks as beasts and unworthy of human dignity (*The Black Image in the White Mind* [New York: Harper & Row, 1972], 97–99, 101–15, 125–26).

[55] W. E. B. Du Bois stated: "But while race differences have followed mainly physical race lines, yet no mere physical distinctions would really define or explain the deeper differences—the cohesiveness and continuity of these groups. The deeper differences are spiritual, psychical, differences—undoubtedly based on the physical but infinitely transcending them" ("The Conservation of Races," in *W. E. B. Du Bois Speaks: Speeches*

such as "negritude," "soul," and most recently "Afrocentricity" express in new and altered form the continued desire to capture transcendent threads of racial "oneness." Frantz Fanon described the quest for cultural identity and self-recovery as "the whole body of efforts made by a people in the sphere of thought to describe, justify and praise action through which that people has created itself and keeps itself in existence."[56] These efforts seek to negate white stereotypes of blacks and in their place insert a black worldview or standpoint. Of critical importance here are the dialogic racial representations effected by blacks themselves against negative representations—or more precisely, blacks' appropriation of the productive power of language for the purpose of resistance.[57]

Such a discursive rendering of race counters images of physical and psychical rupture with images of wholeness. Yet once again, race serves as myth and as a global sign, for it superimposes a "natural" unity over a plethora of historical, socioeconomic, and ideological differences among blacks themselves. This is not to understate the critical liberating intention implicit in blacks' own usage of the term "the race," when referring to themselves as a group. But the characterization obscures rather than mirrors the reality of black heterogeneity. In fact, essentialist or other racialized conceptions of national culture hardly reflect paradigmatic consistency. Black nationalism itself has been a heteroglot conception, categorized variously as revolutionary, bourgeois reformist, cultural, religious, economic, or emigrationist.[58] Race as the sign of cultural identity has been neither a coherent nor static concept among African-Americans. Its perpetuation and resilience have reflected shifting, often monolithic and essentialist assumptions on the part of thinkers attempting to identify and define a black peoplehood or nation.

Acceptance of a nation-based, racialized perspective even appears in the work of black women scholars, who seek to ground a black feminist standpoint in the concrete experience of race and gender oppression. Notwithstanding the critical importance of this work in contesting racism and sexism in the academy and larger society, its focus does not permit sufficient exploration of ideological spaces of difference among

---

and Addresses, 1890–1919, ed. Philip S. Foner [New York: Pathfinder, 1970], 77–79, 84); see also Appiah's critique of Du Bois (n. 7 above), 23–29.

[56] Frantz Fanon offers this definition of national culture in contradistinction to one based on "an abstract populism that believes it can discover the people's true nature" (*The Wretched of the Earth* [New York: Grove, 1968], 233).

[57] Raymond Williams asserts: "Language has then to be seen as a persistent kind of creation and re-creation: a dynamic presence and a constant regenerative process" (*Marxism and Literature* [New York: Oxford University Press, 1977], 31).

[58] See Bracey, Meier, and Rudwick, eds. (n. 48 above), xxvi–xxx; Winant and Omi (n. 5 above), 38–51.

black women themselves. For example, sociologist Patricia Hill Collins identifies an ethic of caring and an ethic of personal accountability at the root of Afrocentric values and particularly of Afrocentric feminist epistemology, yet she does not investigate how such values and epistemology are affected by differing class positions.[59] In short, she posits but does not account for the *singularity* of an Afro-American women's standpoint amid diverse and conflicting positions of enunciation.

The rallying notion of "racial uplift" among black Americans during the late nineteenth and early twentieth centuries illustrates the problematic aspects of identifying a standpoint that encompasses all black women. Racial uplift was celebrated in the motto of the National Association of Colored Women—"lifting as we climb." The motto itself expressed a paradox: belief in black womanhood's common cause and recognition of differential values and socioeconomic positions. Racial uplift, while invoking a discursive ground on which to explode negative stereotypes of black women, remained locked within hegemonic articulations of gender, class, and sexuality. Black women teachers, missionaries, and club members zealously promoted values of temperance, sexual repression, and polite manners among the poor.

"Race work" or "racial uplift" equated normality with conformity to white middle-class models of gender roles and sexuality. Given the extremely limited educational and income opportunities during the late nineteenth–early twentieth centuries, many black women linked mainstream domestic duties, codes of dress, sexual conduct, and public etiquette with both individual success and group progress.[60] Black leaders argued that "proper" and "respectable" behavior proved blacks worthy of equal civil and political rights. Conversely, nonconformity was equated with deviance and pathology and was often cited as a cause of racial inequality and injustice. S. W. Layten, founder of the National League for the Protection of Colored Women and leader of one million black Baptist women, typified this attitude in her statement of 1904: "Unfortunately the minority or bad Negroes have given the race a ques-

[59] E. Frances White's perceptive analysis of African-Americans' contestation of the discursive representation of Africa calls attention to the conservative implications of Afrocentric feminism. See E. Frances White, "Africa on My Mind: Gender, Counter Discourse and African-American Nationalism," *Journal of Women's History* 2 (Spring 1990): 90–94; Patricia Hill Collins, "The Social Construction of Black Feminist Thought" (n. 50 above), 765–70, and *Black Feminist Thought: Knowledge, Consciousness, and the Politics of Empowerment* (Boston: Unwin Hyman, 1990), 10–11, 15. Also for a good critique, see bell hooks, *Yearning: Race, Gender, and Cultural Politics* (Boston: South End Press, 1990).

[60] Evelyn Brooks Higginbotham, "Beyond the Sound of Silence: Afro-American Women in History," *Gender and History* 1 (Spring 1989): 58–59.

tionable reputation; these degenerates are responsible for every discrimination we suffer."[61]

On a host of levels, racial uplift stood at odds with the daily practices and aesthetic tastes of many poor, uneducated, and "unassimilated" black men and women dispersed throughout the rural South or newly huddled in urban centers.[62] The politics of "respectability" disavowed, in often repressive ways, much of the expressive culture of the "folk," for example, sexual behavior, dress style, leisure activity, music, speech patterns, and religious worship patterns. Similar class and sexual tensions between the discourse of the intelligentsia (the "New Negro") and that of the "people" (the "folk" turned proletariat in the northern urban context) appear in Hazel Carby's discussion of black women novelists of the Harlem Renaissance during the 1920s.[63]

Today, the metalanguage of race continues to bequeath its problematic legacy. While its discursive construction of reality into two opposing camps— blacks versus whites or Afrocentric versus Eurocentric standpoints— provides the basis for resistance against external forces of black subordination, it tends to forestall resolution of problems of gender, class, and sexual orientation internal to black communities. The resolution of such differences is also requisite to the liberation and well-being of "the race." Worse yet, problems deemed too far astray of respectability are subsumed within a culture of dissemblance. The AIDS crisis serves as a case in point, with AIDS usually contextualized within a Manichean opposition of good versus evil that translates into heterosexuality versus homosexuality or wholesome living versus intravenous drug use. At a time when AIDS is a leading killer of black women and their children in impoverished inner-city neighborhoods, educational and support strate-

---

[61] National Baptist Convention, *Journal of the Twenty-fourth Annual Session of the National Baptist Convention and the Fifth Annual Session of the Woman's Convention, Held in Austin, Texas, September 14–19, 1904* (Nashville: National Baptist Publishing Board, 1904), 324; also, I discuss the politics of respectability as both subversive and conservative in Evelyn Brooks Higginbotham, *Righteous Discontent: The Women's Movement in the Black Baptist Church, 1880–1920* (Cambridge, Mass.: Harvard University Press, 1992), in press, chap. 7.

[62] Houston A. Baker, Jr., in his discussion of the black vernacular, characterizes the "quotidian sounds of black every day life" as both a defiant and entrancing voice (*Afro-American Poetics: Revisions of Harlem and the Black Aesthetic* [Madison: University of Wisconsin Press, 1988], 95–107); see also Houston A. Baker, Jr., *Blues, Ideology and Afro-American Literature: A Vernacular Theory* (Chicago: University of Chicago Press, 1984), 11–13. Similarly, John Langston Gwaltney calls the "folk" culture of today's cities a "core black culture," which is "more than ad hoc synchronic adaptive survival." Gwaltney links its values and epistemology to a long peasant tradition. See Gwaltney, ed. (n. 50 above), xv–xvii.

[63] Carby, *Reconstructing Womanhood* (n. 49 above), 163–75; also Henry Louis Gates, Jr., "The Trope of a New Negro and the Reconstruction of the Image of the Black," *Representations* 24 (Fall 1988): 129–55.

gies lag far behind those of white gay communities.[64] Black women's groups and community organizations fail to tackle the problem with the priority it merits. They shy away from public discussion in large measure because of the historic association of disease and racial/sexual stereotyping.

Conclusion

By analyzing white America's deployment of race in the construction of power relations, perhaps we can better understand why black women historians have largely refrained from an analysis of gender along the lines of the male/female dichotomy so prevalent among white feminists. Indeed, some black women scholars adopt the term *womanist* instead of *feminist* in rejection of gender-based dichotomies that lead to a false homogenizing of women. By so doing they follow in the spirit of black scholar and educator Anna J. Cooper, who in *A Voice from the South* (1892) inextricably linked her racial identity to the "quiet, undisputed dignity" of her womanhood.[65] At the threshold of the twenty-first century, black women scholars continue to emphasize the inseparable unity of race and gender in their thought. They dismiss efforts to bifurcate the identity of black women (and indeed of all women) into discrete categories—as if culture, consciousness, and lived experience could at times constitute "woman" isolated from the contexts of race, class, and sexuality that give form and content to the particular women we are.[66]

On the other hand, we should challenge both the overdeterminancy of race vis-à-vis social relations among blacks themselves and conceptions of the black community as harmonious and monolithic. The historic reality of racial conflict in America has tended to devalue and discourage attention to gender conflict within black communities and to tensions of class or sexuality among black women. The totalizing tendency of race

[64] See Bruce Lambert, "AIDS in Black Women Seen as Leading Killer," *New York Times* (July 11, 1990); Ernest Quimby and Samuel R. Friedman, "Dynamics of Black Mobilization against AIDS in New York City," *Social Problems* 36 (October 1989): 407–13; Evelynn Hammonds, "Race, Sex, Aids: The Construction of 'Other,'" *Radical America* 29 (November–December 1987): 28–36; also Brandt (n. 42 above), 186–92.

[65] Anna Julia Cooper stated: "When and where I enter in the quiet, undisputed dignity of my womanhood without violence and without suing or special patronage, then and there the whole Negro race enters with me" (*A Voice from the South,* reprint of the 1892 ed. [New York: Negro Universities Press, 1969], 31).

[66] Alice Walker, *In Search of Our Mothers' Gardens: Womanist Prose* (New York: Harcourt, Brace, Jovanovich, 1983), xi–xii; also see, e.g., Elsa Barkley Brown's introductory pages and historical treatment of Maggie Lena Walker, black Richmond banker in the early twentieth century, which reflect this perspective ("Womanist Consciousness: Maggie Lena Walker and the Independent Order of Saint Luke," *Signs* 14, no. 3 [Spring 1989]: 610–15, 630–33).

precludes recognition and acknowledgment of intragroup social relations as relations of power. With its implicit understandings, shared cultural codes, and inchoate sense of a common heritage and destiny, the metalanguage of race resounds over and above a plethora of conflicting voices. But it cannot silence them.

Black women of different economic and regional backgrounds, of different skin tones and sexual orientations, have found themselves in conflict over interpretation of symbols and norms, public behavior, coping strategies, and a variety of micropolitical acts of resistance to structures of domination.[67] Although racialized cultural identity has clearly served blacks in the struggle against discrimination, it has not sufficiently addressed the empirical reality of gender conflict within the black community or class differences among black women themselves. Historian E. Frances White makes this point brilliantly when she asserts that "the site of counter-discourse is itself contested terrain."[68] By fully recognizing race as an unstable, shifting, and strategic reconstruction, feminist scholars must take up new challenges to inform and confound many of the assumptions currently underlying Afro-American history and women's history. We must problematize much more of what we take for granted. We must bring to light and to coherence the one and the many that we always were in history and still actually are today.

Department of History
University of Pennsylvania

---

[67] I am using "micropolitics" synonymously with James C. Scott's term "infrapolitics." According to Scott, the infrapolitics of subordinate groups not only constitute the everyday, prosaic, "unobtrusive" level of political struggle in contradistinction to overt protests but also constitute the "cultural and structural underpinning" of more visible discontent (*Domination and the Arts of Resistance: Hidden Transcripts* [New Haven, Conn.: Yale University Press, 1990], 183–92).

[68] White (n. 59 above), 82.

Critical Clitoridectomy: Female Sexual Imagery and Feminist Psychoanalytic Theory

Paula Bennett

Of what cannot be seen, of what is hidden, there is no possible symbolic use. [JACQUES LACAN]

The difficulty in defining an autonomous form of female sexuality and desire . . . is not to be overlooked or willfully bypassed. It is perhaps even greater than the difficulty in devising strategies of representation which will, in turn, alter the standard of vision . . . *of what can be seen*. [TERESA DE LAURETIS]

Biology is possibility. [EVE KOSOFSKY SEDGWICK]

ALTHOUGH THIS ESSAY is not about Emily Dickinson, it begins with her. In 1976, I gave a paper titled "The Language of Love: Emily Dickinson's Homoerotic Poetry" before the Gay Academic Union in New York City (Bennett 1977). In the paper, I cited references to what appeared to be cunnilingus and to what I called "clitoral imagery" in Dickinson's poetry. In particular, I focused on one poem, "Forbidden Fruit a flavor has," in which the orality and use of clitoral symbolism seemed especially stunning and therefore defensible:

This article originated in a talk given at Southern Connecticut State University (spring 1990) at the invitation of Vara Neverow-Turk. I would like to thank the following people whose criticism and support did so much to enable my thinking: Mary Carpenter, Clem Hawes, Barbara Johnson, Teresa de Lauretis, Vara Neverow-Turk, Vernon Rosario, Camille Roman, the *Signs* editorial staff and external readers, and Eve Kosofsky Sedgwick, who in a personal communication so graciously provided the epigraph that encapsulates (and for me, clarified) this essay's themes. Such as it is, this article is dedicated to her.

[*Signs: Journal of Women in Culture and Society* 1993, vol. 18, no. 2]

Forbidden Fruit a flavor has
That lawful Orchards mocks—
How luscious lies within the Pod
The Pea that Duty locks—

[1955, 949]

Discussing this poem was difficult for me, despite having a sympathetic audience. On the one hand, I believed what I said; on the other, I could not believe it. It seemed too bizarre, too impossible to be true. For ten years, I let the paper lie. I had stumbled onto something, but I did not know what. Nor was I ready to pursue the implications of my discovery. Convinced that only lesbians would agree with me and profoundly suspicious of my own motivations, I published the paper in a gay journal that folded the next year and forgot about it.

In 1986, I returned to the question of Dickinson's sexual imagery at a very different time and as a very different person. My knowledge of Dickinson had deepened and so had my comfort with my own sexuality. Equally important, lesbian studies had become an area of legitimate academic pursuit, and its exploration of female sexuality relevant to women at large. No longer interfering with my own insight, I read with new eyes. What I found astonished me. The few poems I had pounced on in 1976, in an attempt to validate my own sexuality as much as anything else, were not isolated phenomena. Clitoral imagery—peas, pebbles, beads, berries, nuts, buds, crumbs, pearls, pellets, dews, gems, jewels, drops, and (as I have argued elsewhere) bees (Bennett 1990, 171–73)— was central to Dickinson's writing. So far I have counted—for what else does one do in such circumstances?— 287 of these small, round, and frequently hard objects, objects whose insignificance Dickinson stresses even when attributing inestimable value to them.

The high value Dickinson places on littleness is, in fact, distasteful to many readers. They associate it with a trivializing femininity and with the poet's so-called little-girl voice. When discussing Dickinson's poetry in *My Life a Loaded Gun* (1986), I expressed much the same attitude myself. However, on the basis of the research I have done since then on Dickinson and other nineteenth-century American women poets, I now believe that such judgments are culturally constructed. That is, they are not an objective assessment of worth but result, rather, from our embeddedness in the hierarchical binaries of phallocentric thought, binaries that automatically and unilaterally identify that which is little with that which is weak, worthless, and pejoratively feminine. To Dickinson and to many other nineteenth-century women writers, the little could also be great, the insignificant could be meaningful and valuable.

Clitoral symbols—that is, symbols of small but precious objects—are ubiquitous in nineteenth-century American women's writing.[1] Indeed, given that this symbolic network not only covers the buds, berries, and seeds favored by Victorian women poets but jewels as well (according to Robert Scholes, "jewel" or "gem" is the clitoris's only secondary meaning in classical Greek [1982, 130]), clitoral symbolism is one of the dominant forms of female sexual symbolism in Western culture generally, the others being vaginal and uterine.[2] Like these other forms of symbolism, clitoral symbols are also used by men and women alike. Yet, despite the fact that modern sexology (with, perhaps, an excess of enthusiasm) has not only debunked Freud's argument for the primacy of the vaginal orgasm but elevated the clitoris to the sine qua non of female orgasmic pleasure (Gallop 1988, 71–87),[3] and despite the fact that Naomi Schor (1981), Gayatri Spivak (1981), and Barbara Johnson (1989) all have called attention to the clitoris's theoretical relevance, feminist psychoanalytic theory has had nothing to say concerning the clitoris's possible significance for treatments of women's sexuality in art, let alone in life. Instead—largely, I believe, as a result of the influence of Sigmund Freud and Jacques Lacan—feminist theorists have maintained a singular silence regarding this little organ. The clitoris, which for two millennia prior to Freud was viewed as (to quote one mid-nineteenth-century gynecologist [Meigs 1851, 130]) the "prime seat" of female erotic sensibility if never the only one, remains effectively erased in their work.[4]

[1] The omnipresence of small but highly valued objects in nineteenth-century women's writing was first observed by Ellen Moers (1985, 244); she does not identify the objects as clitoral, however.

[2] Freud discusses vaginal and uterine symbolism in *The Interpretation of Dreams* ([1900] 1959) but, as I shall discuss later, never apparently identified clitoral symbolism. The locus classicus for a discussion of uterine imagery in women's art is Erik Erikson's influential essay, "Womanhood and the Inner Space," in *Identity, Youth and Crisis* (1968, 261–94). Havelock Ellis ([1900] 1936, 5) identified the myrtle berry as a clitoral symbol in classical Greek literature. To my knowledge, this is the only reference to such symbolism prior to my own 1976 discussion; this reference is of particular importance however, as Freud was familiar with Ellis's work, making his own lapse that much more pointed.

[3] Gallop's treatment of twentieth-century sexology's recovery of the clitoris is entirely oppositional, but she is correct that the flood of literature on the clitoris following Masters and Johnson left little space for other forms of female sexuality, most notably, for the experience of women who find vaginal penetration stimulating. If nothing else, the latter's testimony suggests the degree to which anatomy is not destiny and sexuality is not predetermined or locatable in only one spot. Although I want to put an end to the clitoris's theoretical invisibility—or, more accurately, an end to the phallus's presumed monopoly on symbolic expression—I have no wish to claim that female sexuality is limited to this one site.

[4] According to Thomas Laqueur, "the clitoris, like the penis, was for two millenia both 'precious jewel' and sexual organ, a connection not 'lost or mislaid' through the ages, as Scholes would have it, but only (if then) since Freud" (1990, 234).

Given in particular feminist psychoanalytic theory's concern with evolving nonphallocentric constructions of female sexuality, this is, to put it bluntly, a remarkable development and one that demands explanation. In discussing the use of clitoral symbolism by Dickinson and other nineteenth-century bourgeois American women poets, I hope to bring this silence to an end and, by so doing, to make the "invisible" visible, giving it presence and a name. More than this, however, I also hope to explore the consequences for feminist psychoanalytic theory of a construction of female sexuality that takes the clitoris centrally into account.

Let me stress that the nineteenth-century "clitorocentric" representation of women's sexuality I describe in this article is not the only way in which a nonphallocentric female sexuality can be constructed. Nor is it necessarily more representative of individual women's sexual experience than the very different versions offered, for example, by Jane Gallop (1988), Luce Irigaray (1985b), and Hélène Cixous (1983; Cixous and Clement 1986). As these and other theorists, Johnson (1989) in particular, insist, female sexuality, like female pleasure, is multiply sited. It presents, therefore, multiple ways in which it can be constructed—as well as experienced—by individual women. In sex, as Eve Kosofsky Sedgwick (1990) so cannily puts it, nothing is "axiomatic," least of all the way in which we define our experience to ourselves (24–26).[5]

Nevertheless, as Thomas Laqueur points out (1990, 236–37), the facts of the flesh remain. Of all human organs, female and male, the clitoris is uniquely adapted to a sexual mission, being better supplied with nerve endings proportionate to its size than any other human body part, the penis included. Pleasure, moreover, is its only object. Quite unlike the penis, which is also employed in reproduction and excretion, the clitoris has no reason beyond pleasure for being.

This being the case, the clitoris's presence or absence in theoretical treatments of female sexuality—as in the body itself—is of no small consequence to women. As Spivak (1981) has argued, "The pre-comprehended suppression or effacement of the clitoris relates to every move to define woman as sex object, or as a means of reproduction—with no recourse to a subject-function except in terms of those definitions or as 'imitators' of men" (181). Investigating the clitoris's effacement is therefore a passage into understanding the historical and theoretical suppres

---

[5] Sedgwick (1990) writes, "To alienate conclusively, *definitionally,* from anyone on any theoretical ground the authority to describe and name their own sexual desire is a terribly consequential seizure. In this century, in which sexuality has been made expressive of the essence of both identity and knowledge, it may represent the most intimate violence possible" (26). I would submit that this is also true of the body, accounting for much of the hostility psychoanalytic theory provokes in those who do not accept its initial premises.

sion of women—their absorption into what Spivak calls the "uterine social organization" (183) of the family and the state. To the extent that male domination is based on women's sexual subordination to and within the family, the "excess" this organ represents—the excess of absolute sexual autonomy—is a threat to individual men and to male rule generally. Like Spivak, I believe that the issue of clitoridectomy—whether taken literally or figuratively, whether performed in the body or through language—is consequently the place where theory and politics come together. Put another way, as Schor (1981) and Johnson (1989) demonstrate, however it is treated—whether as absent, present, or deliberately excised—the clitoris is something feminists cannot afford to ignore.

To demonstrate the potential richness of clitoral symbolism, I would like to discuss one more Dickinson poem before turning to the work of other nineteenth-century American women poets. Because of the way in which this particular poem was edited, it provides an unusually clear demonstration of how precise these poets' sexual vocabulary—a vocabulary mediated through images rather than words—could be. Like many Dickinson poems, "Crisis" was left in rough draft with some variants underlined. Assuming that these underlinings indicated Dickinson's final choices, her editor, Thomas Johnson, "finished" the poem for his one-volume edition of her work. Whether inadvertently or deliberately, however, he neutralized the poem's sexual content in the process, something Dickinson herself was apparently reluctant to do. In figure 1 (following page), Johnson's completed version (Dickinson 1960, 604) is on the left; the version that appears in his variorum edition of Dickinson's poetry, and which more closely approximates Dickinson's original manuscript (1955, 982–83), is on the right. Only the first three lines in both versions are the same.

Although a sexual reading of Johnson's poem (I am reluctant to call it Dickinson's) is possible, it is hardly obligatory. Words such as "sweet," "heart," "dowers," "rose," "rapture," and "sighing" possess erotic connotations, to be sure, but the final "rescinded bud" is ambiguous enough to leave the poem open. By selecting the sexually neutral "rescinded" and dispensing with Dickinson's other alternatives, Johnson has masked the bud's explicit sexuality and hence the primary erotic reading of the poem. The bud may represent desire, but it could also stand for a number of other human experiences, from sex to heaven, that, according to Dickinson, can be enjoyed more ecstatically in hope than in having.

The sexual specificity of the "bud" in the variorum version, on the other hand, is impossible to evade, and the result is, ironically, in some ways a far more problematic poem. For if Dickinson is talking of the difference between a consummated and an unconsummated relationship (the full-blown rose that has enjoyed its sweet "crisis" vs. the "rescinded"

Crisis is sweet and yet the Heart
Upon the hither side
Has Dowers of Prospective
To Denizens denied

Inquire of the closing Rose
Which rapture she preferred
And she will point you sighing
To her rescinded Bud.

Crisis is sweet and yet the Heart
Upon the hither side
Has Dowers of Prospective
Surrendered by the Tried —
Witheld to the arrived —
                              Debarred —
                              denied
To Denizen denied

Inquire of the proudest Rose
                    fullest
                    closing
Which *rapture* — she preferred
                    triump[h]
                    Hour —
                    moment
And she ~~would~~ tell you sighing —
                    answer
                    will point undoubtedly
And she will point you fondly —
                              longingly
                              sighing
The transport of the Bud —
                    rapture
To her surrendered Bud
                    rescinded
The Hour of her Bud —
                    session of
To her rescinded Bud
                    receding
                    Departed —
                    Receipted Bud
                    Expended

FIG I

bud that presumably has not), why does she depict the bud's experience as orgasmic? Why, that is, does she refer to "transport," "rapture," "triumph," "surrender"? And why does the speaker claim that the rose prefers "the hour" — or "session" — "of her bud" ("receding," "departed," and "expended" as it is) to the "real" thing: marriage, the sweet "crisis" of those who are permanent "denizens" of the state of matrimony? (Of such spatial metaphors, Karen Lystra [1989] writes that nineteenth-century couples viewed marriage as a quasi-physical threshold "and intercourse was supposed to wait until they crossed over to the 'other side'" [71].) Why, that is, has Dickinson so unequivocally sexualized the bud unless she means to suggest that for some women "antic-ipatory" sex—that is, the sexual pleasure achieved through clitoral masturbation—is preferable to the so-called fulfilled sex of marital inter-course and vaginal penetration, accounting, as she says, for the rose's preference for "the hither [nearer] side."[6]

On the basis of Dickinson's handling of the "bud" in "crisis is sweet," I believe that this is what she is saying. But like bourgeois men and women generally in the period, she does not say it directly. She uses a highly elaborated vocabulary of images instead. It is this vocabulary in all its dreamlike multiplicity of meaning that permeates her poetry, filling it with erotic suggestion. In employing these "dreamlike" images, however, Dickinson was not writing in ignorance of their latent sexual content. Rather, she was using a semiprivate code that, on one level or another, most bourgeoisie of her day would have recognized for what it was—a highly nuanced discourse of female erotic desire—even though few, if any, might have publicly admitted to using or understanding it as such. (As Lystra [1989] and others point out, such splits between public ad-mission and private knowledge typify the Victorian approach to sexuality and have misled more than one scholar respecting the extent of bourgeois sexual awareness. See Gay [1984, 71–168, and 466–68].)

The erotic use of this image discourse, commonly called the "Lan-guage of Flowers," was rooted in *Canticles,* and its appearance in work by male and female artists both on the Continent and in the United States in Dickinson's day could not have been more widespread. Indeed, flower language was so widely deployed for sexual purposes that Freud, writing in the first decades of the twentieth century, could casually refer to its erotics as " 'popular' symbolism" and assume his audience would not demur—as they most certainly did in many instances respecting phallic symbolism ([1900] 1959, 374).

At the beginning of the modernist era (1910–20), writing drawing on the Language of Flowers (particularly women's) was roundly denigrated by masculinist critics for being excessively feminine and sentimental—as, for example, in T. E. Hulme's sneering reference to "roses, roses all the way."[7] But this judgment was hardly unbiased. Men like Hulme, engaged

---

[6] Lystra's characterization of masturbation as "the ultimate symbol of private free-dom and atomistic individualism" (1989, 106) suggests its possible appeal to Dickinson, for whom individualism, freedom, and privacy were virtually synonymous goods. Insofar as masturbatory sex also tends in women to be clitoral, these associations also may help explain why the clitoris—like female masturbation—became increasingly problematic in the nineteenth century with the rise of privacy and the attendant difficulties privacy cre-ated for the social control of sex (see Rosario 1992).

[7] As quoted by Sandra M. Gilbert and Susan Gubar (1988, 154). Taken from Hulme's "A Lecture on Modern Poetry" (1914), the full citation reads: "Imitative poetry springs up like weeds, and women whimper and whine of you and I alas, and roses,

in what Sandra M. Gilbert and Susan Gubar (1988, 125–62) describe as a "war between the sexes," had little stake in seeing women's flower poems as powerful statements of female erotic desire. Ignoring this imagery's sexual potential (a potential they nevertheless exploited in their own work, as T. S. Eliot's "hyacinth girl" in "The Waste Land" testifies), they condemned women's flower poetry as sentimental and trivializing instead.

Nevertheless, from the Bible to Baudelaire to Georgia O'Keeffe and Judy Chicago, to a host of minor and major artists and writers in between—including the pre-Raphaelites, decadents, and academics who composed the bulk of the Victorian and Edwardian art worlds (Dijkstra 1986)—the Language of Flowers has been Western culture's language of women. Most specifically, it has been the language through which woman's body and, even more particularly for this article, women's genitals have been represented and inscribed.

Throughout the nineteenth century, this language, presumably with varying degrees of awareness, was used in the United States by sex educators, letter writers, artists, craftswomen, pornographers, dreamers, and poets alike.[8] While the degree of intentionality in any given instance can never be pinned down (nor need be, since all that matters, finally, is the ambience of sexuality this imagery creates), the failure by present-day commentators to decode it in women's writing has led to major misunderstandings of nineteenth-century bourgeois women's sexuality and of the sexual content of their poetry. Given that these women were sur-

---

roses all the way. It becomes the expression of sentimentality rather than of virile thought.' " Hulme's heavily gendered comment is part of a general move by British and American male modernists to reappropriate poetry, which had become a largely "female" genre by 1900. See Gilbert and Gubar 1988, 141–62. What happened to women's poetry and to women's sexuality at the turn of the century eerily parallel each other, and for both the stigmatization of the Language of Flowers as sentimental was crucial.

[8] For example, Gay quotes the following piece of "cloying" advice from Dr. Mary Wood-Allen's *Teaching Truth:* "Let us imagine that she [the mother] has gathered a few morning-glories, and, showing the child the bright-hued flower-cup, says: 'Would you like to hear the story of Mr. and Mrs. Morning Glory and their children?' " (Gay 1984, 324). And Lystra (1989) cites a similarly "flowery" passage from the erotic courtship letters passed between Robert Burdette and his fiance Clara Baker, a well-respected clubwoman: "[I] half-expected, when my wanton hand followed the guiding of my hot desire, that it would rest upon a dimple-grotto, sealed with the tender veil of virginity, and smooth as the child's own cheek. And lo, the silken vines that meshed and fringed the throbbing fountain of a Woman's Love! My Little Girl—My 'Sweet White Violet' " (97–98). While such passages do not "prove" conclusively that Victorian women poets consciously identified their "buds" with the clitoris, they do establish that the sexual subtext of the Language of Flowers was familiar to bourgeois men, women, and children alike. Such passages also suggest that the horror and embarrassment evinced by Freud's patients—and Whitman's readers—at hearing sexuality discussed explicitly did not necessarily mean the ideas themselves were foreign to them. Freud, like Whitman, was violating well-established taboos—but, as Edith Wharton makes clear in *The Age of Innocence,* these taboos were against explicit speech, not against actual knowledge or veiled forms of communication.

rounded by art (from their Bibles to the very pictures on their walls) that associated women sexually with flowers, given, indeed, that their everyday language contained terms such as "wallflower" and "deflower" based on this association, it is inconceivable that these poets remained uniformly ignorant of the latent sexual potential of the imagery they used, especially when they themselves use it in such highly suggestive as well as woman-centered ways. It is, therefore, all the more significant not only that they privilege clitoral images—buds, berries, seeds, and small compact flowers such as snowdrops and crocuses—but that they identify with these images in ways most male writers simply do not.[9]

Here, for instance, is the middle stanza from "No Concealment" by Lydia Huntley Sigourney (1848), the premier American woman poet of her day and a highly sophisticated writer despite the "sentimental" reputation with which she is burdened today:

> Think'st thou to be conceal'd, thou little seed,
>   That in the bosom of the earth art cast,
> And there, like cradled infant, sleep'st awhile,
>   Unmoved by trampling storm or thunder blast?
> Thou bid'st thy time; for herald Spring shall come
>   And wake thee, all unwilling as thou art,
> Unhood thy eyes, unfold thy clasping sheath,
>   And stir the languid pulses of thy heart;
> The loving rains shall woo thee, and the dews
>   Weep o'er thy bed, and, ere thou art aware,
> Forth steals the tender leaf, the wiry stem,
>   The trembling bud, the flower that scents the air.
> And soon, to all, thy ripen'd fruitage tells
> The evil or the good that in thy nature dwells.
>   [90–91]

In the final couplet, Sigourney signals the presence of a sexual allegory by shifting away from transparent images of simple description—the seed's

[9] To take two examples from the enormous body of similar work produced by comparable male poets of the period, in Henry Timrod's "The Rosebuds" (1899) and Edmund Clarence Stedman's "Seeking the May-Flower" (1908), the speakers unequivocally identify the titular images with women. Of the full contents of the sexual fantasy elicited by his beloved's "rosebuds," Timrod writes "How far my fancy dared to stray, / A lover's reverence needs not say" (62), while the "eager, wandering hands" of Stedman's speaker fill his lady's lap with "pink, pale flowers" that are "Like her, so pure, so sweet, so shy" (318). Whether viewed singularly or multiply, whether identified with the clitoris, the breasts, babies, or the vagina (male writers, like female writers, work all these possibilities), these buds and flowers are the woman's possessions and they are celebrated as such. Where they become liminal, not surprisingly, is in the work of gay men, Whitman and Robert Mapplethorpe, e.g., or heterosexual men with very strong female identifications, like Thomas Wentworth Higginson (see Looby 1992a, 1992b).

blossoming—to images of moral judgment—the "ripen'd fruit" that may eventually spoil. As this shift indicates, concealed within her seemingly innocuous depiction of a flower's growth is the subtextual narrative of a woman's (sexual) unfolding—an unfolding whose unconcealable product will be either "evil or . . . good."

And here is Harriet Prescott Spofford's "Snow Drop" (1882). Spofford, the author of, among other works, the short story "The Amber Gods," with its spirited defense of female sexual power, is known today (unlike Sigourney) for the intensity of her erotic effects. Yet in this brief poem, she, like many another Victorian woman poet, focuses on the most seemingly innocent of little flowers, the pure white snowdrop, even while claiming for it a life energy sufficient to fuel the stars:

> Only a tender little thing,
>   So velvet soft and white it is;
> But March himself is not so strong,
>   With all the great gales that are his.
>
> In vain his whistling storms he calls,
>   In vain the cohorts of his power
> Ride down the sky on mighty blasts—
>   He cannot crush the little flower.
>
> Its white spear parts the sod, the snows
>   Than that white spear less snowy are,
> The rains roll off its crest like spray,
>   It lifts again its spotless star.
>
> Blow, blow, dark March! To meet you here,
>   Thrust upward from the central gloom,
> The stellar force of the old earth
>   Pulses to life in this slight bloom.
>
> [1882, 30]

Now let us turn to Amy Lowell's "The Weather-Cock Points South" ([1919] 1955). Born in the nineteenth century but writing in the twentieth, Lowell bridges the earlier era and our own more explicit, post-Whitmanian, post-Freudian day. Yet, though she had the possibility to do otherwise, she too selects the Language of Flowers when speaking erotically. Indeed, her title suggests she chose this discourse precisely because it offered her a specifically nonphallocentric direction from which to approach her topic: woman-to-woman love. In the waxlike jewel, the flower bud, she found the images she needed to represent woman to herself—not as a space to be entered but as a presence to be uncovered and adored:

I put your leaves aside,
One by one:
The stiff, broad outer leaves;
The smaller ones,
Pleasant to touch, veined with purple;
The glazed inner leaves,
One by one
I parted you from your leaves,
Until you stood up like a white flower
Swaying slightly in the evening wind.

White flower,
Flower of wax, of jade, of unstreaked agate;
Flower with surfaces of ice,
With shadows faintly crimson.
Where in all the garden is there such a flower?
The stars crowd through the lilac leaves
To look at you.
The low moon brightens you with silver.

The bud is more than the calyx.
There is nothing to equal a white bud,
Of no colour, and of all,
Burnished by moonlight,
Thrust upon by a softly-swinging wind.
                                        [(1919) 1955, 211]

Finally, let me cite, since I would not have dared do so earlier, the first four stanzas of "The Crocus Soliloquy" by Hannah F. Gould (1833). Unlike the three previous poets, Gould, a contemporary of Sigourney's, does appear to epitomize all that was presumably naive, awkward, trivializing—and unintentionally funny—in nineteenth-century American women's poetry. In fact, it is not too much to say that in this poem she is the very Emmeline Grangerford of flowers:

Down in my solitude under the snow,
    Where nothing cheering can reach me—
Here, without light to see how to grow,
    I'll trust to nature to teach me.

I will not despair, nor be idle, nor frown,
    Locked in so gloomy a dwelling;
My leaves shall run up, and my roots shall run down,
    While the bud in my bosom is swelling.

Soon as the frost will get out of my bed,
From this cold dungeon to free me,
I will peep up with my little bright head,
And all will be joyful to see me.

Then from my heart will young petals diverge,
As rays of the sun from their focus;
I from the darkness of earth will emerge,
A happy and beautiful Crocus.

[1833, 240]

Yet even here, in a poem as apparently unsophisticated as this, the Language of Flowers has enabled the author to describe the utter self-containment, the complete autonomy, of clitorally based female sexuality (a sexuality that nature, not one's husband, "teaches") with extraordinary, indeed, forbidding precision. In its appropriation of the sun, usually taken as a symbol of male sexual power, to represent this self-containment, as in its shift from a closed to a rayed flower shape to express the moment of orgasm itself, Gould's poem is little short of astonishing. (In all fairness to Gould, let me add that she writes more skillfully in other poems.)

Given the way in which Gould positions her flower as being alone in its "solitude," it is worth noting that she, like Dickinson, never married. Whether consciously or not, therefore, her poem's subtextual topic may be masturbation. That is, she may have treated the flower's "sexuality" in terms congruent with her own. What matters, however, is that even here, in a poem such as this, written naively and awkwardly, and in all likelihood without full awareness, the Language of Flowers has enabled the articulation of sexual feelings and knowledge the author obviously possessed. Far from being muted within women's culture, Hannah Gould's sexuality, like that of the other poets I have discussed, speaks through it loud and clear.

What then is the version of female sexuality that emerges from a study of these poems? To begin with, it is a largely self-contained sexuality, concentrating on the bud more than on the flower, and it is clitorocentric and paradoxical in essence. Like the clitoris, which becomes erect with stimulation, the bud, or little seed, is a spear; it is sheathed; it possesses a hood; it trembles and pulses; it is tender, soft, and white. Pure—and powerful—in itself, it abides in the cold body of a female earth, hidden and folded into itself until ready to bloom and burst into life. Then it is an energy nothing can stop, a "stellar force," a "sun," thrusting upward until its petals spread, yielding (as Dickinson asserts) its hour or moment of rapture (the French *jouissance*) and risking (as Sigourney warns) its potential for evil as well as for good.

While these poets ground their sexuality differently—Dickinson and Gould suggesting masturbation, Spofford and Sigourney employing a heterosexual frame, and Lowell describing love between women—for each of them (as for Lowell's beloved) the bud is the source and center of life and, in some sense, the final end of desire. However small or hidden it is, its power like its pleasure is located finally within itself. A littleness that is paradoxically great ("The bud is more than the calyx"), it is a seed that, lit by its own interior force, is also a "sun." And paradoxically structured in this way, it is able to function and flourish outside the complementarity that, according to Freud and Lacan, constitutes the phallic economy of man's unilateral presence and woman's unilateral lack. Far from being created by (or absorbed in) the male logos—a logos whose breath/spirit, in the Spofford poem, the bud may be said explicitly to resist—this sexuality possesses a life and significance of its own. Both "A" and "not-A" at the same time, both little and great, the bud is how female sexuality is defined or constructed in these poems, whether by lesbians or heterosexuals, whether in alloerotic or autoerotic terms.

Bourgeois nineteenth-century American women evolved this very different, nonphallocentric perspective on female sexuality, I believe, as part of an effort to understand themselves at a time when women in Western culture were just beginning to know themselves as a truly distinctive "other" sex rather than as inferior and incomplete men.[10] Profoundly influenced by a cultural ideology that gendered nature's transient beauties as female, they used the popular erotic symbolism of their day—flowers and, above all, buds—as "natural" symbols for the difference they sought to inscribe. In the sexual symbology that developed from this set of identifications, difference between men and women still produced meaning; where women were concerned, however, the clitoris (not the penis-which-they-lacked) was the primary signifier. The clitoris was that which was present, and it was men who were erased or conceptualized as other, whether as "herald Spring" or "dark March."

Given that bourgeois men and women were theoretically divided into separate spheres in this period, it is not surprising that women evolved a concept of "separate but equal" female sexuality. But what is astonishing is that in these poems the vaginal and the uterine have been so completely subordinated to the clitoral. In an age when presumably motherhood and domesticity were all and when many authorities, both female and male, declared bourgeois women to be "passionless" (Cott 1978), these poets

[10] See Laqueur 1990, 194–207 and passim. I do not believe that it is an accident that the Language of Flowers achieved currency at the same time that Western medicine began to define women as a separate biological sex, sometime in the eighteenth century. Both scientific and poetic discourses were responding, as Laqueur documents, to profound changes in the cultural construction of women, changes that had less to do with the knowledge of anatomy per se than with the way in which anatomical differences were interpreted (Laqueur 1990, 149–92).

base their paradoxical construction of female sexuality on the power of inwardly felt and directed desire. In these poems, men are at best casual initiators, at worst direct threats to this quintessentially female scene. Babies play no role in it at all. It is the responsive flowering of the bud—not the flower's power to procreate or passively to provide satisfaction for others—that inspired these poets to write.[11] The result is a construction of female sexuality that by the very paradoxicality of its definition (small is great) falls outside the phallocentric order and the heterosexualized and hierarchical complementaries this order predicts.

But if the clitoris can thus supply an alternative and autonomous site for definitions of female pleasure and desire, why then, one must wonder, has twentieth-century feminist psychoanalytic theory been so reluctant to discuss it? Why, that is, have so many theorists maintained a Freudian- and Lacanian-authorized silence on this particular topic, a silence that neither female sexual symbolism nor the female sexual response in themselves supports? While, as noted earlier, there are many ways in which a nonphallocentric female sexuality can be and has been constructed, including those that look to maternity and reproduction, those that emphasize the preoedipal bond, and those that celebrate the multiple erogeneity of the female body, surely one privileging the organ that is the "primary" if not the only "seat" of female erotic sensibility ought to rank among them. Yet with the aforementioned exceptions of Schor (1981), Spivak (1981), and Johnson (1989) (none of whom addresses the clitoris's presence in women's writing), no feminist psychoanalytic theorist with whom I am familiar has taken the clitoris's symbolic potential seriously, let alone attempted to theorize its relation to desire. One theorist, Jane Gallop, subjects what she sees as lesbian-feminism's politically motivated privileging of the clitoris to blistering attack (1988, 107–8). Far too often, it is not mentioned at all.

To understand why feminist psychoanalytic theory thus far has been unable to incorporate the clitoris into its thinking on female sexuality, the best place to begin is with Freud. And to understand Freud's treatment of the clitoris, one must see it as part of the general anxiety he exhibits whenever confronting the female genitalia in what might best be called their unreconstructed state—that is, as present rather than lacking. From Karen Horney on (see Chesler 1972, 75–85), feminist critics of Freud

[11] David Halperin (1990) observes that men have historically projected their own sexual issues onto women, nowhere more dramatically than in their insistence on "the interdependence of sexual and reproductive capacities" in female sexuality. The ability to "*actually* isolate . . . sexual pleasure and reproduction, recreative and procreative sex" is, in fact, a feature of female—not male—physiology, he writes (142–43). Halperin goes on to warn that " 'femininity' must continue to remain a mystery so long as it is defined wholly by reference to 'masculinity'—whether as a lack of male presence or as the presence of a male lack" (149).

have observed that this anxiety is basic to his formulations of human psychosexual development. Nowhere is it more naked or virulent, however, than in his brief essay "Medusa's Head"([1922] 1950), an essay whose central symbol Cixous brilliantly re-visions in "The Laugh of the Medusa" (1983).

For Freud, there was nothing laughable—or joyful—about Medusa. Instead, he identifies her decapitated head with the "terrifying genitals of the Mother." When the young boy views these genitals, Freud posits, he turns to stone. That is, he is psychologically castrated by the sight of his mother's "castrated" state, symbolized in Medusa's case by the multiplicity of phalli that as snakes adorn her head. (In the logic of dreams and myths, Freud asserts, many equals none.) To "avert" this evil, the boy displays his genital in turn. "To display the penis (or any of its surrogates)," Freud explains, "is to say: 'I am not afraid of you. I defy you. I have a penis.' Here, then," he concludes, apparently without irony, "is another way of intimidating the Evil Spirit" ([1922] 1950, 106). This is not the place to analyze the analyst, tempting though the idea is. But it is worth noting that the little boy's (Freud's) need to "display the penis (or any of its surrogates)" seems, by the rules of conventional logic, to derive from his overestimation of female power, not the reverse. The head is terrifying because it possesses so many phalli, not because it lacks one.

And it may well have been Freud's need to contain this presumably psuedo-"masculine" excess of female sexuality—an excess that greatly troubled other medical men of his day also (Barker-Benfield 1976; Chauncey 1982; Masson 1986)—that led him to construe psychosexual development the way he did. For in making the issue of castration the centerpiece of gender development for both sexes, Freud not only managed to "display" his own penis but at the same time he reconstructed women as "lack," a "lack" his theory of the vaginal orgasm (which, in effect, "castrates" women) serves only to reinforce (Laqueur 1990, 240 – 43). "The elimination of clitoridal sexuality is a necessary precondition for the development of femininity," Freud announced in "Some Psychological Consequences of the Anatomical Distinction between the Sexes" ([1925] 1950, 194), and eliminate it he did.

Whether in the form of cauterization or actual clitoridectomy, medical assaults upon the clitoris were routinely performed by many nineteenth-century gynecologists in order to bring under control socially undesirable forms of female sexuality such as masturbation, lesbianism, and "nymphomania" (Bullough and Voght 1976; Masson 1986; Baker Brown [1866] 1987; Showalter 1990). Psychologically speaking, as Thomas Laqueur argues (1990), Freud's theory of the vaginal orgasm does the same thing, albeit more humanely. It seeks to recontain female sexuality by "castrating" women, denying them the sexual agency and active power

that would make them sexual subjects in their own right—and consequently terrifying indeed to this man who based both his career and his
gender on men's genital superiority to women. Freud did not simply
invent the myth of the vaginal orgasm, however, although that was sufficient to leave numberless women anxious and confused respecting their
sexuality for sixty years (Laqueur 1990, 1233–43; Hite 1976). He "castrates" female sexual discourse and symbology as well.

Where phallic symbolism receives thirty-seven pages in the *Interpretation of Dreams* ([1900] 1959), vaginal and uterine symbolism together
receive ten. Clitoral symbolism—of which, apparently, Freud remained
ignorant to his death—receives none: a striking blind spot indeed in this
master decoder of sexual symbolism. Freud's lapse may be explained by
the privileged role he gives the penis in psychosexual development and by
the contempt he heaps on the clitoris because of its "inferior" size. But it
is difficult not to believe that a profound fear of independent female
sexual potency underlies his blindness as well.

As Scholes (1982) and Johnson (1989) have argued, despite its "small"
size the clitoris presented a sizable impediment to Freud's theory of sexual complementarity and, therefore, to his entire construction of women
as sexually subordinate to men. His response was to render the clitoris
invisible—not only assimilating it to the phallus as an inadequate penis
whose "masculine" and supplementary pleasures mature women eventually abandon, but, like other interpretaters within these fields, blinding
himself to its traces in language, literature, and art.[12] And it is this
inheritance—one that, as Irigaray insightfully demonstrates, employs
blindness to rationalize male dominance—that he bequeathed to his heirs
(1985a, 13–129). Accepting Freud's theory of phallic presence (and, at
least where the clitoris is concerned, women's complete insufficiency if
not exactly their lack), they, too, have been unable to see the innumerable
nonphallic symbols of female sexual potency that actually exist.

For feminist psychoanalytic theory, the consequences of this Freudian
blind spot have been as negative as Spivak suggests they must be whenever the "suppression or effacement of the clitoris" is involved (1981,
181). For it is only by rendering the clitoris accidental (as it were) to
female sexuality (and thus, effectively, eliminating it) that complementarity is made possible. In the binary terms of Freud's phallocentric definition, without the clitoris, women are what men are not; as Cixous puts
it, they are dark where men are light, passive where men are active, empty

---

[12] It is worth repeating here Laqueur's (1990) caveat that "there is nothing in nature
about how the clitoris is construed. It is not self-evidently a female penis, and it is not
self-evidently in opposition to the vagina" (234). The clitoris and the penis have, in fact,
very little besides excitability in common, and they situate their respective possessors
very differently in respect to sexual pleasure and reproduction.

where men are full (Cixous and Clement 1986). Thus deprived by Freud of that which makes her different but "equal" to men, the Freudian woman becomes man's negative obverse: not-A to his A. Her sexual and reproductive system thus neatly matched to his, she is, as Spivak observes, absorbed into the "uterine social organization" of family and state (1981, 183). Under such circumstances, she can never also be what she is in herself—independent and autonomous in respect to her own sexual power.

In insisting that Freud's construction of women was written into the deep structures of language, Lacan made theoretical escape from this phallocentric systemization of sexual difference and representation virtually impossible. Insofar as sexual difference is defined only through the presence or absence of the phallus (symbolic or otherwise), female sexuality can only be understood in the complementary terms of phallocentrism, as these are the terms by which it is produced in the first place. Given this Lacanian-defined double bind, it is no wonder that many recent lesbian theorists, in particular, have chosen to follow Wittig and declare themselves "not woman" (Wittig 1981, 1982; Butler 1990). By accepting the hegemony of the phallus as the signifier of difference, feminist psychoanalytic theorists, both lesbian and heterosexual, have yielded so much territory to Freud and Lacan that they have left themselves virtually no ground on which to stand that is not already precontaminated by the ideas they wish to resist. That is, insofar as they agree that the system of representation and sexual definition that prevails in Western culture is phallocentric-as-Lacan-defines-phallocentrism, they have, theoretically at any rate, no terms by which to describe female sexuality that (1) are not phallocentric and (2) do not presuppose the suppression or the effacement of the clitoris.

To take only one example (but one of particular poignancy since the author describes clitorally based sexuality even though she never identifies it as such), let us look at Judith Roof's moving and eloquent tribute to lesbian sexuality, "The Match in the Crocus: Representations of Lesbian Sexuality" (1989). While Roof is clearly critiquing phallocentric systems of representation in this essay, by refusing to name the clitoris as the explicit locus of the alternate sexuality she depicts, she ends up, I would argue, leaving the phallus's dominance as signifier of difference all but entirely in place. If, as she concludes, lesbian sexuality is the "gap" through which the "other-than-phallus" can be glimpsed (114–15), this "gap," as she also admits, can never be other than derivative, since it is predicated on the phallus's dominance as signifier to begin with.

Roof's essay begins with a quotation from *Mrs. Dalloway* in which Virginia Woolf struggles through a series of approximations to express what Roof calls the "unrepresentability" (102) of lesbian sexuality—in

Woolf's words, an "illumination, a match burning in a crocus, an inner meaning almost expressed." Woolf's difficulty in finding words for Clarissa Dalloway's desire, Roof argues, is a symptom of the "crisis" that lesbian sexuality "provokes . . . in a system of representation which is reliant upon a symmetry, if not sameness, between the sexes" (100). Because the lesbian does not desire the penis—the natural and visible complement to her own presumed lack—she threatens the schema on which "normative heterosexuality" is based. To Roof, lesbian sexuality suggests therefore "a present yet hidden and invisible third term in the phallic register of representation," a term lying outside "the phallic matrix" (103).

It is for this reason, Roof insists, that lesbian sexuality is "other-than-phallus." But because this third term is both present and unrepresentable at once, she argues, it can only be "approximated" in images that suggest but do not actually reveal or make visible what it is like (112–13). "Modeled after female genitalia seen other than as lack," lesbian sexuality "re-creates the conditions of its own representational impossibility: it can be there," Roof writes, "but it cannot be seen in its own terms since such terms do not exist" (103).

To support this conception of the unrepresentable yet present lesbian sexuality, Roof cites two examples, one from *Mrs. Dalloway* and one from Violette Leduc's *La Batarde*. I quote briefly the key lines from each. Speaking of Clarissa, Woolf's narrator says " 'Then came the most exquisite moment of her whole life passing a stone urn with flowers in it. Sally stopped; picked a flower; kissed her on the lips. . . . And she felt that she had been given a present, wrapped up . . . a diamond, something infinitely precious . . . which . . . the radiance burnt through' " (111). Leduc writes, " 'She waited: that was how she taught me to open into a flower. She was the hidden muse inside my body. Her tongue, her little flame, softened my muscles, my flesh'." Like Clarissa's well-wrapped but "infinitely precious" diamond, the narrator's "hidden spot" in *La Batarde* is, Roof comments, also "hidden again by lips" (112).

It is also hidden by Roof's language. "Without its wrapping, without the petals of the crocus," she explains, "the miracle match burns out, fades, or is transformed into the priapus. Revealed, it is no longer neither one nor two as Irigaray describes it, but monolithic, at once phallus and absence of phallus" (113). To name this "other-than-phallus," Roof claims, would be to render the lesbian "a function of the symmetry by which all complementary parts fit into the whole, reenfolded in the system of binary oppositions by which we represent and understand sexual difference and sexuality" (114). Rather than be caught by what she sees as ineluctable alternatives—since both desire and the clitoris can, she assumes, only be spoken of in phallic terms—Roof refuses in effect to speak at all. Despite her enormous sensitivity to lesbian erotic language, and despite the obvious clitoral symbolism of the images Woolf and Leduc employ, the word "clitoris" never appears in her text. Rather, lesbian sexuality remains throughout a mystified and mystifying "other-than-phallus." Radiant, diffuse, yet withal unrepresentable and unseen, it has—or appears to have—no organic or symbolic base.

Roof clearly wants to locate lesbian desire in the body; yet by refusing to name a bodily locus for that desire she reinstates the very phallic primacy she sets out to deconstruct. Caught in the meshes of a language and a point of view that (as she herself asserts) has consistently alienated twentieth-century bourgeois women from their own sexuality, Roof does not name the clitoris because, apparently, she believes that by naming it she will evoke the phallus (either as phallus or as absence of phallus). Lacking a conception of the clitoris as part of an independent female sexual symbology, the only exit from phallocentrism she can imagine, as she herself admits, is one that phallocentrism itself predicts. "Thus," she concludes of her analysis of Woolf and Leduc, "though the working of phallocentric representation is revealed, the position of representations by women is also exposed as derivative, dependent on the system they attempt to subvert. Other, like the unconscious, like woman, is finally only expressed in the breaks and paradoxes resulting from play on the phallus and yet perhaps that is the only way to escape" (115).

It is precisely because Roof's essay is so sensitive to the wealth and power of female textuality and sexuality that it makes clear the price paid by feminist theorists working with a Freudian-Lacanian model of sexual difference and representation. In accepting the phallus's monopoly on symbolic expression even while attempting to deconstruct it, Roof is caught within its toils. There is no way for her to represent lesbian desire except by an intensification of lack—a lack of words, an absence of an autonomous and independent symbology, a darkness to which she can only bring, as she says so beautifully, a radiant but indescribable light.

Yet as many feminist theorists, from Irigaray to Roof herself, insist, female sexuality (including lesbian sexuality) is a good deal more than lack. And, even more to my point, it has been extensively represented through a wide variety of nonphallocentric imaginings. Put another way, Cixous is quite simply wrong when she asserts that "with a few rare exceptions, there has not yet been any writing that inscribes femininity; exceptions so rare, in fact, that, after plowing through literature across languages, cultures, and ages, one can only be startled at this vain scouting mission" (1983, 282).

As the female sexual symbolism discussed in this essay demonstrates, women in Western culture do have a highly representational nonphallocentric sexual symbology of their own. This symbology, which covers not just the clitoris but all the primary and secondary sexual organs, is rich, prolific, dense, and ubiquitous. It has given rise to great art from biblical times *(Canticles)* to our own era. Equally important, whether on a conscious or unconscious level, it has enriched thousands of individual women's lives through activities such as embroidery, pottery, weaving, jewelry making, gardening, and arranging flowers. It may even be related to women's supposed preoccupation with what Susan Glaspell acutely termed "trifles"—that is, with the "little" crafts, activities, and concerns that so many men—along with not a few women—affect to disdain. And it is an integral and ubiquitous part of Western representations of sexuality, so ubiquitous, in fact, that, as noted earlier, Freud could dismiss significant aspects of it as "popular" symbolism.

But this symbology—together with the sexual power it inscribes—has been passed over or underestimated by psychoanalytically oriented critics precisely because, without a notion of clitoral symbolism, it has been impossible to establish just how autonomous and independent of male sexual symbology it actually is. Trained as male readers of the female bodily text, post-Freudian critics can "see" woman as container (house, enclosed space, tunnel, vase, rose) and, as Cixous makes clear, can project her onto the oceanic and the diffused. But we have been unable to see her in those symbols (bud, pearl, berry, seed, jewel) that make her the agent of her own desire, an autonomous desiring subject in her own right. Worse, we have been taught to despise art privileging such symbols simply because it is not "great" like men's—that is, because it does not emulate, replicate, or praise the phallic.

There are probably a number of reasons why the clitoris's signifying power has eluded us for so long, but the most obvious (if also the riskiest to speak about) is this issue of size. As readers of the bodily as well as the symbolic text, we learn to value that which is large and to dismiss as insignificant as well as inferior all that is small, Freud's "little penis" included.[13] (One could note here, e.g., Lacan's automatic assumption that the penis's capacity for tumescence—along with its visibility—makes it the appropriate signifier of sexual difference.)[14] Yet by such tests, much

[13] In one of his more astonishing non sequiturs, Freud announces in his essay on fetishism that "the normal prototype of all fetishes is the penis of the man, just as the normal prototype of an organ felt to be inferior is the real little penis of the woman, the clitoris" ([1927] 1950, 204). This assumption (which Freud treats as axiomatic) that smallness = inferiority is so basic to our culture that it requires an act of will to step back and realize how absurd it is—or how much mischief it works. Naomi Schor (1987) has dealt with the aesthetic fallout of this reaction at length, but only in the context of male-authored texts. Her use of an epigraph from Woolf is on target, however: "Let us not take it for granted that life exists more fully in what is commonly thought big than in what is commonly thought small" (1).

[14] "One might also say that by virtue of its turgidity, it is the image of the vital flow as it is transmitted in generation" (Lacan [1966] 1982, 82).

CRITICAL CLITORIDECTOMY 135

that is central to women's art—and lives—must fail. I think here, sadly, not only of my own long resistance to pursuing the idea of clitoral imagery, but of Adrienne Rich's denigration of Dickinson's emphasis on littleness in "Vesuvius at Home": "Most of us, unfortunately, have been exposed . . . to Dickinson's 'little-girl' poems, her kittenish tones . . . or the poems about bees and robins" (1979, 106). In this deservedly influential essay, Rich recuperates Dickinson's (phallic-sized) volcanos as powerful figures for women's rage; but not even she could recognize in Dickinson's paradoxical handling of littleness parallel statements of an independent female sexual and textual power. It was, I might add, for the same reason that the title of my first book referenced a gun.

Sentimental they may have been, but the nineteenth-century poets discussed in this essay were not afraid to celebrate the small or to see in it an image of power. And because they could, they were able not only to accept the clitoris's littleness but to rejoice in its wildness—its place outside the reproductive economy and the exchange of women. Indeed, it was precisely because they were able to situate their sexuality in the "separate sphere" of sexual difference that these poets were empowered to speak. Sharing a cultural construction of female sexuality based on the assumption that women differed essentially from men, and living at a time when women took pride in their independent culture, these writers imagined a form of female sexual autonomy most twentieth-century feminist theorists caught in the thickets of Freud's phallocentrism (and our era's all-too-rigid heterosexist assumptions) are still struggling to achieve.[15]

In *Trifles,* Susan Glaspell ([1919] 1987) presents an allegory of women's reading, a reading that takes place in relation to puns and images that speak to women's lives. Mrs. Hale and Mrs. Peters, the sheriff's wife (a woman "married" to the penis as well as to the law), discover the truth of Minnie ("mini" or "little") Wright's crime. But they only do so because they read with women's eyes the enormous significance of the

[15] " 'We do not advocate the representation of women because there is no difference between men and women,' " Laqueur quotes one nineteenth-century feminist as saying, " '*but rather because of the difference between them*' " (1990, 197; see also 194–207). Situated in a "separate sphere" and no longer seen as "lesser" versions of men, nineteenth-century bourgeois women could argue legitimately that men could not speak for them. They had to speak for themselves. A similar opening up of "critical space—a conceptual, representational, and erotic space—in which women could address themselves to women," occurred, as Teresa de Lauretis observes, with the second wave and, of course, is meeting with analogous attempts to recontain it—of which Lacanism is in my opinion one (see de Lauretis 1988, 155). Lesbian poststructuralist approaches to sexual difference, which are among the most recent offshoots of Lacanism, ultimately have the same recontaining effect insofar as they silence women as a category (see Butler 1990). While I sympathize with such theorists' desire to deconstruct heterosexual binarism, I find their work exceedingly problematic as a result.

"trifles" constituting women's lives: the little "fancy box," the silk-wrapped songbird dead within it. Like the jewel box they subtly mimic, these trifles are the mute if eloquent symbols of the female sexual power Minnie's husband loathed (feared?) and sought to crush. And in accepting the enormous significance of these trifles, Mrs. Hale and Mrs. Peters liberate themselves along with Minnie. But, as Glaspell makes clear, they would never have read the "text" Minnie left them had they not remained in the kitchen and let the men go off on their own.[16]

However it is constructed, sexual difference exists together with sexual differences. But as long as Freud and Lacan set the terms by which we read and thus, as Elizabeth Grosz comments, reduce all possibilities to A or not-A, either phallus or absence of phallus, alternative ways of understanding and representing difference will remain virtually impossible to see (1990, 124).[17] Worse, this privileging of a psuedotranscendent psychosexual/psycholinguistic perspective will continue to interfere with and distort the theoretical analysis of the material conditions that are the real source of the inequities for which the phallus stands as a misleading symbol at best.

Phallocentrism as defined and accounted for within the Lacanian framework of feminist psychoanalytic theory is a myth. Women are not necessarily "invisible" within our system of representation nor are their genitals definitionally without signifying power. That women (like members of other minoritized and colonized groups) nevertheless experience themselves as invisible or "lacking" seems beyond dispute. The causes of this lack are political, however, and they can be changed. In moving to change them, like Spivak I can think of no better place to begin than with a construction of female sexuality that takes the clitoris centrally into account.

Without the clitoris, theorists have no physical site in which to locate an autonomous sense of female sexual agency. As a result, women's sexuality thus can be readily absorbed, as Spivak argues, into the social

---

[16] I am profoundly indebted to Annette Kolodny (1985, 55–57) and Elaine Hedges (1986) for their readings of Glaspell's text. See also Moers for the sexual symbolism of the jewel box (1985, 253). While, as noted earlier, Moers does not identify such images as specifically clitoral, her entire treatment of female imagery (243–64), esp. in its emphasis on small and round objects (under which Moers classifies birds, among other things), begs this identification. For Minnie, the bird was her "jewel," the most precious thing in her life. Hence the "fancy box," mimicking a jewel case (as well as a coffin), and hence her decision to wring "John" Wright's neck in precisely the way he "wrung" the bird's (or hers). (Marie de France, by the way, employs the same motifs—outraged husband, dead bird with broken neck, precious box/casket, etc.—in "Rossignol" [ca. 1170–90] and may be Glaspell's source. In the *Lais,* of course, such images are undeniably erotic. See Reynolds 1990, 102–3.)

[17] As Grosz (1990) observes, Lacan's is not "Saussurian 'pure' . . . difference . . . ('A' and 'B')," which allows for an infinite number of other possibilities, but "difference based on the privileging of a single term ('A' and 'not-A')" (124). And this is why it is so utterly inadequate as a theoretical basis for the understanding of sexual difference and its representation.

organization of the family and the state. With the clitoris, theorists can construct female sexuality in such a way that women become sexual subjects in their own right, taking their sexual, social, creative, and political power into their own hands. No longer married (like Mrs. Peters) to the penis or the law, they can become (as Mrs. Hale's name suggests) by themselves healthy and whole.

Department of English
Southern Illinois University—Carbondale

References

Baker Brown, Isaac. (1866) 1987. "On Some Diseases of Woman Admitting Surgical Treatment." In *The Sexuality Debates,* ed. Shiela Jeffreys, 27–41. New York and London: Routledge & Kegan Paul.

Barker-Benfield, G. J. 1976. *The Horrors of the Half-Known Life: Male Attitudes toward Women and Sexuality in Nineteenth-Century America.* New York: Harper & Row.

Bennett, Paula. 1977. "The Language of Love: Emily Dickinson's Homoerotic Poetry." *Gai Saber* 1:13–17.

————. 1986. *My Life a Loaded Gun: Female Creativity and Feminist Poetics.* Boston: Beacon.

————. 1990. *Emily Dickinson: Woman Poet.* Iowa City: University of Iowa Press.

Bullough, Vern L., and Martha Voght. 1976. "Homosexuality and Its Confusion with the 'Secret Sin' in Pre-Freudian America." In *Sex, Society and History,* ed. Vern L. Bullough, 112–24. New York: Science History Publications.

Butler, Judith. 1990. *Gender Trouble: Feminism and the Subversion of Identity.* New York and London: Routledge.

Chauncey, George. 1982. "From Sexual Inversion to Homosexuality: Medicine and the Changing Conceptualization of Female Deviance." *Salamagundi* 58:114–46.

Chesler, Phyllis. 1972. *Women and Madness.* Garden City, N.Y.: Doubleday.

Cixous, Hélène. 1983. "The Laugh of the Medusa." In *The Signs Reader: Women, Gender & Scholarship,* ed. Elizabeth Abel and Emily K. Abel, 279–97. Chicago and London: University of Chicago Press.

Cixous, Hélène, and Catherine Clement. 1986. *The Newly Born Woman,* trans. Betsy Wing. Minneapolis: University of Minnesota Press.

Cott, Nancy F. 1978. "Passionlessness: An Interpretation of Victorian Sexual Ideology, 1790–1850." *Signs: Journal of Women in Culture and Society* 4(2):219–36.

de Lauretis, Teresa. 1988. "Sexual Indifference and Lesbian Representation." *Theatre Journal* 40(2):155–77.

Dickinson, Emily. 1955. *The Poems of Emily Dickinson,* ed. Thomas H. Johnson. Cambridge, Mass.: Harvard University Press, Belknap Press.

————. 1960. *The Complete Poetry of Emily Dickinson,* ed. Thomas H. Johnson. Boston: Little, Brown.

Dijkstra, Bram. 1986. *Idols of Perversity: Fantasies of Feminine Evil in Fin-de-Siècle Culture.* New York and Oxford: Oxford University Press.

Ellis, Havelock. (1900) 1936. *Studies in the Psychology of Sex,* vol 3. New York: Random House.

Erikson, Erik. 1968. *Identity, Youth and Crisis.* New York: W. W. Norton.

Freud, Sigmund. 1950. *Collected Papers,* vol. 5, ed. James Strachey. London: Hogarth.

―――. (1900) 1959. *The Interpretation of Dreams,* trans. James Strachey. New York: Basic.

Gallop, Jane. 1988. *Thinking through the Body.* New York: Columbia University Press.

Gay, Peter. 1984. *The Bourgeois Experience: Victoria to Freud,* vol 1. New York and Oxford: Oxford University Press.

Gilbert, Sandra M., and Susan Gubar. 1988. *No Man's Land: The Place of the Woman Writer in the Twentieth Century,* vol 1. New Haven, Conn., and London: Yale University Press.

Glaspell, Susan. (1919) 1987. *Trifles.* In *Plays by Susan Glaspell,* ed. C. W. E. Bigsby. Cambridge and New York: Cambridge University Press.

Gould, Hannah F. 1833. "The Crocus Soliloquy." In *Flora's Interpreter: or, the American Book of Flowers and Sentiments,* ed. Sarah J. Hale, 240. Boston: Thomas H. Webb & Co.

Grosz, Elizabeth. 1990. *Jacques Lacan: A Feminist Introduction.* London and New York: Routledge.

Halperin, David. 1990. *One Hundred Years of Homosexuality and Other Essays on Greek Love.* New York and London: Routledge.

Hedges, Elaine. 1986. "Small Things Reconsidered: Susan Glaspell's 'A Jury of Her Peers.'" *Women's Studies* 12(1):89–110.

Hite, Shere. 1976. *The Hite Report.* New York: Dell.

Irigaray, Luce. 1985a. *Speculum of the Other Woman,* trans. Gillian C. Gill. Ithaca: Cornell University Press.

―――. 1985b. *This Sex Which Is Not One,* trans. Catherine Porter with Carolyn Burke. Ithaca, N.Y.: Cornell University Press.

Johnson, Barbara. 1989. "Is Female to Male as Ground Is to Figure?" In *Feminism and Psychoanalysis,* ed. Richard Feldstein and Judith Roof, 255–68. Ithaca, N.Y.: Cornell University Press.

Kolodny, Annette. 1985. "A Map for Rereading: Gender and the Interpretation of Literary Texts." In *The New Feminist Criticism: Essays on Women, Literature, and Theory,* ed. Elaine Showalter, 46–62. New York: Pantheon Books.

Lacan, Jacques. (1966) 1982. "The Meaning of the Phallus." In *Feminine Sexuality: Jacques Lacan and the ecole freudienne,* ed. Juliet Mitchell and Jacqueline Rose, 74–85. New York and London: W. W. Norton.

Laqueur, Thomas. 1990. *Making Sex: Body and Gender from the Greeks to Freud.* Cambridge, Mass., and London: Harvard University Press.

Looby, Christopher. 1992a. " 'As Thoroughly Black as the Most Faithful Philanthropist Could Desire': Erotics of Race in Higginson's *Army Life in a Black Regiment.*" Unpublished manuscript, University of Chicago, Department of English.

————. 1992b. " 'The Roots of the Orchis, the Iuli of Chesnuts': The Odor of Male Solitude." Unpublished manuscript, University of Chicago, Department of English.

Lowell, Amy. (1919) 1955. "The Weather-Cock Points South." In *The Complete Poetical Works of Amy Lowell*, 211. Boston: Houghton Mifflin.

Lystra, Karen. 1989. *Searching the Heart: Women, Men, and Romantic Love in Nineteenth-Century America*. New York and Oxford: Oxford University Press.

Masson, Jeffrey Moussaieff. 1986. *A Dark Science: Women, Sexuality and Psychiatry in the Nineteenth Century*. New York: Farrar, Straus & Giroux.

Meigs, Charles. 1851. *Woman: Her Diseases and Remedies*, 2d ed. Philadelphia: Lea & Blanchard.

Moers, Ellen. 1985. *Literary Women: The Great Writers*. New York: Oxford University Press.

Reynolds, Margaret. 1990. *Erotica: Women's Writings from Sappho to Margaret Atwood*. New York: Fawcett Columbine.

Rich, Adrienne. 1979. " 'Vesuvius at Home': The Power of Emily Dickinson." In *Shakespeare's Sisters: Feminist Essays on Women Poets*, ed. Sandra M. Gilbert and Susan Gubar, 99–121. Bloomington: Indiana University Press.

Roof, Judith. 1989. "The Match in the Crocus: Representations of Lesbian Sexuality." In *Discontented Discourses: Feminism/Textual Intervention/Psychoanalysis*, ed. Marlene S. Barr and Richard Feldstein, 100–116. Urbana and Chicago: University of Illinois Press.

Rosario, Vernon, III. 1992. "Phantastical Pollutions." Unpublished manuscript, Harvard University, History of Medicine.

Scholes, Robert. 1982. *Semiotics and Interpretation*. New Haven, Conn.: Yale University Press.

Schor, Naomi. 1981. "Female Paranoia: The Case for Psychoanalytical Feminist Criticism." *Yale French Studies* 62:204–19.

————. 1987. *Reading in Detail: Aesthetics and the Feminine*. New York and London: Methuen.

Sedgwick, Eve Kosofsky. 1990. *Epistemology of the Closet*. Berkeley and Los Angeles: University of California Press.

Showalter, Elaine. 1990. *Sexual Anarchy: Gender and Culture at the Fin de Siècle*. New York: Viking.

Sigourney, Lydia Huntley. 1848. "No Concealment." In *The American Female Poets*, ed. Caroline May, 90–91. Philadelphia: Lindsay & Blakiston.

Spivak, Gayatri Chakravorty. 1981. "French Feminism in an International Frame." *Yale French Studies* 62:154–84.

Spofford, Harriet Prescott. 1882. *Poems*. Boston: Houghton Mifflin.

Stedman, Edmund Clarence. 1908. *The Poems of Edmund Clarence Stedman*. Boston and New York: Houghton Mifflin.

Timrod, Henry. 1899. *Poems of Henry Timrod*. Boston and New York: Houghton Mifflin.

Wittig, Monique. 1981. "One Is Not Born a Woman." *Feminist Issues* 1(2):47–54.

————. 1982. "The Category of Sex." *Feminist Issues* 2(2):63–68.

Criticism

No Lost Paradise: Social Gender and Symbolic Gender in the Writings of Maxine Hong Kingston

Leslie W. Rabine

The question of gender, of what it is, how it works, and how it determines our lives as men and women, receives divergent answers in contemporary feminist theory. The notion that gender is a social construct rather than an innate essence[1] has been complicated in recent years by theories of feminists influenced by French critical theory and Lacanian psychoanalysis for whom gender is a symbolic construct. Whether French or Americans schooled in French theory, these feminists see gender as produced in and through language systems.[2]

[1] See Alice Echols, "The New Feminism of Yin and Yang," in *Powers of Desire: The Politics of Sexuality*, ed. Ann Snitow, Christine Stansell, and Sharon Thompson (New York: Monthly Review Press, 1983), 440; Zillah R. Eisenstein, *Feminism and Sexual Equality: Crisis in Liberal America* (New York: Monthly Review Press, 1984); Heidi Hartmann, "The Unhappy Marriage of Marxism and Feminism: Towards a More Progressive Union," in *Women and Revolution: A Discussion of the Unhappy Marriage of Marxism and Feminism*, ed. Lydia Sargent (Boston: South End Press, 1981); and Gayle Rubin, "The Traffic in Women: Notes on the 'Political Economy of Sex,'" in *Toward an Anthropology of Women*, ed. Rayna Reiter (New York: Monthly Review Press, 1975). The theorists they most often associate with a universal female principle are Mary Daly, Robin Morgan, and Adrienne Rich (see, e.g., Echols, 442).

[2] For some of the most prominent French theories of gender, see Hélène Cixous, *La jeune née* (Paris: Union Générale d'Editions, 1975); Luce Irigaray, *This Sex Which Is Not One*,

[*Signs: Journal of Women in Culture and Society* 1987, vol. 12, no. 3]

Hélène Cixous, for instance, taking off from the notion that linguistic signs are not positive entities but products of a system of difference, sees our particular form of gender difference as the paradigm by which we conceive the particular pattern of difference that shapes our symbolic order. This pattern is based not on true difference but on hierarchical oppositions. One term, the masculine, posits itself as the primary term and represses the other (feminine) term, replacing it with its mirror opposite, a secondary term, derived from itself. This symbolic law of opposition, operating in different systems—"discourse, art, religion, the family, language"[3]—always "comes back to the man/woman opposition,"[4] and wherever it operates, it works to absorb the other into the same. Without seeing gender as biological, Cixous, and those who in different ways also seek to subvert this law of opposition, do see it as fundamental, grounding the very structures of subjectivity, representation and language.[5] For this reason, those theories, which have been called "French feminist" and which I will here call "symbolic feminist," provide tools for analyzing gender more precisely and deeply through analyses of discourses.

But the blind spot in the discursive practices of symbolic feminism is that they tend to repress the social dimension of gender by collapsing the social into the symbolic. The notion that linguistic structures and social structures are coextensive can lead to reestablishing a hierarchal opposition in which the specificity of the social is repressed and becomes the secondary, derived term of the symbolic. It may be true, as Jacqueline Rose says, that "there is no feminine outside language . . . because the 'feminine' is constituted as a division in language, a division which pro-

trans. Catherine Porter with Carolyn Burke (Ithaca, N.Y.: Cornell University Press, 1985); and Julia Kristeva, *La révolution du langage poétique* (Paris: Editions du Seuil, 1974), translated as *The Revolution in Poetic Language*, by Margaret Waller (New York: Columbia University Press, 1984). For American versions of poststructuralist theories of gender, see Jane Gallop, *The Daughter's Seduction* (Ithaca, N.Y.: Cornell University Press, 1982), and *Reading Lacan* (Ithaca, N.Y.: Cornell University Press, 1985); and Kaja Silverman, *The Subject of Semiotics* (New York: Oxford University Press, 1983).

[3] Cixous, 64.

[4] Hélène Cixous, "Castration or Decapitation?" trans. Annette Kuhn, *Signs: Journal of Women in Culture and Society* 7, no. 1 (Autumn 1981): 41–55, esp. 44.

[5] Cixous's and Irigaray's insistence that gender is fundamental has led to a debate on the extent to which they are essentialists in their notions of femininity. Toril Moy argues that their texts contain a contradiction between a deconstructive view of gender and an essentialist view and that the essentialist view constitutes a flaw in their theories (see Moy, *Sexual/Textual Politics* [London: Methuen, 1985]). Naomi Schor argues, however, that this contradiction between deconstructive and essentialist writing on gender is productive and one of the strengths of Cixous's and Irigaray's writing (see "Introducing Feminism" [paper delivered at symposium of the UCLA Faculty Critical Theory Study Group, University of California, Los Angeles, March 15, 1986]).

duces the feminine as its negative term."⁶ But while the social cannot be thought outside of language, an exclusive theoretical focus on language structure can lead to strategies that seek to liberate the "feminine" while leaving intact the oppression of social women.

The strategies used by symbolic feminism to transform our phallocentric gender system bring into play both its strengths and its blind spot. In various ways the theorists seek to replace a sociosymbolic order based on the logic of opposition with one based on the logic of difference or to displace the absolute difference *between* masculine and feminine so as to reveal multiple differences *within* each sex and each speaking being.⁷ In other words, the hierarchized dichotomy between a superior masculine essence embodied by men and an inferior feminine essence embodied by women would give way to an infinity of different and alternating gender positions. Fixed gender identity that protects the rigidly guarded identity of the masculine subject and denies feminine subjecthood would give way to subjects in flux. Since our oppositional order represses the feminine and substitutes for it a femininity that stands in as the secondary term derived from masculinity, the repressed feminine becomes, in the works of writers like Cixous and Luce Irigaray, the site where the play of sexual difference can emerge through discursive practices that Cixous calls "feminine writing."⁸

As Cixous and others have pointed out, masculine and feminine are not necessarily embodied by biological men and women. Therefore, men can also engage in feminine writing and in deconstructing a phallocentric gender system. What this analysis leaves out, however, is that our social order transforms biological bodies into social men and women, into occupiers of relatively privileged and relatively oppressed social positions that the oppressed cannot simply choose to abandon and that few privileged people would want to abandon. Sexed bodies become the visible signs through which a system of hierarchal social roles is enforced by economics, politics, the family, religion, and other institutional constructs so that individuals whose bodies are visibly marked "female" find themselves forced into oppressive positions. In such a social order men, or individuals whose bodies are marked male, can and do engage in feminine discursive practices while occupying positions of privilege and while continuing to

⁶ Jacqueline Rose, "Introduction—II," in *Feminine Sexuality: Jacques Lacan and the école freudienne,* ed. Juliet Mitchell and Jacqueline Rose (New York: W. W. Norton & Co., 1982), 55.

⁷ These terms come from Barbara Johnson, *The Critical Difference: Essays in the Contemporary Rhetoric of Reading* (Baltimore: Johns Hopkins University Press, 1978).

⁸ See esp. Hélène Cixous, "The Laugh of the Medusa," trans. Keith Cohen and Paula Cohen, in *New French Feminisms,* ed. Elaine Marks and Isabelle de Courtivron (New York: Schocken Books), 245–64.

exclude women from them. Strategies of feminine writing can subvert symbolic gender while leaving social gender oppression intact if they do not also adopt social feminist strategies of institutional transformation. The following analysis of Maxine Hong Kingston's writing seeks to reconcile insights of symbolic and social feminism. If feminine writing expresses difference, then it cannot simply take the form practiced by French theorists but must also take many different forms. Although Kingston's writing does not put into play a subject in boundless flux, it is a "feminine writing" of a different kind. Two aspects of Kingston's writing, its double ambivalence to the culture her parents brought from China and to the U.S. culture that also claims her, as well as its complex textuality, make the fixed polarities of oppositional logic unstable. In various interviews Kingston has said that her writings aim to "claim America"[9] for Chinese-Americans, and she disclaims that they are representative of China or Chinese-Americans.[10] Her individual expression of a Chinese-American culture marginalized by Anglo-American culture sets the laws of gender systems into motion.

Like the feminine writing of Cixous and Irigaray, Kingston's writing violates the law of opposition, making gender dichotomies proliferate into unresolvable gender differences. In conjunction with this instability of male and female, her texts also set to spinning fixed oppositions of theme and form—between fiction and autobiography, history and myth, parents and children, and finally, writing and oral legend. Unlike Cixous and Irigaray, Kingston's proliferation of gender arrangements remains rooted in the social world and so reveals not only how gender systems change across cultural boundaries but also how the distinction between symbolic and social gender changes between cultures. These two forms of gender, distinct and interrelated, illuminate, contradict, and reinforce each other. By making their contradictions work for her, Kingston performs a writerly liberation that also has social implications. The following reading will first study Kingston's work as a unique kind of feminine writing that in its own way fractures the logic of opposition into a play of difference and will then study how this play of difference, especially between writing and oral legend, clarifies relations between social and symbolic gender.

---

[9] Elaine H. Kim, *Asian American Literature: An Introduction to the Writings and Their Social Context* (Philadelphia: Temple University Press, 1982), 209.

[10] Maxine Hong Kingston, interview by Arturo Islas, in *Women Writers of the West Coast Speaking of Their Lives and Careers*, ed. Marilyn Yalom (Santa Barbara, Calif.: Capra Press, 1983), 12.

Gender opposition/gender difference

While in *The Woman Warrior* and *China Men*[11] gender determines one's place in the family and society, and certainly one's place in power relations, there are no gender essences. Women can have opposite qualities. They can be strong and aggressive, like Maxine's mother Brave Orchid, or meek and passive, like her aunt Moon Orchid. They can be both at different times, like Maxine herself, who as a child is talkative and athletic in Chinese school, silent and passive at American public school. Kingston does away with the illusion of a universal feminine, placing among her confusing and painful childhood experiences the attempts to be "American feminine."

Though neither sex possesses essential qualities, gender oppositions do play a determining role in organizing Kingston's textual world. *The Woman Warrior* tells the stories of the women in Kingston's family, and *China Men* tells the stories of the men. The members of each sex are shadow creatures in the world and in the book of the other sex. But Kingston seems to emphasize gender boundaries *between* the two books all the better to reorganize and play with these boundaries *within* each book. Each book incorporates legends from the oral tradition into autobiographical, bio-graphical, and historical stories; and in each book the starring legend concerns a character who crosses over the boundary into the other gender. *The Woman Warrior* takes its title from the legend of Fa Mu Lan, the swordswoman who disguises herself as a man by dressing in male armor so that she can take revenge against greedy landlords and barons for the injustices done to her family. *China Men* opens with the legend of Tang Ao, who in Kingston's version travels to the Land of Women, where he is forced to have his feet bound, his ears pierced, his eyebrows plucked, to don constricting clothing and makeup, and, in short, to become a member of the weaker sex.[12] Both legends are metaphors for a textual practice in *The Woman Warrior* and *China Men* that displaces and transforms boundaries.

This double deployment of gender, with the logic of the "difference between" genders practiced between the two books and the logic of the "difference within" each gender practiced within each text, is expressed by Kingston in two statements. One appears in an interview with Elaine Kim, and the other is a poetic statement in *The Woman Warrior*. Kim reports, "Kingston says that she wrote *The Woman Warrior* and *China Men*

[11] Maxine Hong Kingston, *The Woman Warrior: Memoirs of a Girlhood among Ghosts* (New York: Random House/Vintage Trade Books, 1977), hereafter referred to as *WW*, and *China Men* (New York: Ballantine Books, 1980), hereafter referred to as *CM*.

[12] The story of Tang Ao in the Land of Women comes from the Chinese eighteenth-century classic novel by Li Ju-Chen, *Flowers in the Mirror*, trans. and ed. Lin Tai-Yi (London: Peter Owen, 1965). In the novel, it is Tang Ao's brother-in-law who is forced to become a member of the weaker sex in the Land of Women.

together, having conceived of them as an interlocking story about the lives of men and women. But the women's stories 'fell into place,' and she feared that the men's were anti-female and would undercut the feminist viewpoint."[13] Kim reports Kingston as saying: "I feel I have gone as deeply into men's psyches as I can, and I don't find them that different. I care about men . . . as much as I care about women. . . . Given the present state of affairs, perhaps men's and women's experiences have to be dealt with separately for now, until more auspicious times are with us."[14]

This statement about gender opposition as a destructive and, it is hoped, temporary condition bears a striking contrast to Fa Mu Lan's mystic vision in *The Woman Warrior* of gender difference as the basis of time and movement themselves:

> I saw two people made of gold dancing the earth's dances. They turned so perfectly that together they were the axis of the earth's turning. They were light; they were molten, changing gold— Chinese lion dancers, African lion dancers in midstep. I heard high Javanese bells deepen in midring to Indian bells, Hindu Indian, American Indian. Before my eyes, gold bells shredded into gold tassles that fanned into two royal capes that softened into lions' fur. Manes grew tall into feathers that shone—became light rays. Then the dancers danced the future. . . . I am watching the centuries pass in moments because suddenly I understand time, which is spinning and fixed like the North Star. And I understand how working and hoeing are dancing; how peasant clothes are golden, as king's clothes are golden; *how one of the dancers is always a man and the other a woman.*[15]

Gender is as necessary as it is arbitrary.

The language here replaces the logic of separation with a logic of difference. It is difference, rather than separation, that allows change, motion, integration, and connection to happen. This couple is reminiscent of the Tao in the *I Ching* where Yin, the masculine, and Yang, the feminine, are constantly in the process of changing into each other and where their changes engender chains of transformations similar to those Kingston here expresses in a poetic mode.

The logics of opposition and difference vie with each other in theme and narrative structure as well. In *China Men*, Kingston is the woman warrior who takes vengeance *for* the family by reporting the vicious racism her male relatives combatted in America and the uncredited contributions

---

[13] Kim, 209.
[14] Ibid.
[15] *WW*, p. 32 (emphasis added).

they made to building this country. In *The Woman Warrior*, Kingston takes vengeance *against* the family, expressing her rage against an institutionalized hatred for women, and especially girls.

Corresponding to this thematic opposition, the narrative structures of the two books, as Suzanne Juhasz has shown, also differ from each other.[16] The narrative structure of *China Men* is based, like much traditional male narrative, on a linear and circular quest to return to a lost paradise. In *The Woman Warrior*, which relates Kingston's girlhood memoirs, there is no lost paradise, not in China the mythical homeland, or in childhood, or in her relationship to her mother; and its absence structures the text. This absence, moreover, may have significance beyond the poetic power it anchors in *The Woman Warrior: Memoirs of a Girlhood among Ghosts*, for Kingston is not the only writer to evoke it. Other second-generation women from immigrant communities in the United States, like Anzia Yezierska and Sandra Cisneros, have also written semiautobiographical works structured on the lack of a lost paradise.[17]

The narrative structure of femininity

The Woman Warrior is structured in a double and simultaneous movement that traces the girl's anguished but never totally completed struggle to break away from her girlhood world and the incomplete return after the incomplete break. The narrator, in telling her story, simultaneously relives the young girl's negative feelings for her mother, her family, the community, and its myths and also measures the distance that bestows on them their positive and irreplaceable value: "I looked at their ink drawings of poor people snagging their neighbors' flotage with long flood hooks and pushing the girl babies on down the river. And I had to get out of hating range. . . . I refuse to shy my way anymore through our Chinatown, which tasks me with the old sayings and the stories. The swordswoman and I are not so dissimilar. May my people understand the resemblance soon so that I can return to them."[18] A double voice writes these words, a voice that is at the same time both in and out of hating range, the voice of a writer who in a certain sense has already returned to write about her people, to claim and

---

[16] Analyzing the narrative techniques of *The Woman Warrior* and *China Men* in the framework of Nancy Chodorow's theory and in relation to the search for a home as I am doing here, Suzanne Juhasz comes to almost opposite conclusions on issues of narrative structure and the search for a home (Suzanne Juhasz, "Maxine Hong Kingston: Narrative Technique and Female Identity," in *Contemporary Women Writers*, ed. C. Rainwater and W. J. Soheik [Lexington: University Press of Kentucky, 1985], 173–89).

[17] Sandra Cisneros, *The House on Mango Street* (Houston: Arte Publico Press, 1983); Anzia Yezierska, *The Bread Givers* (1925; reprint, New York: Persea Books, 1975).

[18] *WW*, 62.

transform their stories, but who writes as the girl who cannot return. Throughout *The Woman Warrior*, these two voices, while remaining two, never really separate from each other any more than Kingston can really separate from her mother and her people. Her story, like those of Cisneros and Yezierska, is about separation and the impossibility of separation.

In the works of all three writers, women's contradictory attitude toward their culture has both social and psychological reasons. The culture of each—Chinese-American, Jewish-American, Chicano—in addition to providing their personal identity, also provides an area of resistance against the dominant culture that dehumanizes people not only through racism but also through a homogenizing and sterile rationalism. Yet the childhood culture, infused in the works of all three authors with what Kingston calls "woman hatred,"[19] provides small haven. The myths that nourish the imagination and the spirit also relegate women to an inferior position; and the community, instead of suffusing them with warmth, suffocates them, limits them to a role of serving men, and hinders their growth. "Living among one's own emigrant villagers can give a good Chinese far from China glory and a place. . . . But I am useless, one more girl who couldn't be sold."[20] A woman from an immigrant group in the United States can find that between the two cultures she has no place.

This insoluble ambivalence can be explored through psychoanalytical theories about mother-daughter relationships, theories that analyze the way that male and female infant relationships to the mother affect the development and structure of the masculine and feminine psyche.[21] Boys separate completely from the mother, developing a subjective structure based on lack (or as Freudians have said, on castration) and, therefore, on the desire to fill it. Fulfillment is fantasized as a return to the lost unity with the mother and the state of nature she represents or, in other words, to a lost paradise. But girls do not go through this complete separation, so that their subjectivity is shaped not by a linear desire for something imagined as

[19] Maxine Hong Kingston, "Reservations about China," *Ms. Magazine* (October 1978), 67–79, esp. 67.

[20] *WW*, 62.

[21] The most influential of these theories is that of Nancy Chodorow, *The Reproduction of Mothering: Psychoanalysis and the Sociology of Gender* (Berkeley and Los Angeles: University of California Press, 1978). See also Dorothy Dinnerstein, *The Mermaid and the Minotaur: Sexual Arrangements and Human Malaise* (New York: Harper & Row, 1976). While these theories are grounded in Western notions of the oedipal conflict, I am mentioning them here in the hope that they can help to analyze the texts in question since the oedipal quest structure of *China Men* contrasts so strikingly to the nonlinear composition of *The Woman Warrior* and since Kingston has pointed out that her writing is unmistakably American (see Maxine Hong Kingston, "Cultural Misreadings by American Reviewers," in *Asian and Western Writers in Dialogue: New Cultural Identities*, ed. Guy Amirthanayagam [London: Macmillan, 1982], 55–65). It is significant in this respect that the heroes of *China Men* eventually decide that their "lost paradise" is to be found not in China but in the United States.

lost, but by a conflict between two needs: they desire both to remain close to the mother and to break into autonomy.

Luce Irigaray, in her poetic work *Et l'une ne bouge pas sans l'autre*, expresses the violence and insolubility of this conflict. For the narrator, the acultural, asymbolic unity with the mother suffocates and paralyzes her: "And I can no longer run toward what I love. And the more I love, the more I become captive, held in sluggish fixity." With great effort, she gains autonomy from the mother, but her only alternative is to turn to the father. She becomes a "mechanical scholar,"[22] learning the sterile power-hungry culture of the father, which for Kingston, Cisneros, and Yezierska would also be the racist or anti-Semitic dominant culture. Irigaray explores constructing a new cultural relationship with the mother, but only as an impossible fantasy, at least for now.

The narrator of *The Woman Warrior* weaves her ambivalence to her community and culture into her ambivalence toward her mother, who communicates to her the culture and its myths and who interprets the community for her.[23] In a scene relating an interchange between the adult Maxine and her mother, the narrator says, "How can I bear to leave her again?"[24] And in the same scene she also expresses the contrary desire to get away: "'When I'm away from here,' I had to tell her, 'I don't get sick. . . . I can breathe. . . . I've found some places in this country that are ghost free. And I think I belong there.'"[25] Yet it is the mother's ghosts who breathe life into the daughter's writing.

Feminine narrative/masculine narrative

In *The Woman Warrior* this conflictual texture provides the internal structuring principle; in *China Men* the relationship to the father forms the external framework in which Kingston molds the lives and thoughts of the men in her family and the immigrant community. In *China Men*, the theme of revenge, which permeates the *Woman Warrior*, becomes secondary to the theme of being exiled from home, precisely the theme of the lost paradise, whose absence in *The Woman Warrior* so marked the structure and the female experience recounted. Both books describe with

[22] Luce Irigaray, *Et l'une ne bouge pas sans l'autre* (And one doesn't stir without the other) (Paris: Editions de minuit, 1979), 7, 12 (my translation).
[23] For a study of the ambiguity of the mother in *The Woman Warrior*, see Stephanie A. Demetrakopoulos, "The Metaphysics of Matrilinearism in Women's Autobiography: Studies of Mead's *Blackberry Winter*, Hellman's *Pentimento*, Angelou's *I Know Why the Caged Bird Sings*, and Kingston's *The Woman Warrior*," in *Women's Autobiography: Essays in Criticism*, ed. Estelle C. Jelinek (Bloomington: Indiana University Press, 1980).
[24] *WW* (n. 11 above), 118.
[25] Ibid., 126–27.

nostalgia the loving rituals accompanying the birth of boys, and both express bitterness over the silence accompanying the birth of girls. Within the texts, these rituals express parental love and make childhood an Edenic place from which girls are excluded. But there are sociohistoric reasons for this difference as well. In *China Men*, the grandfathers and great-grand-fathers, admitted to the United States as agricultural and railroad workers, long to go home because the cruel treatment they receive deprives them of a worthwhile life. But in *The Woman Warrior*, the place Maxine's family calls "home" is the country where families sell their daughters into slavery and where daughters-in-law are tortured. "Home" is a place she does not want to go.

Yet Kingston's writing makes permeable this boundary between the apparently mutually exclusive experiences of men and women. Most of the legends incorporated into *China Men* are about exiles who wander in search of returning home, and, in at least two of these legends, exile is symbolized by the men being transformed into women. To be a woman, whose birth is not recognized by the family, is to be a permanent exile, without any home, without a place. To be a man who loses one's home is to cross over into the feminine gender. *China Men*, about men who have been forced to cross over into the feminine gender, is written by a woman, who, in the act of writing, has also, like the woman warrior, crossed over, albeit voluntarily, into the masculine gender and assumed the voice of the men she writes about.

The Woman Warrior recounts not only how the boys' births were celebrated while the girls' were ignored but also how her brother was royally welcomed home from Vietnam by the family, while she was never welcomed home from Berkeley. That scene of bitterness in *The Woman Warrior*[26] is transformed into the triumphant conclusion of *China Men*, where the brother, having gone to Hong Kong and discovered he does not belong there, fulfills the family's quest by coming "back home" to California. In the course of the male family quest in *China Men*, the meaning of "home" for the men of the family gradually shifts from China to America. It is Great Uncle who pronounces this shift: " 'I've decided to stay in California.' He said, 'California. This is my home. I belong here.' He turned and, looking at us, roared, 'We belong here.' "[27]

Ironically, it is through this hated Great Uncle, who calls girls maggots, that Maxine finally discovers a home of sorts, a place where she "belongs." In *China Men* she describes herself hiding from her great uncle because he treats her like a servant:

I did not want to see him or hear him or be in his bossy presence. . . .
I liked hiding in the dark, *which could be anywhere*. The cel'ar door

[26] Ibid., 56.
[27] *CM* (n. 11 above), 184.

sloped overhead, a room within the storeroom within the basement. I listened to footsteps above the rafters. He would not come
down to the basement, where he had to duck the pipes and walk
stooped. I was safely tucked away among the bags of old clothes and
shoes, the trunks and crates the grown-ups had brought with them
from China, the seabags with the addresses in English and Chinese,
the tools, the bags and bottles of seeds, the branches of seeds and
leaves and pods hanging upside down, and the drying loofahs. . . . I
thought over useless things like wishes, wands, hibernation. I
talked to the people whom I knew were not really there. I became
different, complete, an *orphan*; my partners were beautiful cow-
girls, and also men, cowboys who could talk to me in conversations;
I named this activity Talking Men. . . . *I belonged here.*[28]

Through this dreamlike landscape, Kingston writes her own version of
what Freud calls the "family romance."[29] Giving access to a childhood
imaginary realm freed from the bitter memories of childhood experience,
this room within a room within a room (recalling the Jungian passageway to
the unconscious) transforms old China from a threatening family law into a
conglomeration of mythic symbols—crates, bags, dried plants, English and
Chinese writing—evoking dream instead of duty and waiting to be translated into fantasy and then into text. Like a dream, the memory performs
the work that translates the materials of the unconscious into language. A
buried, internal place that is not a place but a darkness, this place could be
anywhere. A nonplace of writerly productivity, the antechamber of the
unconscious, it is in the father's house (and in the father's book); in fact, it is
at the foundation of the father's house but hidden from the fathers, unseen
and unrecognized by them. It resembles Sarah Kofman's description of the
unconscious that "doesn't have a place. Like writing it is a-topical. It
disrupts the domestic economy and turns the house upside down." The
unconscious, says Kofman, is "*unheimlich*"—uncanny but also without a
home.[30]
    While at the foundation of the family institution, Maxine is yet outside
of the family, an orphan. Her situation contrasts with that of Ch'ü Yüan,
China's Homer, and the subject of the last legend in *China Men*.[31] Kingston, relating Ch'ü Yüan's exile, calls him, too, an "orphan," because he
"cannot go home."[32] Ch'ü Yüan's male tragedy is precisely Maxine's escape

---

[28] *CM*, 180–81 (emphasis added).
    [29] Sigmund Freud, "Family Romance," in *The Standard Edition of the Complete Psycho-
logical Works*, trans. and ed. James Strachey, vol. 9 (London: Hogarth Press, 1962).
    [30] Sarah Kofman, *Lectures de Derrida* (Paris: Editions Galilée, 1984), 55 (my translation).
    [31] See Jaroslav Prusek, *Chinese History and Literature* (Dordrecht: D. Reidel Publishing
Co., 1970); and Dorothea Hayward Scott, *Chinese Popular Literature and the Child* (Chicago:
American Library Association, 1980).
    [32] *CM*, 258.

154   *Rabine*

from female tragedy. The orphaned state that marks for him the loss of home marks for her the discovery of a home that does not exist anywhere. It is constructed through and exists only in the logic of ambiguity that weaves her texts, a logic that overturns the law of opposition.

Violating the law of gender: A logic of ambiguity

Kim sees the "portrayal of ambiguity as central to the Chinese American experience," which is neither mainstream American nor Asian-Chinese.[33] This ambiguity, which instead of finding resolution is transformed into the warp and woof of Kingston's writing, is also the result of love/hate relationships to the immigrant Chinese culture and to the childhood myths and memories experienced in that culture. Without a childhood imaginary realm and the access to the unconscious it opens up, we would be little more than robots. The power of the childhood imaginary realm also increases the power of marginalized cultures in the United States to resist a social order that tends to turn us all into robots. But its very necessity to us constitutes its danger since it can also draw one back into paralytic unity with the mother, as well as accommodate one to the limits of patriarchal institutions. Kingston's ambiguity shuttles between the necessity and the danger of this childhood imaginary realm.

As feminists, many of us seek in pre-Greek and pre-Judaic matriarchal myth and in an idyllic mother-daughter bond a healing alternative to patriarchal technocracy. Kingston, in writing the healing journey into myth, also encourages a questioning of myth as an unequivocally positive answer to women's oppression. The same narrator who glorifies the mythical woman warrior Fa Mu Lan also praises antimythical rationalism: "I had to leave home in order to see the world logically, logic the new way of seeing. I learned to think that mysteries are for explanation. I enjoy the simplicity. Concrete pours out of my mouth to cover the forests with freeways and sidewalks. Give me plastics, periodical tables, TV dinners."[34] *The Woman Warrior* also raises questions about the liberating quality of the mother archetype and the idyllic quality of a matriarchal community since, like other more theoretical works, it portrays in its own poetic register a Chinese cultural structure that can incorporate matriarchal relationships into a patriarchy as oppressive as any other.[35]

[33] Kim (n. 9 above), xvii. See also Frank Chin, Jeffery Paul Chan, Lawson Fusao Inada, and Shawn Hsu Wong, *Aiiieeeee! An Anthology of Asian-American Writers* (Washington, D.C.: Howard University Press, 1974); David Hsin-Fu Wand, *Asian-American Heritage: An Anthology of Prose and Poetry* (New York: Washington Square Press, 1974); and Kai-yu Hsu and Helen Palubinskas, *Asian American Authors* (Boston: Houghton Mifflin Co., 1972).

[34] *WW*, 237.

[35] The incorporation of matriarchy into patriarchy in Chinese family structure is examined in Julia Kristeva, *Des Chinoises* (Paris: Des Femmes, 1974); and P. Steven Sangren, "Female

Even legends, as they are told within the context of an oppressive community, are at first presented as sending anything but a liberating message. *The Woman Warrior* begins by showing the traditional community and its oral tradition at its worst. The heroine's mother tells her a hair-raising story of an aunt in China, pregnant out of wedlock, whom the villagers terrorized to the point that she took revenge by drowning herself and her newborn baby (girl) in the family well. It is a cruel story, cruelly told by the mother for a cruel motive: "Don't let your father know that I told you. He denies her. Now that you have started to menstruate, what happened to her could happen to you. Don't humiliate us. You wouldn't like to be forgotten as if you had never been born."[36]

Oral culture, which on one level transmits an unquestioning acceptance of women's subservience, is anything but idealized here. Yet, like everything in *The Woman Warrior*, it branches into ambiguities. Themes and language, like the relation to the mother, split and separate within their unity. The text suggests that the mother's stated motives for telling the story also hide an opposite motive, that of telling the forbidden story in a secret pact with her daughter for the pleasure of telling it. In repeatedly enjoining her daughter from telling this story—"Don't tell anyone you had an aunt. Your father does not want to hear her name"[37]—is the mother not also seeking her own release from silence and giving Maxine the means and material to break the injunction? Kingston's motive in telling the story of the aunt, "No Name Woman," is indeed to violate the paternal/community injunctions to silence and, beyond that, to destroy their power and authority. She not only breaks the silence but also transforms the oral story into writing and by this act denies the power of the community that maintains its cohesiveness through the oral tradition. A story that is oppressive when orally transmitted within the context of family and community is liberating when transformed into writing.[38]

Yet Kingston's act is just as ambiguous as her mother's. Like the cruel mother, she, too, tells the story for the pleasure of telling it and, moreover, to preserve the culture whose authority she seeks to destroy. This act of cultural preservation, itself born of ambiguity, splits into another ambiguity. Her act preserves culture not just by keeping old stories alive but by engaging in the tradition of ancestor worship. Other ancestral spirits have "their descent lines providing them with paper suits and dresses, spirit

Gender in Chinese Religious Symbols: Kuan Yin, Ma Tsu, and the 'Eternal Mother,'" *Signs* 9, no. 1 (Autumn 1983): 4–25.

[36] *WW* (n. 11 above), 5.

[37] Ibid., 18.

[38] Suzanne Juhasz has a different analysis of *The Woman Warrior* as an autobiography that integrates fantasy, in "Towards a Theory of Form in Feminist Autobiography: Kate Millet's *Flying* and *Sita*; Maxine Hong Kingston's *The Woman Warrior*," *International Journal of Women's Studies* 2, no. 2 (1979): 62–75.

money, paper houses, paper automobiles." Of her aunt, Kingston says, "I alone devote pages of paper to her, though not origamied into houses and clothes."[39]

She observes the customs of ancestor worship in such a way as to destroy its fundamental principle, that of maintaining patriarchal descent intact. She pays homage to the woman who ruptured the descent line and so had to be excluded from it in order to preserve it unbroken. By establishing a descent line with this woman, Kingston reaffirms the damage to the true patriarchal descent line and replaces it with a competing, illegitimate line. She adheres to it not just by offering paper to the spirit of her aunt but also by carrying on the aunt's tradition of engaging in the one act that destroys the essence of patriarchal descent: illegitimate birth. She gives birth not only to the aunt who was "forgotten as if she had never been born," but also to a book that violates the father's law. From the very first sentence of the book: "You must not tell anyone,"[40] the text performs its own transgression of the paternal law concerning language, sexuality, generation, and gender. An illegitimate conception, it imitates No Name Woman, who "crossed boundaries not delineated in space."[41] Crossing boundaries of gender and genre, both desiring and rejecting her family, her mother, her family's culture, and its traditions, Kingston's writing enacts what the swordswoman learns in her mystical vision of the dancing couple, that nothing is identical to itself but is always something else as well. The "difference between," the logic of opposition, the law of gender that protects patriarchal geneology, gives way to the difference within.

The legendary figures in *The Woman Warrior* are also textual figures in which the logic of ambiguity spins its relays. Each of them plays a different role in elaborating a kind of feminine writing. While one such figure is of course Fa Mu Lan, another figure is Ts'ai Yen (Lady Wen-Chi), legendary poetess of the second century. The last episode of *The Woman Warrior*, which suggests Kingston's reconciliation with her mother and her culture, retells the legend in which Ts'ai Yen was kidnapped by a barbarian general, had two children by him, and fought in his army, but after twelve years she "was ransomed and married to Tung Ssu so that her father would have Han descendents."[42] According to Caroline Ong, Ts'ai Yen would have been considered, as a person who lived among the barbarians and had barbarian children, a greater outcast than No Name Woman.[43] She is legendary because she later redeemed herself by returning to China and leading a life of exemplary filial piety. According to Robert Rorex and Wen Fong, Ts'ai Yen's return is associated in the Chinese tradition with the idea of

[39] *WW*, 18–19.
[40] Ibid., 3.
[41] Ibid., 9.
[42] Ibid., 243.
[43] Personal communication with Caroline Ong, June 1985.

"the superiority of Chinese civilization over cultures beyond her borders; the irreconcilability of the different ways of life; . . . and above all, the Confucian concept of loyalty to one's ancestral family and state."[44]

Needless to say, Kingston changes the meaning in rewriting the legend, or, to put it more precisely, she deprives it of a single, definite meaning or truth and makes it alternate between different meanings. In concluding that Ts'ai Yen's words were later adopted by the Chinese because they "translated well,"[45] Kingston suggests that Ts'ai Yen is a parable for her own writing as translation of the Chinese oral tradition into American-English writing. Yet like many of the legends that Kingston juxtaposes in biography and autobiography, the legend of Ts'ai Yen is a parable that does not work. By inserting legend among the contemporary stories, Kingston follows the conventions of parable, inviting the reader to create interpretive parallels between the two narrative chains, but at a certain point the parallels fall apart.

The mother herself, the model "talk-storier," also uses myths as analogies to interpret experience. Yet Kingston recounts her mother's proliferation of parables in a satiric way. Brave Orchid, in one of her own acts of Fa Mu Lan–style warfare, plots to avenge her sister Moon Orchid against Moon Orchid's husband and his second wife. Explaining to Moon Orchid how she will win her husband back, Brave Orchid says: "You are the Empress of the East, and the Empress of the West has imprisoned the Earth's Emperor in the Western Palace. And you, the good Empress of the East, come out of the dawn to invade her land and free the Emperor."[46] This parable wildly distorts the situation. Like Kingston's legends, Brave Orchid's myth of the empresses carries a double message: legends are meant to be interpreted as analogies for experience, and legends cannot be interpreted as analogies for experience. The message on interpretation cannot itself be interpreted except as split within itself.

This happens because contradictory analogies alternate within the legend of Ts'ai Yen and the other legends retold in *The Woman Warrior* and *China Men*. The figure of Ts'ai Yen flashes back and forth between being an analogy for Maxine Hong Kingston in relation to her mother, and for the mother, Brave Orchid, in relation to her daughter. In the mother's eyes the daughter has gone to live among the barbarians, yet it is the mother herself who has left China to live in a barbarian land and sings songs of her homesickness. When Kingston says of Ts'ai Yen that "her words seemed to be Chinese, but the barbarians understood their sadness and

---

[44] Robert A. Rorex and Wen Fong, "Introduction," in *Eighteen Songs of a Nomad Flute: The Story of Lady Wen-Chi* (a fourteenth-century handscroll in the Metropolitan Museum of Art) (New York: Metropolitan Museum of Art, 1974), 1.

[45] *WW*, 243.

[46] Ibid., 166.

anger" and that "her children did not laugh, but eventually sang along,"[47] she could be speaking either about herself translating her own sadness and anger toward her mother into poetry, or she could be talking about her mother's oral stories.

Who is the real outcast poetess, who the real woman warrior, Maxine or Brave Orchid? Both legendary figures, Ts'ai Yen and Fa Mu Lan, merge the mother and daughter but also separate them since they can both fit the figure, but not at the same time. The figure of Ts'ai Yen, like the figure of Fa Mu Lan, as it alternates between embodying Kingston and embodying her mother, is different within itself. It creates both a difference and a relationship between mother and daughter. Through Ts'ai Yen, the daughter's conflict, evoked by Irigaray, between merging and separating is not resolved (how could it be?), but it is harmonized in poetry. The fantasy of the legendary poetess is on a formal level a fantasy of transforming the conflict from pain into beauty and from paralysis into harmonious movement. Like the myth of the empresses in relation to Moon Orchid's American experience, the alternating form of the Ts'ai Yen analogy distorts the relationship between mother and daughter but also clarifies a not-yet-existing possibility.

The figure of Fa Mu Lan takes this contradictory form in a different direction. Like her daughter Maxine, Brave Orchid also plots elaborate strategies of revenge—against male privilege in the episode of the sister's husband or against a society in which she does not feel at home, as in the episode of the druggist's delivery boy.[48] Like her daughter, she also fantasizes her revenge in a proliferation of extravagant stories. In contrast to her daughter, however, she puts them into practice with great theatrical flourish, although they backfire on her in equally dismal failures. Maxine identifies with Fa Mu Lan in fantasy but recoils in embarassment when her mother takes on the role of the swordswoman in real life.

The scenes in which the mother plots revenge cast identification with Fa Mu Lan into a more overtly comic and satirical light that reflects on both the vengeful mother and the embarrassed daughter. The comedy casts doubt on the use of the Fa Mu Lan legend itself as an ideal, a model, and a metaphor for Kingston's text. The woman warrior, affirmed and doubted as the metaphor of the text, embodies an ambiguity toward writing itself. She figures a quality essential to a certain kind of women's writing—a literature whose angry, poetic revenge against racial and sexual injustice is not diminished by a turning back on itself in self-questioning and self-amusement. Such self-questioning avoids dogmatism or indulgence in self-pity.

The legend that introduces *China Men*, Tang Ao in the Land of

---

[47] Ibid., 243.
[48] Ibid., 196–98.

Women, also presents itself as a parable for the text while raising doubts about the parallels it suggests. Recounting with apparent relish the treatment of Tang Ao by the female rulers, it is a revenge story, since treating a man like a woman is in itself a form of revenge. The conventions of parable lead to the interpretation that for Kingston to tell her father's stories is also a form of vengeance, especially since he would never tell them to her, taking refuge in what his daughters interpret as a punishing silence alleviated by strings of antifemale curses. Kingston's revenge consists in forcing him to be interpreted by a disdained woman and to be absorbed into a woman's language. While telling his stories is on the one hand an act of love, it is, on the other hand, an act of vengeance, also a way of usurping power from the father. Since opposition to the father proves futile, Kingston, borrowing from Fa Mu Lan's store of military strategy, defeats and transforms patriarchal power by immersing herself in it.

Like the figures of Fa Mu Lan and Ts'ai Yen, Tang Ao is a metaphor both for the father and for Kingston as writer. In writing China Men, Kingston travels to the Land of Men and assumes the voice of her male relatives. Her version of the legend, in which Tang Ao becomes indistinguishable from a woman, also suggests that the arbitrary and fictional quality of gender, both unstable and rigid, makes it dangerous to play with for both men and women, both Kingston and Tang Ao, in this double crossover.[49]

Symbolic gender and social gender

The danger and necessity of crossing the gender boundary is related to the problem of crossing the genre boundary or of bringing legends from the oral tradition into a written text. Some feminine theorists for whom gender is a symbolic structure also see writing and the spoken word as gendered. Theorists like Julia Kristeva and Kofman associate writing with the feminine and voice with phallocentrism.[50] In Kingston's text, writing and orality are gendered as well but in a different way. This difference opens up the collapse between symbolic and social gender discussed earlier in this essay.

[49] The story of Tang Ao also shows the uncanny ability of writing to produce connections. The story, part of the oral tradition, is a modified version of an episode from Li Ju Chen's Flowers in the Mirror (n. 12 above). Although Kingston does not make an explicit connection between the oral legend and the novel, the coincidental similarities between China Men and Flowers in the Mirror are remarkable. Li Ju Chen is known as China's feminist author. He sets off the action in his novel by a double act of revenge that "disturbs the principle of the sexes" by putting a woman emperor on the throne. Tang Ao has a daughter who spends the last half of the novel searching for her father, who will not communicate with her.

[50] Julia Kristeva, "Le Texte clos," in Semeiotike: Recherches pour une sémanalyse (Paris: Editions du Seuil, 1969).

According to these French theorists, the logic of metaphysical opposition that helps to shape gender operates everywhere, even creating an
opposition between speech and writing. In this opposition, the spoken
word has the status of the primary, privileged term, and writing, the
derived, secondary term. Western symbolic orders (as distinct from
Chinese) limit writing to the concept of phonetic writing and reduce it to
nothing more than a transcription of the spoken word. In colloquial usage,
writing means merely the marks that transcribe sounds, but Kofman,
following Derrida, reverses and displaces this opposition. She contends
that writing in a more general sense, as the marks of difference, spacing,
repetition, always inhabits speech. This "graphic element" makes possible
the production of meaning. It is the "inscription of energy,"[51] without
which a speaking subject, in a necessary disruption of its own unity and
stability, could not produce language. Writing, like the feminine, is associated with difference, disruption of oneness, in a culture that represses
difference. Kofman sees a "complicity between logocentrism and phallocentrism." For her "the voice of truth," or the voice that claims absolute
truth for itself, is "that of the law, of God, of the father." Conversely,
writing as a "form of disruption of presence, like woman, is always abased,
reduced to the lowest rung."[52]

According to this theory, the spoken word, enforced and guaranteed by
the presence of the speaker, can create the illusion of emitting a single,
absolute truth. It thus upholds the power of patriarchy that posits the
absolute truth of the father's authority and the absolute opposition between
a superior masculine essence and an inferior feminine essence. Writing
opens up ambiguity, the difference within each word, person, or entity
that makes it nonidentical to itself rather than the differences between
pure, self-identical, unalterable essences.

For Kingston, whose writing denies the father's truth, the relation
between writing and the spoken word is not so much reversed and displaced as double and contradictory.[53] In her interview with Arturo Islas,
she says: "[T]he oral stories change from telling to telling. . . . Writing is
static."[54] Yet in the texts the oral tradition, although at times a source of
pleasure, transmits patriarchal authority, while writing releases the freedom of internal difference and is the medium of rebellion. An examination
of the contradiction will show that in *The Woman Warrior* and *China Men*,

---

[51] Kofman (n. 30 above), 64.

[52] Ibid., 25.

[53] Kingston's difference from European and Euro-American theorists in this respect may
come from her incorporation of material from a Chinese symbolic order that, not based on
phonetic writing, is not logocentric or is not logocentric in the same way. For a development of
this hypothesis, see Kristeva, *Des Chinoises* (n. 35 above), 57–63.

[54] Kingston, interviewed by Islas (n. 10 above), 18.

the relation between writing and orality operates in two different ways because the texts distinguish between social gender and symbolic gender. According to Caroline Ong, the legend of Fa Mu Lan, as transmitted in oral culture, communicates a lesson, a patriarchal "truth" about absolute filial piety and the battle of absolutes, with good triumphing over evil,[55] and Kingston does at one point indicate that her mother used the legend to chide her for insufficient filial devotion. Ong shows how Kingston, in transforming the oral legend into writing, transforms it from a story about absolutes and patriarchal authority to a story glorifying feminine freedom and ambiguity. It becomes a story about the freedom to live outside the rigid categories of a patriarchal family, free from guilt and conflicts about the family. Kingston also changes it from a story communicating a single moral to a story with multiple and contradictory meanings at different levels. The orally transmitted stories of No Name Woman and Ts'ai Yen, intended to teach, respectively, a negative or positive moral about filial duty, are transformed in similar ways.

Yet it is the mother who transmits the power of "talk-story," while the father, "a silent magician," whose "magic was also different from my mother's"[56] transmits the power of the written tradition, in which he received a classical education. Kingston inherits the oral tradition from her mother: "I too had been in the presence of great power, my mother talking-story. . . . I had forgotten this chant [of the Woman Warrior] that was once mine, given me by my mother."[57] Even the stories about the fathers and grandfathers in *China Men* come from the women, guardians of the oral tradition: "Without the female story teller, I couldn't have gotten into some of the stories. . . . Many of the men's stories were ones I originally heard from women."[58]

But the writing with which she transforms the oral tradition is given to her by, or stolen from, her father. *China Men* recounts how her father took her as a young child to the gambling hall where he worked:

We put away our brooms, and I followed him to the wall where sheaves of paper hung by their corners, diamond shaped. "Pigeon lottery," he called them. "Pigeon lottery tickets." Yes, in the wind of the paddle fan the soft thick sheaves ruffled like feathers and wings. He gave me some used sheets. Gamblers had circled green

[55] Caroline Ong, "The Woman Warrior/The Woman Writer: An analysis of Maxine Hong Kingston's novel *The Woman Warrior* according to Julia Kristeva's essay 'The Bounded Text' from *Desire in Language*," (Irvine: University of California, Department of French and Italian, 1985, photocopy).
[56] *CM* (n. 11 above), 236.
[57] *WW* (n. 11 above), 24.
[58] Kim (n. 9 above), 208.

and blue words in pink ink. They had bet on those words. You had to
be a poet to win, finding lucky ways words go together. My father
showed me the winning words from last night's games: "white jade
that grows in water," "red jade that grows in earth," or—not so
many words in Chinese—"white water jade," "redearthjade,"
"firedragon," "waterdragon." He gave me pen and ink, and I linked
words of my own: "rivercloud," "riverfire," the many combinations
with *horse, cloud,* and *bird.* The lines and loops connecting the
words, which were in squares, a word to a square, made designs too.
So this was where my father worked and what he did for a living,
keeping track of the gamblers' schemes of words."[59]

In spite of Kingston's comments on writing as static, this scene of
writing, like Mallarmé's "Never Will a Throw of the Dice Abolish Chance,"
shows that if gamblers are poets, poets must also be gamblers, casting their
lot in the infinity of chance connections writing makes between words. The
very repetitiveness of writing makes the connections fall into dazzling
kaleidoscopic patterns. One of the chanciest tricks of writing's combinatory
power is that it always escapes the writer, always says more and otherwise
than she intends it to say. The writer, absent from the act of communication, does not have the same illusion of authority as the speaker. Read by
many different people, in many different contexts, writing also changes
every time it is read, and it furthermore, as Kingston has pointed out, gives
rise to new talk-stories outside the patriarchal tradition. For all these
reasons, it throws the single-minded moral of patriarchal "truth" in the
stories to the winds.

While many of the "talk-stories" in Kingston's books express the pleasure with which they were written, many scenes that represent talking in
The Woman Warrior associate it—or its mirror opposite, the impossibility
of talking—with the most painful memories of childhood. Writing, by
contrast, as in the scene of the gambling hall, is associated with the most
pleasant memories. After relating her fantasy identification with Fa Mu
Lan, Kingston ironically contrasts it to her conflict-ridden girlhood in
Stockton. She portrays the pain of this time in terms of a loss of the spoken
word: "When one of my parents or the emigrant villagers said, 'Feeding
girls is feeding cowbirds,' I would thrash on the floor and scream so hard I
couldn't talk."[60] When, as a young adult, she tries to fight against racist
bosses and unjust city officials, in imitation of the woman warrior, she can
only squeak and whisper "in my bad, small-person's voice that makes no
impact."[61] However, during the one period of her life, just before high

[59] *CM,* 240.
[60] *WW,* 54.
[61] Ibid., 57.

school, when she can talk, she reproduces the cruelty, absolutism, and authoritarianism of oral culture in her behavior toward the most silent of the Chinese girls. Voice is here associated with "the worst thing I had yet done to another person."[62] The injustice of talk and the pain of silence as represented by the text contrast with the rebellious power of the text itself as it transforms talk and "talk-story" into writing.

A summary of the role of writing and the oral word in Kingston's texts brings forth the distinction between social gender and symbolic gender. On a symbolic level, writing is associated with feminine difference and the spoken word with patriarchal absolutism, but the social act of story telling belongs to the realm of women, and the social act of writing belongs to the realm of men. It is that realm, the secret "father places" that Kingston sets out to "win by cunning."[63] Kingston says during the Fa Mu Lan story, "Chinese executed women who disguised themselves as soldiers or students, no matter how bravely they fought or how high they scored on the examinations."[64] In the culture that Kingston describes (as well as in contemporary culture), writing belongs to men privileged to express the feminine within them, while the oral tradition, although it seems the province of women, serves, as in the orally transmitted legends of Fa Mu Lan, Ts'ai Yen, and No Name Woman, to accommodate them to patriarchy. The privileged members of patriarchy can afford to give themselves a certain freedom from their own phallocentric symbolic order, but they cannot afford to give it to the oppressed who might use it to overthrow the order.

In the first part of China Men, Maxine's father, the intellectual, differs from his peasant brothers. He is the favorite of the mother, and as an intellectual he does not do hard farm labor so that his hands stay smooth. In an analysis of the role of intellectual castes within society, Julia Kristeva calls such an intellectual "a twin of the opposite sex," an outsider who is yet accepted by society.[65] Maxine's father, whose story is introduced by that of Tang Ao, is also a feminine man, but there is a night and day contrast between the femininity of the two men. Tang Ao is made into a social woman, an oppressed being, while the father as an intellectual is allowed to play the role of the feminine without being outcast, humiliated, or deprived of male status.

As a writer, then, Kingston is heir to her father the classical scholar. In this, too, she resembles Fa Mu Lan, who "took her father's place in battle."[66] The swordswoman, disguised as a man, resembles the male intellectual. She is outside the community yet accepted; she lives outside

---

[62] Ibid., 210.
[63] CM, 238.
[64] WW, 46.
[65] Kristeva, La révolution du langage poétique (n. 2 above), 92 (my translation).
[66] WW, 24.

its laws, duties, and classifications and yet is not an outcast but an honored member. She is a twin of the opposite sex, able finally to express with freedom the feminine within herself, only because she has become a social man. Her male armor hides her forbidden pregnancy, so that in direct contrast to the horror of No Name Woman's childbearing, hers is enjoyed in tranquil bliss. Her male armor also hides the writing, the words of revenge inscribed on her back. "The swordswoman and I are not so dissimilar," says Kingston. "What we have in common are the words at our backs."[67] But Fa Mu Lan has to hide the writing under the male armor in order to be able to express it.

The writerly feminine, as mentioned at the beginning of this essay, can be in our social order the feminine of a privileged being, of a social man. And, with few exceptions, it has to be. For a social woman to write in our social order, she has to be able to don, whether legitimately or illegitimately, male privilege. To write in a public way means not only to set words to paper but also to have these words printed, published, distributed, sold, advertised, and reviewed by male-dominated institutions. Such is our present sociosymbolic order that feminine difference has to be expressed in a way acceptable to these institutions in order even to be recognized as feminine difference. Winning back from the "father places" the power of symbolic feminine freedom for social women has indeed been the task of woman warriors. But here, too, the parallel between Kingston as writer and Fa Mu Lan is both appropriate and inapplicable, for in writing *The Woman Warrior* Kingston has to a certain extent shed her male armor and, writing/fighting as a social woman, is in this respect dissimilar from the fantasy heroine.

Department of French and Italian
University of California, Irvine

[67] Ibid., 62–63.

The Sultan and the Slave: Feminist Orientalism and the Structure of *Jane Eyre*

Joyce Zonana

> I proposed to myself to display the folly of those who
> use authority to bring a woman to reason; and I chose
> for an example a sultan and his slave, as being two
> extremes of power and dependence. [JEAN FRANÇOIS MAR-
> MONTEL]

O N T H E D A Y following Jane Eyre's betrothal to her "master" Rochester, Jane finds herself "obliged" to go with him to a silk warehouse at Millcote, where she is "ordered to choose half a dozen dresses." Although she makes it clear that she "hated the business," Jane cannot free herself from it. All she can manage, "by dint of entreaties expressed in energetic whispers," is a reduction in the number of dresses, though "these . . . [Rochester] vowed he would select himself." Anxiously, Jane protests and "with infinite difficulty" secures Rochester's grudging acceptance of her choice: a "sober black satin and pearl-gray silk." The ordeal is not over; after the silk warehouse, Rochester takes Jane to a jeweller's, where "the more he bought me," she reports, "the more my cheek burned with a sense of annoyance and degradation" (Brontë [1847] 1985, 296–97).[1]

The shopping trip to Millcote gently figures Rochester as a domestic despot: he commands and Jane is "obliged" to obey, though she feels degraded by that obedience. At this point in the narrative, Jane is not yet aware that in planning to marry her Rochester is consciously choosing to

I am indebted to the anonymous readers for *Signs* who helped clarify and refine my argument. Nancy Easterlin, Jimmy Griffin, Cynthia Hogue, Peter Schock, and Les White provided valuable comments on early drafts, while Ruth Walker always listened and encouraged. Mark Kerr helped with the initial research; Maria McGarrity assisted in the final stages. For her excellent copyediting, I am grateful to Jeanne Barker-Nunn.

[1] Hereafter, unidentified page numbers in text refer to the Penguin edition of *Jane Eyre*.

[*Signs: Journal of Women in Culture and Society* 1993, vol. 18, no. 3]

become a bigamist. Yet the image she uses to portray her experience of his mastery as he tries to dress her "like a doll" (297) signals that not only despotism but bigamy and the oriental trade in women are on Jane's mind. Riding with Rochester back to Thornfield, she notes: "He smiled; and I thought his smile was such as a sultan might, in a blissful and fond moment, bestow on a slave his gold and gems had enriched" (297). The image is startling in its extremity: surely Jane seems to overreact to Rochester's desire to see his bride beautifully dressed.

Yet by calling Rochester a "sultan" and herself a "slave," Jane provides herself and the reader with a culturally acceptable simile by which to understand and combat the patriarchal "despotism" (302) central to Rochester's character. Part of a large system of what I term feminist orientalist discourse that permeates *Jane Eyre,* Charlotte Brontë's sultan/slave simile displaces the source of patriarchal oppression onto an "Oriental," "Mahometan" society, enabling British readers to contemplate local problems without questioning their own self-definition as Westerners and Christians.[2] As I will demonstrate, in developing her simile throughout her narrative, Jane does not so much criticize (in the words of Mary Ellis Gibson) "domestic arrangements and British Christianity from the point of view of the 'pagan' woman" (1987, 2) as define herself as a Western missionary seeking to redeem not the "enslaved" woman outside the fold of Christianity and Western ideology but the despotic man who has been led astray within it.[3]

---

[2] Although the feminist orientalism I discern in the novel is parallel to the "figurative use of blackness" earlier identified by Susan L. Meyer (1989, 250), it also has significant differences. Whereas Meyer focuses on the opposition "white/black," I examine the opposition "West/East." The two forms of opposition are related but not identical: the one privileges skin color or "race," and the other "culture," a phenomenon that may be associated with but that is not necessarily reducible to "race." Meyer's essay admirably demonstrates how *Jane Eyre* uses racial oppression as a metaphor for class and gender oppression. However, in systematically linking gender oppression to oriental despotism, *Jane Eyre* focuses on a form of oppression that is, from the first, conceived by Westerners in terms of gender.

[3] Gibson, one of the few critics to note how the sultan image pervades *Jane Eyre,* makes the sanguine assumption that Brontë's critique of Eastern despotism "extends to British imperialist impulses themselves," leading Gibson, like many critics, to find the novel's conclusion "strange" (1987, 1, 7). As I shall show, however, Jane's concluding paean to her missionary cousin in India is thoroughly grounded in the novel's figurative structure. Gayatri Spivak, for her part, argues that Brontë's novel reproduces the "axiomatics of imperialism" (1985, 247) and that its "imperialist project" remains inaccessible to the "nascent 'feminist' scenario" (249). My argument emphasizes less the acts of political domination that constitute imperialism than how its ideology (and specifically its orientalism) infects the analysis of domestic relations "at home" and posits that orientalism is in fact put to the service of feminism. See also Suvendrini Perera's discussion of how "the vocabulary of oriental misogyny" became "an invisible component in feminist representations" in the nineteenth century (1991, 79). Perera's chapter on *Jane Eyre,* published after the research for this article had been completed, focuses on sati as the text's "central image" (93), while my reading emphasizes the use of the harem as the

THE SULTAN AND THE SLAVE   167

Brontë's use of feminist orientalism is both embedded in and brings into focus a long tradition of Western feminist writing. Beginning early in the eighteenth century, when European travelers' tales about visits to the Middle East became a popular genre, images of despotic sultans and desperate slave girls became a central part of an emerging liberal feminist discourse about the condition of women not in the East but in the West. From Mary Wollstonecraft to Elizabeth Barrett Browning to Margaret Fuller and Florence Nightingale, one discovers writer after writer turning to images of oriental life—and specifically the "Mahometan" or "Arabian" harem—in order to articulate their critiques of the life of women in the West. Part of the larger orientalism that Edward Said has shown to inform Western self-representation, the function of these images is not primarily to secure Western domination over the East, though certainly they assume and enforce that domination.[4] Rather, by figuring objectionable aspects of life in the West as "Eastern," these Western feminist writers rhetorically define their project as the removal of Eastern elements from Western life.

Feminist orientalism is a special case of the literary strategy of using the Orient as a means for what one writer has called Western "self-redemption": "transforming the Orient and Oriental Muslims into a vehicle for . . . criticism of the West itself" (Al-Bazei 1983, 6).[5] Specifically, feminist orientalism is a rhetorical strategy (and a form of thought) by which a speaker or writer neutralizes the threat inherent in feminist demands and makes them palatable to an audience that wishes to affirm its occidental superiority. If the lives of women in England or France or the United States can be compared to the lives of women in "Arabia," then the Western feminist's desire to change the status quo can be represented not as a radical attempt to restructure the West but as a conservative effort to make the West more like itself. Orientalism—the belief that the East is inferior to the West, and the representation of the Orient by means of unexamined, stereotypical images—thus becomes a major premise in the formulation of numerous Western feminist arguments.

The conviction that the harem is an inherently oppressive institution functions as an a priori assumption in the writing I examine here. Even

central image of gender oppression. Western feminist uses of both sati and the harem function equally, as Perera points out, to objectify the "colonized or imagined 'oriental' female subject" (82).
[4] See Said 1979 for the definitive exposition of orientalism as a "Western style for dominating, restructuring, and having authority over the Orient" (71).
[5] Al-Bazei's excellent study does not consider the specifically feminist adaptation of this strategy. Interestingly, however, Al-Bazei identifies Byron's Turkish Tales as a crucial locus for the development of "self-redemption" as the dominant mode of nineteenth-century literary orientalism. Byron's influence on Brontë has been well documented, and further study might establish a link between his Turkish Tales and Brontë's feminist orientalism.

in the twentieth century, such an assumption continues to appear in Western feminist discourse, as Leila Ahmed (1982) and Chandra Mohanty (1988) demonstrate. Actual research on or observation of the conditions of the harem is rare, and what little that has been written tends toward either defensive celebration or violent condemnation. The defenses are written with an awareness of the condemnations; their authors must challenge the Western feminist imagination that unquestioningly perceives polygamy as sexual slavery and domestic confinement as imprisonment. The attempt to introduce a genuinely alternate vision is fraught with the difficulties both of documenting the actualities of life in the harem and of achieving a transcultural perspective, though some writers have made the effort.[7]

This article does not claim to demonstrate any truth about the harem that would definitively contradict or even modify the Western views presented here, nor does it systematically engage in the effort to achieve an objective estimate of the harem; rather, it seeks only to show how assumptions about the East have been used to further the Western feminist project instead of either spurring research and theorizing about the actual conditions of harem life or establishing genuine alliances among women of different cultures. For what is most crucial about what I am calling feminist orientalism is that it is directed not toward the understanding or even the reform of the harem itself but toward transformation of Western society—even while preserving basic institutions and ideologies of the West. Coming to recognize the feminist orientalism in *Jane Eyre* and other formative Western feminist texts may help clear the way for a more self-critical, balanced analysis of the multiple forms both of patriarchy and of women's power, and it may also, indirectly, help free global feminism from the charge that it is a Western movement inapplicable to Eastern societies.[8]

That *Jane Eyre,* like so many nineteenth-century British texts, has a diffusely orientalist background has long been recognized and for the

[6] For a recent defense of polygamy in the context of Western Mormonism, see Joseph 1991. Earlier in this century, Demetra Vaka argued that women living in harems were "healthy and happy," possessing a "sublimity of soul . . . lacking in our European civilization" (1909, 29, 127–28). Ahmed 1982 argues that the harem can be construed as an inviolable and empowering "women's space" that enables Islamic women to have "frequent and easy access to other women in their community, vertically, across class lines, as well as horizontally" (524).

[7] See, e.g., Makhlouf-Obermeyer 1979; Gordon (1865) 1983; Delplato 1988; Croutier 1989; Gendron 1991; Leonowens (1872) 1991.

[8] See Ahmed 1982 for a pointed analysis of how fundamentalist Islamic movements "target" feminism as " 'Western' and as particularly repugnant and evil" (533). Similarly, Hatem 1989 shows how in the late nineteenth and early twentieth centuries "European and Egyptian women were influenced by modern national ideologies and rivalries . . . prevent[ing] them from using each other's experience to push for a more radical critique of their own societies" (183).

most part attributed to the influence of the *Arabian Nights,* a book known to have been a staple of the Brontës' childhood reading.[9] The first simile in the novel, in the fourth paragraph of the first chapter, places Jane, "cross-legged, like a Turk" (39) in the window seat of the Gateshead breakfast room. Not much later, Jane takes down a book of "Arabian tales" (70); she reveals that she is fascinated by "genii" (82); and eventually she makes it plain that the *Arabian Nights* was one of her three favorite childhood books (256). Other characters in the novel also display a loose familiarity and fascination with the Orient: the Dowager Lady Ingram dresses in a "crimson velvet robe, and a shawl turban" (201); her daughter Blanche admits that she "dote[s] on Corsairs" (208); Rochester worries when Jane assumes a "sphinx-like expression" (329).

The specifically feminist quality of *Jane Eyre*'s orientalism, however, has not been recognized, perhaps because feminist orientalism has remained until recently an opaque, underexamined aspect of Western intellectual history. (Ahmed 1982, Spivak 1985, Mohanty 1988, and Perera 1991 are important exceptions.) The feminist orientalism of *Jane Eyre,* furthermore, is only made explicit in the sultan/slave simile, and, although the chords struck in this passage resonate throughout the entire novel, they cannot properly be heard without an understanding of the full eighteenth- and nineteenth-century background that generates them. Before turning to that background, however, it may be helpful briefly to set in relief this key episode in which Jane not only compares Rochester to a sultan but engages with him in an extended discussion of women's rights and uses her comparison of him to a sultan as a means by which to secure more rights for herself.

Among the more interesting features of this passage is the fact that Jane does not tell Rochester that she is mentally comparing him to a sultan. She simply asks him to stop looking at her "in that way." Rochester is astute enough to understand Jane's unspoken reference, suggesting that feminist orientalist discourse is so pervasive as to be accessible to the very men it seeks to change: '"Oh, it is rich to see and hear her!' he exclaimed. 'Is she original? Is she piquant? I would not exchange this one little English girl for the Grand Turk's whole seraglio—gazelle-eyes, houri forms, and all!' " (297). Rochester suggests that he will take Jane instead of a harem, though Jane bristles at the "Eastern allusion": " 'I'll not stand you an inch in the stead of a seraglio,' I said; 'so don't consider me an equivalent for one. If you have a fancy for anything in that line, away with you, sir, to the bazaars of Stamboul, without delay, and lay out

---

[9] See, e.g., Conant 1908; Stedman 1965; Ali 1981; Caracciolo 1988; Workman 1988.

in extensive slave-purchases some of that spare cash you seem at a loss to spend satisfactorily here' " (297).

~ When Rochester jokingly asks what Jane will do while he is "bargaining for so many tons of flesh and such an assortment of black eyes," Jane is ready with a playful but serious response: "I'll be preparing myself to go out as a missionary to preach liberty to them that are enslaved—your harem inmates among the rest. I'll get admitted there, and I'll stir up mutiny; and you, three-tailed bashaw as you are, sir, shall in a trice find yourself fettered amongst our hands: nor will I, for one, consent to cut your bonds till you have signed a charter, the most liberal that despot ever yet conferred!" (297–98). Although Jane promises Rochester that she will "go out as a missionary" to "Stamboul," the focus of her remarks is the reform of Rochester himself within England. Her concern is that she herself not be treated as a "harem inmate," and her action, immediately following this conversation, succeeds in accomplishing her goal.

It is precisely Jane's experience of degrading dependency, playfully figured here as the relation of rebellious harem slave to despotic Eastern sultan, that leads her to take the step that ultimately reveals Rochester as more like a sultan than Jane had imagined. For it is at this point that Jane makes and executes the decision to write to her Uncle John in Madeira, in the hope that he will settle some money on her. "If I had ever so small an independency," she reasons, "if I had but a prospect of one day bringing Mr. Rochester an accession of fortune, I could better endure to be kept by him now" (297). Jane's letter to John Eyre alerts Rochester's brother-in-law, Richard Mason, to Rochester's plans to become a bigamist, and Jane is freed from a marriage that would, in her own terms, have thoroughly enslaved her.

Jane's comparison of Rochester to a sultan proves to be no exaggeration. The narrative makes plain that it is because she sees him in this way that she later is able to free herself from a degrading relationship with a man who has bought women, is willing to become a bigamist, and acts like a despot. The plot thus validates the figurative language, making of it much more than a figure. This Western man is "Eastern" in his ways, and for Jane to be happy, he must be thoroughly Westernized. To the extent that Brontë has Jane Eyre present hers as a model life—"Reader, I married him"—she suggests that her female readers would also be well advised to identify and eliminate any such Eastern elements in their own spouses and suitors.

More than ten years ago, Peter A. Tasch observed that in having Jane call Rochester a "three-tailed bashaw," Brontë "was echoing the refrain in a song by George Colman the Younger for his extravaganza *Blue Beard*." Tasch further notes that "the idea of an English girl in the 'grand

Turk's' seraglio demanding liberty forms the theme of another stage comedy, [Isaac Bickerstaffe's] *The Sultan; or, A Peep into the Seraglio"* (1982, 232). Tasch may well be correct in identifying these specific sources for Brontë's allusions; yet the image of a harem inmate demanding liberty had by 1847 become so ingrained in Western feminist discourse that Brontë need not have had any specific text in mind; her audience, whether familiar with *Blue Beard* and *The Sultan* or not, would have had a full stock of harem images by which to understand and applaud Jane's sultan/slave simile.

The stage was set for the Western use of the harem as a metaphor for aspects of Western life as early as 1721, in Baron de Montesquieu's *Persian Letters*. The letters in Montesquieu's novel, written primarily by two "Persian" men traveling in Europe, offer dramatic images of both Eastern and Western ways of structuring domestic and political relations. Usbek and Rica, the travelers who report on the oddities of Western ways, are in constant contact with the women and eunuchs they have left behind in the harem. The Western reader moves between defamiliarized visions of Europe and "familiar" images of Persia, eventually coming to see, in the words of one modern commentator, that in the seraglio, constructed as the heart of oriental despotism, "It is myself, and our world, finally, that I rediscover" (Grosrichard 1979, 32–33, translation mine; for further commentary on the self-reflexive function of Western representations of the harem, see Richon 1984 and Alloula 1986).

Montesquieu's work focuses primarily on the nature of political despotism, using images of the Eastern and Western domestic enslavement of women as metaphors for the political enslavement of men. The condition of women is not Montesquieu's central concern, but because the harem is his functional model of despotism, the novel repeatedly returns to the question of "whether it is better to deprive women of their liberty or to leave them free" (Montesquieu [1721] 1923, 107) and draws recurrent analogies between the status of women in the East and the West. In its closing pages, *Persian Letters* portrays a full-scale rebellion in the seraglio: in the absence of their masters, the women have taken new lovers and sought to undo the system of surveillance that has kept them imprisoned.

As Katie Trumpener notes, "the last—and perhaps most powerful— voice in the book is Roxanna's" (1987, 185), the voice of a formerly enslaved harem inmate who willingly accepts her death as the price of her freedom: "How could you think that I was such a weakling as to imagine there was nothing for me in the world but to worship your caprices; that while you indulged all your desires, you should have the right to thwart me in all mine? No: I have lived in slavery, and yet always retained my freedom: I have remodeled your laws upon those of nature; and my mind has always maintained its independence" (350). Although Montesquieu may have had other applications in mind, the voice of his rebellious Roxanna came to be the voice adopted by later writers seeking to expose the oppression of women.

Thus, as Pauline Kra has shown, after Montesquieu French literature of the eighteenth century regularly used the "harem theme" to "demonstrate the subordinate status of women" in the West (1979, 274). Martha Conant notes that Jean François Marmontel's 1761 popular Moral Tale, "Soliman II," features the conquest of a sultan by a "pretty European slave, Roxalana," who appears to echo Montesquieu's heroine. Roxalana's heart was "nourished in the bosom of liberty," and her expostulations "against the restraints of the seraglio" succeed in converting the sultan (1908, 205–7). In English literature as well the harem came to function as a metaphor for the Western oppression of women. Samuel Johnson's 1759 *Rasselas* includes an exposé of the oppressiveness of the harem and a defense of women's rights to intellectual development;[10] the heroine of the 1775 play Tasch identifies as a source of *Jane Eyre* (and which Conant traces to Marmontel) is named "Roxalana"; and Defoe's feminist heroine of *The Fortunate Mistress* calls herself "Roxanna" (Trumpener 1987, 187–88). The name of Montesquieu's rebellious harem inmate seems to have been so consistently associated with the demand for female rights that when Mary Wollstonecraft has a character in *Maria or the Wrongs of Woman* seek liberation from an oppressive husband, the man responds by invoking her literary model: "Very pretty, upon my soul! very pretty, theatrical flourishes! Pray, fair Roxana, stoop from your altitudes and remember that you are acting a part in real life" ([1798] 1975, 116).

To the extent that Montesquieu demonstrates for Western readers that the oriental institution of the seraglio can shed light on Western practices, one can say that his text inaugurates feminist orientalist discourse. But it is in Wollstonecraft's 1792 *Vindication of the Rights of Woman,* the founding text of Western liberal feminism, that one finds the fullest explicit feminist orientalist perspective. Like many of the enlightenment thinkers on whom she drew—including, of course, Montesquieu— Wollstonecraft uncritically associates the East with despotism and tyranny. Her text is replete with images that link any abuse of power with "Eastern" ways: she is not above likening women who seek to dominate their

[10] Jane Eyre's friend Helen Burns reads *Rasselas* at Lowood; though Jane's "brief examination" of the book convinces her it is "dull" (Brontë [1847] 1985, 82), the text's presence within *Jane Eyre* signals Brontë's familiarity with—and interest in highlighting—a key source of feminist orientalism. Kringas 1992 points out that *Rasselas* not only exposes the oppressiveness of the harem but, by juxtaposing the experiences of Nekayah and Pekuah, specifically links the lives of women in the harem with the lives of uneducated, middle-class women outside the seraglio (33).

husbands with "Turkish bashaws" ([1792] 1982, 125). Yet she reserves her fullest scorn for the gendered despotism that she sees as a defining feature of Eastern life and a perverse corruption of Western values. Any aspect of the European treatment of women that Wollstonecraft finds objectionable she labels as Eastern. Thus, she finds that European women's "limbs and faculties" are "cramped with worse than Chinese bands" (Wollstonecraft [1792] 1982, 128); Western women are educated in "worse than Egyptian bondage" (221); their masters are "worse than Egyptian task-masters" (319). Upper-class women, "dissolved in luxury," have become weak and depraved "like the Sybarites" (130); if women do not "grow more perfect when emancipated," Wollstonecraft advises that Europe should "open a fresh trade with Russia for whips" (319).

Yet it is "Mahometanism"—and the "Mahometan" institution of the seraglio or harem—that Wollstonecraft singles out as the grand type for all oppression of women. Any Western writer who treats women "as a kind of subordinate beings, and not as a part of the human species" is accused of writing "in the true style of Mahometanism" ([1792] 1982, 80). This is because what she believes about "Mahometanism" embodies for Wollstonecraft the antithesis of her own central claim: that women, like men, have souls. Although Ahmed asserts that she can find "no record . . . in the body of orthodox Muslim literature of the notion that women are animals or have no souls," she notes that views such as Wollstonecraft's are a staple of Western writing about Islam (1982, 526). Ahmed attributes the creation of this purported fact about Islamic culture to the same Western men who have insisted on the "inferiority of Western women" (523). Yet in Vindication of the Rights of Woman, a founder of modern feminism reproduces and intensifies the spurious "fact" about "Mahometanism," indeed, using it as a cornerstone of her argument for women's rights in the West.

A peculiarity of language may have led to or enforced Wollstonecraft's conviction that Muslims believe that women do not have souls. The Oxford English Dictionary (OED) notes that the Italian word seraglio, meaning "place of confinement," was used to render the Turkish serai, "lodging" or "palace." N. M. Penzer also observes that "the modern seraglio is directly derived from the Italian serraglio, 'a cage for wild animals,' " while the original Persian words, sara and sarai, meant simply "building" or "palace" (1936, 16). As late as the seventeenth century in England one finds seraglio used to refer to "a place where wild beasts are kept" (OED) as well as to the private apartments of women. Thus, when Wollstonecraft speaks of women being reduced to "mere animals" who are "only fit for a seraglio" (83), she invokes both meanings of seraglio and may have thought herself well justified in her view that "Mahomet-ans" regarded women as animals.[11]

Wollstonecraft is so committed to her notion of Islamic culture that she goes so far as to accuse Milton, demonstrably a Christian thinker, of writing in the "true Mahometan strain" when he specifies the nature of Eve, "our first frail mother": "I cannot comprehend his meaning, unless, in the true Mahometan strain, he meant to deprive us of souls, and insinuate that we were beings only designed by sweet attractive grace, and docile blind obedience, to gratify the senses of man when he can no longer soar on the wing of contemplation" ([1792] 1982, 100–101).[12] Although Wollstonecraft here locates what she calls Mahometan belief at the center of Western Christian culture, she does not waver from her conviction that the West is fundamentally distinct from—and superior to—the East, claiming that the "despotism that kills virtue and genius in the bud" does not "hover over Europe with that destructive blast which desolates Turkey" (131).

Thus, for Wollstonecraft, the English husband "who lords it in his little harem" (167) is more guilty than his Eastern counterpart, for the despotism incarnate in the harem is not natural to Europe. Unlike the "Turk," the English husband goes against the grain of his race and cul-ture, as does any Western woman who accepts such "Eastern" treatment of her. For example, Wollstonecraft responds to Rousseau's wish that " 'a young Englishwoman cultivate her agreeable talents, in order to please her future husband, with as much care and assiduity as a young Circas-sian cultivates hers, to fit her for the harem of an Eastern bashaw' " (183) by criticizing the woman who could accept such a life: "In a seraglio, I grant, that all these arts are necessary; . . . but have women so little am-bition as to be satisfied with such a condition? . . . Surely she has not an soul immortal who can loiter life away merely employed to adorn her person, that she may amuse the languid hours, and soften the cares of a fellow-creature" (112–13).

Though the Western emphasis on the marriageability of girls makes "mere animals" of them, "weak beings" who "are only fit for a seraglio" (Wollstonecraft [1792] 1982, 83), it is only "Mahometan" women who can accept such bondage: "If women are to be made virtuous by author-

---

[11] In this context, it may also be worth noting that *harem,* derived from the Arabic *haram,* designates places that are " 'holy,' 'protected,' 'sacred,' 'inviolate,' and lastly 'for-bidden' " (Penzer 1936, 15). In Western usage, the holiness of *harem* is elided, and the caging aspect of *seraglio* is introduced.

[12] Samuel Johnson had levied a similar charge against Milton, claiming in his 1779 *Life* of Milton that "there appears in his books something like a Turkish contempt of females as subordinate and inferior beings. . . . He thought woman made only for obedi-ence, and man only for rebellion" (85).

ity, which is a contradiction in terms, let them be immured in seraglios and watched with a jealous eye. Fear not that the iron will enter their souls—for the souls that can bear such treatment are made of yielding materials, just animated enough to give life to the body" (311).

If the seraglio exists unchallenged as an Eastern institution, Wollstone-craft implies, it is because "Mahometan" teachings are accurate in their representation of Eastern women: their souls are barely "animated." In the West, however, women are made of sterner stuff, and the seraglio—or anything that resembles it—has no place. The feminism of Wollstone-craft's *Vindication of the Rights of Woman* ultimately reduces itself to what would have been in her time a relatively noncontroversial plea: that the West rid itself of its oriental ways, becoming as a consequence more Western—that is, more rational, enlightened, reasonable.

Whether through direct influence or simply because the ideas on which she drew were circulating freely within the culture, the feminist oriental-ist strategy introduced by Wollstonecraft came to pervade nineteenth-century feminist discourse. Said has noted that orientalism characteristi-cally emerges in Western writing as a "set of representative figures, or tropes," and he argues that to observe it "the things to look at are style, figures of speech, setting, narrative devices" (1979, 71, 21). In *Persian Letters* and *Vindication of the Rights of Woman*—as in *Jane Eyre*—the figures and tropes of the Orient are deeply woven into the fabric of the entire text. Other examples of feminist orientalist discourse are typically less elaborated and appear to be no more than random, casual allusions. Yet the very casualness of these allusions suggests that the writers are drawing upon a fully developed cultural code implicitly shared with their readers. There is no need to argue for or to prove any individual defini-tion of Eastern ways nor any specific analogy between East and West, for the entire belief system that makes the individual references possible is taken for granted.

Among the elements that feminist writers return to again and again are three aspects of the Eastern treatment of women that Wollstonecraft had emphasized: (1) the central belief that women do not have souls, which justifies and explains the other practices; (2) the excessive sexuality of the harem, embodied partly in polygamy but also in luxury, indolence, and the trade in women; and (3) the enforced confinement, undereducation, and inactivity of women in the harem that reduces them to animals or children. A few more examples may help to establish the full context of the discourse that allowed Brontë to structure her novel as the drama of a Western woman oppressed by Eastern beliefs and practices.

One of the more extended instances of nineteenth-century feminist orientalism appears in the work of Wollstonecraft's daughter, Mary Shel-ley. Although it seems that Shelley did not fully share her mother's com-

mitted feminist activism, in her novel *Frankenstein* she nevertheless created a striking female character who insists on her existence as a soul.[13]
This character, Safie, not only echoes the words and philosophy of Wollstonecraft but is also dramatically figured as a "lovely Arabian," a
woman who barely escapes "being immured" within a harem:

> Safie related, that her mother was a Christian Arab, seized and
> made a slave by the Turks; recommended by her beauty, she had
> won the heart of the father of Safie, who married her. The young
> girl spoke in high and enthusiastic terms of her mother, who, born
> in freedom, spurned the bondage to which she was now reduced.
> She instructed her daughter in the tenets of the religion, and taught
> her to aspire to higher powers of intellect, and an independence of
> spirit, forbidden to the female followers of Mahomet. This lady
> died; but her lessons were indelibly impressed on the mind of Safie,
> who sickened at the prospect of again returning to Asia, and the
> being immured within the walls of a haram, allowed only to occupy
> herself with puerile amusements, ill-suited to the temper of her soul,
> now accustomed to grand ideas and a noble emulation for virtue.
> [Shelley (1818) 1974, 119]

"Let woman share the rights, and she will emulate the virtues of man,"
Wollstonecraft had written at the end of her *Vindication* ([1792] 1982,
319). Shelley echoes this sentiment in the person of her "lovely Arabian,"
inscribing it in the same orientalist frame as had her mother.

Feminist orientalism emerges again in the work of Anna Jameson,
whose *Memoirs of the Loves of the Poets* is designed to show "the
influence which the beauty and virtue of women have exercised over the
characters and writings of men of genius" ([1824] 1890, vii). Hardly a
feminist of the order of Wollstonecraft, Jameson is nevertheless deeply
disturbed by the belief that women do not have souls, attributing it to the
"Mahometan" East, where women are "held in seclusion, as mere soulless slaves of the passions and caprices of their masters" (25). Like Wollstonecraft, Jameson also discerns Eastern values operating in the West:
she calls Lord Byron the "Grand Turk of amatory poetry," explaining
that despite the beauty of his "female portraits," there is "something very
Oriental in all his feelings and ideas about women; he seems to require
nothing of us but beauty and submission" (507). One is reminded of
Wollstonecraft's critique of Milton's "Mahometan" prescriptions for

---

[13] See Zonana 1991 for an extended argument that Safie in fact articulates *Frankenstein*'s thematic center. For a more qualified view of Shelley's feminism, see Poovey
1984. See also Spivak 1985 for the view that *Frankenstein* resists its culture's pervasive
orientalism.

Eve: "sweet attractive grace, and docile blind obedience" (Wollstonecraft [1792] 1982, 100).

Jameson and Shelley echo one another when they repudiate the belief that women do not have souls. Yet they do not directly address the sexual practices that can be said to follow from this belief—polygamy and the buying and selling of women—though, as Alain Grosrichard has shown, polygamy tended to be a key feature of Western meditations upon the Orient (1979, 177–82). Later in the nineteenth century, however, while European male painters reveled in voyeuristic and vaguely pornographic representations of the multiplicity of female bodies available to masters of the harem, feminist writers learned to approach issues of sexuality by putting them in oriental terms. Prostitution, the marriage market, and the habit of keeping mistresses are all now figured as Eastern intrusions into a Western ideal of monogamous romantic love and marriage.

For example, when Jemima Bradshaw, a character in Elizabeth Gaskell's 1853 novel *Ruth,* contemplates the financial basis of her forth-coming marriage, she invokes a feminist orientalist image: "She felt as if she would rather be bought openly, like an Oriental daughter" [(1853) 1985, 240). In America, Margaret Fuller similarly compares the "selling" of English "daughters to the highest bidder" with "sending them to a Turkish slave-dealer." "You know how it was in the Oriental clime," she reminds her readers, though she defends the "Turkish" practice as less degrading than its Western counterpart, for "it is not done in defiance of an acknowledged law of right in the land and the age" ([1845] 1971, 139, 133, 139). What seems to be a healthy respect for difference is in fact a ratification of Western superiority. Like Wollstonecraft, Fuller accepts "Oriental" practices in the Orient—but not in the more temperate, enlightened West.

Likewise, when Elizabeth Barrett Browning justifies her discussion of prostitution in *Aurora Leigh,* she explains she is working to rid England of oriental prejudice: "I am deeply convinced that the corruption of our society requires not shut doors and windows, but light and air: and that is exactly because pure and prosperous women choose to *ignore* vice, that miserable women suffer wrong by it everywhere. Has paterfamilias, with his Oriental traditions and veiled female faces, very successfully dealt with a certain class of evil? What if materfamilias, with her quick sure instincts and honest innocent eyes, do more towards their expulsion by simply looking at them and calling them by their names?" (1897, 2:445) When Barrett Browning writes of "shut doors and windows" and "veiled female faces," she also indirectly hints at another central aspect of the life of Eastern women in the imaginations of Western feminists: the confinement of the harem. This is the aspect emphasized when Walter Besant, in 1897, comments on the "Oriental prejudice" that keeps British women out of certain professions and that earlier in the century resulted in their "seclusion . . . in the home, and their exclusion from active and practical life" ([1897] 1989, 2:1653, 2:1652).

And it is this aspect that emerges most tellingly in the writing of Florence Nightingale. "If heaven and hell exist on this earth, it is in the two worlds I saw that morning—the Dispensary and the Hareem," she writes at the conclusion of her 1849 tour of Egypt ([1849–50] 1988, 208). Nightingale's may be the most dramatic nineteenth-century feminist condemnation of the harem: it is for her literally hell on earth. What makes it so for Nightingale is not (at least not explicitly) its sensuality, nor its domination by a male despot, nor even the slavery of its women. Rather, what Nightingale finds horrifying about the harem are its all too familiar boredom and confinement: "A little more of such a place would have killed us . . . Oh, the *ennui* of that magnificent palace, it will stand in my memory as a circle of hell! Not one thing was there laying about, to be done or to be looked at" (208).

Although Nightingale is describing an actual visit to a harem, her description is conditioned both by her preexisting cultural images of the harem and the experience of her own life as a woman in England.[14] Her words echo those of Pekuah in Johnson's *Rasselas,* even as they anticipate her own analyses of family life in England. Pekuah had noted of the harem that "the diversions of the women . . . were only childish play, by which the mind accustomed to stronger operations could not be kept busy. . . . They had no ideas but of the few things that were within their view, and had hardly names for anything but their clothes and their food" (Johnson [1759] 1977, 135). Nightingale herself writes: "The very windows into the garden were woodworked, so that you could not see out. The cold, the melancholy of that place! I felt inclined to cry" (Nightingale [1849–50] 1988, 208). In *Cassandra,* written a few years later, Nightingale condemns the "cold and oppressive conventional atmosphere" of women's family life, noting that women are forced to abandon "intellect as a vocation," taking it only "as we use the moon, by glimpses through . . . tight-closed window shutters" ([1852] 1980, 29, 37). Nightingale's description of domestic confinement, whether in Egypt or England, recalls one of Wollstonecraft's most chilling descriptions of women "immured in their families groping in the dark" ([1792] 1982, 87).

It is this image of domestic immurement that most obviously haunts *Jane Eyre* and shapes its very structure. Examining this narrative structure, one sees that each household in which Jane finds herself is con-

---

[14] See Barrell 1991 for a provocative discussion of how tourists such as Nightingale brought their own fantasies and preoccupations to their descriptions of the sights in Egypt.

structed to resemble a harem; each of her oppressors is characterized as a Mahometan despot; and each of her rebellions or escapes bears the accents of Roxanna, the harem inmate declaring her existence as a free soul. At Gateshead, at Lowood, at Thornfield, and at Moor House, one discovers a series of communities of dependent women, all subject to the whim of a single master who rules in his absence as much as his presence and who subjects the imprisoned women to the searching power of his gaze.[15] In each of these households, Jane finds her own power of move-ment and of vision limited; even when she is most in love with Rochester at Thornfield, she recognizes that he stands in her way, "as an eclipse intervenes between man and the broad sun" (Brontë [1847] 1985, 302).

The pattern of home as harem is established at Gateshead, where the household consists of John Reed, Mrs. Reed, Eliza and Georgiana Reed, Jane, and the two female servants, Bessie and Abbott. There are also a male "butler and footman" (60), though these are shadowy presences, nameless men inconsequential in the dynamics and management of the household. The "master" is young John Reed, a boy of fourteen who demands that Jane call him "Master Reed" (41) and against whose ar-bitrary rule Jane has no appeal: "the servants did not like to offend their young master by taking my part against him, and Mrs. Reed was blind and deaf on the subject: she never saw him strike or heard him abuse me, though he did both now and then in her very presence" (42).

Like the sultans described by Montesquieu and the eighteenth-century travelers, John considers the privileges of seeing and knowing to be his. What enrages him in the novel's opening scene is that Jane is out of his sight. Hidden behind the curtain of the window seat, reading and looking out the window, she has usurped his role as the "Turk." "Where the dickens is she?" John asks his sisters, and when Eliza finds Jane for him, John castigates his cousin not only for "getting behind curtains" but also for reading: "You have no business to take our books" (42). In the course of his tirade, John calls Jane a "bad animal" (41) and a "rat" (42); later she will become a "wild cat" (59). John's descriptions of Jane as beast and his wish to keep her from educating herself through books may recall Wollstonecraft's definition of the "true style" of Mahometanism: the view of women as "domestic brutes" ([1792] 1982, 101), "not as a part of the human species" (80).

The sexuality of the harem is absent from the Reed home, but the indolent, pampered sensuality that so offends Wollstonecraft is not. In the opening scene, Mrs. Reed lies "reclined on a sofa by the fireside . . .

---

[15] Grosrichard convincingly demonstrates that, in the Western construction of the seraglio, "To be the master . . . is to see. In the despotic state, where one always obeys 'blindly,' the blind man is the emblematic figure of the subject" (73, translation mine). See also Bellis 1987 for an exploration of the politics of vision in *Jane Eyre*.

with her darlings about her" (39). John is constantly plied with "cakes and sweetmeats," even though he "gorged himself habitually at table, which made him bilious, and gave him a dim and bleared eye with flabby cheeks" (41). John is the effete, attenuated tyrant made weak by his abuse of power, familiar from Wollstonecraft's characterizations of "bashaws." The Reed sisters are "universally indulged" (46) and "elaborately ringleted" (60); their mother dresses regularly in silks. The luxury of Gateshead, associated as it is with the degeneracy and despotism of the harem, is something Jane learns to abhor, and this abhorrence informs her later attempts to resist Rochester's desire to see her "glittering like a parterre" (296).

Jane, not unlike Montesquieu's Roxanna, rebels against her imprisonment within Master Reed's "harem." Her physical violence is expressed against John, but she reserves her strongest words for Mrs. Reed, the adult who has enforced the "young master's" wishes: "If anyone asks me how I liked you, and how you treated me, I will say the very thought of you makes me sick, and that you treated me with miserable cruelty. . . . You think I have no feelings, and that I can do without one bit of love or kindness; but I cannot live so: and you have no pity" (68). Like Roxanna, Jane exposes the hypocrisy of her keeper, insisting on the freedom of her mind and on her desire for and right to genuine love.

Jane's outburst leads to her departure from Gateshead, though she soon finds herself in another institution that even more closely resembles the harem that haunts the Western feminist imagination. Lowood, "a large and irregular building" through which on her arrival Jane is led "from compartment to compartment, from passage to passage" (76), perfectly embodies the confinement of the harem. The building is oppressive, dark, and gloomy, and the garden is no better: "a wide enclosure," it is "surrounded with walls so high as to exclude every glimpse of prospect" (80). These walls not only limit the vision of the institution's "inmates" but they are "spike-guarded" (107) to prohibit freedom of movement.

Within the confines of this dwelling, Jane discovers "a congregation of girls of every age. . . . Their number to me appeared countless" (76). Over this community of women rules the redoubtable Mr. Brocklehurst, "the black marble clergyman" (98) whom Jane perceives as a "black column," a "piece of architecture" (94). Like John Reed, Brocklehurst's characteristic gesture is to gaze searchingly upon his assembled dependents. When he makes his first appearance at Lowood, he "majestically surveyed the whole school" (95); a few moments later he "scrutinize[s]" the hair of the terrified girls. As with John Reed, Jane seeks to hide from this master's eyes: "I had sat well back on the form, and while seeming to be busy with my sum, had held my slate in such a manner as to conceal my face" (97). Jane does not escape Brocklehurst's look, however, and is forced to suffer the humiliation of his description of her as a liar. Jane is freed by the good offices of Miss Temple, and later, when the scandal of Brocklehurst's despotic rule is revealed (significantly, it takes the death of a number of the inmates to cause this revelation) he is stripped of some of his power. Lowood becomes a fairly happy home for Jane, though a "prison-ground" nonetheless (117).

It may be objected that the ascetic aspects of Lowood accord ill with the suggestion that it is figured as a harem. Certainly Lowood harbors neither the sensuality nor the overt sexuality associated with the harem. Yet its structure, with one man controlling an indefinite number of dependent women, mimics that of the seraglio. Further, Brocklehurst's wish to strip the girls of all adornment, of all possibilities of sensual gratification, has its parallel in the sultan's wish to keep the women of the harem restrained from any sexuality not under his control. That Brocklehurst is figured in plainly phallic terms only underscores his identification as a sultan whose perverse pleasure here consists in denying pleasure to the women he rules. For his wife and daughters, however—women over whom presumably he can exert even greater control—Brocklehurst allows a greater sensuality: these women are "splendidly attired in velvet, silk, and furs" (97).

When Jane leaves Lowood for her "new servitude" at Thornfield (117), she happily anticipates entering the domain of Mrs. Fairfax, an "elderly lady" (120) whom she believes to be the mistress of a "safe haven" (129), a "snug" and secure realm of feminine "domestic comfort" (127). To her initial dismay, Jane discovers that this new household of women also has a "master," the absent yet omnipotent Mr. Rochester. Jane first meets Rochester on the moonlit lane connecting Thornfield to the town of Hay, unaware he is her master. She perceives this stranger to have a "dark face, with stern features and a heavy brow" (145); later she will call his skin "swarthy," his features "Paynim" (212). The man has fallen from his horse, and Jane offers to assist him. Before accepting her help, however, he subjects her to intense "scrutiny" in order to determine her identity (146).

Jane reveals that she is the governess at Thornfield; Rochester offers no information about himself, except to say, when Jane fails in her effort to lead his horse to him: "I see . . . the mountain will never be brought to Mahomet, so all you can do is to aid Mahomet to go to the mountain" (146). Though uttered in jest, these words do not bode well for Jane's relationship with her master. Rochester gives himself the one name that, to a nineteenth-century audience, would unambiguously identify him as a polygamous, blasphemous despot—a sultan. After such an introduction, it comes as no surprise when Rochester chooses to dress "in shawls, with a turban on his head" for a game of charades, nor that Jane should see him as "the very model of an Eastern emir" (212).

The most striking identification of Rochester as an oriental despot—again a characterization that comes from his own lips—occurs when he begins to contemplate marriage with Jane. The intimacy between master and dependent has begun to develop and, in the course of guardedly discussing his past with the governess, Rochester admits that he "degenerated" when wronged by fate (167). As Jane and the reader will later learn, he is referring to his marriage with Bertha Mason, and his subsequent indulgence in "lust for a passion—vice for an occupation" (343). With no knowledge of the details of Rochester's "degeneration," Jane nevertheless encourages him to repent, though Rochester insists that only pleasure, "sweet, fresh pleasure" (167), can help him. Jane suggests that such pleasure "will taste bitter" (167) and warns Rochester against "error." Rochester, apparently referring to his wish to love Jane, replies that the "notion that flitted across my brain" is not error or temptation but "inspiration": "I am laying down good intentions, which I believe durable as flint. Certainly, my associates and pursuits shall be other than they have been. . . . You seem to doubt me; I don't doubt myself: I know what my aim is, what my motives are; and at this moment I pass a law, unalterable as that of the Medes and Persians, that both are right" (168–69).

Rochester's aim is to find happiness with Jane; his motives are to redeem himself from his association with Bertha; the unalterable law that he makes his own has its antecedent in the one decreed by King Ahasuerus—"written among the laws of the Persians and the Medes, that it not be altered"—when he banishes his Queen Vashti and vows to "give her royal estate unto another that is better than she" (Esther 1.19). Ahasuerus, to whom Jane will later compare Rochester (in the same chapter in which she compares him to a sultan [Brontë (1847) 1985, 290]), had been angered by Vashti's refusal to come at his command. His counselors point out that the queen's refusal to be commanded might "come abroad unto all women" (Esther 1.17), and the Persian king passes his law so that "every man should bear rule in his own house" (Esther 1.22). Rochester's decision to banish Bertha and marry Jane is dangerously like Ahasuerus's replacement of Vashti by Esther; Jane's resistance signals her engagement in both the reform of her master and the liberation of her people.

The conversation between Jane and Rochester about Rochester's "Persian" law offers readers clear signals about how they should perceive Rochester's relationship to Jane. Expressed as a conflict between Judeo-Christian law and Persian arrogance, the conflict can also be understood as Jane's struggle to retain possession of her soul, to claim her rights as a Western, Christian woman. Thus, when Rochester begins his actual proposal to her, Jane insists, "I have as much soul as you" (Brontë [1847] 1985, 281). Later, when she resists his wish to take her to a "white-washed villa on the shores of the Mediterranean," where, as his mistress, she would live a "guarded" life (331), she expresses her triumph in precisely the same terms: "I still possessed my soul" (344).[16]

It is at Thornfield, of course, that the confinement and sexuality of the seraglio/harem are most fully represented. Rochester has a wife whom he keeps literally caged in a "wild beast's den" (336), "a room without a window" (321). In her first explicit view of Bertha Mason, Jane depicts her in the ambiguous, nonhuman terms Wollstonecraft had applied to harem inmates: "What it was, whether beast or human being, one could not, at first sight tell: it grovelled, seemingly, on all fours; it snatched and growled like some strange wild animal: but it was covered with clothing, and a quantity of dark, grizzled hair, wild as a mane, hid its head and face" (321). Referred to by Jane as a "clothed hyena" (321), Bertha incarnates a brute sensuality that apparently justifies her imprisonment. Rochester calls her his "bad, mad, and embruted partner" (320), whom he married without being "sure of the existence of one virtue in her nature" (333).

When Rochester takes his first wife, he is himself acting purely on the basis of his own "excited" senses (332), not seeking a rational companion. He discovers in Bertha a "nature wholly alien" to his own, a "cast of mind common, low, narrow, and singularly incapable of being led to anything higher, expanded to anything larger" (333). Bertha is characterized here as a woman without a soul. This Western man has married a figuratively Eastern woman, an "embruted" creature who, through the marriage bond, becomes a "part of" him (334). When Rochester, responding to the "sweet wind from Europe," decides to leave Jamaica and "go home to God" (335), his behavior continues to be governed by the "most gross, impure, depraved" nature that is permanently "associated" with his own (334). Instead of remaining faithful to his wife, he roams Europe seeking "a good and intelligent woman, whom I could love" (337). Of course he finds only the "unprincipled and violent," "mind-

---

[16] The other Old Testament reference to a "law of the Medes and Persians, which altereth not" occurs in chap. 6 of the book of Daniel. Here the Persian king Darius orders that anyone who petitions "any God or Man" other than the king "shall be cast into the den of lions" (Dan. 6.7). Daniel prays to the God of the Hebrews; the king casts him in the lion's den; Daniel's miraculous deliverance converts Darius to an acknowledgment of the "living God" (Dan. 6.26). Jane Eyre names Daniel as one of her favorite books in the Bible early in the novel (Brontë [1847] 1985, 65); Daniel's ordeal, as well as Esther's, serves as a model for her own resistance to her master's desire to strip her of "soul." I am indebted to Jimmy Griffin for bringing to my attention the relevant biblical passages.

less," and faithless mistresses his money buys him (338). Rochester knows that "hiring a mistress is the next worse thing to buying a slave" (339), yet he persists on this course—even with Jane—because, the narrative suggests, his association with Bertha has deformed him into a polygamous, sensual sultan.

Thus Brontë appears to displace the blame for Rochester's Eastern tendencies on the intrusion of this "Eastern" woman into his Western life. Though Jane protests in Bertha's behalf—"you are inexorable for that unfortunate lady" (328)—Rochester's account of his first marriage serves as the narrative explanation of his own oriental tendencies. The fact that he does not reform until Bertha dies suggests how powerful her oriental hold on him has been.[17]

Bertha, of course, is West Indian, not "Mahometan," and she scarcely resembles the conventional image of an alluring harem inmate—no "gazelle eyes" or "houri forms" here. Indeed, as Susan L. Meyer convincingly shows, she is consistently figured as a "nightmare" vision with "savage," "lurid," and "swelled" black features (1989, 253–54) and associated with the oppressed races subject to British colonialism. Yet, as Grosrichard points out, "The West Indies can end by rejoining, in the imagination, the East Indies" (1979, 32, translation mine). Bertha's characterization in other significant ways recalls the terms used by Wollstonecraft to depict the fate of "Mahometan" women: she is soulless, regarded as "not . . . a part of the human species," and her all-too-real imprisonment at Thornfield invokes the root meaning of *seraglio:* a place where wild beasts are kept. One might say that Bertha's characterization as a "clothed hyena" manifests the Western view of the underlying reality of the harem inmate, the philosophical view of women that underpins both their confinement within the harem and their more conventional adornment.[18]

Thus, to note Bertha's "blackness" and her birth in Jamaica need not preclude seeing that she is also, simultaneously, figured as an "Eastern" woman. Indeed, in Bertha's characterization a number of parallel discourses converge: she is the "black woman who signifies both the oppressed and the oppressor" (Meyer 1989, 266); she is Jane's "dark double" who enacts both Jane's and Brontë's repressed rage at patriarchal oppression (Gilbert and Gubar 1979, 360); she is the Indian woman consumed in sati (Perera 1991); she is Vashti, King Ahasuerus's uncontrollable queen; and she is a harem inmate whose purported soullessness justifies and enforces her own oppression. Bertha is overdetermined; as

---

[17] See Meyer 1989 for fuller discussion of how contact with the Other serves to besmirch the Englishman in *Jane Eyre.*

[18] The reader may be reminded of Horace Walpole's comment that Mary Wollstonecraft was a "hyena in petticoats" (Wollstonecraft [1792] 1982, 17).

the "central locus of Brontë's anxieties about oppression" (Meyer 1989, 252) and as the spark for the redemptive fire that clears the way for Jane's fulfillment, she serves to focus a number of different systems of figuration that structure the novel.

Indeed, Brontë equivocates still further in her presentation of Bertha, never fully indicating whether she is inherently soulless or only made so by Rochester's treatment of her. In a few significant passages, Brontë allows her narrative to suggest that Bertha, like Jane, is consciously aware of and legitimately enraged by her enslavement. On the eve of the doomed wedding, Bertha enters Jane's room, not to harm her as Rochester fears but to rend the veil, which Rochester in his "princely extravagance" had insisted upon buying (Brontë [1847] 1985, 308). Jane sees in the veil an image of Rochester's "pride" (309). When Bertha rends it "in two parts" and "trample[s] on them" (311), her action may be explained as emanating from her resentment of and jealousy toward Jane. Or, it may be viewed as a warning to Jane about the "veiled" existence she would have to lead as Rochester's harem slave.

That Bertha kills herself in her attempt to burn down the house of her master can also be linked to Roxanna's ultimately self-destructive rebellion in *Persian Letters*. Defying the master who has enslaved her, she asserts her freedom only to find death as its inevitable price. As long as the despotic system is in place, no woman can truly be free, yet the suicide of a rebellious woman serves as a powerful condemnation—and potential transformation—of that system.[19] Thus it is no accident that Rochester is blinded in the conflagration caused by Bertha's rebellion. Stripped of his despotic privilege to see, he can no longer function as a sultan. Despite her earlier promises to "stir up mutiny" in the harem (298), Jane owes her freedom not to her own rebellion but to that of the actual "harem-inmate," the "dark double" who acts as her proxy.

After Bertha's death, Rochester is free to reform, and this reform is significantly figured as a conversion: "Jane! you think me, I dare say, an irreligious dog: but my heart swells with gratitude to the beneficent God of this earth just now. . . . I did wrong. . . . Of late, Jane—only—only of late—I began to see and acknowledge the hand of God in my doom. I began to experience remorse, repentance, the wish for reconcilement with my Maker. I began sometimes to pray" (471). The man who had passed a "Persian" law to justify his own behavior here acknowledges the authority of the Christian God who mandates monogamy and respect for the souls of women. Despite the many critiques of Christian ideology and practice that abound in *Jane Eyre*, Brontë's feminist orientalism here

---

[19] See Donaldson 1988 for a similar argument about the self-assertion implicit in Bertha's suicide; Perera 1991, on the contrary, sees Bertha's death as a denial of her subjectivity.

takes priority, as she obscures the patriarchal oppression that is also a part of Christianity.

And by ending her novel with the words of the Christian missionary St. John Rivers, himself one of the domestic despots Jane has had to defy, Brontë leaves the reader with an idealized vision of Christianity as the only satisfactory alternative to Eastern, "Mahometan"—and even Hindu—despotism. While this reversal in the characterization of St. John and the expressed attitude toward Christianity has struck many readers as a self-contradictory shift in Brontë's focus, it in fact confirms and seals the pattern begun with Jane's promise to "go out as a missionary to preach liberty to them that are enslaved" (297).

The novel's concluding paean to St. John and to Christian values takes place against the backdrop not of a vaguely conceived Middle East but of the Far East, India. The groundwork establishing India as another locale for gendered oriental despotism had been laid early in the novel, in the same chapter that features the "sultan/slave" simile. Back at Thornfield after the trip to Millcote, Jane objects to a "pagan" tendency in Rochester (301). Her master has just sung a song to her in which a woman swears "to live—to die" with her beloved (301). Jane seizes on the seemingly innocent phrase and asserts that she "had no intention of dying" with Rochester: "I had as good a right to die when my time came as he had: but I should bide that time, and not be hurried away in a suttee" (301).

Though this identification of India as another Eastern site for the oppression of women is not in my view extensively developed throughout the text, it returns in the novel's conclusion, as well as in the penultimate section of the novel, when Jane faces the threat of being "grilled alive in Calcutta" (441) if she chooses to accompany St. John to India. For during her stay at Moor House, Jane once again encounters a man with a "despotic nature" (434) who rules over a household of dependent women and who threatens not only to immure but also to immolate her (430).

At first Jane finds Moor House less oppressive than her earlier homes. Yet when Jane consents to give up her study of German in order to help St. John learn Hindustani, she discovers another form of "servitude" (423) and she experiences the kiss that St. John gives her as a "seal affixed to my fetters" (424). Jane's subjection to St. John is in fact stronger than any she has felt before. "I could not resist him," she uncharacteristically admits (425). Part of Jane's difficulty in resisting St. John's wishes is that they come cloaked in Christian doctrine. Jane recognizes the despotism in St. John, knowing that to accede to his wishes would be "almost equivalent to committing suicide" (439). Yet because St. John is a "sincere Christian" (434), not an "irreligious dog," she has a harder time extricating herself from the seductions of his proposal that she marry him and accompany him to India: "Religion called—Angels beckoned—God commanded" (444).

Brontë here reveals the motive behind feminist orientalism as a mode of cultural analysis as well as a rhetorical strategy. Jane finds it possible to resist Rochester because he calls himself and acts in ways that clearly echo the Western conception of "Mahomet," not Christ. But a man who assumes the language and posture of Christ is harder to combat. Jane ultimately does find the strength to resist St. John, however, when he unwittingly sets her a challenge that obviously mimics the behavior of a Western feminist's notion of a sultan.

What St. John asks of Jane is that she abandon her already established love for Rochester. With this demand, he manifests what was, to Western feminists, perhaps the most threatening feature of "Mahometan" practice: interference with a woman's free choice of love object. Indeed, what had motivated Roxanna's rebellion in *Persian Letters* was not her desire to escape confinement nor her position as one of many wives. Rather, it was her desire to be free to love another man, coupled with her abhorrence of her sexual "master." In denying Jane her freedom to love (and in promising to impose the forms of sexual love upon her), St. John becomes the most brutal (and literal) of her harem masters and thus the one who evokes from her the greatest effort of rebellion.[20]

Yet in the concluding paragraphs of the novel, St. John—the archetypal Christian man—is redeemed from the flaw in his own nature. By her resistance to his desire to enslave her, Jane frees him from his own oriental tendencies. If she is not a slave, he cannot be a master. Brontë makes explicit the implication behind Wollstonecraft's assertion that the women of the harem have souls "just animated enough to give life to the body." A woman of soul, as Jane has by now firmly established herself to be, has the power not only to resist the harem but to transform it: as Jane had once promised Rochester, "you, three-tailed bashaw as you are, sir, shall in a trice find yourself fettered amongst our hands" (298).

St. John, like Rochester, becomes a true Christian after his encounter with Jane and thus is free to pursue her orientalist project. For St. John, as a Christian missionary in India, "labours for his race" with the same impulses as do Jane and her author: "Firm, faithful, and devoted, full of energy and zeal, and truth . . . he clears their painful way to improvement; he hews down like a giant the prejudices of creed and caste that encumber it" (477). Jane Eyre ends her story with St. John's words—"Amen; even so, come, Lord Jesus!" (477)—because they exter-

---

[20] See Leonowens (1872) 1991 for a fuller elaboration of this idea: the greatest horror of the harem, for Leonowens, is not polygamy, not confinement, not enforced sexual submission, but denial of the freedom to love.

188   *Zonana*

nalize and make global what has been her own internal and local project all along: the purging of oriental elements from her society, the replacement of "Mahometan" law by Christian doctrine. In voicing these words, St. John is recommitting himself to the specifically Christian project of combating alien religious forms. Thus, although the novel's primary focus is the occidentalization of the Occident, it ends with the vision of the occidentalization of the Orient that simultaneously underlies and expands that focus. Readers, both male and female, are encouraged to follow both St. John and Jane in the task of clearing the thicket of oriental "prejudices" abroad, at home, and within their own souls. It remains for readers in the twentieth century to clear yet another thicket, the tangle of feminist orientalist prejudice that continues to encumber Western feminist discourse.

Department of English
University of New Orleans

References

Ahmed, Leila. 1982. "Western Ethnocentrism and Perceptions of the Harem." *Feminist Studies* 8(3):521–34.

Al-Bazei, Saad Abdulrahman. 1983. "Literary Orientalism in Nineteenth-Century Anglo-American Literature: Its Formation and Continuity." Ph.D. dissertation, Purdue University.

Ali, Muhsin Jassim. 1981. *Scheherazade in England: A Study of Nineteenth-Century English Criticism of the "Arabian Nights."* Washington, D.C.: Three Continents.

Alloula, Malek. 1986. *The Colonial Harem,* trans. Myrna Godzich and Wlad Godzich. Theory and History of Literature, vol. 21. Minneapolis: University of Minnesota Press.

Barrell, John. 1991. "Death on the Nile: Fantasy and the Literature of Tourism, 1840–1860." *Essays in Criticism* 41(2):97–127.

Barrett Browning, Elizabeth. 1897. *The Letters of Elizabeth Barrett Browning,* ed. Frederic G. Kenyon. 2 vols. New York: Macmillan.

Bellis, Peter J. 1987. "In the Window-Seat: Vision and Power in *Jane Eyre.*" *ELH* 54(3):639–52.

Besant, Walter. (1897) 1986. *The Queen's Reign.* In *Norton Anthology of English Literature,* ed. M. H. Abrams. 5th ed. New York: Norton.

Brontë, Charlotte. (1847) 1985. *Jane Eyre.* New York: Penguin.

Caracciolo, Peter L., ed. 1988. *"The Arabian Nights" in English Literature: Studies in the Reception of "The Thousand and One Nights" into British Culture.* New York: St. Martin's.

Conant, Martha Pike. 1908. *The Oriental Tale in England in the Eighteenth Century.* New York: Columbia University Press.

Croutier, Alev Lytle. 1989. *Harem: The World behind the Veil.* New York: Abbeville.

Delplato, Joan. 1988. "An English 'Feminist' in the Turkish Harem: A Portrait of Lady Mary Wortley Montagu." In *Eighteenth-Century Women and the Arts,* ed. Frederick M. Keener and Susan E. Lorsch. Westport, N.Y.: Greenwood.

Donaldson, Laura E. 1988. "The Miranda Complex: Colonialism and the Question of Feminist Reading." *Diacritics* 18(3):65–77.

Fuller, Margaret. (1854) 1971. *Woman in the Nineteenth Century.* New York: Norton.

Gaskell, Elizabeth. (1853) 1985. *Ruth.* New York: Oxford.

Gendron, Charisse. 1991. "Images of Middle-Eastern Women in Victorian Travel Books." *Victorian Newsletter,* no. 79, 18–23.

Gibson, Mary Ellis. 1987. "The Seraglio or Suttee: Brontë's *Jane Eyre.*" *Postscript* 4:1–8.

Gilbert, Sandra, and Susan Gubar. 1979. *The Madwoman in the Attic: The Woman Writer and the Nineteenth-Century Literary Imagination.* New Haven, Conn.: Yale University Press.

Gordon, Lucie Duff. (1865) 1983. *Letters from Egypt.* London: Virago.

Grosrichard, Alain. 1979. *Structure du Serail: La Fiction du Despotisme Asiatique dans L'Occident Classique.* Paris: Editions Seuil.

Hatem, Mervat. 1989. "Through Each Other's Eyes: Egyptian, Levantine-Egyptian, and European Women's Images of Themselves and of Each Other." *Women's Studies International Forum* 12(2):183–98.

Jameson, Anna. (1829) 1890. *Memoirs of the Loves of the Poets: Biographical Sketches of Women Celebrated in Ancient and Modern Poetry.* Boston and New York: Houghton Mifflin.

Johnson, Samuel. (1779) 1975. *Lives of the English Poets: A Selection,* ed. John Wain. London: Everyman.

———. (1759) 1977. *Rasselas.* In *Selected Poetry and Prose,* ed. Frank Brady and W. K. Wimsatt. Berkeley: University of California Press.

Joseph, Elizabeth. 1991. "My Husband's Nine Wives." *New York Times,* May 23.

Kra, Pauline. 1979. "The Role of the Harem in Imitations of Montesquieu's *Lettres Persanes.*" *Studies on Voltaire and the Eighteenth Century* 182:273–283.

Kringas, Connie George. 1992. "The Women of *Rasselas:* A Journey of Education and Empowerment." M.A. thesis, University of New Orleans.

Leonowens, Anna. (1872) 1991. *The Romance of the Harem,* ed. Susan Morgan. Charlottesville: University Press of Virginia.

Makhlouf-Obermeyer, Carla. 1979. *Changing Veils: A Study of Women in South Arabia.* Austin: University of Texas Press.

Marmontel, Jean François. 1764. *Moral Tales by M. Marmontel Translated from the French.* 3 vols. London.

Meyer, Susan L. 1989. "Colonialism and the Figurative Strategy of *Jane Eyre.*" *Victorian Studies* 33(2):247–68.

Mohanty, Chandra. 1988. "Under Western Eyes: Feminist Scholarship and Colonial Discourses." *Feminist Review* 30(Autumn):61–88.

Montesquieu, Charles de Secondat Baron de. (1721) 1923. *Persian Letters*, trans. John Davidson. London: Routledge.

Nightingale, Florence. (1852) 1980. *Cassandra*. New York: Feminist Press.

——. (1849–50) 1988. *Letters from Egypt: A Journey on the Nile, 1849–1850*. New York: Widenfeld & Nicolson.

Penzer, N. M. 1936. *The Harem: An Account of the Institution as It Existed in the Palace of the Turkish Sultans with a History of the Grand Seraglio from Its Foundation to Modern Times*. London: Spring Books.

Perera, Suvendrini. 1991. *Reaches of Empire: The English Novel from Edgeworth to Dickens*. New York: Columbia University Press.

Poovey, Mary. 1984. *The Proper Lady and the Woman Writer: Ideology as Style in the Works of Mary Wollstonecraft, Mary Shelley, and Jane Austen*. Chicago: University of Chicago Press.

Richon, Olivier. 1985. "Representation, the Despot and the Harem: Some Questions around an Academic Orientalist Painting by Lecomte-du-Nouy (1885)." In *Europe and Its Others*, ed. Francis Barker, Peter Hulme, Margaret Iverson, and Diana Loxley. Vol. 1. Colchester: University of Essex.

Said, Edward. 1979. *Orientalism*. New York: Vintage Books.

Shelley, Mary Wollstonecraft. (1818) 1974. *Frankenstein or the Modern Prometheus: The 1818 Text*, ed. James Rieger. New York: Bobbs-Merrill.

Spivak, Gayatri Chakravorty. 1985. "Three Women's Texts and a Critique of Imperialism." *Critical Inquiry* 12(1):243–61.

Stedman, Jane W. 1965. "The Genesis of the Genii." *Brontë Society Transactions* 14(5):16–19.

Tasch, Peter A. 1982. "Jane Eyre's 'Three-Tailed Bashaw.' " *Notes & Queries* 227(June):232.

Trumpener, Katie. 1987. "Rewriting Roxane: Orientalism and Intertextuality in Montesquieu's *Lettres Persanes* and Defoe's *The Fortunate Mistress*." *Stanford French Review* 11(2):177–91.

Vaka, Demetra (Mrs. Kenneth Brown). 1909. *Haremlik: Some Pages from the Life of Turkish Women*. Boston and New York: Houghton Mifflin.

Wollstonecraft, Mary. (1798) 1975. *Maria or the Wrongs of Woman*. New York: Norton.

——. (1792) 1982. *Vindication of the Rights of Woman*. London: Penguin.

Workman, Nancy V. 1988. "Scheherazade at Thornfield: Mythic Elements in *Jane Eyre*." *Essays in Literature* 15(2):177–92.

Zonana, Joyce. 1991. " 'They Will Prove the Truth of My Tale': Safie's Letters as the Feminist Core of Mary Shelley's *Frankenstein*." *Journal of Narrative Technique* 21(2):170–84.

Dancing Out the Difference: Cultural Imperialism and Ruth St. Denis's "Radha" of 1906

Jane Desmond

Introduction

AN ANALYSIS of the mechanisms through which meaning is generated is central to any reevaluation of dance history and its canon. I will be arguing in this article for the application of poststructuralist theory to the writing of dance history and also for the wider opening of feminist scholarship to considerations of live performance.[1] Women's studies, although it has generated a great deal of scholarly writing on the social construction of gender and the visual and verbal representation of women in literature, visual arts, and the mass media, has yet to engage fully with the specific richness of performance. Study of performance can include not only historical analysis of visual representations, their construction and reception, but also consideration of the special case of construction of meaning through display of the body—a body that is at once "real" and "representational" as it exists in performance. If "the feminine" itself can be conceived of as a socially constituted masquerade, as Mary Ann Doane and others have noted, then an analysis of performance has wide potential application for work in feminist studies.[2]

My thanks to Jennifer Wicke and Virginia Domínguez for commenting on earlier drafts of this article and to Victoria Vandenberg for research assistance.

[1] Susan Leigh Foster's excellent *Reading Dancing: Bodies and Subjects in Contemporary American Dance* (Berkeley and Los Angeles: University of California Press, 1986) is, as of this writing, the only extended treatment of dance history to draw on theories of semiotics and on the historiographic work of Hayden White to construct a new model for a poetics of dance. This work focuses on developing paradigms for approaching various types of choreography but does not make race, gender, or class central components of its analysis.

[2] See Mary Ann Doane, "Film and the Masquerade: Theorizing the Female Spectator," *Screen* 23, nos. 3–4 (September/October 1982): 74–89, for a discussion of related concerns and references to relevant articles.

[*Signs: Journal of Women in Culture and Society* 1991, vol. 17, no. 1]

Dance scholarship
Although dance scholarship has expanded dramatically in the last fifteen years or so, it remains far behind related fields of arts criticism both in the amount of work and in the level of analysis. Within the bounds of traditional history and criticism, several excellent scholars have emerged in the last two decades,[3] but the discipline as a whole is still waging a battle for acceptance within the academy and remains relatively closed to current work in related fields such as literary theory. There are many reasons for this: as the most ephemeral of all the arts, dance leaves the fewest traces (most dances have not been recorded in any way), making historical reconstruction and analysis exceedingly difficult. And, because it deals most directly with the mute (and most often female) body, dance remains suspect in institutions of higher learning.

Most dance writing is still concerned with technical and artistic judgment, historical reconstruction, reportage, and description, or even social history; but deeper analyses of the ideological functions of dances as works of art are still relatively rare. Only in the last few years have dance critics and historians begun to consider issues that have engaged literary critics and feminist scholars for much more than a decade. Gender, while it may be noted, is rarely analyzed as a constitutive factor.[4]

Furthermore, we are still in the early stages of developing theoretical tools suitable for our object of investigation: the human body, most often the female body, moving in performance. I want to show how theoretical tools drawn from other disciplines can be adapted to dance criticism, as well as how any investigation of gender in dance must be linked to concurrent analysis of other markers of cultural otherness, such as race and class. I hope that in return the particular structure of dance as live performance will open new avenues of theoretical investigation, furthering development of current theories about perception, pleasure, and the mapping of meaning onto the gendered body.

[3] See, e.g., work by Marcia Siegel and Sally Banes such as Sally Banes, *Democracy's Body: Judson Dance Theatre, 1962–1964* (Ann Arbor: UMI Research Press, 1983) and Marcia Siegel, *The Shapes of Change: Images of American Dance* (Berkeley and Los Angeles: University of California Press, 1979).

[4] In the last few years, some exceptions have begun to appear. See Ann Daly's interesting work on gender and ballet in her "Classical Ballet: A Discourse of Difference," *Women and Performance* 3, no. 2, issue 6 (1987–88): 57–66; and Marianne Goldberg's discussion of gender in Martha Graham's work, "She Who Is Possessed No Longer Exists Outside," *Women and Performance* 3, no. 1, issue 5 (1986): 17–27. Suzanne Shelton's meticulously researched biography of Ruth St. Denis, *Divine Dancer* (New York: Doubleday, 1981), on which I will draw throughout this article, discusses sexuality as a factor in St. Denis's work but does not analyze it in detail. Neither does Foster's consideration of St. Denis, although gender is noted.

Ruth St. Denis
My object of analysis is an important 1906 piece, "Radha," choreographed and performed by Ruth St. Denis. St. Denis is usually presented as one of the major figures in the history of American dance, and she is always cited, along with Loie Fuller and Isadora Duncan, as one of the three "mothers" of modern dance. Any reevaluation of the dance history canon must consider St. Denis's work.

With her husband, Ted Shawn, she started the Denishawn school of dance, one of the first professional schools of "aesthetic" dancing, in 1915, and toured throughout the country in the early decades of this century. Doris Humphrey, Charles Weidman, and Martha Graham, the leading choreographers of the next generation, all served an apprenticeship with Denishawn. St. Denis's work was seen on the vaudeville circuit (often the first professional aesthetic dancing that many Americans encountered) and was performed in elite theaters as well. The bulk of her repertoire, which she continued to perform well into the 1960s, consisted of dances inspired by ethnic styles ranging from American Indian to Japanese. The scale of the works varied from solo pieces to large spectacles. Denishawn dancers even appeared in D. W. Griffith's 1916 film, *Intolerance*. In the 1920s St. Denis's company toured Asia, presenting its orientalia to enthusiastic crowds. Although St. Denis's aesthetic was largely rejected as too decorative by Humphrey and Graham, and her works are not regularly performed today, her contribution to the rise of modern dance in America cannot be denied.

Most dance histories discuss St. Denis's "showmanship" and refer to her dances as part of the turn-of-the-century American passion for exotica.[5] But such observations do not take us deeply into the ideological structure and function of the work itself. While we can never imagine with certainty the meaning of an art work for a particular audience, we can venture an analysis of its structures of meaning. I will argue that by adapting contemporary insights drawn from literary criticism, film theory, and work on race and colonialism, we can come closer to understanding not only what "Radha" means, but how its range of meanings may be produced. I will argue that "Radha" presents a hyperbolization of categories of otherness, mapping markers of race,

[5] For works that discuss "Radha" as part of the general passion for the exotic at the turn of the century, see Elizabeth Kendall, *Where She Danced: The Birth of American Art Dance* (1979; reprint, Berkeley and Los Angeles: University of California Press, 1984); Nancy Lee Chalfa Ruyter, *Reformers and Visionaries: The Americanization of the Art of Dance* (New York: Dance Horizons Press, 1979); Christina L. Schlundt, "Into the Mystic with Miss Ruth," *Dance Perspectives*, no. 46 (Summer 1971). Foster and Shelton also situate the work in terms of exotica.

orientalism, and sexuality onto the white middle-class female body. Thus, "Radha" can be said to function as a site of condensation and displacement of desire.

"Radha"

Spectacle
The dance opens and closes with visions of the Hindu goddess Radha posed in spiritual contemplation, partially hidden by a screen. The longest portion of the dance, however, consists of five variations celebrating the pleasures of the senses, and a whirling "delirium of the senses" episode that plunges the dancer into postorgasmic darkness. In both its theatrical structure and its visual arrangement on the stage, "Radha" is a spectacle displaying the female body (see fig. 1).

It is spectacular first in the sense of not being narrative. Although there is a thin story line to the dance, and it fits the barest requirements of narrative—stasis, disruption, stasis—the majority of stage time is devoted to the display of the body in a way that does not drive a narrative forward by providing new information or character development.[6] Second, the spectacular aspects of the dance are enhanced by an emphasis on surface decoration. The stage is set with soft amber lighting, wisps of incense, and an ornate backdrop (or—in a later version—a stage set) representing a Jain temple. St. Denis's costume, a short jacket and gauzy skirt, is accented with "jewels" and trimmed with shiny material. Flowers adorn her hair and jewelry her ankles and arms. Midriff and feet are bare. That a critic for *Variety* referred to the "semi-nudity of the woman" tells us how this costuming was perceived at the time.[7]

The choreography itself reiterated the decorative aspect of the design. As Suzanne Shelton notes, St. Denis believed that "each gesture and pose should objectify an inner emotional state," and "Radha" was conceived as "an elaborate network of spatial and gestural symbols" connoting such feeling states as rapture, despair, or inspiration.[8] Authorial intent aside, "Radha"—having been blocked out with saltcellars on the kitchen table—was a series of simple circular or square spatial patterns composed of relatively simple movements.

---

[6] For a discussion of the relation of narrative and spectacle, see Laura Mulvey's breakthrough article, originally published in 1975, "Visual Pleasure and Narrative Cinema," reprinted in her *Visual and Other Pleasures* (Bloomington: Indiana University Press, 1989), 14–28.
[7] Quoted in Shelton, 54.
[8] Ibid., 62.

These movements were the turns and flourishes of the skirt dancer's repertoire mixed with a smattering of balletish steps and Delsartean limb movements. Never having studied Indian dance, St. Denis drew on the images of India available to her in books and punctuated her simple phrases with poses that recalled oriental icons and "popular images of the late Victorian era," such as the femme fatale.[9] Many of these poses were performed in profile, enhancing the two-dimensional quality of the figure-ground relationship. Radha, brought out of her ornate enclosure like a precious jewel, becomes a moving ornament against an elaborately decorated backdrop until, after displaying her valuable beauty, she is enclosed again, still tantalizingly visible but unattainable, within the carved fretwork of her diadem. Every aspect of staging can be seen as contributing to this fetishistic display. A closer look at the choreography will clarify the presentation.

Description and close analysis[10]

The curtain rises to reveal the goddess Radha sitting in the lotus position on a pedestal. (In later versions she is partially hidden from view behind an ornately carved screen, which will be opened by the head priest.) A procession of Brahman priests enters, carrying sacrificial offerings. (The priests were performed by Indian sailors and clerks rounded up for the purpose.)[11] When the priests are seated in a semicircle, framing a space for Radha to enter, she comes to life. Watched by her priests, she enters the sacred space to begin the dance of the five senses. In a progression from the senses of far distance to the more intimate ones (taste and touch), Radha dances to music from Delibes's orientalist opera, *Lakme.*

In the opening dance of sight, Radha holds a strand of pearls in each hand as she revolves in place. Then, in small steps phrased to the music, she moves from side to side in front of her watching priests, posing occasionally with one leg gently lifted to the front. Exchanging the pearls for bells, she begins the playful, rhythmic dance of hearing during which she surrounds her body with a cascade of sounds. Throbbing music initiates the dance of smell as Radha manipulates a garland of marigolds in a series of simple waltzing steps and poses. At the close of the section she arches back, trailing the blossoms along the front of her body, one

---

[9] Ibid.
[10] I rely on my viewing of a 1941 filmed version of St. Denis performing "Radha," a print of which is housed in the Dance Collection of the Lincoln Center Library, New York. I draw also on Shelton's verbal reconstruction of the dance, based on her viewing of the same film and supplemented by her review of St. Denis's papers housed at Lincoln Center.
[11] Kendall, 51.

hand crushing the flowers to her face. So far we have seen the dancer's body in association with nature and signs of luxurious ornamentation. Things heat up for the dance of taste, which follows. Drinking deeply from a simple clay bowl, she whirls with abandon, ending in the seductive vulnerability of a deep back bend before she falls to the ground. Kneeling, with her skirt spread around her, she starts the dance of touch by caressing one hand with the other. Languorous music accompanies her movements as she slides her hands voluptuously over her body, ending with fingertips to her lips.

After the "foreplay" of the preceding episodes, the "delirium of the senses" section unfolds, the music quickening to a frenzied tempo. Spinning, possessed, Radha whirls with her skirts swishing wildly until she suddenly falls to the ground, and "writhes and trembles to a climax, then lies supine as darkness descends."[12] The lights come up on a chastened Radha, lifting her arms in supplication. After tracing the petals of a lotus blossom on the floor, she withdraws to her shrine. The final image shows her sitting on her pedestal, transformed by *samadhi*, self-realization.

Aesthetic dancing

St. Denis's aesthetic dancing arose during a time of complex social change in America. At the turn of the twentieth century, changing gender roles joined with racial and ethnic differences and class antagonisms to create a volatile social mixture.[13] To contextualize St. Denis's work, I will consider two aspects of turn-of-the-century culture: changing social attitudes toward the body, and popularization of the "exotic" in cultural forms.

American Delsarte movement

In the latter decades of the nineteenth century, a growing emphasis on "physical culture" was allied with a number of reform and educational movements, such as women's dress reform and physical education.[14] Prominent among these physical training regimes was the American Delsarte movement, based on the teachings of French music and drama teacher Francois Delsarte (1811–71). Seeking to analyze and classify human expression, he developed a technical training system based on "an elaborate and mystical science of aesthetics deriving from his personal

---

[12] Shelton (n. 4 above), 61.
[13] See John Higham, "The Reorientation of American Culture in the 1890's," in his *Writing American History: Essays on Modern Scholarship* (Bloomington: Indiana University Press, 1970), 73–102.
[14] Kendall (n. 5 above), 22.

FIG 1 Ruth St. Denis in "Radha," 1906. (Photo reprinted by permission of Performing Arts Research Center, New York Public Library at Lincoln Center, New York.)

interpretation of the Christian Trinity."[15] In the Delsarte system, the codification of gesture was linked to "a spiritual labeling of every part of the body according to certain zones—Head, Heart, and Lower Limbs, which corresponded to Mind, Soul, Life."[16]

Although intended for the elocutionary training of professional speakers and actors in the 1870s, the expressive principles of Delsarte's aesthetic theory were being practiced throughout the United States by the late 1880s, especially by women, in the drawing rooms of middle- and upper-class households. American proponents of Delsartism stressed relaxation techniques, "energizing" exercises, rhythmic gymnas- tics, "natural" movement based on spiraling curves, statue-posing, and pantomime. Statue-posing and pantomime were deemed "the ultimate in refinement and gentility" and helped open a "wedge for the entrance of respectable women into the field of theatrical dance" at a time when the theater was regarded in the United States as morally suspect.[17]

Through Delsarte, movement was analyzed and linked to meaning and morality. "Natural" movement was thought to provide authenticity of expression. The body became a signifier of Truth. Writing in 1954 about the Delsarte system, Ted Shawn, St. Denis's lifelong partner, states, "The spontaneous movements of the body cannot lie . . . all human beings move under the government of universal laws, and gesture is the universal language by which we can speak to each other with immediacy, clarity, and truth, and which no barrier of race, nationality, language, religion or political belief can diminish in communicative power."[18]

The changes in American society at the turn of the century coincided with massive colonial expansion in which Europe consolidated control of most of what is now known as the Third World. During this time, a popular and elite fascination with non-European cultures coincided with a rise in such "sciences" of codification as ethnography. The "exotic" was extremely fashionable in scholarly endeavors as well as "high" art and "low" art forms.

In some high art contexts, the exotic was cast as a utopian vision of the past glories of classical civilizations. The past seemed to offer an antidote to the chaotic urban conditions that threatened the middle and upper classes. At the 1893 Chicago Columbian Exposition, the monumental White City, built in neoclassical style, typified this urge in elite cultural production.[19] Popular images of the exotic, however, were less utopian

---

[15] Ruyter (n. 5 above), 17.
[16] Kendall, 24.
[17] Ruyter, 29.
[18] Ted Shawn, *Every Little Movement: A Book about Francois Delsarte* (New York: Dance Horizons Press, 1963), 90.

and were perceived by the cultural elite as merely gratifying the senses rather than providing spiritual uplift. For example, historian John Kasson describes the exposition's Midway as "exuberant chaos," and a "hurly-burly of exotic attractions: mosques and pagodas, Viennese streets and Turkish bazaars, South Sea Island huts, Irish and German castles, and Indian tepees."[20] A prime attraction was the Persian Palace of Eros where Little Egypt and her cohorts danced the hootchy-kootchy. Described at the time as a "suggestively lascivious contorting of the abdominal muscles" that was "almost shockingly disgusting," this attraction proved immensely popular.[21]

Exotic popular amusements like the Midway and Luna Park on Coney Island, which attracted both middle- and working-class patrons, supplied an ornate aesthetic that Kasson has termed the "oriental orgasmic." The essentialist strains of Delsartism and orientalism mixed well. St. Denis's achievement in "Radha" was to combine the oriental orgasmic with Delsartism's transcendent spirituality into a spectacular form that could play successfully not only on the vaudeville circuit but also at the garden parties of the elite and in the art theaters of America and Europe.

Ruth St. Denis and "Radha"

The multiple strains of orientalism, popular culture, and artistic spiritualism that are found in St. Denis's work have their beginnings in her childhood. The daughter of a well-educated progressive mother, she was drilled in Delsarte exercises and exposed to Eastern spiritualism through theosophy and through the orientalist performance of leading American Delsarte exponent Genevieve Stebbins. As a young adult, St. Denis became a believer in Christian Science, and throughout her career she combined the spirituality of the Delsarte system with her own adaptations of Christian Science teachings, which emphasized that "spirit is the immortal truth; matter is mortal error."[22]

Some scholars have seen a feminist dimension in Christian Science, founded by Mary Baker Eddy, because it asserts the androgynous nature of God. In the social sphere, this concept means that in order to be complete persons, both men and women had to have "a harmonious balance of masculine and feminine traits."[23] But equally important to

[19] John Kasson, *Amusing the Million: Coney Island at the Turn of the Century* (New York: Hill & Wang, 1978), 17.

[20] Ibid., 24.

[21] Ibid., 26.

[22] Mary Baker Eddy, quoted in Shelton (n. 4 above), 47.

[23] Margery Fox, "Protest in Piety: Christian Science Revisited," *International Journal of Women's Studies* 1, no. 4 (July/August, 1978): 411.

Christian Science were notions of morality that promoted "purity" and chastity.[24] Inheriting the traditional Christian dualism between the spiritual and material realms, Christian Science did away with the hierarchy of that dualism by denying the material world altogether, subsuming it into a monism of Spirit. As Susan Hill Lindley has argued, the feminism of Christian Science was "ambiguous," and Eddy's resolution of this dualism that traditionally denigrated both women and the material "was no real solution to the tension, for it denied rather than redeemed the 'lost half.' "[25]

But, the spiritualism of Christian Science combined with the Delsarte system, which allowed women a new freedom of expression through movement, may have provided St. Denis a way "around" the strictures associated with the body's materiality and sensuality. While building a career on her own physical display, she steadfastly asserted her identity as a mystic and her dancing as spiritual uplift. In a poem titled "White Jade" describing an early dance of the same name, St. Denis writes, "My own body is the living Temple of all Gods. The God of Truth is in my upright spine. The God of Love is in the Heart's rhythmic beating. The God of Wisdom lives in my conceiving mind . . . . The God of Beauty is revealed in my harmonious body."[26] In this rhetorical fiat, the material body is not so much denied as transposed into the figuration of transcendental values.

Through her dance, St. Denis declared that she was presenting the mystic's experience of unity with God. In preparation for each performance of "Radha," St. Denis writes, she would meditate for half an hour to "realize my contact with the one Mind," so that by the time she stepped onstage, she felt she "was truly the priestess in the temple."[27]

Just as in Christian Science the body was subsumed into Spirit, St. Denis subsumed the sensual aspects of her dancing into a vaunted mysticism framed both as religion and as art. In doing so she, like her contemporary Isadora Duncan, was able to extend the bounds of propriety in the public display of the partially clothed female body. At a time when bare feet were cause for shock, St. Denis in her revealing costume earned reviews declaring, "Every lascivious thought flees shy into the farthest corner . . . . [She has] freed our souls from the clutches of everyday life."[28]

St. Denis's dancing was not always so uplifting. With the support of her mother, who accompanied her to New York, she got her start at the

[24] Susan Hill Lindley, "The Ambiguous Feminism of Mary Baker Eddy," *Journal of Religion* 64, no. 3 (July 1984): 326.
[25] Ibid., 331.
[26] St. Denis quoted in Schlundt (n. 5 above), 24.
[27] Ibid., 21.
[28] Ibid.

age of fifteen as a skirt dancer in a dime museum variety show. Surrounded by specimens like triple-headed calves, she danced six shows a day, punctuating her routines with acrobatic roll-overs and her specialty, the slow-splits. On the bill with St. Denis one week in 1894 were an albino musician and Lillie the Trick Dog. This may not seem an auspicious start for a dancer who was later to be hailed as the solution to "the world's enigma," but it provided the basis for an artistic savvy that "aspired to the loftier echelons of fine art" while never losing the "genius of lowbrow."[29]

The myth surrounding St. Denis's first moment of choreographic revelation combines mass consumer culture with the spiritual aspirations assigned to high art. In 1904, while on tour in a David Belasco production of *DuBarry,* St. Denis was struck by a drugstore poster advertising Egyptian Deities cigarettes: the bare-breasted goddess Isis sat surrounded by huge columns and flowering lotus. An inscription carved in stone above her head assured the buyer that "No Better Turkish Cigarette Can Be Made." St. Denis later wrote, "My destiny as a dancer had sprung alive in that moment. I would become a rhythmic and impersonal instrument of spiritual revelation. . . . I have never before known such an inward shock of rapture."[30]

In dance histories, this incident is usually repeated and valorized as a moment of artistic inspiration. What should be noted, however, is how it reveals the forces of commodification, appropriation of the exotic, rapturous denial of the physical in favor of the spiritual, and display of the female body as a site of revelation that were to mark St. Denis's work throughout her career. All of these are exemplified in "Radha."

The dance ("Egypta") that the poster inspired was not completed until several years later, but the idea of an Eastern goddess was transposed into an Indian setting for "Radha," which catapulted St. Denis into the artistic circles of the cultural elite. First publicly performed in 1906, "Radha" played in New York at Proctor's vaudeville house on Twenty-third Street,[31] with St. Denis appearing between acts by a pugilist and a group of trained monkeys.[32] Soon, however, a New York socialite and oriental

---

[29] Shelton, 67, 21.

[30] Ibid., 46.

[31] Vaudeville at this time reflected both its "coarser" origins in variety shows for male audiences and its newer respectability as it targeted a growing middle-class (male and female) audience. St. Denis's work, a respectable presentation of sexuality, fit well with changing codes of performance. Shelton (n. 4 above) notes: "As ladies began to patronize high-class variety, the atmosphere of the theater became even more self-conscious, with elaborate rationales required to justify the display of female bodies. Scantily clad women appeared as 'living statues' or in tableaux that duplicated famous paintings or biblical episodes" (25).

[32] Ibid., 54.

enthusiast, Mrs. Orland Rowland, took an interest in St. Denis's work and arranged a private matinee for her society friends. "Radha" became a hit. Newspaper notices assured her success with headlines such as "Yes, Society Did Gasp When Radha in Incense-Laden Air 'Threw Off the Bondage of the Earthly Senses,' " and hundreds of eager spectators were turned away from subsequent performances.[33] St. Denis was launched on the high art circuit and soon found an influential supporter in Stanford White, but her work never lost its cross-class appeal. Lean times periodically sent her back to vaudeville to finance her work.

By thus contextualizing "Radha" in terms of the popularity of exotica at the turn of the century, the rise of "barefoot dancing," and various strains of spiritualism, I have touched on issues of gender, orientalism, and changing representations of women. Many dance historians stop their analysis at this point. But I still want to consider in detail the ideologies of these various discourses and their mode of activation in the construction of "Radha."

"Orientalism"

Edward Said defines "orientalism" as "a political vision of reality whose structure promoted the difference between the familiar (Europe, the West, 'us') and the strange (the Orient, the East, 'them')."[34] Through an act of "imaginative geography,"[35] it both created and then served the maintenance of the two worlds. It articulates a "relationship of power, of domination, and of varying degrees of cultural hegemony."[36] "Orientalism" in Said's usage refers not only to the changing political-historical relations between Europe and Asia but also to the discovery and study of various oriental cultures by Westerners and to a body of assumptions, images, and fantasies held by Westerners about the Orient.[37] It is this latter category that is my concern here. Although Said traces historical changes in the specific constitution of these images and fantasies, he maintains that a pervasive "latent Orientalism," circulating both inside and outside of scholarly disciplines, has remained remarkably consistent for several hundred years.[38]

Above all, the Orient is conceived of as unchanging and eternal. Occasionally these characteristics are valorized as "seminal" and "pro-

---

[33] Ibid., 58.
[34] Edward Said, *Orientalism* (New York: Random House, 1978), 43.
[35] Ibid., 90.
[36] Ibid., 5.
[37] Ibid., 90.
[38] Ibid., 206.

found," as in reference to "the wisdom of the East."[39] Yet, most of the attributes assigned to the Orient are opposite to those valorized in the West. The East is primitive, childlike, and backward; it is eccentric, irrational, chaotic, and mysterious; it is sensual, sexual, fecund, and despotic. Most important, the Orient is deemed incapable of speaking for itself. It is not Europe's "interlocutor, but its silent Other."[40] The Western orientalist, as artist or scholar, "makes the Orient speak, describes the Orient, renders its mysteries plain for and to the West."[41]

By the end of the nineteenth century, the East was clearly constructed as a site requiring explication, investigation, illustration, discipline, reconstruction, or redemption.[42] The East's otherness offended European standards of sexual propriety, threatened domestic seemliness, and "wore away Eastern discreteness and rationality of time, space, and personal identity. In the Orient, one was suddenly confronted with unimaginable antiquity, inhuman beauty, boundless distance."[43]

By the last decades of the nineteenth century, the "unchanging" nature of the East was seen as a source of regeneration for a Western world caught in an unsettling rise of industrialism and materialism.[44] Said has characterized this idea of regeneration as a secular post-Enlightenment myth based on Christian imagery of death and rebirth through salvation.[45] In "Radha," St. Denis acts out a similar scenario of redemption within the imaginative geography of the Orient.

Following Said, we could thus look at "Radha," with its cresting tide of physical excitement overcome by spiritual purification, as illustrating the threatening chaotic sensuality of the East and its ultimate discipline and redemption through the triumph of spirituality or the law of ultimate truth. From this point of view, "Radha" projects a vision of the East as a site of imaginary pilgrimage both for sensual indulgence and physical

---

[39] Ibid., 208.
[40] Ibid., 93.
[41] Ibid., 20.
[42] Ibid., 40, 206.
[43] Ibid., 167.
[44] Notions of regeneration were not limited to the West. Said notes that in view of the conditions under colonialism, the Western "Orientalist found it his duty to rescue some portion of a lost, past classical Oriental grandeur" (ibid., 29) in order to ameliorate conditions in the present. In other words, the Westerner could now represent the Orient as it was, is, or should be, not only to himself but also to the Orientals, restoring to them glimpses of their past glories. St. Denis participated in this process when she toured the Orient in 1925–26. Her dances, constructed primarily from library research and from inspiring pictures, were warmly received in India, Japan, and other countries. In India, her respectability may have contributed to a renewal of prestige for traditional classical dancing. However, as one critic noted (see Shelton [n. 4 above], 199), there may have been some irony in the situation for the Indian audiences as they watched a white woman dance a temple dance that was, at the time, usually performed by prostitutes.
[45] Said (n. 34 above), 115.

awakening (the same notion later popularized in E. M. Forster's *Passage to India*, e.g.) and for spiritual rejuvenation of an America in the throes of change.

But if "Radha" is "about" the East, it is even more about the West. As James Clifford has noted in his criticism of Said's book, Said's argument at times suffers too much from the dichotomy we/they he attempts to describe.[46] In fact, Western discourse about "the East" reflects a continually changing historical process of self-definition by "the West." We can see "Radha" as a portrayal of Western desires and ambivalences displaced onto an orientalized, gendered body. The association between the cultural otherness of the Orient and the construction of gender in the West is the key to this linkage.

Orientalism and the otherness of gender and race

As a site of unlimited desire and deep generative energies, the Orient is figured as female.[47] Trinh T. Minh-ha describes the construction of the feminine in Western culture in practically the same language Said uses in depicting the Orient. "Woman," she says, "can never be defined. . . . She wallows in night, disorder, immanence, and is at the same time the 'disturbing factor (between men)' and the key to the beyond."[48]

Both "woman" and "the East" are constructed by Western patriarchy as "natural" categories of difference requiring explication, investigation, illustration, discipline, reconstruction, or redemption. Knowledge of both is eroticized as a stripping bare, an exposing of hidden meaning. The vocabulary itself reveals a scopic economy of difference in which the act of seeing is equated with mastery. As Said notes, a recurrent motif in nineteenth-century writing is the "vision of the Orient as spectacle, or tableau vivant."[49] That both the Orient and woman are cast as speechless renders self-narrative and history impossible and creates the necessary conditions for visual spectacle as site or source of knowledge. These double specular economies of difference come together in St. Denis's performance of "Radha." Here the mute colonized female body represents the sensuality of both the "female" and the Orient. Similarly, the higher spirituality attached to the "wisdom of the East" meets current notions of the women's sphere as the province of moral guardianship.

---

[46] James Clifford, "On Orientalism," in *The Predicament of Culture: Twentieth-Century Ethnography, Literature, and Art,* ed. James Clifford (Cambridge, Mass.: Harvard University Press, 1988), 255–76.

[47] Said, 188.

[48] Trinh T. Minh-ha, "Difference: 'A Special Third World Women Issue,' " *Discourse* 8 (Fall–Winter 1986–87): 30.

[49] Said, 158.

"Radha" is thus doubly sexualized and doubly chaste. The tensions between these seemingly incommensurable attributes—goddess/whore, Eastern/Western, and sexual/chaste—are all articulated across the material presence of the female body. The dance signals the underlying dialectical relation of opposites in any binary construction. It also points to the changing dimensions of women's roles at the turn of the century and the reconstruction of female physicality as it was reflected in the health reform movement.

Freud's description of woman's sexuality as the dark continent reminds us of the intimate relationship among orientalism, gender, and a third register of otherness: race. In discussing this phrase, Sander Gilman asserts that Freud "ties the image of female sexuality to the image of the colonial black and to the perceived relationship between the female's ascribed sexuality and the Other's exoticism and pathology."[50] The reason Freud's statement was legible to his contemporaries is that, like female sexuality and the imaginative geography of colonialism, the "dark races" were represented as objects to be illuminated, mapped, and controlled.

Early nineteenth-century race theory[51] joined with social Darwinism in the latter half of the century to provide intellectual currency for white ideas about the biological basis of racial inequality.[52] Like gender, the concept of race entailed notions of difference that were seen as irreducibly linked to the body and, therefore, as "natural." Both women and nonwhites were thus consigned to the "lower" realm of nature. The same dynamic of dominance based on natural difference that was exemplified in white colonialism also undergirds patriarchy.

Reading "Radha"

In "Radha" I find a construction of meaning that depends on manipulating these codes of difference into an overlapping structure. Race, gender, and cultural otherness double one another, with each register reinforcing the next to produce a hyperbole of "Otherness." Dancing, as a nonverbal display of the body—most often the female body—provides an especially rich mode of articulation for this process.

[50] Sander Gilman, "Black Bodies, White Bodies: Toward an Iconography of Female Sexuality in Late Nineteenth-Century Art, Medicine, and Literature," in *"Race," Writing, and Difference,* ed. Henry Louis Gates, Jr. (Chicago: University of Chicago Press, 1986), 257.

[51] Race theories proposed a division of races into advanced (white) and backward (nonwhite) categories, just as orientalist thought divided the world into the strong, progressive, advanced West and the weak, primitive, degenerate East. Colonial expansion was seen as proof of the triumph of the fittest.

[52] Said, 206.

As I have noted in the preceding discussion, orientalist thought has constructed the East as feminine. Racial thinking has similarly tied otherness to the body. Display of the "colored" Eastern female body then carries with it a surplus of signifiers of difference. The litany of difference can be summarized as sexual (i.e., desirable yet terrifying), mute, natural, essential, universal, unchanging, and visually knowable. The female body is the nodal point that interpolates racial and cultural difference in "Radha." Its investigation is also the main content of the dance and the vehicle for spectacle.

Mechanisms of meaning

The structure of this dance reveals the spectacle of a woman lost in a rising tide of self-pleasure, a goddess delirious with her own sexuality. It shows a woman renouncing, of her own accord, the powerful pleasure of her own body for a chaste spiritual union with the transcendent. It shows the careful marking out and celebration of each aspect of a woman's physicality, her five senses explored one by one moving in sequence, so that the spectator is drawn into an ever more intimate relationship with her body. This spectacle is displayed in front of a semicircle of male viewers on stage and equally directed outward to the audience.

When it is described in this way, the scopophilic aspects of the piece become apparent. Drawing on psychoanalytic film theories of spectatorship and voyeurism, I maintain that the woman's body is fragmented and fetishized, not only visually but conceptually, into each of the five senses—the woman *is* the five senses, each displayed separately for investigation by the viewer.[53] The woman, observed "unawares" by the audience in the darkened theater, is caught in a vortex of pleasure. She is further situated as object of the male gaze through the relayed looks of the priests on stage. Their presence also signals the religiosity of the act. (Being priests, they provide no competition for a white heterosexual male viewer in the audience but do provide adequate gender identification.)

At first glance, it appears that any displeasure that may be aroused in a male viewer by the woman's ability to sexually satisfy herself is soon banished by the reassurance that she rejects her own pleasure/power for spiritual fulfillment. The potential terror of female sexuality would thus

[53] Laura Mulvey's article (n. 6 above), remains a cornerstone for psychoanalytic critical theories of spectatorship in film. She draws on Lacan's extension of Freud's work on ego formation and the construction of sexual subjectivity to develop a theory of visual pleasure based on voyeurism and fetishism. Her work opposes notions of the social construction of the female as spectacle, i.e., "to-be-looked-at," to that of the male as active narrative agent. These ideas have important implications for developing a related theory of spectatorship for live performance. Following Mulvey, I believe that staging "Radha" as a spectacle (see "Spectacle" section under "Radha," above) enhances the voyeuristic and fetishistic production of pleasure.

be constrained by the patriarchal law of the Father in the form of religion, which would demonstrate the control that orientals, women, and all people of color were seen as requiring. However, the dance also unites the goddess/whore duality within the figure of one woman, thus allowing for several possible readings. One reading reassures the male viewer that even "asexual" women are really "women," that is, defined by and reducible to their bodies. Other readings might hold that women themselves are repositories of both relationships to sexuality, indulgence, and control; or that woman's pleasure in her own body is so seductive as to involve a constant struggle between expression and renunciation; or even that the pleasure of the senses is itself a transcendent spiritual experience. That is, the recuperative effect of the religious framing remains ambiguous, allowing for multiple responses.

Scopophilic pleasures of this sort are allowed in high art under certain conditions. St. Denis's contemporary, the Austrian writer Hugo von Hofmannsthal, characterized this requirement when he stated that, although "Radha" "borders on voluptuousness, . . . it is chaste."[54] The mechanism that allows this audience/performer link can be described as what Michel Foucault calls the "confessional" mode.

The pleasures of the confessional mode

One way of looking at the dynamics of meaning in "Radha," with its religious discourse, is in the form of a Christian confessional. The confessional structure is a ritual expression, a truthful telling of forbidden behavior, especially—as Foucault emphasizes in The History of Sexuality—sexual behavior. It requires a speaker and listener (performer and audience).[55] The act of telling "exonerates, redeems, and purifies" the confessor, and promises him or her salvation.[56] Its redemptive promise simultaneously allows, while disavowing, the illicit pleasures of prurient interest on the part of the audience.

Foucault indicates how the range of the confessional form expanded after the Reformation. By the end of the nineteenth century this range extended into a series of relationships, including those between psychiatrists and patients and delinquents and experts, and it also took several rhetorical forms such as autobiographical narratives and published letters.[57] I would add to this list the relationship between Radha and her audience as it functioned in performance. It was the supposed moral superiority of the viewing audience that was being played to and rein-

---

[54] Quoted in Shelton (n. 4 above), 47.
[55] Michel Foucault, The History of Sexuality, vol. 1, An Introduction (New York: Random House, 1987), 61.
[56] Ibid., 62.
[57] Ibid., 63.

forced in Radha's display and renunciation of the pleasures of her own
body. Linda Nochlin has, in her discussion of orientalist painting, called
this type of viewing experience a "tongue-clicking and lip-smacking response."[58]
The confessional mode interlocked with St. Denis's own way of conceiving of her work. St. Denis's belief in the Delsartean meaningfulness of
movement, and her conviction that her dancing demonstrated the unity
of the individual spirit with god (formulated in Christian Science as
androgynous, or beyond sexuality), framed her work in moral justifica-
tion. The confessional mode, as a way of structuring a relationship between performer and spectator, framed sexuality as art and art as moral
uplift. Given St. Denis's position as a woman choreographer, then a
rarity, I believe that her utilization of these discourses of morality enabled
her to subvert the contemporary standards for "respectable" women's
display of their own sexuality. In doing so, however, she also reproduced
traditional patriarchal designations of that sexuality.
The tensions between the sexuality of the work and its artistic and
spiritual framing are reflected in the contemporary critical response. Von
Hofmannsthal captured the crux of the dance: "It is consecrated to the
senses, but it is higher." Similarly, a British critic called "Radha" athletic
in its actuality and ascetic in its refinement. The reviewer for the *Boston
Herald* could not help noting that St. Denis's "body is that of a woman
divinely planned" but insisted that "there is no atmosphere of sex about
her."[59]
Foucault's work can take us farther in a consideration of sexuality and
spectatorship. Foucault points out the similarity between two modes of
production of truth, the confessional and the scientific discourse.[60] Both
were utilized in the expanding nineteenth-century discourses of sexuality,
and both implied a will to knowledge that reflected a socially inscribed
power to investigate, to judge, and ultimately to reform or punish. In
"Radha," both of these discourses come together. The ethnographic urge
to represent the other for the pleasure and uses of the representer[61]
combines with the display of sexuality sanctified by the confessional

[58] Linda Nochlin, "The Imaginary Orient," *Art in America* 71, no. 5 (May 1983):
125.
[59] Quotes from Shelton, 64. Note also that Shelton, who calls "Radha" a "ritual orgasm," acknowledges the mixed message in the piece and its oriental eroticism. But in
her discussion of these qualities she merely states, "This mixed message stemmed from
St. Denis' own stage personality and, by extension from the quality of the gestures,"
which reflected her background as an unassuming New Jersey farm girl (64–65). The
intricate dialectic between East and West remains submerged in a discussion of individual artistry.
[60] Foucault, 64.
[61] Houston A. Baker, Jr., "Caliban's Triple Play," in Gates, ed. (n. 50 above), 386.

code. The result for the audience is a doubly inscribed "right to look," further enhanced by racial ideologies.[62]

In white Western discourse, both nonwhites and non-Westerners are coded as extremely or excessively sexual. The dark (St. Denis used dark body paint in the first versions) goddess from the erotic East, then, implies a surfeit of sexuality. Even when St. Denis switched to a body suit of her own flesh color in later versions, either for reasons of propriety or merely for convenience, she was still perceived as a Hindu goddess, and we know that at that time in North America, Hindus were perceived as black. In one of the first performances, when a Hindu first entered carrying a tray of incense, an audience member jeered in black dialect, "Who wants de Waitah?"[63] The racial implication was so clear that the company did not tour south of the Mason-Dixon line because of the Jim Crow laws.

St. Denis was, of course, known by her audience to be white. Her portrayal of a woman of color had the effect of sexualizing her in the audience's mind. This is similar to the device used in nineteenth-century odalisque paintings where the association of black women with whites served as a clue to the sexual knowledge or availability of the white women.[64] Similarly, while St. Denis is Western, she is here linked to the sensuous, eternal feminine represented by the East.

These several dynamics function to enhance the audience's right to look sexually at the respectable white middle-class woman on the stage.[65] The racial and cultural displacement of "Radha" is precisely what enhances the success of the confessional mode in the context of art. It is this hyperbole of otherness and its reinforcing linkages between ideological notions of race, gender, and non-Westernness that, I suspect, was the key to this dance's popularity.

Conclusions

But if we leave the analysis at that, we fail to consider fully the dynamics of live performance. After all, the representation of Radha is not

---

[62] I am using the term "right to look" as it is developed by Jane Gaines in her "White Privilege and Looking Relations: Race and Gender in Feminist Film Theory," *Cultural Critique* 4 (Fall 1986): 59–79. She refers to culturally proscribed economies of vision as they are delineated along lines of race, gender, and class.

[63] Quoted in Shelton, 54.

[64] Gilman (n. 50 above), 240.

[65] The class alignment or consignment of successful performers during that time was complex. "Respectable" artists often socialized with the elite, yet remained a class apart, somewhat beyond the pale. In terms of her class origins, St. Denis came from a family relatively poor in economic capital, but rich in educational capital (to use Bourdieu's distinction). Her mother was trained as a doctor, although she did not practice, and her father was an inventor. Certainly, St. Denis's self-presentation in her adult life ("respectably" married to her partner Ted Shawn, e.g.) indicated an alignment with the middle class.

a story, where the priestess Radha might be imagined, or a painting, where she might be displayed and observed, but a live performance. As I have already mentioned, the middle-class white woman's body is central to the production of pleasure in the relationship of these three markers of otherness as discussed above. But it is also the factor that ultimately confounds binary constructions of meaning. In the ludic or dreamlike space of performance, the performer is both white and nonwhite, Western and Eastern, and female while usurping the male role of choreographer. (Remember that at that time, although most dancers were female, very few dances were choreographed by women.)

What issues of spectatorship and the production of meaning do these complications raise? At the very least, they unsettle the binarisms of the ideologies that undergird racism, sexism, and orientalism. The element of mastery, however, implied by the right to represent the "other," remains.

But if we look at the choreography, with its combination of skirt-dancing turns, ballet steps, and "Indian" gestures, something else becomes apparent. The dance itself serves as a sign of the cultural process of "othering" through representation—an ongoing process of construction that is always self-reflexive with regard to the culture that produces it. The representative codes of vaudeville skirt-dancing collide with iconic signs of Indianness, mixing with and overlaying one another as a sign of cultural interaction and continually renegotiated meaning.[66]

Although there is no Brechtian self-reflexivity built into the theatrical structure of "Radha," implicit in every performance is the spectator's awareness of the construction of an illusion.[67] Because of its existence as a temporal art—and a three-dimensional one that is dependent on the physical presence of the performer in the same space as the audience (i.e., not sculpture, not film, not literature)—live performance must produce a convincing linkage of similarity and difference.[68] The performer is both himself or herself and the character who is portrayed. Performance presents this as a dialectical relationship, always in negotiation.

[66] For a consideration of issues of negotiation in colonialism, see Homi Bhabha's "Of Mimicry and Man: The Ambivalence of Colonial Discourse," *October*, no. 28 (Spring 1984), 125–33.

[67] Brecht's theories of theater emphasized the notion of distanciation, or the "alienation effect." By means of such devices as self-reflexivity his plays keep spectators aware that they are participating in the construction of a fiction; thus they avoid the conventions of realism that serve to naturalize ideology. See Bertolt Brecht, *Brecht on Theatre*, ed. and trans. John Willett (New York: Hill & Wang, 1964).

[68] The situation is somewhat different with film. While the image composed of reflected light is less material than a play in performance, the evidentiary nature of the photographic image carries with it a strong coding of realism. In some ways, film can allow for a stronger identification (and temporary loss of the sense of self as separate from the fiction) than live performance. The complexities of this relationship between film and live performance will have to be considered as film theory is adapted to performance analysis.

Drawing on psychoanalytic film theories of spectatorship, I could argue that St. Denis as a white Westerner provides an avenue of psychological identification for her white Western audience. Framed by the
essentialist, transcendent spirituality of the piece, the audience is brought
into ego identification with the white as nonwhite and the Western as
Eastern. At the same time, the voyeuristic and fetishistic aspects of the
dance (enhanced by its construction as spectacle) objectify it as separate
from the observer. A "colored" white woman (since this is not caricature
of the minstrel-show variety) also evokes an ambiguous response. While
"mixing" sexualizes the white woman, it simultaneously indicates a potential mixing of the races, legally proscribed at the time. If ideologies are
based on binary constructions of difference necessary to the maintenance
of hegemony, performance thus indicates the ambiguity of such binary
constructions and their true dialectical function in the production of
meaning.

Certainly St. Denis's rise to fame and her ability to present herself in
respectable theaters as a woman alone on the stage is emblematic of the
social changes in the women's sphere at the turn of the century. Still, her
work remains conservative in its assertion of spirituality as the realm of
woman and also in its presentation of woman's body as sexualized. One
of St. Denis's achievements was to unite these supposed opposites.

Some critics have begun to pose questions theorizing the body in performance.[69] Questions of the power of representation become more complex when acted out on and through a material body. Is the female
appropriation of sexual display in live performance, even within patriarchal norms, an act that in some way threatens the hegemony of patriarchy? That so much of the sexual pleasure in "Radha" is danced as
self-pleasure (especially Radha's self-caressing) on the one hand asserts a
new self-empowerment for woman and on the other belongs to traditional structures of pornographic viewing.[70]

In any performance, the venue and the particularities of audience are
essential to the generation of meaning. Certainly the meanings activated
by the first performance, for spectators who had just watched boxing and
were soon to see trained monkeys, were somewhat different from those
generated by the same piece in a "respectable" theater, framed as "art."
Different still is the reception of "Radha" by our students today who
dutifully sit through St. Denis films in dance history seminars.

---

[69] For interesting discussions of related concerns, see Elinor Fuchs, "Staging the Ob-
scene," *Drama Review* 33, no. 1 (Spring 1989): 33–57; and Jill Dolan, *The Feminist
Spectator as Critic* (Ann Arbor: U.M.I. Research Press, 1988).

[70] For an analysis of the visual structures of pornographic viewing, see Annette
Kuhn, "Lawless Seeing," in her *The Power of the Image: Essays on Representation and
Sexuality* (Boston: Routledge & Kegan Paul, 1985), 19–47.

What the investigation of a piece like "Radha" can provide is an example of the necessity of unraveling the multiple strains of ideological meaning that are present in any work of performance and that are variously activated in specific viewing situations. For instance, similar doublings of race, exotica, and sexuality are played out in Josephine Baker's famous "banana dance." As a black woman, however, her construction as "exotic" never played as successfully in North America as in Europe.

As we reconsider the canon of dance history and integrate it with gender studies, it is not enough to ask how St. Denis conceived of her work, or how it relates to the dance history that precedes and follows it. Nor it is enough to ask how St. Denis's work reflected the changing roles of women in her day, or to note stylistic similarities between dance and other types of artistic products in the same historical period. All of these investigations produce valuable information and should not be ignored. But as scholars we must also look more deeply at the mechanisms of meaning on which the performance hinges and investigate the role of live display of the female body in activating those mechanisms, as I have attempted to do in this article. Only by more fully comprehending the production of ideology in every sphere of social construction, including the female body in performance, can we begin to sever the invisible links that bind racism, sexism, and cultural imperialism so tightly together.

Institute of the Arts, and Dance Program
Duke University

Poetry as a Strategy of Power:
The Case of Riffian Berber Women

Terri Brint Joseph

Although anthropological studies of the Middle East generally acknowledge the low status of Islamic women, the complex "mosaic" of national, ethnic, and tribal social organization makes it difficult to make accurate, significant statements about the area as a whole. Even when focused on a single country, anthropological accounts arrive at conflicting conclusions about the role of women. Ethnographers of Morocco like Westermarck, Coon, Hart, and Gellner have concentrated on the exercise of formal, public power and thus have stressed the hegemony of men over women.[1] This notion of monolithic masculine dominance and feminine subjugation has been somewhat modified by recent studies of women's ability to influence male decisions, a "power behind the throne" theory articulated by Roger Joseph.[2] Maher and Nelson have also argued that women wield some direct power through female systems of network and alliance. And

The data on which this study is based were collected during eighteen months of fieldwork in 1965–66 in the Rif Mountains of Morocco. The author wishes to thank the Berbers for their patience, interest, and hospitality; Roger Joseph for his unstinting intellectual rigor and assistance; and Cheryl and David Evans, Katherine Frank Clark, Donald Heiney, James McMichael, John C. Rowe, Maria Ruegg, Barbara Herrnstein Smith, Diane Wakoski, and the anonymous reviewers of *Signs: Journal of Women in Culture and Society* for their comments and encouragement. Portions of this essay were delivered orally at the California Folklore Society (1974, 1976) and the Modern Language Association (1977).

1. Edward Westermarck, *Marriage Ceremonies in Morocco* (London: Macmillan & Co., 1906); Carleton Stevens Coon, *Tribes of the Rif* (1931; reprint ed., New York: Kraus Reprint Co., 1970); David Montgomery Hart, *The Aith Waryaghar of the Moroccan Rif: An Ethnography and History* (Tucson: University of Arizona Press, 1976); and "The Land and the People" and "Social Organization," in *Morocco: Subcontractor's Monograph HRAF-62* (New Haven, Conn.: Human Relations Area Files, Inc., n.d.); Ernest Gellner, "Introduction" and "Political and Religious Organization of the Berbers of the Central High Atlas," in *Arabs and Berbers*, ed. Ernest Gellner and Charles Micaud (London: Trinity Press, 1973).
2. Roger Joseph, "Sexual Dialects and Strategy in Berber Marriage," *Journal of Comparative Family Studies* 7 (1976): 471–81.

[*Signs: Journal of Women in Culture and Society* 1980, vol. 5, no. 3]

from a different perspective Mernissi has insisted that, with the exception of a few influential men, Moroccan males are as powerless and dispossessed as Moroccan females.[3] This variety of contradictory views makes it all the more important to engage in very specific studies that can help us ascertain the status and relative power of women in Islamic societies. The present study focuses on a delineated area—the Rif Mountains of northern Morocco—a particular people—the Riffian Berbers of the Beni-Waryaghar and Ibbucoya tribes—and a single question—the role played by the songs which Berber women compose for and then perform at wedding ceremonies. It attempts to analyze how women express themselves in a public arena *within* the formal, institutionalized structure of *male society*, rather than a female network system for covert influence. It explores the degree to which songs constitute strategic devices, weapons which can help women have a voice in the community and gain control over their lives.

Social Structure and Economy of the Berbers

The Berbers, speaking dialects of the Hamitic and unwritten language whose name they bear, form an ethnic and linguistic group within the larger Arabic culture of Morocco. The indigenous inhabitants of the country, they were gradually converted to Islam between the seventh and eleventh centuries A.D. by Arab missionaries and invaders. Today they are centered in the Atlas and Riffian Mountain ranges; the latter runs south of the Mediterranean coastal plain from Tangier to Melilla, in the northern section of the country. The Beni Waryaghar and Ibbucoya, the central Riffian tribes studied for this essay, live in the Al-Hoceima Province, once held under the Spanish Protectorate but a part of the Moroccan regime since the country gained independence from Spain and France in 1956.

In a country noted for its poverty, the Rif is one of the poorest sections. Its comparatively mild climate is offset by deforestation and soil erosion on the slopes. The Central Rif has only two major rivers, the Nekkor and the Rhis, as its water supply, and its essential crops of barley and maize are dependent on rainfall. Since the Rif is subject to years of drought alternating with flash floods, its food supply is uncertain and, even in good years, can only support a limited number of people. Overpopulation which has been a recurrent problem, was controlled in the

3. Vanessa Maher, *Woman and Property in Morocco: Their Changing Relation to the Process of Social Stratification in Middle Atlas* (London: Cambridge University Press, 1974); Cynthia Nelson, "Public and Private Politics: Women in the Middle Eastern World," *American Ethnologist* 1, no. 1 (1974): 551–63; Fatima Mernissi, *Beyond the Veil: Male-Female Dynamics in a Modern Muslim Society* (New York: John Wiley & Sons, 1975). Mernissi's view has been challenged in a review by Daisy Dwyer in *Signs: Journal of Women in Culture and Society* 2, no. 2 (1976): 470–73.

pre-Protectorate days through the blood feud and since independence through large-scale emigration to the cities of Morocco, Algeria, and Europe. A settled, agricultural people, the Riffians work their steeply terraced land with hand tools, using oxen or cattle to plow only the flatter lands of the valleys. The meager crops are supplemented with vegetables grown in irrigated gardens near the rivers; nuts and fruits from orchards; and meat, cheese, and milk from the small herds of goats and sheep owned by more prosperous families. In spite of careful husbandry, malnutrition and disease are endemic in the Rif. To give but one index, at the time this field study was made the infant mortality rate, *within a week of birth,* was over 50 percent.

Women have only one access to the cash economy—the sale of eggs from their flocks of chickens and turkeys. Their days are an endless round of tasks connected with food preparation, child care, and home maintenance. Because the Riffians practice sexual segregation of women of childbearing age, these chores are associated with stages in the life cycle. From a very early age, a girl gathers firewood for her mother, assists in caring for younger children, and helps keep the house clean. As soon as she is old enough, she and her brothers take the flocks out to pasture every day, clean their pens in the household, and remove their droppings from the dirt floor. When strong enough, usually at adolescence, she gathers water from the nearest river or spring and carries it on her back in a jug which, when filled, weighs about thirty pounds. She also has increased child-care duties and plays a more responsible role in preparing meals. When she marries, a young woman will probably no longer work outside the home, unless the family cannot afford the luxury of losing some of her labor by segregating her.

Men in the Rif work in a seasonal pattern. During plowing and reaping periods, which are brief but intense, they labor for long hours in the fields. Much of their year, though, is leisurely and allows time for visiting, conversation, and forming political alliances. Women's tasks may be less intense but must be repeated on a daily basis and leave little time for relaxation; a woman is dependent socially on visits from relatives and women past menopause. Once a woman is no longer of childbearing age, her activities broaden again; meals may be prepared by her daughters-in-law, freeing her to visit neighbors and friends. Older women, especially if they are widows or have husbands who do not object to their appearing in public, may visit the women's markets and participate in religious sisterhoods.

The life of the Berber woman contrasts sharply with that of a relatively prosperous Arab woman in a Moroccan town. Whereas the townswoman will have at least one female servant and considerable leisure which she, veiled and in her *jaballa,* devotes to visiting the mosque, the baths, her friends and neighbors, her Riffian counterpart rarely has paid help within the home, goes unveiled, has a heavy share of household responsibilities, and may have a limited circle of associates. These differences are reflections of two polarities: town/country and Arabic/ Berber. One explanation for the differences between Berber and Arabic norms is that, until subjugated by European powers in the twentieth century, the Rif had always been *bled-es-siba*, land of dissidence, as opposed to *bled-al-mahkzen*, land of the regime or government. Because the Riffians lived in such an isolated and impenetrable area, they could refuse to pay tribute to the sultans of Morocco or serve in their armies and could practice their own way of life. They had minimal interference from the central government and limited contact with it.

The tribal organization of the Riffians is based formally on a lineage system which establishes specific rights and obligations in a reciprocal relationship with agnatic kin and a secondary set of obligations through the affinal bonds of marriage. This lineage system is considered normative by formalist Moroccanists like Westermarck and Coon, even though it ignores the alliance relationships with neighbors, friends, and associates which Berber men devote considerable time and energy to developing, and—what is more important—takes no account of the role of women in tribal life. In "Sexual Dialectics and Strategy in Berber Marriage," Roger Joseph has questioned the normative account of mate selection in the Rif which flatly states that fathers arrange marriages for their children and select their mates. Although this explanation would seem to be verified by the exclusive presence of males when the marriage contract is drawn up und the details of the dower or *sadak* recorded, Joseph has analyzed the specific behavior of both sexes and argued that the mothers of the bride and groom can exercize control over mate selection. In discussing the sexual dialectic between men and women of the Rif, Joseph characterizes the two models which have been used to study the Berbers as the "formalist" and the "interactionist." While formalists stress discrete kinship units within the segmentary lineage system that are closed and relatively stable, interactionists like Geertz focus on individuals negotiating in dyadic or face-to-face relationships which are subject to constant readjustments as each participant maneuvers for advantage and makes corresponding concessions. It is Joseph's contention that a study of both models reveals "an interplay between norms and acts"[4] that manifests the influence of women.

Joseph has emphasized the role of the mothers of the bride and groom, but not that of the potential brides and their attempts to affect the choice of their mates. It should be understood that in Berber society all able-bodied adults of both sexes are expected to conform to the Koranic injunction to marry; neither men nor women are allowed the option of remaining single. Within these limitations, however, young women are far more powerless than young men; indeed they are usually considered the most powerless members of society except for young children. It is, in fact, through their songs that females between the ages

4. Joseph, p. 471.

of thirteen and twenty try to compensate for their powerlessness; they attempt to seize the initiative in courtship and to usurp their fathers' public roles as the figures who choose spouses for their offspring.[5]

Form and Composition of the Songs

Extremely brief, the Berber song is made up of a single couplet. Each of the two lines is roughly twelve syllables long, although some contain only nine and others as many as fifteen. Each song is introduced by a traditional chorus which can be repeated as often as the singers wish:

> Ayah-rala boyah-ayah rala boya
> Ayah-rala boyah-ayah rala boya
> Ayah-ra (la) boyah etc.

Most Riffians interviewed for this study regard this chorus as a series of sounds with no meaning. They say it is used because "it is the custom." Several informants, however, reported that the initial *a* is a vocative like the English "oh"; *yah-rala* was said to be a form of *la la,* madame, or lady, in this case the bride's mother; and *boyah* a form of *baba,* father. One anthropological account has translated the refrain as "Oh look, oh look, look at the bride."[6]

Rather than use formulaic or set material such as Lord and Parry have identified in oral narratives,[7] Berber singers engage in self-conscious composition, scrutinizing their work and subjecting it to numerous revisions. Indeed, there seem to be no Berber girls who are unable to compose and perform original songs. Composing is not only a privilege but a responsibility. It is expected that each girl will be a poet just as it is expected that each woman will bake bread for her family. One Berber song uses the complaint, "I have no songs," as a metaphor to suggest that its singer is unattractive and that no one wants to marry her:[8]

5. Young men try to influence their fathers' decisions by threatening to divorce an unwanted bride. Divorce is extremely easy for a man—who needs only repeat to his wife three times that she is divorced—and almost impossible for a woman to obtain. She can, however, drive her husband to divorcing her by threatening to use witchcraft against him. Such a step is rarely taken, however, since her father would have to return to the groom's family a large portion of the wedding settlement, already spent on food for the guests, and would mean that she would lose custody of all her children once they had been weaned.

6. *Morocco: Subcontractors's Monograph HRAF-62,* p. 178.

7. Milman Parry, *The Making of Homeric Verse: The Collected Papers of Milman Parry,* ed. Adam Parry (London: Oxford University Press, 1971); Albert B. Lord, *The Singer of Tales* (Cambridge, Mass.: Harvard University Press, 1964).

8. All interpretations of the songs are based on native explications. Since they sometimes seemed far-fetched, I made it a practice to collect at least three interpretations from separate informants and found remarkable consistency in their understanding of the songs.

Madesrah wuware na-we thanen-awanu
Ra-la thasherethine agmathunt sufero
[I have no songs! I'm like a rock which has fallen in a well. . . .
Oh, my friend, catch the rock with a string.]

The complaint is used ironically in a song whose very composition dis-
proves the singer's lack of songs; in the second line, the poet asks a girl
friend to help her find a young man. Although some songs are better or
worse than others according to Berber notions of poetic value, all of the
women interviewed in the Rif during a period of eighteen months for
this study were able to compose songs.

Although the poems are short, it is not unusual for a young woman
to spend several months working on a few couplets, searching for the *mot
juste* as she readies her lyrics for the weddings which occur after the
harvest in late summer and early September. While going about her
daily tasks, she composes her songs by singing the lyrics softly or chant-
ing them under her breath, introducing changes by a process of conscious revision. If she replaces a word or a phrase in the lyrics, she can
usually give a good reason: the revision enhances the meaning or sounds
better with the other words in the song.

The Performance

Songs are performed at Berber weddings either in front of the
houses of the bride and groom or on a central patio located within the
walls of the house. The stage is a cleared area in front of an open fire,
around which the guests are seated or stand. The audience is comprised
of men of all ages, young women who are not yet married, older women
past the age of childbearing, and young children of both sexes. Young,
married women usually stay in the house itself, but they listen to the
songs and watch the performance through windows if they can. The
older women who stand behind the men in the audience, although they
do not sing, add to the performance by ululating (making a shrill sound
by trilling their tongues against the roof of their mouths) at various
dramatic moments during the singing. The men in the crowd, especially
the young bachelors, shout encouragement, cheer, and applaud
throughout the evening.

On the first day of the wedding, the performance begins at sunset
and lasts until dawn. It is then resumed on the second and third eve-
nings, and the girls try to present a variety of songs, even though they
sing several times each evening. They perform in groups of four, dressed
in their finest, floor-length gowns, and wearing dark glasses which render their faces mysterious in the flickering light of the fire.[9] Although

9. These dark glasses are obviously a recent innovation in the Rif. Although fire-
crackers are now used instead of gunplay to frighten evil spirits at the wedding, I was

these dark glasses are supposed to function as disguises, members of the audience have no difficulty in recognizing the singers, and, in fact, much of the point of their songs would be lost were the singers to remain anonymous. It may be, however, that the glasses, operating as a fictive mask, make it easier for the girls to step beyond the role ascribed to young women of the Rif; it is this violation of normal decorum and restraint which gives the songs their particular import and potential power.

Berber women in groups of four sing the "rala boyah" chorus in unison although each presents her own lyrics as a solo. Holding tambourines and small drums called *tabours,* the young women do a side-shuffle dance as they sing, keeping time with their hand instruments. After the chorus is completed, the first singer presents her song. If the audience likes it, the men will cheer and shout *yallah* to encourage the quartet as it breaks into another round of the chorus; the tempo quickens, and the side-shufflle gives way to the *shidhih,* in which the girls undulate, moving their hips, waists, and breasts in circular movements while the audience shouts more encouragement. After a few minutes of dancing, the tempo slows, the girls resume their side shuffle, the second girl sings her song, and so on, until each of the quartet has performed. The girls exit to a last chorus of "rala boyah" and are replaced by a new quartet.

During this performance, the girls clearly flaunt sexual energy, perform provocative dances, and, dressed in their most seductive finery, expose themselves to public scrutiny. For the songs serve the vital function of a rite of passage for these girls within the framework of a larger rite of passage, the wedding itself. While the bride and groom are being initiated to their new status as married adults, the girls who sing at the wedding, like debutantes in Western societies, are being "presented" to the community as young women who have come of age and can be scrutinized by the parents of prospective grooms as well as by the young bachelors themselves. While the bride and groom are formally ratifying their relationship, the girls performing are setting in motion a train of events which may determine their own weddings. The Berbers themselves, of course, are consciously aware of the wedding as the context for the songs, as one lyric specifically indicates:

Eh-ham rid gazar nunkor swatad er henne
Wo-men gabridan saad enesh ma tuniye.
[River Nekkor has risen, bringing tea and henna
When luck was divided among us, I alone was forgotten.]

---

unable to determine what, if any, custom the dark glasses have replaced. It seems unlikely that they replace an earlier use of the veil, since it is always regarded as an Arabic custom by the Berbers.

The singer associates a year of abundant rainfall ("River Nekkor has risen") with the prosperity necessary for many families to meet the expenses of weddings for their sons. The composer singles out for attention the sweet mint tea which is offered to the wedding guests, and henna, which is ritually applied to the bride and groom during the ceremonies of "The Big Henna" and "The Little Henna." In a year when all of her age mates are engaged or getting married, only the singer remains single.

The songs play their part in the very continuity of tribal society which requires marriage, the founding of families, and the rearing of children for its survival. While the adolescent girls sing, the girls who have not yet reached puberty try to memorize the songs of the performers, waiting expectantly for the day when they, too, will be allowed to sing. They are thus going through a socialization process, receiving informal training for their own future role as women.

Songs as Social Criticism

Over and beyond their sexual and social functions, the Berber songs essentially allow young women to address the entire community. The freedom to address the tribe *(tackbitch)* or community *(dchar)* as a whole, people of both sexes and all ages, is granted to any young woman who wishes to perform; it is, however, a privilege unique to young, single women. Married, divorced, or widowed women are not permitted to perform. Men, even the most powerful leaders, cannot address the entire community. Although they utilize tribal gatherings to speak to men of all ages, they can communicate with only those women who are members of their own family or are related to them by marriage. If they wish to reach other women of the tribe, males must use their mothers, wives, sisters, or daughters as emissaries.

The songs women perform at weddings are often explicitly critical of Berber life. The range of subjects for social critique is theoretically as broad as any singer's interests; the following song, for example, attacks not only native society but the countries of Europe that hire Berber labor, create new emigration patterns in tribal life, and contribute to social upheavals:

> Afer runil ekanit Nesar hend g-kesan
> Ay! *Alemania!* nefishan emsan.
> [A piece of packing cord has sullied a water glass. . . .
> Oh, Germany! You have given illusions to beggars!]

In this song, the drinking glass, a fragile, expensive item which must be imported to the Rif, represents Germany and other European countries which send representatives to Morocco to recruit Berbers to work in their factories. The singer describes the glass as being cheapened and dirtied by a piece of packing cord, a metaphor for those Berber men, usually of poor families and low social standing in the Rif, who sign contracts and go to Europe to work. By living inexpensively abroad, these men amass what the Berbers consider a fortune, which they often use, upon their return, to buy land and to try to marry girls of proud lineage. These young men are regarded with a mixture of contempt and respect by the settled Berber community. The girl who composed this song is voicing a criticism shared by the larger Berber community when she claims that the boys are still "beggars" and their hopes of entering Berber society an "illusion." Yet emigration is a powerful mechanism in the Rif and allows young men to have greater control over their choice of spouses. With the cash accumulated abroad a young man can threaten to arrange—and pay for—his own wedding should his father be too insistent about a potential bride who is not his own choice.[10] Two other songs by Berber women attack the *Makhzen* or Moroccan government. These songs date from the time when the government pressed impoverished tribesmen into service to construct the road that cuts through the Rif from Tetuan to Mellilla. In the first the government comes under fire for paying its workers so little that they are unable to buy the head scarves for their wives that Berber decency requires; in the second, for forcing Berber men into labor that takes them far from their homes:

E-hudem abred e-hudmen opeyuz
Themrarin incid quren suz-uzh.
[The workers who labor with picks on the road!
Their women must wander bareheaded.]

A-breth n-tumobil hudminth a breth-n-kum
Uk-seer thetwon the-bre-then red-n-hum.
[The highway? The workers must make their own road.
The women of Tetuan aren't theirs and cannot be seen through their
    veils.]

The first song contrasts a Berber custom, the wearing of a head scarf by girls and women, with the Arabic custom, referred to in the second, of veiling the face. Although rural Berber women tend to go unveiled, some who have moved to towns like Al-hoceima have adopted the custom in imitation of Arabic women.

In a modern song that criticizes the government for levying an admission price at a local beach in the town of Al-hoceima, the phenomenon of tourism itself is scrutinized:

10. For a more detailed discussion of immigration and its impact on the Rif, see David Hart's *Aith Waryaghar*, pp. 93–95.

Shebab n-Al-hoceima hisrah su sekn
Kenu alemanan hezrah tibe serkun
[The young boys of Al-hoceima dive from the shining cliffs
You, the Germans, sprawl on the blazing sand.]

When the Playa Quemada beach was taken over in 1966 for the use of two government hotels and a fee of one dirham was charged for admission to what had once been a public beach, the Berbers felt the fee was aimed at discouraging them from using the beach. Rather than pay admission, the Berber men perform the dangerous feat of diving from the cliffs above the beach while the tourists lie on the sand below, acquiring the suntans the Berbers, with their liking for fair skin, consider unattractive. The song's social criticism is aimed at the invading tourists and the *makhzen* for forcing the Berbers to pay to use their own beach. Although the song was composed by a young woman who lived in Al-hoceima, it was taken up by the rural girls who had some contact with the town, and it became popular in the countryside, even though inlanders had little personal interest in tourists nor a stake in using the Playa Quemada beach. Several informants explained its appeal in the tribal area by saying that the new admission price was similar to the government's infringements on other aspects of Berber life since Morocco's independence.

The Love Songs

The woman who performs her songs at a wedding uses them not only as social criticism but as strategies to defend herself, attack others, encourage suitors, announce an engagement, remind young men of the tribe that she is in love, shame or ridicule an unwanted swain, or justify her decision to break an engagement. Even the most ordinary love song represents a form of social criticism since it implicitly attacks three powerful stereotypes often expressed by Berber men: (1) women, especially young girls, are too foolish or uninformed to hold strong opinions about something as important as the choice of a mate; (2) they are merely pawns in the male game of strengthening past affinal relationships or establishing new ones through marriage; (3) unmarried girls, segregated from contact with nonrelated males, have no opportunity to develop positive or negative feelings toward any particular young man. Yet men not only accept these songs, they like them, memorizing their favorites to quote or chant in conversation.

Some of the most interesting and problematic songs of the Rif are addressed to young men who have already entered into successful negotiations with the composer's father. Since these negotiations will lead to marriage, the singer, if she does not care for him, must discourage

the young man so thoroughly in her lyrics that he will voluntarily with-
draw his offer:

A thsib-banah-tasebnath: astsah ho fades
Jemah sucarinik-nish d shik udentes
[I am going to wash my fringed head scarf; I shall hang it on the *fades*
  bush:
Take your sugar away! You and I aren't good together.]

In this song, the singer places in explicit opposition the formal negotiations of the masculine world and her own, informal system for getting
what she wants. The reference to sugar is an economical way of saying:
"You came to my house and asked my father for my hand; he has
encouraged you, accepting your proposal, but I don't want to marry
you." In Berber society sugar is considered the most expressive symbol
of the affection which unites an engaged or married couple. It is also
used as a signal between the boy and the girl's father to open or close
negotiations for a wedding. On the occasion of his first visit to the girl's
home, the young man (or his representative) will present her father with
five or six hard cones of tightly packed sugar. If the father is amenable to
the idea of accepting the young man as a son-in-law, he will strike a cone
with a hammer and break the sugar into lumps which will be used to
sweeten the mint tea that he will share with the young man. If the father
does not wish to encourage the young man, he will either return the
cones or ostentatiously use household sugar in preparing the tea. With
nothing overt having been said by either party, the young man has
declared his intentions, and the girl's father has indicated his willingness
or reluctance to open formal negotiations.

Moreover, by washing her head scarf, the composer of the song is
metaphorically washing her hands of her lover. This cleansing is an act
of purification as well; she will become a new woman who has broken
with the past. The *thasebneth*, which is made of brightly colored and
patterned silk with a long, soft fringe, is considered the most beautiful
head scarf worn by Berber women and is worn only on special occasions
when a woman wishes to be particularly attractive. The poet's use of the
fades (pistacia lentiscus) intensifies the cleansing imagery of the lyric, since
ashes from the *fades* bush are used by Berbers to make soap. By hanging
her head scarf to dry in a conspicuous location outside the home, the girl
is not only rejecting her suitor but making a public declaration of the
rupture and of her own freedom to consider other offers of marriage.
There is also, of course, a veiled threat to use the newly washed scarf for
flirtatious purposes.

The audience listening to this song would know what particular
young man was seeking the singer in marriage, even though no names
are mentioned in the lyric. It is unlikely that a suitor subjected to a

rejection witnessed by the entire community would continue to press for marriage. Of course, the composer takes the risk that the young man will persist, that the negotiations will go through, and that she will find herself married to the butt of her song. It is only because the songs are trusted to be generally effective that a young woman can afford to gamble, wagering her desire to extricate herself from an unwanted match against the unpleasant possibility of finding herself married to a man she has spurned in public.

Berber poets exercise considerable license in their songs, in sharp contrast to the normal decorum and modesty required of a young Berber virgin. In the following song, a young woman abuses a suitor with impunity, something which she would never do to his face.

> Math zwed *el vino* nhara methumnat
> Math zwed *el vino* math kul bid tazeyat?
> [Did you drink wine today or yesterday?
> Did you drink wine glass by glass or the whole bottle at once?]

The singer is saying that the boy must have been drunk and, by extension, out of his mind, to have asked for her hand; he was as drunk as if he had consumed an entire bottle of wine before setting out to make arrangements with her father. Since the drinking of wine is expressly forbidden by the Koran, an injunction which rural Berbers take seriously, the singer's accusation would be an embarrassment both to the boy and to his family. It is doubtful if the young man, after this verbal face slapping, would pursue any further his plans to marry the girl.

Whatever the verbal license of the singers, the victims of their lyrics are expected to suffer in dignified silence. At a wedding which took place on the Bulma Peak in the Rif Moutains in the summer of 1966, a young man became so incensed about a song which he considered insulting that he and a group of his friends began throwing stones at the singer. The adult males in the audience quickly intervened, the boys were forcibly ejected from the compound, and the evening continued without further incident. Most of the wedding guests were shocked by the boys' behavior and observed that however insulting a girl's song might seem to any given young man she has a right to sing it. This freedom to overstep the boundary of ordinary Riffian courtesy is one of the most powerful weapons which songs give Berber women.

Many of the Berber lyrics are efforts at self-justification or defense. In one song the composer, accused of a sexual transgression, defends her own life:

> Nanis eguma wutchma anrret a-hisen
> anri ahzezbo huma urensen.
> [The boys have challenged my brother, "It would be better

to kill that wanton your sister!"
Then let them kill me to silence their lying tongues!]

A group of young men, probably disgruntled suitors, accuses the singer of sexual immorality. So serious is this allegation in the Rif that the brother would be within his rights if he defended the family honor and killed the girl. In the song, the poet shows her brother believes in her innocence, and, by openly confronting unpleasant gossip, she transforms a dangerous situation into an opportunity to defend her reputation. Only by exposing the problem to the whole community is she able to combat her accusers and maintain her good name. In another song of defense, the poet uses the public forum of the wedding to appease a fiancé who has broken their engagement because she admired the young men of Al-hoceima on a visit to the town:

> Themdenth n-Alhoceima arras wah ebaden
> Thene esother a-lefeno zugen.
> [The city of Al-hoceima with its strong walls!
> It was there I fell from the esteem of my darling.]

The poet admits that her head was turned by the "strong walls" or attractive young men of the town, but this public confession serves to minimize her misdemeanor. In fact, upon hearing the girl sing this song at a wedding, the fiancé decided that he had been too harsh and their marriage took place within a month. The songs are a recognized channel for redressing wrongs and for allowing the young women of the tribe to speak in their own defense. One lyric specifically mentions this function:

> Suneth ezranino ashar riz-bubenik
> Mirme gar thar-ruth wuh ah-wuth u wa sherenik
> [Fill your ears and your heart with my songs!
> Tell my denouncer he lied!]

Like occidental love poetry, Berber lyrics are often songs of celebration, lamentation, and seduction. One typical love song is written as a dialogue, in which the fiancé poses a question in the first line which the composer answers in the second:

> Eni mi shem rahgah a yah denub
> Donue gui a lefino mani tigguth i-kultub
> [He asked me, "Where shall I put you, my poor little one?"
> Put me, my darling, where you put your book.]

The singer asks her lover to place her in his hip pocket, where he carries his book, so that she can be with him all the time. *Denub*, "poor little thing," is a word that is usually used for young children and is a term of affection when applied to an adult. The other endearment in the song, *lefino,* is the first-person singular possessive of the noun *lef,* the word that signifies the trusted allies who laid down their lives for a man in the days of the blood feud; it is the strongest word for "beloved" or "darling" in the Rif and has no literal equivalent in English. In a representative example of a lament, the singer voices her loneliness for a fiancé who has gone to Europe to work in a factory:

> Lefino e-sahwar ge-fotographia
> Ah-we or-resewer afefraz-a-nita
> [His face in the window of the photographer's shop
> The portrait can't speak, but how it resembles my darling!]

Such a song, with its reference to her fiancé's passport photograph on display in the window of the photographic shop in Al-hoceima, allows her also to remind other young men that she is engaged and is waiting for her young man to return.

Songs of seduction sung at weddings must veil their eroticism in order to be performed in public.[11] According to a Berber male informant, the following lyric is "the song most in love of any," or it is as explicitly erotic as any song which can be sung before an audience:

> Ath-sarsh temese hokahmom owahnu
> Athadosun waman athaso lefeno athesu.
> [I shall lower a candle at the mouth of the well.
> If the water rushes upwards, my lover will drink.]

The song begins with the commonplace activity of fetching water at the well, but moves into the realm of the extraordinary as the water under-

---

11. Songs which are too blatantly sexual for the wedding ceremony are reserved for private encounters between the composer and her man. The following lyrics are two cases in point:

> Arge we-u-fen thakamun a tereyuk
> Ager wuht unbtho atere fath-e-nuk
> [God, if you can find him, send me a breakfast of his kisses
> When the flowers bloom great thirst slays.]

> Wala mathak-e-nir menrarer thuggwazen
> Ebasheno thetfah mazwa thatubsen
> [By God I swear I shall not tell all that I hide beneath my gown:
> Breasts hard and round as apples and under them, a bowl.]

A Berber bride is supposed to be a virgin at marriage, and the cloth stained with her hymenal blood is exhibited to the guests at the wedding. But if the groom has been the girl's lover, his mother will often kill a chicken and use its blood for the cloth to prevent scandal. Should his wife not be a virgin, the groom has the option of sending her back to her father's house in disgrace and reclaiming his *sadat;* but if he likes her and she can put her sexual experience with another man in a sympathetic light, he will often keep her nonetheless.

goes a miraculous transformation and becomes a fountain. The reference to a candle, which suggests that it is night rather than day, implies a tryst at the well. Even more, many Berbers claim that this lyric contains an explicitly sexual metaphor: The well symbolizes the girl's vagina, the candle the boy's penis, the flame their sexual passion, and the act of drinking that of sexual intercourse. Since the lyric can be read more literally, however, it falls within the Berber concept of propriety and can be performed without causing offense.

The Songs and the Reality of Women's Lives

Although Riffians make a conscientious effort to keep adolescent boys and girls apart as part of the ideology of sexual segregation, the songs reveal that unmarried boys and girls spend enough time in each other's company to form attachments and antipathies. Since both sexes have tasks to perform which take them outside the home, parental supervision is necessarily limited. Unmarried boys make it a habit to appear at the well, river, or spring when the girls arrive to fetch water. A boy who is struck by the appearance or manner of one of the young women will accompany her part of the way to her house, staying several feet behind her; this pretense at social distance enables young people to insist that they are not together if challenged by adults. If the boy likes the girl he will begin to linger along the path just out of sight of her home in order to follow her to the well or as she goes about her errands. A few words will be exchanged, and if the girl is friendly they will walk abreast of each other when no one is in sight and perhaps disappear into a grove of olive trees to converse privately. Such encounters are "dates" in Riffian society and help young people conduct courtships and make decisions about whom they wish to marry. Despite these social patterns which have existed for at least several generations, adults, especially parents discussing their children, assume that little or no communication takes place between adolescent boys and girls. Adults maintain this social blindness because the society tries to uphold sexual segregation and clings to a formal model in which the fathers of the bride and groom arrange the marriage of their offspring. And these partial fictions are maintained in the face of the evidence from the song lyrics, heard at ten or fifteen weddings a year, which are presented and understood as true statements, not as imaginative constructs.

Although the Berbers pay lip service to a formal model in which the father of the bride arranges her marriage without consulting her wishes, the songs reveal a different world in which the bride accepts or rejects various suitors on the basis of their attractiveness to her; her father, if he appears in the lyrics at all, is a shadowy figure who simply carries out the wishes of his strong-willed daughter. One possible reason why Berber girls are allowed to expose social fictions and to challenge certain aspects of their patriarchal society may be that the performance of songs occurs during a rite of passage, what Victor Turner in *The Ritual Process* has called a marginal or liminal event (from *limen,* "threshold" in Latin), in which the participants are on a threshold between two social categories and are ambiguous figures who are not fully members of either.[12] This liminality also extends to the guests at the wedding, whose own status groups are being changed by the marriage. The parents and families of the bride and groom are bidding farewell to their offspring as children and, like the elders of the community, must accept them henceforth as married adults; and the adolescent friends, the age mates of the bride and groom, must adapt themselves to the change in the couple's social role. Within the liminal event, *reversal* of social categories and *inversion,* in which the high exchange places with the low, seem to be consistent features. The Berber wedding shows a paradigm of reversal in power relationships: unmarried girls, who are less powerful in ordinary Berber life than any group except'small children, suddenly become figures of authority who are allowed to address all the members of their society and to use their creativity to achieve their own ends. The powerful father of a singer (and with him, all the adult males who expect to oversee the marriages of their children) is reduced to being a passive member of the audience while his daughter is the center of attention, singing words which her audience not only carefully listens to but often actually memorizes, as she comments boldly on the attractions and weaknesses of various young men in the crowd. The girl's performance, then, allows her to play "queen for a day," but because her usurpation of power takes place within the formal structure of the marriage rites she is expected to resume her docile, obedient demeanor after the wedding, and not attempt to exercise authority until the next time she performs in public. The irony of this expectation is that the girl seizes the moment of her performance to encourage relationships which will continue after the wedding or to permanently dismiss an unwanted suitor. Her songs can have far-reaching consequences and affect the shape of her life long after the wedding is over.

The Berbers recognize that the songs are critiques of their existing mores, but when asked why such songs are allowed to be performed in public they reply in amazement that a wedding would not be a wedding without the songs, that Berber women have always sung at weddings. The more thoughtful suspect that it would be unfair to force a woman into an unwanted marriage without giving her a chance to prevent it through her lyrics. In fact, apart from the songs, a woman has no way of discouraging an unwanted or hated fiancé except by threatening or at-

12. Victor Turner, *The Ritual Process: Structure and Anti-Structure* (Chicago: Aldine Press, 1969).

tempting suicide. However, the songs may also be perceived as a mechanism which, while giving women the impression of gaining power, ultimately supports the patriarchal system, for in spite of the rebelliousness of many of the lyrics the act of performance itself is also a mode of participation in a "marriage market," a display of wit, talent, and attractiveness to an audience that includes potential mates. Whatever the specific content of any given lyric, the singers never attack the institution of marriage itself in their songs. Their aim is to discourage unwanted suitors and to ensure engagement to their preferred young men. Notwithstanding the difficulties of determining their exact revolutionary force, the Berber songs expose the problems and deficiencies inherent in traditional views of male-female relationships in the Middle East and to the need for further, more intensive studies.

Department of English and Comparative Literature
University of California, Irvine

Womanism: The Dynamics of the Contemporary Black Female Novel in English

Chikwenye Okonjo Ogunyemi

> We are not white. We are not Europeans. We are black
> like the Africans themselves. . . . We and the Africans will
> be working for a common goal: the uplift of black people
> everywhere. [ALICE WALKER, *The Color Purple*]

What does a black woman novelist go through as she comes in contact with white feminist writing and realizes that Shakespeare's illustrious sisters belong to the second sex, a situation that has turned them into impotent eunuchs without rooms of their own in which to read and write their very own literature, so that they have become madwomen, now emerging from the attic, determined to fight for their rights by engaging in the acrimonious politics of sex? Does she precipitately enter the lists with them against Euro-American patriarchy and, in their victory, further jeopardize the chances of her race in the sharing of political, social, and economic power? Does she imitate their war effort and throw the gauntlet down to challenge black patriarchy? Does she fight the sexual war some of the time and the racial war at other times? Does she remain indifferent to the outer sex war and, maintaining a truce in the black sexual power tussle, fight only the race war?

Many black female novelists writing in English have understandably not allied themselves with radical white feminists; rather, they have explored the gamut of other positions and produced an exciting, fluid

[*Signs: Journal of Women in Culture and Society* 1985, vol. 11, no. 1]

corpus that defies rigid categorization. More often than not, where a white woman writer may be a feminist, a black woman writer is likely to be a "womanist." That is, she will recognize that, along with her consciousness of sexual issues, she must incorporate racial, cultural, national, economic, and political considerations into her philosophy.

It is important to establish why many black women novelists are not feminists in the way that their white counterparts are and what the differences are between them. African and Afro-American women writers share similar aesthetic attitudes in spite of factors that separate them. As a group, they are distinct from white feminists because of their race, because they have experienced the past and present subjugation of the black population along with present-day subtle (or not so subtle) control exercised over them by the alien, Western culture. These extraliterary determinants have helped to make the black female novel in English what it is today and partly account for the conflict between white and black women over strategies and priorities in sexual politics. To illustrate the black womanist aesthetic, I will cite many novels by black women in both African and Afro-American literatures without going into detailed analysis of them; my intention is to establish that womanism is widespread and to pinpoint the factors that bind black female novelists together under this distinct praxis. On the African side I will refer to Bessie Head's *When Rain Clouds Gather, Maru,* and *A Question of Power* (South Africa); Flora Nwapa's *Idu* and *One Is Enough* (Nigeria); Ama Ata Aidoo's *Our Sister Killjoy* (Ghana); and Mariama Bâ's *So Long a Letter* (Senegal). On the Afro-American side my references turn primarily on Margaret Walker's *Jubilee*; Paule Marshall's *The Chosen Place, the Timeless People* and *Praisesong for the Widow*; Toni Morrison's *The Bluest Eye* and *Song of Solomon*; and Alice Walker's *The Third Life of Grange Copeland* and *The Color Purple.*

* * *

Since the feminist novel is still evolving, the following descriptive statements are tentative and hypothetical but serve as a working base: the feminist novel is a form of protest literature directed to both men and women. Protesting against sexism and the patriarchal power structure, it is unapologetically propagandist or strident or both. It demands that its readers, whether the male oppressors or the female oppressed, be aware of ideological issues in order that it may change their attitudes about patriarchy. For a novel to be identified as feminist, therefore, it must not just deal with women and women's issues but should also posit some aspects of a feminist ideology.[1] A reader can expect to find in it some

1. Ama Ata Aidoo dismisses the assumption that all material dealing with women is necessarily feminist: "I am not a feminist because I write about women. Are men writers

combination of the following themes: a critical perception of and reaction to patriarchy, often articulated through the struggle of a victim or rebel who must face a patriarchal institution; sensitivity to the inequities of sexism allied with an acceptance of women and understanding of the choices open to them; a metamorphosis leading to female victory in a feminist utopia, or a stasis, signifying the failure to eliminate sexism; a style spiced with the acrimony of feminist discourse. As with recipes, so with works of art; results are variable. Womanist novels, while they too may possess these characteristics to a greater or lesser degree, lay stress on other distinctive features to leave an impression markedly different from that of feminist works. This divergence, I think, necessitates the separate classification I have given to black female novels.

Consider *Jane Eyre*, a complex and far-reaching novel that Sandra Gilbert and Susan Gubar, in their scintillating analysis, identify as part of the feminist tradition.[2] The feminist character of the novel is apparent in the portrait of Jane as a rebel against patriarchal institutions, represented by such domineering male figures as the Reverend Brocklehurst, Edward Rochester, and St. John Rivers. For the white feminist reader the novel's ending is a positive one: Jane triumphs through achieving acknowledged equality with her husband, Rochester.

For the discerning black reader, however, *Jane Eyre* is not just a feminist novel, but a disarmingly realistic appraisal of white survival ethics. David Cecil in his *Early Victorian Novelists* saw in the Heathcliff–Edgar Linton clash in Emily Brontë's *Wuthering Heights* an economic (and, I might add, a racial) dimension, an interpretation that can be extended to the Bertha-Rochester relationship. The indomitable West Indian mulatto, Bertha Rochester, exploited for her sexual attractiveness and wealth, is locked up because the patriarchal Rochester says she is mad.[3] Rochester,

---

male chauvinist pigs just because they write about men? Or is a writer an African nationalist just by writing about Africans? . . . Obviously not . . . no writer, female or male, is a feminist just by writing about women. Unless a particular writer commits his or her energies, actively, to exposing the sexist tragedy of women's history; protesting the ongoing degradation of women; celebrating their physical and intellectual capabilities, and above all, unfolding a revolutionary vision of the role [of women]," he or she cannot be pronounced a feminist. "Unwelcome Pals and Decorative Slaves—or Glimpses of Women as Writers and Characters in Contemporary African Literature," in *Medium and Message: Proceedings of the International Conference on African Literature and the English Language* (Calabar, Nigeria: University of Calabar, 1981), 1:17–37, esp. 33.

2. Sandra M. Gilbert and Susan Gubar, *The Madwoman in the Attic: The Woman Writer and the Nineteenth-Century Imagination* (New Haven, Conn.: Yale University Press, 1979), pp. 338 ff.

3. David Cecil, *Early Victorian Novelists* (London: Constable & Son, 1935); cf. Jean Rhys, *Wide Sargasso Sea* (New York: W. W. Norton & Co., 1967). In this fictional interpretation of *Jane Eyre*, Rhys presents Mrs. Rochester as a Creole. See also Elaine Showalter, *A Literature of Their Own: British Women Novelists from Brontë to Lessing* (London: Virago Ltd., 1978), p. 124.

as is typical of exploitative white masters, likes her wealth and her sexual possibilities but dislikes the tint of her skin, the color that, among other factors, made her vulnerable to him in the first place. He casts her aside,[4] has affairs, and attempts to marry a white woman as if the black one has metamorphosed into an invisible woman; for the "mad" Bertha, it is a catch-22 situation. She therefore fights for survival. She wreaks vengeance on the polygynously inclined Rochester and his female accomplice, "virtuous, plain Jane," who should know better than to supplant another female to secure a husband. Bertha burns down Thornfield, the white patriarchal edifice, to the chagrin of the white man and woman. To right the inequities of patriarchy, from the black viewpoint, the white woman must accept a more lowly situation in life, having as mate a man in reduced circumstances, with whom she is equal. So far, so good. However when Brontë allows Bertha, betrayed on all sides by white women— Adele's mother; her guard, Grace Poole; and her rivals for Rochester's love, especially Jane—to die as the patriarchy collapses, she creates a tragic vision of feminism for a black reader. Such an ending makes the novel ambivalent; or is it, perhaps, that the feminist utopia is for white women only? For black women who would be feminists the lesson is simple: in fighting the establishment, the black woman must not be so mad as to destroy herself with the patriarchy. The fact that this lesson has been learned by many black women novelists partly explains their lack of enthusiasm for feminism's implied endorsement of total white control. Hence their womanist stance.

The works of Nigeria's Buchi Emecheta, who has been living in exile in England for almost twenty years and started to write after a marital fiasco, are something of an exception. Emecheta's two autobiographical novels, *In the Ditch* (1972) and *Second-Class Citizen* (1974), are deeply grounded in the British and Irish feminism in which she was nurtured. Adah, Emecheta's alter ego in these novels, is rebellious. Unlike Bertha Mason—a predecessor of Adah's insofar as they are both black women alone in a white society—she successfully fights patriarchy, experienced as the British welfare state (*In the Ditch*). She also triumphs over her Nigerian husband, Francis (*Second-Class Citizen*), bestial in his sexuality and economic irresponsibility, even though he is backed by a long Nigerian patriarchal tradition. In England, Adah transcends the female predicament by obtaining a divorce (which would be frowned on in Nigeria), and she also copes with the burden of caring for five children in a hostile environment.

Following the tradition of feminists, Emecheta, in her later nonautobiographical works whose titles suggest their feminist slant—*The Bride*

---

4. Kate Millett (*Sexual Politics* [London: Sphere Books, 1972], p. 39) asserts that black men are more ready to stand by their white women than white men are prepared to protect their black women.

Price (1976), *The Slave Girl* (1977), *The Joys of Motherhood* (1979), *Double Yoke* (1982)—tends to feminize the black male, making him weak, flabby, and unsuccessful. This disquieting tendency also calls into question Emecheta's opinion about women. She presents the black male as the "other," a ridiculous "object," to borrow Simone de Beauvoir's apt vocabulary. He is destined to be "killed" by Emecheta but is incongruously resurrected, perhaps in the author's last-minute bid to remain faithful to Nigerian patriarchal reality. Her heroines are mostly strong characters who struggle against patriarchy only to die in childbirth, become enslaved in marriage, or die insane, abandoned by the children they nurtured. Emecheta's destruction of her heroines is a feminist trait that can be partly attributed to narcissism on the part of the writer.[5] The African feminist writer's position is complicated by the fact that her work sometimes lacks authenticity, since the traditional African woman she uses as protagonist is, in reality, beset by problems of survival and so is hardly aware of her sexist predicament; the feminist desire to present her as rebellious can, in the context of this reality, be merely ludicrous.

If the feminist literary movement desires the illumination of female experience in order to alter the status quo for the benefit of women,[6] the African woman writer's dilemma in a feminist context becomes immediately apparent. Black women are disadvantaged in several ways: as blacks they, with their men, are victims of a white patriarchal culture; as women they are victimized by black men; and as black women they are also victimized on racial, sexual, and class grounds by white men. In order to cope, Emecheta largely ignores such complexities and deals mainly with the black woman as victim of black patriarchy. This preoccupation is atypical of black women writers, though Emecheta's indefatigable zeal for black feminism could become catching.

* * *

Interviewed during the feminist book fair in London in June 1984, the white South African journalist Beata Lipman was forthright about the state of women's writing in South Africa. According to her, "Racism is a more urgent matter than sexism,"[7] a statement that can be extended to many Third World areas if we substitute hunger, poverty, or backwardness for "racism." Much as she downplays her power, the white woman

5. Compare Myra Jehlen, "Archimedes and the Paradox of Feminist Criticism," *Signs: Journal of Women in Culture and Society* 6, no. 4 (Summer 1981): 575–601, esp. 598.

6. Cheri Register, "Literary Criticism," *Signs: Journal of Women in Culture and Society* 6, no. 2 (Winter 1980): 268–82, esp. 269.

7. "The Feminist Book Fair," *West Africa* (June 18, 1984), p. 1263. The East African writer Grace Ogot considers other dimensions, such as "economic struggle" and the generation gap; see Oladele Taiwo, *Female Novelists of Modern Africa* (London: Macmillan Publishers, 1984), p. 162.

has an authority that the black man or woman does not have. Moreover, while the white woman writer protests against sexism, the black woman writer must deal with it as one among many evils; she battles also with the dehumanization resulting from racism and poverty. What, after all, is the value of sexual equality in a ghetto? Black women writers are not limited to issues defined by their femaleness but attempt to tackle questions raised by their humanity. Thus the womanist vision is racially conscious in its underscoring of the positive aspects of black life. The politics of the womanist is unique in its racial-sexual ramifications; it is more complex than white sexual politics, for it addresses more directly the ultimate question relating to power:[8] how do we share equitably the world's wealth and concomitant power among the races and between the sexes?

White feminists consistently compare the situation of white women with that of "slaves," "colonials," the "black minority," "serfs in a feudal system," the "Dark Continent."[9] Since these are demeaning positions to which black people have been assigned and which they still hold in many parts of the world, such comparisons alienate black readers because they underscore yet trivialize black subordination. Indeed, the white feminist stance arouses black suspicion that whites will further suppress blacks to make provision for a female victory in the white, sexual, political game. The black woman writer, therefore, whether in Africa or somewhere in the diaspora, tends to believe that white feminism is yet another ploy, perhaps unintentional, against her and hers. The common black heritage of subjugation by whites, both directly and by the introjection of white values and mores, has determined the nature of modern black life, which S. E. Ogude rightly recognizes as a living tradition of suffering and humiliation.[10] To generate public awareness and understanding of this central fact through the writing of stories that are tellingly appropriate and instructive is the black woman writer's first concern. She is thus not as primarily or exclusively interested in sexism as is the feminist.

The intelligent black woman writer, conscious of black impotence in the context of white patriarchal culture, empowers the black man. She believes in him; hence her books end in integrative images of the male and

8. Millett, pp. 38–39. She notes that socially the white female has a "higher status" than the black male who is in turn "higher" than the black female.

9. Ibid., p. 33. Millett inherits some of her phraseology from Simone de Beauvoir (*The Second Sex*, trans. H. M. Parshley [Harmondsworth: Penguin Books, 1972], p. 609); see also Barbara Charlesworth Gelpi, "A Common Language: The American Woman Poet," in *Shakespeare's Sisters: Feminist Essays on Women Poets*, ed. Sandra M. Gilbert and Susan Gubar (Bloomington: Indiana University Press, 1979), pp. 269–79, esp. p. 269; Elaine Showalter, "Feminist Criticism in the Wilderness," in *Writing and Sexual Difference*, ed. Elizabeth Abel (Brighton: Harvester Press, 1982), pp. 9–35, esp. p. 31. Recent feminist writing resembles Afro-American male literature from the Harlem Renaissance to the 1960s.

10. S. E. Ogude, "Slavery and the African Imagination: A Critical Perspective," *World Literature Today* 55, no. 1 (Winter 1981): 21–25, esp. 24.

female worlds. Given this commitment, she can hardly become a strong ally of the white feminist until (perhaps) the political and economic fortunes of the black race improve. With the world power structure as it is, what would the relevance be of a black female character's struggle to be equal to such a black man as, for example, on the Afro-American side, Richard Wright's bestialized Bigger Thomas or Ralph Ellison's eternally hibernating Invisible Man or James Baldwin's sterile Leo Proudhammer; or, on the African side, as Ngugi wa Thiong'o's treacherous male or Wole Soyinka's drifting interpreter or Chinua Achebe's insecure Okonkwo? Just as Baldwin rejects integration into the burning house of the United States, the black woman instinctively recoils from mere equality because, as in Aidoo's *Our Sister Killjoy*, she has to aim much higher than that and knit the world's black family together to achieve black, not just female, transcendence.[11]

Aidoo might have been speaking for most black women writers when she diagnosed the African woman writer's disease: "Life for the African woman writer is definitely 'not crystal stair.' It is a most peculiar predicament. But we also share all, or nearly all the problems of male African writers"—sharing experience that white female writers do not have with their male counterparts.[12] For the African man or woman, there are the basic problems of writing in a borrowed language and form; for most blacks the difficulties in getting published when there are so few black publishing houses remains a critical issue. Then, too, many African novels are slight or lack the profundity found in many black American ones. The tradition of African art with its simplicity and ephemerality—as can be seen in African architecture as well as in oral and performed literatures— has been bequeathed to African women writers. Yet they have to produce novels in a milieu that hankers after the complex and the enduring. At the same time, who will read what they produce when a large proportion of the home audience hates reading or cannot read—a predicament shared by black Americans?

Writing from a position of power, the white female writer does not face such difficulties. Instead she concentrates on patriarchy, analyzing it, attacking it, detecting its tentacles in the most unlikely places. Patriarchy, as it manifests itself in black ghettos of the world, is a domestic affair without the wide reverberations it has in white patriarchy where the issue is real world power. The ultimate difference between the feminist and the womanist is thus what each sees of patriarchy and what each thinks can be

11. Amiri Baraka, "Afro-American Literature & Class Struggle," *Black American Literature Forum* 14, no. 1 (Spring 1980): 5–14, esp. 12. Baraka treats the black female predicament from an economic, racial, and social viewpoint: "Third World women in this country suffer a triple oppression, if they are working women, as workers under capitalism—class oppression, national oppression and oppression because of their sex."

12. Aidoo (n. 1 above), p. 32.

changed. Black sexism is a microcosmic replication of Euro-American racism, a concept Alice Walker recognizes. In *The Color Purple*, Nettie writes that the Olinka in not educating girls are "like white people at home who don't want colored people to learn."[13] It follows that for the black woman racism and sexism must be eradicated together.

Since the 1960s, when the idea of independence and nationalism blew through Africa and the diaspora, the white woman has intensified her feminist drive for equality with white men, a position that complicates her response to racial issues and to black feminism. Many white feminist critics have confirmed black suspicion of duplicity by rarely dealing with black women's writing, curtly dismissing it on the pretext of their ignorance of it.[14] This neglect has a positive side in that it has encouraged the emergence of black women critics. The conflict between the white and black positions is concretized in black women's antagonism toward their white counterparts' sexual politics. It shows in the consistently unsympathetic portrayal of white female characters in novels by black women writers—a situation that signals the extent of the conflict between white feminists and black womanists.

A revealing example of this hostility is Aidoo's portrait of the German Marja, wife of Adolf (Hitler?) in *Our Sister Killjoy*. First Marja appears as a tempter when she presents the black girl, Sissie, with numerous offers of fruits in symbolic gestures that lead finally to a sexual advance. Sissie recoils at what she considers abominable, though her horror is mixed with Baldwinian tenderness, and rejects feminism while she moves toward womanism.[15] Similarly, in *A Question of Power* Head demonstrates, through the portrait of Camilla, that the white woman yearns to control black men and women by humiliating them. She is stopped by an open confrontation.

The Afro-Americans have dealt with the white woman even more viciously than have African writers—understandably, since the racist situation is more exacerbating for them than for their average African counterpart. What could be more damaging than Margaret Walker's portrait in *Jubilee* of Big Missy as the hard matriarch or of her daughter, the lily-livered Miss Lillian, in the contrasting stereotype of the fragile, docile woman? Big Missy, for her diabolical treatment of her black slaves, finally receives her just deserts when—with most of her family dead and

13. Alice Walker, *The Color Purple* (New York: Washington Square Press, 1983), p. 145.
14. Deborah E. McDowell, "New Directions for Black Feminist Criticism," *Black American Literature Forum* 14, no. 4 (Winter 1980): 153–58, esp. 153.
15. Black American writers operate in a more liberal atmosphere than their African counterparts and so tend to portray lesbian relationships more sympathetically: see, e.g., Walker's *The Color Purple*; Ntozake Shange's *Sassafrass, Cypress & Indigo*; Paule Marshall's *The Chosen Place, the Timeless People* and *Praisesong for the Widow*, where lesbianism is depicted tangentially. An exception to the rule in African literature is Rebeka Njau, *Ripples in the Pool* (London: Heinemann Books, 1975).

Yankee guns booming as if at the back of her plantation—she starts emitting flatus and becomes incontinent following a massive stroke. As if that were insufficient, Walker finishes the white female by finally portraying Miss Lillian (who is also adept at emitting flatus at gatherings) as insane and helpless, in sharp contrast to the black Vyry, who thrives under hardships created by Big Missy and other white characters.

Paule Marshall is as devastating as Margaret Walker in her portrait of the white woman in *Brown Girl, Brownstones* and even more trenchant in *The Chosen Place, the Timeless People*. In the latter, she makes an important historical point through her white character Harriet, whose wealth had its origins in the slave trade; like Margaret Walker, Marshall asserts that slavery benefited white women as well as white men. The white woman's dubious role in the racial context is further underscored by the behavior of a white woman, the English lover of the black woman, Merle. The incident has the character of a historical parable. Determined to negate Merle's attempts at connecting with her black African roots through marriage (worldwide unity of blacks), the white woman (Britain), in a symbolic, neocolonialist move, sets the African husband and the West Indian wife against each other, recklessly and treacherously destroying the budding relationship between black people in Africa and the diaspora; she has economic control, and her tactics are to divide and rule.

Neofeminism's "socialist connection" smacks of the black flirtation with communism in the 1940s.[16] A black and white female alliance would have similar characteristics. Like the earlier flirtation, such connections would come to nothing much, since Euro-American economy with its present structure will not readily permit blacks or women to win. So black female writers express in their writing what Sheila Rowbotham has surmised about the world economic situation: "A feminist movement which is confined to the specific oppression of women cannot, in isolation, end exploitation and imperialism."[17] If the ultimate aim of radical feminism is a separatist, idyllic existence away from the hullabaloo of the men's world,[18] the ultimate aim of womanism is the unity of blacks everywhere under the enlightened control of men and women. Each is finally separatist—the one sexually, the other racially—and their different goals create part of the disunity in the women's movement.

Recognition of the impact of racism, neocolonialism, nationalism, economic instability, and psychological disorientation on black lives, when superimposed on the awareness of sexism that characterizes black women's writing, makes concern about sexism merely one aspect of

16. Sheila Rowbotham, *Woman's Consciousness, Man's World* (Harmondsworth: Penguin Books, 1973), p. ix.

17. Ibid., pp. 123–24.

18. Rosemary Radford Ruether, *Sexism and God-Talk: Towards a Feminist Theology* (London: SCM Press, 1983), pp. 229 ff.

womanism. Black women writers distinguish womanism from feminism, just as their critical perception of black patriarchy and particular concern for black women distinguish the themes in their works from the acceptance of obnoxious male prejudices against women often found in writing by black men.

* * *

I arrived at the term "womanism" independently and was pleasantly surprised to discover that my notion of its meaning overlaps with Alice Walker's. She employs it to denote the metamorphosis that occurs in an adolescent girl, such as Ruth or Celie, when she comes to a sense of herself as a woman; involved is what Morrison, with her Pecola, refers to as "the little-girl-gone-to-woman" and Ntozake Shange represents through the maturing Indigo in *Sassafrass, Cypress & Indigo*. The young girl inherits womanism after a traumatic event such as menarche or after an epiphany or as a result of the experience of racism, rape, death in the family, or sudden responsibility. Through coping with the experience she moves creatively beyond the self to that concern for the needs of others characteristic of adult womanists. While writing on Nwapa, Alison Perry made a comment on Walker's extended usage of the word that tallies with my understanding of it. According to Perry, "If Flora Nwapa would accept a label at all, she would be more at home with Black American author Alice Walker's term 'womanist,' meaning a woman who is 'committed to the survival and wholeness of the entire people, male and female.'"[19]

Black womanism is a philosophy that celebrates black roots, the ideals of black life, while giving a balanced presentation of black womandom. It concerns itself as much with the black sexual power tussle as with the world power structure that subjugates blacks. Its ideal is for black unity where every black person has a modicum of power and so can be a "brother" or a "sister" or a "father" or a "mother" to the other. This philosophy has a mandalic core: its aim is the dynamism of wholeness and self-healing that one sees in the positive, integrative endings of womanist novels.

Black American female writers share with black males the heritage of the blues, whose spiritual dynamics ensure equilibrium in a turbulent world—perhaps because, as Stephen Henderson points out, there is a connection between the blues and the capacity to experience hope. The blues have had a tremendous impact on the Afro-American womanist novel, and, in contrast to feminist novels, most Afro-American womanist novels, culture-oriented as they are, abound in hope.[20] The Afro-

19. Alison Perry, "Meeting Flora Nwapa," *West Africa* (June 18, 1984), p. 1262.
20. See Annis Pratt, *Archetypal Patterns in Women's Fiction* (Sussex: Harvester Press, 1982), pp. 51 ff.

American female novelist sometimes even employs the mood and structure of the blues in her novels. As Henderson explains, "The blues . . . are
a music and poetry of confrontation—with the self, with the family and
loved ones, with the oppressive forces of society, with nature, and, on the
heaviest level, with fate and the universe itself. And in the confrontation
. . . a woman discovers her strengths, and if she is a Ma Rainey, *she
shares it with the community and in the process becomes immortal*" (emphasis
added).[21]

More often than not, in fiction we have many Ma Raineys—women
without men: examples include Janie Crawford (Zora Neale Hurston's
Their Eyes Were Watching God); Vyry (Margaret Walker's *Jubilee*); Merle
(Marshall's *The Chosen Place, the Timeless People*); Avey Johnson (Marshall's
Praisesong for the Widow); Sula and Nel (Morrison's *Sula*); Pilate and Circe
(Morrison's *Song of Solomon*); Meridian (Alice Walker's *Meridian*); Ruth
(Alice Walker's *The Third Life of Grange Copeland*); Celie and Nettie (Alice
Walker's *The Color Purple*). Many such women can be found in the African
female novel too: Elizabeth (Head's *A Question of Power*); Sissie (Aidoo's
Our Sister Killjoy); Ramatoulaye (Bâ's *So Long a Letter*); Idu (Nwapa's *Idu*);
and Amaka (Nwapa's *One Is Enough*). In the contemporary literary scene,
the Morrisons and Heads and Aidoos and Marshalls are themselves such
matriarchs without men.[22] On one level the depiction of such women can
be regarded as an antipatriarchal statement on the authors' part. On
another these exemplary figures, like Ma Rainey, demonstrate concern
for the family—not for the Western nuclear family (as viewed by feminists) but for the black extended family (as viewed by womanists) with its
large numbers and geographical spread. From this perspective, Sula is a
binding, spiritual force in Medallion; Merle in Bournehills; Sissie amid
black people.

Karen Gasten is therefore mistaken in concluding about *The Third
Life of Grange Copeland* that "what is needed to bring about a healthy
balance in sexual relationships is a generation of Ruths."[23] The book's
purpose is not so much the achievement of that feminist goal but the
integration of the Ruths into the black world—a womanist objective. The
black woman is not as powerless in the black world as the white woman is
in the white world; the black woman, less protected than her white
counterpart, has to grow independent. These factors generate an

21. Stephen E. Henderson, "The Heavy Blues of Sterling Brown: A Study of Craft and
Tradition," *Black American Literature Forum* 14, no. 1 (Spring 1980): 32–44, esp. 32.
22. Elaine Showalter has noted the strange phenomenon that strong, successful female
writers hardly ever portray successful female characters (*A Literature of Their Own* [n. 3
above], pp. 244 ff). This is a feminist rather than a womanist practice, as the strong female
characters cited above easily establish.
23. Karen C. Gasten, "Women in the Lives of Grange Copeland," *CLA Journal* 24, no. 3
(March 1981): 276–86, esp. 286.

affirmative spirit in the womanist novel that is packed full of female achievement.[24] Also, womanists explore past and present connections between black America and black Africa. Like amiable co-wives with invisible husbands, they work together for the good of their people. Charles Chesnutt's Aun' Peggy, the witch-herbalist in *The Conjure Woman*, Hurston's indomitable Janie Crawford, Ayi Kwei Armah's and Ngugi's formidable women—all serve as inspirational sources. Like the younger generation of black aestheticists, black female writers sidetrack the negative spirit of the protest tradition that some feminists still find useful.

In spite of the blues, black women occasionally go mad. Unlike negatively presented white madwomen, the black madwoman in novels written by black women knows in her subconscious that she must survive because she has people without other resources depending on her; in a positive about-face she usually recovers through a superhuman effort, or somehow, aids others. Merle, carrying her national burden of leading Bournehills up a road to progress, recoups her energy after her bouts of insanity and strengthens herself spiritually for the future political struggle by undertaking a pilgrimage to East Africa. In *The Bluest Eye*, the peculiar Pecola goes mad on the surface but acquires an interior spiritual beauty symbolized by the bluest eye (an "I" that is very blue). In this mixed state she acts as the scapegoat so that "all who knew her—felt so wholesome after [they] cleaned [them]selves on her."[25] Merle is comparable to Head's Elizabeth, who—nudged on by self-will, her son, her neighbors, and the medicinal effect of herbal greenery—recovers her sanity to play her part in an agricultural commune. Bâ's Jacqueline recuperates from her nervous breakdown as soon as she understands that her illness is psychosomatic, and she becomes reintegrated into society. After each mental upheaval there is thus a stasis in the womanist novel when the black woman's communion with the rest of the society is established, a consonance that expresses the black way to authenticity and transcendence. Madness becomes a temporary aberration preceding spiritual growth, healing, and integration.

These insights into character portrayal and thematic development have not come easily to the African writer. In an article unfortunately dated in some aspects, Maryse Conde observes that Nwapa and Aidoo "convey the impression that a gifted woman simply has no place in African society." In her analysis this is true "not only because [the gifted woman] cannot find a proper match but because the price she has to pay for her unusual gifts is so high that she would be better born without them," an idea that Juliet Okonkwo reiterates. Conde then concludes,

24. See Barbara Christian, *Black Women Novelists: The Development of a Tradition, 1892–1976* (Westport, Conn.: Greenwood Press, 1980), p. 239.

25. Toni Morrison, *The Bluest Eye* (New York: Holt, Rinehart & Winston, 1970), p. 163.

"Here are two gifted women portraying gifted females like themselves, but ultimately destroying them. These murders are the expression of a deeply-rooted conflict."[26] Perhaps. I suggest that this problem partly arises from the fact that early in their careers the African writers tend to model themselves on white feminists, thus putting themselves at variance with polygamy, which is generally accepted in rural Africa and is gaining ground in urban Nigeria.[27]

Conde's 1972 thesis has since been put into question by the appearance of Nwapa's *One Is Enough* (1981) and, most especially, by Aidoo's assertive *Our Sister Killjoy* (1977). In the latter, the strong-headed Sissie wants black men everywhere to undergo a psychological metamorphosis to assert their manhood in world politics, just as she has successfully represented black womanhood in her role as roving ambassador in Europe. A black man with such mastery can then become equal to and united with her. Here, the Ghanaian Aidoo, an Akan by birth, discards her Western consciousness to embrace the Akan matrilineal culture and outlook. Akan women are generally acclaimed for their independence. There, as a proverb goes, the husband cooks and leaves the food to the woman to relish—though, I must hastily add, the woman's brother dishes it out. So, in the denouement of the work, Aidoo envisages black solidarity between men and women in Africa and the diaspora.

The Senegalese novel *So Long a Letter* by Bâ is grounded in a Fulani world where the foreign religion of Islam has, like Christianity, been ruthlessly imposed on Africans. As Bâ demonstrates, both religions bear partial responsibility for the fact that many Africans have suffered psychological and moral disorientation. She generates tension in the novel by exploring the matrilineal perspective of the Fulanis in opposition to the patriarchal tenets of Islam, which advocates polygyny. Her shortish novel takes the form of a long letter written by Ramatoulaye, the determined heroine, to a friend to tell her about the polygynous situation that has ruined her marriage because of her Western expectation of monogyny. Rather than collapsing, she remains undaunted, with little acrimony. Ramatoulaye will not break another woman's heart by marrying that woman's husband as a second wife, and she even sympathizes with the

26. Maryse Conde, "Three Female Writers in Modern Africa: Flora Nwapa, Ama Ata Aidoo and Grace Ogot," *Présence africaine* 82 (1972): 132–43, esp. 139, 143. Juliet Okonkwo, "The Talented Woman in African Literature," *Africa Quarterly* 15, nos. 1, 2 (1975): 36–47, esp. 45.

27. Compare Gilbert and Gubar, *The Madwoman in the Attic* (n. 2 above), p. 78. If one modifies their observation about the relationship between the female writer and her mad or monstrous characters to suit Nwapa's and Aidoo's conceptual dilemma, one sees that the novelists project "their rebellious impulses" into their heroines but lack the courage to make them succeed, thereby demonstrating the authors' "own self-division, their desire both to accept the strictures of patriarchal society and to reject them," evidence of an early feminism mixed with an unconscious gravitation toward womanism.

other woman who ruined her (Ramatoulaye's) marriage. Men must be men, it seems, but women do not have to be like them. Having accepted men with their libidinous disposition, she can create a stable life around her numerous children, male and female, along with their spouses. This is womanism in action; the demands of Fulani culture rather than those of sexual politics predominate. Though she recognizes the inequities of patriarchy, she never really fights for her "rights"—a position further expressed by the novel's private, epistolary form. It must be pointed out that these two societies—the Akan and the Fulani—though preferable to the strictly patriarchal societies from a woman's viewpoint, are matrilineal and not truly matriarchal. One can therefore postulate that matrilineal and polygynous societies in Africa are dynamic sources for the womanist novel.

Head's *When Rain Clouds Gather* is a womanist novel achieved on different terms: widowhood involving the care of male and female children. In this idyllic novel, bad men are eliminated so that men and women can live together harmoniously. Similarly, ostracism and ethnicism rather than sexism cause the development of the strong woman in Head's *Maru*. In the end, the untouchable Margaret Cadmore marries the chief and touches other people. The disintegrating forces of apartheid in conjunction with the necessity to care for a black male child cause the toughening up and recovery of the insane heroine in Head's *A Question of Power*. Elizabeth frees herself from racial, ethnic, and male bondage to emerge as an intrepid individual, able to cope with bringing up her son and living harmoniously with others and with nature. It is Head's unique South African experience that makes it possible for her to detribalize the African womanist novel by exploring so many possibilities.

In the United States Alice Walker has been equally inventive. To make her point she uses the woman who is docile (but not helpless as her white counterpart would be), hardworking, and pitted against a terrible fate; her heroines suffer from poverty or racism allied with sexism, and sometimes from all three together. Walker is making the point that the black woman's destiny, in general, radically differs from her white counterpart's. About the latter de Beauvoir observes: "But woman is not called upon to build a better world: her domain is fixed and she has only to keep up the never ending struggle against the evil principles that creep into it; in her war against dust, stains, mud, and dirt she is fighting sin, wrestling with Satan."[28] In couching woman's war in domestic and religious terms, de Beauvoir is playful and somewhat Puritanical; her account does not cover the experience of the black woman for whom Satan is not a metaphysical concept but a reality out there, beyond her home, where she must willy-nilly go to obtain the wherewithal for decent survival as well as

28. De Beauvoir (n. 9 above), pp. 470–71.

for a "better world." Ruth's mother, Mem, does so in *The Third Life of Grange Copeland*; Meridian in *Meridian*; Celie and Nettie in *The Color Purple*.

* * *

Writing in the latter half of the twentieth century, the black womanist has been experimenting with old forms used by her predecessors, male and female. It is significant that the African woman writer emerged with the advent of political independence. Handicapped by writing in a second language, she has sometimes tried to put herself on familiar ground by fusing the familiar oral tradition with the foreign written medium, while also playing the role traditionally reserved for woman: enlightening and entertaining the population left in her care. The classics of the female Afro-American novel came after the heyday of the protest tradition and took for granted the ideological backing of the black power movement. Consequently, female novelists in both continents prefer to tell of life as it is, sometimes of life as it is thought to be, and rarely of life as it ought to be.

With some parallels to Jane Austen's clever exploitation of the gothic in *Northanger Abbey*, Head manipulates the mystique of gothicism in her psychological portrait of the mad Elizabeth in *A Question of Power*. As the private, fantastical "movies," which represent the punishment cells, un-reel in Elizabeth's mind and vision, the reader is forced to act the voyeur, transported into an exotic, weird world where the unusual, the eccentric, the traumatic, the frightening, the mysterious become the norm. Elizabeth's interior gothic world is wild, unjust, sexist, as her fight against the two reprehensible men—Dan and Sello—demonstrates. Its power play replicates the outer racist and ethnocentric society whose horrific power mongering leads Elizabeth to a nervous breakdown. Human tenderness and her willpower restore her to a supportable society.

Aidoo's, Bâ's, and Alice Walker's return to the early epistolary form of the novel inherited from eighteenth-century women writers departs from twentieth-century novelistic practice.[29] Their rediscovery of the epistle enables them to exploit its qualities of simplicity, relative intimacy, and candor. As a result, a novel in this form appears more open and more sincere than one written in the autobiographical mode—which tends to be defensively aggressive, narcissistic, self-glorifying, as in the work of some feminists. The letter pretends to be authentic and, like oral narration, gives the impression that the storyteller is not lying. In Aidoo's and Bâ's novels, the correspondents are loving friends. This aura of authenticity has a didactic function, particularly for women readers. Aidoo's use of the

29. According to Showalter (*A Literature of Their Own* [n. 3 above], p. 17), "Most eighteenth-century epistolary novels were written by women."

form in *Our Sister Killjoy* seems a modification of that employed in Baldwin's *The Fire Next Time*: she retains his clarity of vision and makes an objective assessment of the black global predicament. Her feminine nagging tone resembles Baldwin's sermonizing mode, made acceptable by a tenderness extended to friend and foe alike. In its daring experimentation in form, *Our Sister Killjoy* also resembles Jean Toomer's *Cane*. Like Toomer, Aidoo mixes prose, the sketch, poetry, song, and the like to produce something living, fresh, and lyrical—an oral performance in book form.

Alice Walker's *The Color Purple* is also complex and variable in its structure. The first addressee in its epistles is a power-wielding God. White, patriarchal, he acts the role of the indifferent voyeur. When God metamorphoses into "It," neuter but not quite neutral, in the female imagination, life miraculously improves for womanhood. Also included in the book is the correspondence of two loving and trusting sisters. Like rural, sequestered women, some of their letters remain unopened, hidden in a trunk by an interfering male. Walker then brings the truth of their lives to the world, just as Shug, the enlightened black woman who brings the secluded, "private" Celie into the public world of artistic and economic fulfillment. Celie and the letters resemble Emily Dickinson's poems, sewn up and hidden in a wombed trunk, away from public hostility or public honor, but later delivered for many eyes to see.

Each letter in *The Color Purple* represents a patch in the quilt that puts the whole of southern life with its sexism, racism, and poverty on display. One distinct pattern in the enormous quilt, painstakingly stitched together, shows the black woman's development from slavery to some form of emancipation from both white and black patriarchy. Walker's positivistic stance emerges as the expression of her yearning: a vision of a union of the male and the female, the black American and the African, brought about through women's faith that is in turn sustained by (letter) writing.

The letter with its surface innocuousness is indeed subversive. As a literary form that pretends to be private while it is made public, it ensures an open inquiry into those matters that affect one's material well-being, one's spiritual disposition, one's destiny, and one's relationship both to other people and to the environment. Letters in black female writing finally ensure illumination of the black predicament that precedes black integrity.

It is notable that some black women writers intersperse their novels with songs, verse, reiterated phrases. These seem to have the communal function of the call-and-response usually employed during African storytelling sessions. They relieve the tedium of a long speech or a long stretch of narration and involve the audience in the spinning of the yarn. They are effective during public readings of novels. The writers sometimes use them to emphasize climactic points in the narration where the emotion is so intense that prose can no longer serve as a suitable vehicle; so Aidoo does in *Our Sister Killjoy* and Morrison in *Song of Solomon*. In Margaret Walker's *Jubilee* as well as in Marshall's *Praisesong for the Widow* the numerous songs, wise sayings, and dances link the principals with black tradition, black suffering, black beliefs, and black religion. Ntozake Shange achieves a similar result by including weaving, culinary and medicinal recipes, and herbal lore in *Sassafrass, Cypress & Indigo*; she demonstrates their voodoo-like, "chemical" effects in the black lives involved.

* * *

The force that binds many black female novels in English together is, thus, womanism. As a woman with her own peculiar burden, knowing that she is deprived of her rights by sexist attitudes in the black domestic domain and by Euro-American patriarchy in the public sphere; as a member of a race that feels powerless and under siege, with little esteem in the world—the black female novelist cannot wholeheartedly join forces with white feminists to fight a battle against patriarchy that, given her understanding and experience, is absurd. So she is a womanist because of her racial and her sexual predicament.

The long-standing tradition of black American women writers has helped to define the black American woman's situation. The works of Pauline Hopkins, Mary Etta Spenser, Jean Fauset, Nella Larsen, Dorothy West, Ann Petry, and Zora Neale Hurston, among many others, have all helped to this end.[30] (It will be a useful line of research to find out if these authors' underlying philosophy is womanism too.) This long line of black foremothers—and also of forefathers—gives the Afro-American female writer an advantage over her African counterpart who was forefathered (in the written tradition) with a vengeance. Nevertheless, the black woman writer in Africa and in the United States has finally emerged as a spokeswoman for black women and the black race by moving away from black male chauvinism and the iconoclastic tendencies of feminism to embrace the relative conservatism of womanism.[31] She consequently ensures larger horizons for herself and her people. Indeed, in helping to liberate the black race through her writing she is aiding the black woman who has been and still is concerned with the ethics of surviving rather than with the aesthetics of living. Womanism with its wholesome, its religious grounding in black togetherness, is her gospel of hope. Morrison ex-

---

30. The first Afro-American novel by a woman is Frances Harper's *Iola Leroy; or, The Shadows Uplifted* (1892). The first African novel by a woman is Flora Nwapa's *Efuru* (1966). The Afro-American woman's scribal tradition is, of course, over two hundred years old, dating back to Phillis Wheatley, though the oral tradition in Africa far predates Wheatley.

31. Aidoo (n. 1 above), p. 33.

presses its nature when she says of black women, "There is something inside us that makes us different from other people. It is not like men and it is not like white women. We talked earlier about the relationship between my women and the men in their lives. When [the women] sing the blues it is one of those 'somebody is gone' kind of thing but there is never any bitterness."[32]

Department of English
University of Ibadan

32. Bettye J. Parker, "Complexity: Toni Morrison's Women—an Interview Essay," in *Sturdy Black Bridges: Visions of Black Women in Literature*, ed. Roseann P. Bell, Bettye J. Parker, and Beverly Guy-Sheftall (Garden City, N.Y.: Anchor Books, 1979), pp. 251–57, esp. p. 255.

Narrative of Community:
The Identification of a Genre

Sandra A. Zagarell

How seldom a book comes that stirs the minds and hearts of
the good men and women of such a village as this. . . . The
truth must be recognized that few books are written for and
from their standpoint. . . . Whoever adds to this department
of literature will do an inestimable good, will see that a simple, helpful way of looking at life and speaking the truth about
it . . . in what we are pleased to call its *everyday* aspects must
bring out the best sort of writing. [SARAH ORNE JEWETT,
Sarah Orne Jewett Letters, 1885][1]

I wish to thank the Andrew R. Mellon Foundation and Oberlin College for support
for this project. The community of scholars at the Mary Ingraham Bunting Institute
at Radcliffe College in 1985–86 provided a challenging and congenial environment
in which to complete a first draft of this essay and to pursue further work on the
narrative of community; my appointment as visiting scholar at Radcliffe's Henry A.
Murray Research Center provided me with an ideal situation for the following year.
I also wish to thank a number of people who have read and commented on this
essay at various stages in its composition: Elizabeth Ammons, Ava Baron, Lawrence
Buell, Nora Eisenberg, Diana Kahn, Aaron Fogel, Phyllis Gorfain, Linda Grimm,
Güneli Gün, Eileen Julien, Jane Hunter, Gail Riemer, Pam Solo, Carol Tufts, Ana
Cara-Walker, and Allen Zagarell. The questions and comments of two anonymous
readers for *Signs* were also extremely helpful.
    [1] Richard Cary, ed., *Sarah Orne Jewett Letters*, rev. ed. (Waterville, Maine: Colby
College Press, 1967), 51–52.

[*Signs: Journal of Women in Culture and Society* 1988, vol. 13, no. 3]

Is Western literature overwhelmingly about the self? Does post-Enlightenment narrative fiction feature, indeed help fashion, the individualized ego? Certainly the self still predominates in critical discourse. Fredric Jameson and Masao Miyoshi have spoken of the centered self as a dominant concern of Western narrative, explaining the self's centrality historically and politically. Structuralist and post-structuralist theory can be read as an extended assault on the Western belief in the heroic indomitability of the self, and humanists are still celebrating the self as a transhistorical entity. For example, in Wallace Gray's *Homer to Joyce*—a guide to the "great books" held to constitute the core of the Western humanities—the basic assumption is that great literature is about the search for the self.[2] Nevertheless, Western culture has long advanced powerful literary as well as theoretical alternatives to its own preoccupation with the self. In narrative, in fact, at least one tradition with a very different focus has existed for the past century and a half, though it has received relatively little notice and has never been adequately named or described.

I call this tradition the narrative of community. Works belonging to this "department of literature," like Sarah Orne Jewett's *The Country of the Pointed Firs*, take as their subject the life of a community (life in "its *everyday* aspects") and portray the minute and quite ordinary processes through which the community maintains itself as an entity. The self exists here as part of the interdependent network of the community rather than as an individualistic unit. Writers of narrative of community give literary expression to a community they imagine to have characterized the preindustrial era. Narrative of community thus represents a coherent response to the social, economic, cultural, and demographic changes caused by industrialism, urbanization, and the spread of capitalism. It took shape in the first half of the nineteenth century in the United States, Great Britain, and Ireland. At least initially, its main practitioners were

---

[2] Jameson and Miyoshi developed this perspective in their respective papers "The Return to Storytelling: Postmodernism and Third World Literature" and "The 'Great Divide' Once Again: Problematics of the Novel in the Non-Western World" at "The Challenge of Third World Culture," a conference at Duke University, September 25–27, 1986. For connections between the novel and the creation of the self, see Fredric Jameson, *The Political Unconscious: Narrative as a Socially Symbolic Act* (Ithaca, N.Y.: Cornell University Press, 1981), chap. 3. Jameson analyzes twentieth-century structuralism and post-structuralism as symptomatic of changes in the condition of the "subject" in late capitalism (124–25). See also Wallace Gray's preface and Steven Marcus's foreword in Wallace Gray, *Homer to Joyce: Interpretations of the Classic Works of Western Literature* (New York: Macmillan, 1985). The book contains not a single chapter on works by blacks, members of nondominant ethnic groups, or women of these or any other group.

white women of the middle classes. In this essay, I suggest why, during the nineteenth century, narrative of community was written primarily by such women and indicate the roles it played in works by their male counterparts. I then illustrate the genre's essential features with reference to Jewett's *Country of the Pointed Firs* and Flora Thompson's *Lark Rise* (1939)[3] and conclude by considering narrative of community's heterogeneity in the twentieth century. First, however, I give a brief account of the genre's antecedents and distinguishing characteristics and suggest why it has been unrecognized for so long.

*   *   *

When literary attention turned to the world that was being lost with the advent of modernization, writers like Elizabeth Gaskell, George Eliot, Harriet Beecher Stowe, as well as Jewett, imagined that world as one in which community and stability had prevailed. In much of their writing, their purposes included presenting—and preserving—the patterns, customs, and activities through which, in their eyes, traditional communities maintained and perpetuated themselves, and nurturing a commitment to community in readers.[4] Although narrative of community cannot be identified as a full-fledged genre in works written before the middle of the nineteenth century, these purposes and the development of formal means of expressing them are pronounced in some earlier regionalist work in both Great Britain and the United States, most of it by women. In the former this includes Maria Edgeworth's *Castle Rackrent* (London, 1800), which introduced into fiction the use of the vernacular as a metonomy for a folk culture, and Mary Russell Mitford's

---

[3] I concentrate on *Lark Rise*, the first volume of Thompson's trilogy, *Lark Rise to Candleford*, rather than discussing all three volumes because the second and third become more specifically autobiographical, focusing far less on community. The edition of *Lark Rise* to which I refer in this essay is the first volume of Flora Thompson, *Lark Rise to Candleford*, introduction by Hugh Massingham (1939–43; reprint, Harmondsworth, England: Penguin, 1973). The edition of *The Country of the Pointed Firs* I use is Sarah Orne Jewett, *The Country of the Pointed Firs and Other Stories*, ed. Marjorie Pryse (New York: Norton, 1981). These two works will hereafter be cited in the text as *Lark Rise* and *Country*.

[4] In the case of George Eliot, Susanne Graver argues that one of her major intents was to inspire readers with a commitment to community, though in the context of accepting individualism as a point of departure (see *George Eliot and Community: A Study in Social Theory and Fictional Form* [Berkeley and Los Angeles: University of California Press, 1984]). Graver also summarizes the contrast between individual-based, contractual industrial society (gesellschaft) and preindustrial community (gemeinschaft) as formulated by Ferdinand Tönnies, whose thought, she suggests, was much like that of Eliot and her intellectual community (see esp. 14, 30–31).

Our Village (London, 1824–32), which adapted the sketch form
Washington Irving had used in his *Sketch Book* (London, 1819–20)
and replaced his peripatetic "alienated observer" narrator with an
empathetic woman deeply involved in her own village.[5] In the
United States, a number of women working in the village sketch
tradition that became highly popular by the 1820s produced portraits of communities so focused and sustained that the communities
have the quality of local cultures. Narrative of community's broader
antecedents include a diverse mixture of Romantic rural and regionalist literature largely authored by white men, among them
Oliver Goldsmith, William Wordsworth, Sir Walter Scott, and Irving. While regional cultures have some presence in this literature,
a Romantic emphasis on the individual consciousness or, in Scott's
work, on individualized, often heroic characters, overshadows the
portrayal of community life. Moreover, that portrayal is, with the
exception of Scott's, highly generalized, as it is in the *Sketch Book*.[6]

[5] This formulation for Irving's narrator is developed at length in William Hedges,
Washington Irving: An American Study, 1802–1832 (Baltimore: Johns Hopkins University Press, 1965), chap. 6.

[6] Among the writers of village sketches were Lydia Sigourney (*Sketch of Connecticut, Forty Years Since* [Hartford, 1824]); Eliza Buckminster Lee (*Sketches of
a New-England Village, in the Last Century* [Boston, 1838]); and Mary Clavers
[Caroline Kirkland] (*A New Home—Who'll Follow?—Or, Glimpses of Western Life*
[New York, 1839]). John Galt's *Annals of the Parish* (Edinburgh and London, 1821),
which marginalized public history as it foregrounded the texture and continuity of
life in a single Scottish parish during a fifty-year period, is another important regionalist work from the United Kingdom; significantly, Galt resisted the term "novel"
to describe his narrative. Contemporary reviewers saw similarities among many of
the writers I point to in the present essay: comparisons between *Our Village* and
Cranford (London, 1851–53), and *Cranford* and *Country*, e.g., were common. And
there were significant cross-influences among writers: Eliot wrote Gaskell that she
read *Cranford* when writing *Scenes of Clerical Life* (Edinburgh and London, 1858)
and the early parts of *Mary Barton* (London, 1848) just before writing *Adam Bede*
(Edinburgh and London, 1859); Stowe visited Gaskell; and Jewett read *Cranford*,
frequently commented that Stowe's *The Pearl of Orr's Island* (Boston, 1862) provided
her with crucial inspiration, expressed admiration for Eliot's work despite a narrative
voice she found intrusive, read Margaret Oliphant's *Passages in the Life of Mrs.
Margaret Maitland* (London, 1849), and owned Jane Barlow's *Irish Idylls* (London,
1892) (the copy in Harvard University's Widener Library belonged to Jewett). Josephine Donovan documents the village sketch tradition's initial inspiration in Edgeworth and Mitford in *New England Local Color Literature: A Women's Tradition*
(New York: Ungar, 1983). In addition to other antecedents mentioned in my text,
nonliterary works such as William Cobbett's *Rural Rides* (London, 1832) and Gilbert
White's *Natural History and Antiquities of Selbourne* (London, 1789), both of which
Mitford knew well, were important precursors. Narrative of community's roots in
nonnovelistic traditions of narrative, oral as well as written (including storytelling),
need further research.

The pronounced generic heterogeneity of Irving's work[7] underscores the general fluidity of the relationship between genre and individual texts, which must be borne in mind when considering what it means to identify a genre for the first time. As a number of theorists and critics note, genres are not strict classifications and need not be exclusive. Arising in response to cultural-historical circumstances, developing unevenly rather than evolving in an orderly fashion, they stand behind individual works of literature but do not govern them. To put it another way, individual literary works participate in genres rather than belong to them, and a number of genres are often present in a given work—contrapuntally in the alternations between novel and romance in Charlotte Brontë's *Shirley* (London, 1849), loosely interwoven in the melange of Irving's *Sketch Book*—though in some works one genre can be said to predominate strongly. Thus to identify a previously unnamed genre is not to insist that certain books should now simply be reassigned to the new classification—to proclaim, for instance, that *Adam Bede* should no longer be read as a novel. Rather, narrative of community should be understood as a generative principle present in, and in some cases constituting the generic center of, a number of extended prose narratives.[8]

The concept of narrative of community, then, brings to light a cultural impulse that was not, until now, sufficiently clear and makes visible structures and purposes shared by works that have not been grouped together, many of which have been troublesome to those seeking to fit them within prevailing generic categories. It illuminates the common ground among well-known narratives like Gaskell's *Cranford*, lesser-known works such as Margaret Oliphant's *Passages in the Life of Mrs. Margaret Maitland*, and books that have been largely forgotten like Jane Barlow's *Irish Idylls*. Although all the features of a genre need not be present in any given work that

---

[7] Lawrence Buell, *New England Literary Culture* (London: Cambridge University Press, 1986), calls the *Sketch Book* "a loosely connected series of descriptive pieces, interweaving essay and fiction (with a few poems thrown in)" (294).

[8] Peter K. Garrett, *The Victorian Multiplot Novel: Studies in Dialogic Form* (New Haven, Conn.: Yale University Press, 1980), gives a useful account of the emphasis on coherence by some contemporary monologic genre theorists, discusses more deconstructive approaches, and, building on the work of Mikhail Bakhtin, develops the notion of dialogic form, in which works are structured by the interplay between divergent principles (see "Introduction"). Jameson discusses generic shifts and complexities throughout *The Political Unconscious* (n. 2 above). Jacques Derrida, "La loi du genre/The Law of Genre," *Glyph Textual Studies* 7 (Baltimore: Johns Hopkins University Press, 1980), notes that "every text participates in one or several genres, there is no genreless text; there is always a genre and genres, yet participation never amounts to belonging" (212).

participates in it, each genre has a distinctive vision and distinguishing structural characteristics. In the nineteenth century, narrative of community's formal elements reflected its commitment to rendering the local life of a community to readers who lived in a world the authors thought fragmented, rationalized, and individualistic. Narratives of community ignore linear development or chronological sequence and remain in one geographic place. Rather than being constructed around conflict and progress, as novels usually are, narratives of community are rooted in process. They tend to be episodic, built primarily around the continuous small-scale negotiations and daily procedures through which communities sustain themselves. In keeping with the predominant focus on the collective life of the community, characterization typically exemplifies modes of interdependence among community members. Additionally, writers present details of local life as integral parts of the semiotic systems of the community, and readers are urged to recognize local language and activities like washing and gardening as both absolutely ordinary and as expressions of community history and values. Finally, narratives of community represent the contrast between community life and the modern world directly through participant/observer narrators, and these narrators typically seek to diminish this distance in the process of giving voice to it.

Although nineteenth-century narratives of community are structurally akin, national particularities in the conception of community are evident. In the British literature, a long history is often reflected, even (in cases such as *Lark Rise*) reconstructed, and class is seen to have a strong influence on community life, whether community is created by negotiation across classes, as in *Adam Bede,* or within one class, as in *Cranford.* In the United States, on the other hand, the community is generally located in a semi-mythological past marked by an important sign of historical change—after the revolution in Lydia Sigourney's *Sketch of Connecticut* (Hartford, Conn., 1824), before the advent of the railroad in Charlotte Jerauld's *Chronicles and Sketches of Hazelhurst* (Boston, 1850). Moreover, poverty is understood as a consequence of personal capacity or luck, not of class. In the American literature, in fact, everyone in the community is seen to have an equal opportunity to be a member, and exclusion because of race or ethnic background is rarely acknowledged: Sigourney's insistent focus on the destruction of Indian life is an exception.

Since narratives of community are structurally similar, it is useful to ask why the genre was not identified earlier, and why it is possible to see it now. The current widespread questioning of long-accepted definitions and conceptual categories—a questioning fundamental to feminist theory and scholarship, to Marxist and other historically oriented modes of thought, to poststructuralism, and to the many unions among these approaches—has provided a context for the identification of the genre. Within the field of literature, one object of such scrutiny has been the culturally monolithic standard canon of literature. The dominance of a canon thought to encompass the literary masterpieces deflected sustained critical and theoretical attention from "noncanonical" literature. Additionally, the preeminence of "the" canon perpetuated a hierarchy of status among genres and worked against the notion that there remain genres yet to be identified. Complementing recent reconstructions of the canon's history and ideological bases is the questioning of the monolithic self, referred to at the outset of this essay, which has thrown into relief other assumptions that formerly discouraged serious study of extended non-novelistic works of narrative prose. Wallace Gray's equation of "individual" and "great literature" reflects quite clearly the way in which literary criticism, like much theory and like Western culture at large, has often privileged and helped perpetuate the cult of the individual without analyzing the cultural and historical status of literature that is "about" the self. Historically speaking, of course, privileging the individual informs the novel's early appearance, purposes, and structure, as Jameson maintains.[9] Ian Watt identifies post-Cartesian and Lockean philosophy, with their starting point in the individual's experience and in bourgeois society, as the cultural and social matrix for the novel's development: as Watt established it, the rise of the novel keeps pace with the rise of the individual; and the rise, or fall, of individuals—or, as critics of nineteenth-century fiction often put it, the interaction between the individual and society—is what novels are about.[10] In a series of conflations, however, readers and critics have tended not just to equate novels with stories about individuals but also to expect that such stories will always be about growth or decline and to identify all serious literary narrative with the novel. Given such expecta-

[9] Jameson (n. 2 above).
[10] Ian Watt, *The Rise of the Novel* (1957; reprint, Berkeley: University of California Press, 1965). Watt traces the rise of the novel to the rise of philosophic realism, emphasizing the grounding of the latter in individual experience (see esp. 11, 13, 63). J. Hillis Miller's influential *The Form of Victorian Fiction* (Notre Dame, Ind.: University of Notre Dame Press, 1968) employs structuralist principles within an essentially humanistic tradition and privileges the self in discussing the self and community. In contrast, Peter Garrett develops a method for discussing the dialogue between the centered self and the collectivity in Victorian novels. In *Society in the Novel* (Chapel Hill: University of North Carolina Press, 1984), Elizabeth Langland takes a useful step toward formulating an approach to novels in which society, not individual characters, constitutes the major presence.

tions, fictions about modes of life that are collective, continuous, and undramatic, such as *Cranford*, are puzzling; generally, as has been the case for *Cranford*, readers either assume that the work has no story, often delegating it to the supposedly inferior category of the sketch, or impose familiar but inappropriate notions of linear plotting on it.[11]

Literary historians' habit of looking at British and American literature as two fundamentally distinct traditions has also helped perpetuate narrative of community's obscurity.[12] In all these areas, feminist scholarship has been particularly instrumental in reconceptualizing literary history in ways that make an enterprise like the identification of narrative of community possible. Renewed attention to texts by, about, and/or featuring women has shown that the narrative impulse has long included supraindividual concerns,

[11] Readers who have "discovered" in *Cranford* a protagonist with an individual story include Edgar Wright, for whom after the first two chapters "it is about Miss Matty that the episodes develop until they have finally limned her history and character in a narrative that accumulates unity as it proceeds" (*Mrs. Gaskell: The Basis for Critical Reassessment* [London: Oxford University Press, 1965], 104). George V. Griffith, in "What Kind of Book Is *Cranford*?" (*Ariel: A Review of International English Literature* 14, no. 2 [April 1983]: 53–66), usefully summarizes critical debate on how to classify *Cranford*, suggesting that it is not a novel, not fully a serial publication, "in part a series" (like *Our Village* and *Annals of the Parish*), best described as "a last hurrah to a departing way of life and to the narrative techniques of an earlier age and a reluctant welcome to a new age and vision" (64).

[12] That the division is enshrined in curricula and textbooks goes without saying. Moreover, the best work that deals, implicitly or explicitly, with literary representations of modernization does not consider the possibility of a response common on both sides of the Atlantic to the changes and losses modernization entailed. For Great Britain, see esp. Raymond Williams, *The Country and the City* (St. Albans: Palladin, 1975), which toward the end does refer to American literature; and W. J. Keith, *The Rural Tradition: A Study of the Non-Fiction Prose Writers of the English Countryside* (Toronto: University of Toronto Press, 1974). With regard to the United States these subjects are implicitly dealt with by older studies, notably Ima Honaker Herron's *The Small Town in American Literature* (Durham, N.C.: Duke University Press, 1939), which invokes initial British influence but maintains that American literature about the small town became an autonomous tradition after the beginning of the eighteenth century; and Warner Berthoff's *The Ferment of Realism: American Literature, 1884–1912* (New York: Free Press, 1965). Discussing regional fiction, Berthoff maintains that if "there is a single formal genre that is native and peculiar to the American imagination in literature, it is perhaps the circumstantial elegy . . . , the detailed lament for a disappearing, though perhaps only recently and precariously established, order of life" (29). More recent works, including Perry D. Westbrook's *The New England Town in Fact and Fiction* (Ruthford, Penn.: Farleigh Dickinson University Press, 1982) and Buell (n. 7 above), also tend to focus on the literature of a specific American region as though it developed without more than an initial conversation with English literature of a similar impulse, and after her first chapter Donovan, too (n. 6 above), discusses New England writers without reference to British literature.

and Nina Auerbach has specifically identified the prominence of literary focus on communities of women in writing by authors of both sexes. Further, feminist literary historians, especially Ellen Moers and Sandra M. Gilbert and Susan Gubar, have established the existence of women's literary traditions that, beginning in the nineteenth century, self-consciously included both England and the United States.[13] Feminist historical work of the past decade, moreover, has provided a context for the rise of such traditions by elaborating the complicated culture shared by middle-class white women in both countries in the nineteenth century.[14] Since narrative of community was given shape mainly by such women, I have been

[13] Nina Auerbach, *Communities of Women: An Idea in Fiction* (Cambridge, Mass.: Harvard University Press, 1978); Ellen Moers, *Literary Women: The Great Writers* (New York: Doubleday, 1976); Sandra M. Gilbert and Susan Gubar, *The Madwoman in the Attic: The Woman Writer and the Nineteenth-Century Literary Imagination* (New Haven, Conn: Yale University Press, 1979). Two other crucial studies, Elaine Showalter, *A Literature of Their Own: British Women Novelists from Brontë to Lessing* (Princeton, N.J.: Princeton University Press, 1979); and Nina Baym, *Woman's Fiction: A Guide to Novels By and About Women in America, 1820–1870* (Ithaca, N.Y.: Cornell University Press, 1978), reconstruct traditions within national boundaries.

[14] I use the phrase women's culture in this essay in the historical sense: it refers to the culture associated with the sphere of white middle-class women in the nineteenth century. More work has been done on that culture in nineteenth-century America than in nineteenth-century England. Essential is Carroll Smith-Rosenberg, "The Female World of Love and Ritual," *Signs: Journal of Women in Culture and Society* 1, no. 1 (Autumn 1975): 1–29. Nancy Cott, in *The Bonds of Womanhood: "Woman's Sphere" in New England, 1780–1835* (New Haven, Conn.: Yale University Press, 1977), draws explicitly in chap. 1 on generalizations E. P. Thompson has made about nineteenth-century British women, and some of her findings, such as the existence of a connection between women's sphere and preindustrial life, clearly apply to England. That similarities existed in women's culture in nineteenth-century France, England, and the United States is the stated assumption of Erna Olafson Hellerstein, Leslie Parker Hume, and Karen Offen, eds., *Victorian Women: A Documentary Account of Women's Lives in Nineteenth-Century England, France and the United States* (Stanford, Calif.: Stanford University Press, 1981); see pp. 1–5 for a general discussion of commonalities of women's culture in all three countries. For a discussion of British feminists' tendency to use class as a dominant analytic category and American feminists' tendency to employ culture in a similar way, see the introduction to Judith L. Newton, Mary P. Ryan and Judith R. Walkowitz, eds., *Sex and Class in Women's History*, History Workshop Series (London: Routledge & Kegan Paul, 1983), 1–15. Bonnie Thornton Dill, "Race, Class, and Gender: Prospects for an All-inclusive Sisterhood," *Feminist Studies* 9, no. 1 (Spring 1983): 131–50, calls for the explication of different conditions and cultures of black and white, middle- and working-class women; I wish to stress that I do not assume that white women's cultures were identical with those of black women. Additionally, I assume neither that nineteenth-century narrative of community as I identify it here subsumes literature by black Americans of either sex, nor that black Americans did not write narratives of community in that century. The subject needs further research.

able to recognize it only because feminist scholarship has rewritten social and cultural history and attended to these women's lives, their cultural expression, and the particular intertextuality of women's writing.

My identification of narrative of community is thus deeply indebted to feminist scholarship. My work also seeks to extend this scholarship through a shift in the focus of inquiry. Recently reconstructed traditions of nineteenth-century English-language women's literature are marked by writers' concern with patriarchal constructions of femininity and by women's multifaceted efforts to maneuver within or move beyond them. In scholars' tracings of these traditions women's culture has provided a context in a fairly general respect.[15] My elucidation of narrative of community is based on a more detailed pursuit of connections between the culture of certain nineteenth-century women of the middle class and these women's literary expression. Excellent work has been done to establish thematic connections of this sort, but the formulation of the concept of narrative of community is unusual in that it postulates a relationship between women's culture and writing that is also structural.[16] Moreover, while scholars pursuing connections between literature and women's culture have concentrated on writing by women, in the case of narrative of community, there are some similarities between literature by women and that by certain men,

[15] For the nineteenth century, several major, sometimes overlapping, traditions of British and American women's literature have been identified. In the one Gilbert and Gubar have established, women writers, though haunted by misogynist models for and images of women, covertly subverted and rewrote these images and models. In the tradition Showalter (*A Literature of Their Own*) outlines, women writers moved from imitation of male models to near-separatism. In the overplot of the woman's fiction that Baym discusses, the heroine is faced with the dilemma of "mistreatment, unfairness, disadvantage, and powerlessness, recurrent injustices occasioned by her state as female and child," and must learn to accept responsibility for overcoming these obstacles (17). Additionally, Donovan (n. 6 above) maintains that New England women's local-color writing constitutes a women's tradition that goes back to the eighteenth century and is woman-identified.

[16] Lillian Faderman, *Surpassing the Love of Men: Romantic Friendship and Love between Women from the Renaissance to the Present* (New York: Morrow, 1981), and Donovan examine the thematic connections between the literature they discuss and women's culture, while the "trials and triumph" overplot of woman's fiction resembles the bildungsroman. One examination of the connections between women's culture and narrative structure is Elaine Showalter, "Piecing and Quilting," in *The Poetics of Gender*, ed. Nancy K. Miller (New York: Columbia University Press, 1986), 222–47, which connects quilting with theme and form in the work of some American woman writers. See also Joseph Allen Boone's discussion of "centric" narratives by women which feature female community in *Tradition Counter Tradition: Love and the Form of Fiction*, Women in Culture and Society Series, ed. Catharine R. Stimpson (Chicago: University of Chicago Press, 1987).

and I explore briefly narrative of community's presence in the latter. Finally, I understand women's centrality in developing narrative of community to be linked to culturally and historically specific circumstances, and the ties between gender and genre to be relative, not absolute.

*   *   *

Women's connections to preindustrial life are the most striking of several features of nineteenth-century women's culture that are important to the development of narrative of community. Nancy Cott has shown that women's connections lingered far longer than men's, and that they were specific and material, rooted in the rhythms of child care and domestic life. Through them, women's sphere retained much of the character of the preindustrial world well after the public, male world had been reorganized around the requirements of a market economy. Within the domestic sphere, moreover, women maintained a markedly interpersonal, affiliative orientation that may also have been characteristic of preindustrial life.[17] Cott's study elaborates the close ties, moral feeling, ritual, and other forms of bonding through which women's sphere simultaneously inscribed women's exclusion from public life and power and helped shape their strongly relational orientation. The relational quality of women's culture has received much attention from feminist scholars, and the association of women with a commitment to relationships lies at the root of Carol Gilligan's influential study of contemporary women's moral development, *In a Different Voice*. Although Gilligan's book often seems to project an essential, altruistic image of women as "woman," it does articulate very clearly—though perhaps unconsciously—values that were prominent in nineteenth-century women's culture, and it implies that the ethos of that culture retains considerable ideological power, influencing the way many women—certainly many whom Gilligan studied—understand and explain their own lives. Though Gilligan does not write from a historical perspective, we can discern in her comments that for women the totality of human life is "sustained by connection" and that their "maturity is realized through interdependence and care," the bonding and sense of responsibility so important to women's culture in the nineteenth century. Her frequent citation of George Eliot further suggests that the ethic she presents as char-

---

[17] Cott, esp. chap. 1. As Graver (n. 4 above) indicates, nineteenth-century reconstructions of gemeinschaft imagined it as interpersonal and relational rather than as an individual-based industrial society.

acteristic of women at large carries over from the nineteenth century.[18]

Because *In a Different Voice* expresses eloquently and cogently some of the ideology of women's culture, it facilitates the identification of negotiation as a fundamental feature of that culture. In Gilligan's formulation, women have a distinct ability to "attend to voices other than their own and to include in their judgment other points of view."[19] This notion recalls Elaine Showalter's observation that "perpetual negotiation" between spheres was a prominent aspect of nineteenth-century middle-class women's lives and her claim that the same process informs the double-voicedness characteristic of all those who maneuver between a subordinate culture and a surrounding, more powerful, and partly determining, dominant one.[20] The need to maneuver among viewpoints and interests is evident in Carroll Smith-Rosenberg's reconstructions of nineteenth-century American women's negotiations between their positions as wives and their dedication to women friends. It is also pronounced where women's culture intersected or came into contradiction with the public arena. Women may often have performed such negotiation with profound ambivalence. This is Mary Kelley's reading of popular antebellum women novelists, who expressed and tried to contain the disjunction they felt between their private domestic lives and their public literary careers by becoming "literary domestics." Yet negotiation could also cannily inform a bid for power, as in Catharine Beecher's recasting of the moral characteristics assigned to femininity to provide a rationale for women's reform of the public realm. Whatever women's attitude, their need to negotiate made them highly adept at balancing divergent, often contradictory systems of value and discourse and gave them special skill in the kinds of mediation that, as we shall see, are fundamental to narrative of community.[21]

[18] Carol Gilligan, *In a Different Voice: Psychological Theory and Women's Development* (Cambridge, Mass.: Harvard University Press, 1982), 59, 178. For Gilligan's citations of George Eliot, see esp. chap. 5. On the relational quality of nineteenth-century women's culture, see, in addition to Cott, Smith-Rosenberg, and Faderman.

[19] Gilligan, 16.

[20] Showalter ties her formulation of double-voicedness to the work of Gerda Lerner, Carroll Smith-Rosenberg, and anthropologists Shirley and Edwin Ardner in "Feminist Criticism in the Wilderness," *Critical Inquiry* 8, no. 2 (Winter 1981): 179–206. The first conceptualization of double-voicedness of which I am aware is W. E. B. DuBois's discussion of double consciousness in *The Souls of Black Folk* (Chicago, 1903).

[21] In "Politics and Culture in Women's History: A Symposium" (*Feminist Studies* 6, no. 1 [Spring 1980]: 21–64), Mary Jo Buhle points to the importance of one, transformative, kind of negotiation. She notes that "by situating the reform crusades

Narrative of community's relation to these aspects of women's culture is, as I have suggested, structural as well as thematic. The influence of women's culture can be felt in the genre's relational orientation, its double-voicedness, its ties with traditional life. Narrators' constant cross-referencing between the community world and the urban readership exemplifies the perpetual negotiation in which women engaged, while the participant/observer narrator is, like Harry Holyoke in *Oldtown Folks* (Boston, 1869), remarkable for attending to voices other than his own. Narrative of community is, however, in the seemingly paradoxical situation of being at once suffused with qualities of women's culture yet not, as a general rule, woman-centered in a literal sense. Women's culture per se seldom constitutes either the locus of its intended readership, or—except in a work like *Cranford* or *Country*—its explicit subject, and this may have to do with the fact that in the nineteenth century, as Cott observes, women's culture tended to be associated with the preindustrial past common to all. While writers' knowledge of and dedication to communitarianism appear to have derived partly from personal experience of women's culture, these writers presented the values and experiences of such community not, primarily, as properties belonging to women's culture but, more generally, as valuable aspects of a life usually located in the past that they wished to convey to everyone, male and female. *Oldtown Folks'* expressed intent is to "show you New England in its *seed-bed*," "the seed-bed of this great American Republic, and of all that is likely to come of it";[22] Eliot locates *Adam Bede* "sixty years ago" and stresses the links between the "monotonous homely existence" of its community culture and the world of her readers.[23]

Writers apparently felt a certain expansiveness about writing narrative of community that may have been sustained partly by its ties with women's culture and a relative freedom from too oppres-

---

amidst the real experience of mid-nineteenth-century women, we begin to understand the mediation between the presence of distinct cultural values and their transformation into a political arsenal for the self-advancement of a sex. The significance of leaders' ability to tap latent resources and to foster thereby an unprecedented women's mobilization becomes a compelling scholarly goal" (39). On the literary domestics, see Mary Kelley, *Private Woman, Public Stage: Literary Domesticity in Nineteenth-Century America* (New York: Oxford University Press, 1984); on Beecher, see Kathryn Kish Sklar, *Catharine Beecher: A Study in American Domesticity* (New York: Norton, 1976).

[22] *Oldtown Folks*, in Kathryn Kish Sklar, ed., *Harriet Beecher Stowe: Three Novels* (New York: Library of America, 1982), 883.

[23] George Eliot, *Adam Bede* (New York: Washington Square Press, 1964), 171, 173. See esp. chap. 17., "In Which the Story Pauses a Little," for such mediation.

sive constraints of extant literary models: Gaskell's statement to
Ruskin that when she was blue she read Cranford[24] indicates something of this freedom, as does Jewett's sense that literature representing the texture of rural life belonged to its own "department."[25]
At the same time, narrative of community was certainly not fully at
liberty to chart its own course. For one thing, the freedom of not
belonging to a fully developed tradition was often accompanied by
pronounced instability of form and focus, especially since narrative
of community's subject and terms of discourse were different from
and partly in opposition to the individualism that predominated in
so much contemporary fiction. This instability is evident in the fact
that many works that participate in narrative of community are also
quite actively in dialogue with other genres. Adam Bede's negotiations between genres are instructive in this regard. In the development of the major characters, for whom identity and heterosexual
romance are crucial issues, conventional plot predominates and
community life is often a backdrop: thus the process by which
Hetty's feminine identity comes into being as a response to the
gazes of others shapes the structuring of her story. Yet the figure-
ground relationship is also often reversed, with the everyday and
traditional becoming the stronger element. In the presentation of
the Poyser Farm in the chapters "The Hall Farm" and "The Diary,"
for example, the ordinary conversation of Hayslope inhabitants, as
well as everyday activities like churning butter and dusting, are in
the foreground, rendered with vibrant particularity; and despite the
fact that Hetty comes to life here partly under Arthur's gaze and
that of the narrator, even she exists most fully within the fabric of
community life.

In Adam Bede the narrator also mediates insistently, sometimes
strenuously, between the community world of Hayslope and the mid-
nineteenth-century world of the reader: the reflection on "Old Leisure," "gone where the spinning-wheels are gone,"[26] is the most
famous of such mediations. Both of these kinds of negotiations—

---

[24] See J. A. V. Chapple and Arthur Pollard, eds., The Letters of Mrs. Gaskell
(Cambridge, Mass.: Harvard University Press, 1967), 747.

[25] Judith Fetterley, in the "Introduction" to Provisions: A Reader from Nineteenth-Century American Women (Bloomington: Indiana University Press, 1985),
suggests that when American women wrote in literary forms such as the sketch and
essay, they were relatively free from the "anxiety of authorship" and often exuberant
about the values their work embodied and about themselves as writers (see esp. 2–
8). These attitudes may have also obtained for women engaged in writing narrative
of community, even if the same attitudes did not predominate when those women
wrote other kinds of literature.

[26] Eliot, Adam Bede, 504.

among genres, between cultures—help explain why narrative of community is sometimes present in writing by men. Although narrative of community's perpetual negotiation between worlds is closely related to the circumstances of women's culture, such a strategy has never been practiced only by women. Showalter rightly maintains that all members of marginal groups perform it, and negotiation between classes or cultures was in fact pertinent for a number of male writers in whose work traces of narrative of community can be detected, including Charles Dickens, Thomas Hardy, the earlier D. H. Lawrence, and Sherwood Anderson. In fact, the position of these particular men can be said to have been analogous in some respects to that of many women who wrote narratives of community, for their origins were in, or they felt some allegiance to, regional, rural, or working-class ways of life that were not emphatically individualistic.[27] Although in their writing their deepest commitment was to coming to terms with modern life, they also sometimes mediated between the tasks of representing an individual-based, contractual society and expressing a community-based vision.

In the writing of most men who seek to represent community the novel tends to predominate heavily and narrative of community figures as a shadow possibility. There are in Hardy's *The Woodlanders* (London, 1887) glimpses of community in the representation of rural traditions rooted in long-standing skills and rituals, an ethic of loyalty, and a history-drenched language, but community is devastated by commoditization, by aspirations derived from a modern, urban environment to status and gentility, and by the narrowed individualism that characterizes Edred Fitzpiers and, finally, Grace Melbury. Narrative of community has a stronger presence in Dickens's novels: even in *Little Dorrit* (London, 1855–57), one of his grimmest, Bleeding Heart Yard is rendered as an urban community. The Yard, often spoken of as a single entity, exhibits neighborly support, accommodates eccentricity, and even welcomes the foreigner Cavalletto. Yet it is only partially realized and is placed in structural parentheses between the nuclear family and social institutions like the Circumlocution Office and the Marshalsea. It is also offset by the novel's much heavier emphasis on a world darkened by institutional gargantuanism and personal attenuation. Sherwood Anderson's *Winesburg, Ohio* (New York, 1919), on the other hand, stands out as a book specifically structured to accommodate village life. Its episodic chapters are organized around ordinary individuals; discourse is rooted in the vernacular; the narrative is unified

---

[27] Hardy, e.g., experienced rural life at a time when it was still fairly traditional, and Dickens felt an affinity, albeit an ambivalent one, with the urban working class.

264   Zagarell

by the characters' common yearnings and by the presence of George Willard, who plays a participant/observer-like role. Above all, Winesburg's insistence that what may from the outside seem unimportant is actually dense with life and echoing with individual stories links the text to narrative of community. And yet the terms of this insistence also distinguish it dramatically from works like Gaskell's Cranford and Jewett's The Country of the Pointed Firs, in which individual lives and personal histories are part of a larger network. The predominant viewpoint of Winesburg is the individual-based conviction that everyone has a story to tell; further, George Willard's own story becomes increasingly primary, as he becomes a familiar novelistic character, the sensitive young man from the provinces who leaves to forge his destiny. Thus, though Winesburg is informed by a tension between narrative of community and individual-based narrative, its greater allegiance, thematically and structurally, is to the individualistic tradition of the revolt from the village.[28]

George Sturt's Change in the Village (London, 1912), a rendering of life in a Surrey village as the remnant of a "robust [peasant] tradition,"[29] is an exception to men's writing that participates in narrative of community, for in it individualism does not predominate. Here, in the foregrounding of community life and careful attention to practices that link past and present, is the combination of intimate knowledge of community culture and a determination to communicate it to the world beyond that is most characteristic of nineteenth-century narratives of community. Sturt's book, which is about an early twentieth-century village, reminds us that even in the Western world, pockets of preindustrial life persisted into the twentieth century. It suggests, moreover, that twentieth-century ideas of community owe a good deal to the preservation of earlier values. Finally, it exemplifies the fact that the work of writers in which the community, rather than the self, is central has been fundamental in preserving communitarian values. Identifying such literature as the bearer of a culture of community is in fact partly what

[28] My purpose here is to indicate some ways in which narrative of community may be present in works by men, but I have by no means mentioned all pertinent works or possible generic combinations. The connection could be pursued with regard to James Joyce's Dubliners (London, 1914) or William Faulkner's Go Down, Moses (New York, 1942), the first of which could be read as an antinarrative of community. There may be works by white male authors as centered in narrative of community as Country or as committed to maintaining a sustained balance between narrative of community and the novel as Adam Bede. Moreover, there may be many works by men and women of color I have not mentioned.

[29] George Sturt, Change in the Village (London: Duckworth, 1912), 10.

Jewett had in mind in the letter with which this article began. She adapts Matthew Arnold's famous description of the plays of Sophocles—they "saw life steadily . . . and saw it whole"—to the literature of the "everyday." She thus appropriates for the "department of literature" with which she is concerned the culture-building work that Arnold himself repeatedly identified as the writer's greatest social responsibility. Whereas Arnold believed in a high culture that would heal the world and provide continuity with the classics, Jewett and other writers believed in the restorative power of narrative of community and in the genre's capacity to reconnect the present with the common culture of the past. For Jewett, as for Eliot, Stowe, Gaskell, Barlow, and others, the literature of the everyday was neither commercialized nor elitist—not, as Jewett put it in the same letter, "the trashy newspapers" or the "wealth" of high culture—but "belong[ed] to the middle ground." For it was, like the culture it represented, respectful of "the good men and women" of places like Dunnet Landing, and it had faith that their capacity to forge what Jewett would call in *Country* "the golden chain of love and dependence" (*Country*, 90) could be renewed even in what Arnold's sonnet described as "these bad days."[30]

* * *

I have chosen Jewett's *Country* and Thompson's *Lark Rise* to illustrate narrative of community's hallmarks because although in each there are traces of other genres (the novel in *Country*, ethnography in *Lark Rise*), each is most fundamentally conceived as a representation of the life of a self-contained community, and the primary features of narrative of community predominate in both. Moreover, both have always been difficult to place generically. Using them to illustrate narrative of community's elements establishes their structural coherence and its emanation from their informing vision. This approach suggests for *Country* a breadth that has not been fully discerned and highlights the literary distinction of *Lark Rise*, which has generally been approached as a source of historical or anthropological information.[31] In addition, although this discus-

[30] Cary, ed. (n. 1 above), 51.
[31] Debora G. Kodish, "Moving towards the Everyday: Some Thoughts on Gossip and Visiting and Secular Procession," *Folklore Papers of the University Folklore Association* (1980), 93–104, discusses its folkloric dimensions, while Barbara English, "*Lark Rise* and Juniper Hill: A Victorian Community in Literature and in History," *Victorian Studies* 29, no. 1 (Autumn 1985): 6–34, assesses its value as a historical record, identifying it as the glorification of a nostalgia-drenched "Old England."

sion will show that *Country* and *Lark Rise* are fundamentally similar, their similarities coexist with what would once have seemed more essential differences: one is American, the other British; one is nineteenth-century, the other twentieth; one has an established literary reputation, the other is not typically classified as literature at all. Thus they can be paired only when some of the conceptual boundaries that have obscured narrative of community's existence are suspended.[32]

The narrators in *Country* and *Lark Rise* mediate carefully between their positions as participants in community life and their roles as its observers. Marcia Folsom's recent identification of *Country*'s narrator as an empathic observer brings earlier commentators' interest in the involvement of Jewett's narrator in Dunnet life into focus.[33] Even Folsom's formulation can be taken further, for the narrator achieves a delicate balance between what folklorists call ethnic genres and analytic categories alien to the community.[34] The narrative voices in *Country* and *Lark Rise* are exceptionally porous, always hospitable to the language and frame of reference of community members, and this is so partly because the narrators exist primarily in relation to the community, their empathy arising from this positioning. In *Country*, the unnamed narrator, a visitor and "lover of Dunnet Landing" (*Country*, 2), initially makes mildly egocentric professions of affection about the community; these are superseded by an intensified attentiveness to the community's own voices and the experiences they express. Increasingly, she uses the

---

[32] It may appear that the little-known Thompson does not belong in the company of Eliot, Gaskell, Jewett, and Stowe. She did not participate in nineteenth-century middle-class women's culture, and although her childhood and early adulthood took place during the nineteenth century, she wrote during the twentieth. Like other writers of narrative of community, however, Thompson was crucially concerned with portraying a traditional, collective way of life to a modern readership. Further, her literary consciousness and imagination were rooted in the nineteenth century; not only does she invoke Wordsworth and Scott, she makes specific mention of *Cranford*. And her example, like those of some of the male writers mentioned, indicates that interdependence and a commitment to the collective life often existed among the working classes and/or where traces of the peasantry remained. During Thompson's childhood, her home, the Oxfordshire hamlet of Juniper Hill, was one of the many places in England where preindustrial peasant ways persisted into the late nineteenth century and she devoted herself as a writer to resurrecting them. For biographical information on Thompson, see Margaret Lane, *Purely for Pleasure* (New York: Knopf, 1967), chap. 1.

[33] Marcia Folsom, " 'Tact Is a Kind of Mind-Reading': Empathic Style in Sarah Orne Jewett's *The Country of the Pointed Firs*," *Colby Library Quarterly* 18, no. 1 (March 1982): 66–78.

[34] See Dan Ben-Amos, "Analytic Categories and Ethnic Genres," *Genre* 2, no. 3 (September 1969): 275–301.

community's nautical and garden imagery and evaluative expressions ("poor," "pleasant," "dear," "delightful"), while also allowing the characters to speak for themselves. *Lark Rise*'s narrator, also unnamed, describes the community partly from the perspective of the hamlet child Laura, partly from that of an adult whose affection is intensified by her knowledge of life beyond the hamlet and after the 1880s. She always builds exposition and description around country sayings (her term), and her own language has a country tonality, as in the description of one elderly man as a "poor weedy creature" (*Lark Rise*, 59).

Identification with the community, however heartfelt, could represent an effort merely to reproduce community life, but Thompson and Jewett also write to understand and communicate how the community constitutes itself.[35] So, like psychologically inquiring Mary Smith in *Cranford*, historically and theologically analytic Horace Holyoke of *Oldtown Folks*, and the folklorist-narrator of Zora Neale Hurston's *Their Eyes Were Watching God* (Philadelphia, 1937) (who shifts between the voices of black culture in Eatonville, Florida, and a discursive voice directed at other readers), their narrators draw cultural and historical conclusions unthinkable to community members, for whom their life is simply a natural condition. A characteristic passage in which *Lark Rise*'s narrator thinks about the economy and attitudes of country women illustrates the constant interplay between empathy and analysis present in both works:

> Those with an income of ten or twelve shillings a week often had to go short of [commodities], although the management and ingenuity of some . . . was amazing. Every morsel of old rag they could save or beg was made into rugs for the stone floor, or cut into fragments to make flocks to stuff bedding. Sheets were turned outside to middle, and after they had again become worn, patched and patched again until it was difficult to decide which part of a sheet was the original fabric. "Keep the flag flying," they would call to each other when they had their Monday washing flapping on the line, and the seeing eye and the feeling heart, had the possessor of these been present, would have read more than was meant into the saying. They kept the flag flying nobly, but the cost to themselves was great. [*Lark Rise*, 433]

[35] In a letter to Willa Cather, Jewett advised the younger writer to assume "the standpoint of the looker-on who takes [her] material in its relation to letters, to the world" (Annie Fields, ed., *The Letters of Sarah Orne Jewett* [Boston: Houghton Mifflin, 1911], 248).

Only through an insider's empathic experience of the community, this passage insists, can one understand what the world is like to community members. The narrator's account of the women's versatility in economizing is suffused with a first-hand understanding of their circumstances and ingenuity, and the use of community language conveys her grasp of it as the expression of a particular way of experiencing the world. When she reproduces "keep the flag flying," she is commenting on the meanings of the women's task that arise from their economic circumstance and their cultural responses—the shared ethic of fortitude and mutual support. Yet only one with a distancing, interpretive "seeing eye" and "feeling heart" can identify the women's valor fully, and the defamiliarization to which such analysis gives rise is as essential to narrative of community as is the identification facilitated by empathy. Brought to bear on worlds that seemed particularly familiar to readers because they converged with myths about the national past, the combined analysis and empathy act to counteract tendencies to sentimentalize such communities or dismiss them and encourage the kind of serious engagement through which community itself might be resuscitated.

The representation of the everyday complements this sort of compassionate rigor. Both works are dense with details about ordinary activities: one could figure out how to make cough drops from *Country* or cook the customary hamlet dinner, a roly-poly, from *Lark Rise*. But such details are never merely enumerated. The "everyday" is always saturated with meanings in which the personal and the communal unite. In *Lark Rise*, the women's patching and washing are both ordinary work and expressions of a resilience that is prized culturally as well as personally, and the fact that all perform them, cheering each other on, reinforces the women's community identities. Similarly, when Lark Risers invite their neighbors to "come inside an' see our bit o'leazings [grain]" (*Lark Rise*, 28), personal pride, community membership and solidarity, and the expression of absolute material necessity are all contained in the gesture. This conjunction of the personal and cultural in each activity and object creates a symbolism of the everyday—a symbolism scrupulously particular to the community being portrayed. *Country* specifically comments on how to read this kind of symbolism when Mrs. Todd takes the narrator to her cherished pennyroyal grove to reveal that the common herb has intense personal significance, recalling the man she loved but could not marry and the man she married but did not love. Pennyroyal is also the herb she uses most frequently, and henceforth readers grasp the complex of private associations that accompany her appreciation of its medicinal properties. Her experiences also have a strongly felt (though less explicitly articulated) communal dimension: differences in social status separated her from her lover, while the convention that women must marry turned her toward her devoted cousin Nathan, and even her appreciation of pennyroyal is colored by her role as community herbalist.

Finally, in emphasizing that the emblematic quality of the everyday arises from the intersection of the communal and the personal, these writers suggest that the resonance of the "commonplace" had been overshadowed by a prevailing tendency in nineteenth-century literature to claim significance for the ordinary by analogizing it to classical literature or otherwise universalizing it.[36] They also implicitly take to task today's lingering inclination to concentrate on dramatic, reflexive public rituals such as the one anthropologist Clifford Geertz explicates in "Notes on the Balinese Cockfight." That in hanging out sheets and gathering pennyroyal things are not, as they are in the cockfight, "[set] apart from the ordinary course of life," that their symbolic significance specifically derives from their normal context rather than from altering "the established conjunctions between objects and their qualities,"[37] suggests that when the personal and the communal are seen as interwoven, ritual and work, the celebratory and the customary, can be recognized as one. The everyday, these writers show, *is* ritualized, and they provide ways of reading it as such.

Jewett and Thompson place in the narrative center of this environment characters of the sort that gained fictional prominence in the nineteenth century, those Georg Lukács calls the "maintaining individuals" who experience history without becoming major political actors.[38] The two narratives exemplify something of the breadth of characterization possible in a genre that focuses on com-

[36] Eliot and Jewett, though sometimes guilty of both tendencies, also problematized them. The complicated analogy between Mrs. Todd and Antigone with which the pennyroyal sequence concludes suggests that both figures must be understood in the context of their own cultures and daily lives. Early in *Silas Marner*, Eliot contrasts Silas's abstract and isolating love for his gold (a supracultural symbol) with his personalization of a beloved earthenware pot, a local and ordinary object. The personal-cultural nature of the latter registers links between Silas and the community of Raveloe of which he himself is at this point unaware; toward the end of the narrative the pot is evoked as a symbol of the tenacity with which he comes to prize his connectedness to both Eppie and the life of Raveloe (George Eliot, *Silas Marner: The Weaver of Raveloe* [Baltimore: Penguin, 1967], 69, 200).

[37] Clifford Geertz, "Notes on the Balinese Cockfight," in his *The Interpretation of Cultures* (New York: Basic Books, 1973), 446, 447.

[38] Georg Lukács, *The Historical Novel*, trans. Hannah Mitchell and Stanley Mitchell (Boston: Beacon Press, 1963), 39. Lukács attributes the phrase to Hegel.

munity life. In Jewett, the initial point of departure is, in typically American fashion, the individual, but though this approach has contributed to mistaken searches for *Country's* "true" protagonist (variously identified as the narrator, Mrs. Todd, and even Captain Littlepage), the narrative does not feature individualized lives but develops an interdependent community network in which characters are portrayed with reference to how they intersect with and maintain the community. Each character's personality emerges through an activity conceived as fundamentally social, speech. Those who obsessively repeat the same story, Captain Littlepage and, to a lesser extent, Elijah Tilley, are situated vis-à-vis those whose discourse, such as Mrs. Todd's, includes stories of others in the community, the exchange of information, and the collective history vital to community preservation. Moreover, characters are continuously placed within the community setting. Even the most isolated, Captain Littlepage, first appears in a community ritual, a funeral, and when he inflicts on the narrator his preoccupation with a world between life and death, he is established as one incapable of community-building exchange. At the opposite pole is Mrs. Blackett. Described as "one who had long since passed the line that divides mere self-concern from a valued share in whatever Society can give and take" (*Country*, 41), she is always developed through her community-creating effect, from the narrator's testimony, at her first appearance, that "You felt as if [she] were an old and dear friend before you let go her cordial hand" (*Country*, 36) to the collective tributes to her empathy and kindness at the Bowden reunion. Finally, the characterization of Mrs. Todd combines activity that maintains the common life spiritually and physically— herbalism, visits, gossip, storytelling—with a personal sensibility expressed through selective revelation that occurs within community life but does not disrupt it.

Lark Rise's impetus is more ethnographic, its approach to characterization more cumulative, its population denser. Partly because it is British, partly because Lark Risers live perilously "near the bone" (*Lark Rise*, 32) economically and culturally and can survive only by remaining tightly interconnected, characterization takes place within the arena of group life. The narrator often refers to the characters collectively, as "country people," "the besieged generation," "husbands," "wives," "the women," and so forth. Although Thompson, too, presents individuals' stories, these frequently serve to illustrate an aspect of the community's history, customs, or circumstances: "Old Sally" and her husband, for instance, live more productively and comfortably than younger Lark Risers because their house was constructed before the General Enclosure Act of

1801 accelerated the inclosure of what was once common land and because they retain old-fashioned habits of home production. Even though *Lark Rise*'s vision is more continuously collective, however, the narrative features innumerable vividly particularized sketches of characters engaged in culturally specific activities. One example is a little girl dressed "in her mother's best coat with the sleeves turned back to the elbows and her hair done up for the first time that morning, plaited into an inverted saucer at the back of her head and bristling with black hairpins" (*Lark Rise*, 138) who goes out to apply for her first servant's position. Such cameos are woven together by the observations of Laura and her brother Edmond, and their identities, too, are predominantly cultural: their reflections and most intense curiosity and emotions are about Lark Rise, illuminating its life and theirs in connection with it.

The importance of characters of such ordinary dimensions is illuminated by a narrative structure quite different from the linearity of many forms of the novel (bildungsroman, novels of courtship and marriage, some panoramic social novels). Such novels are teleological, plotting the individual lives they feature as dramas arranged around desire, conflict, and choice, dramas that move toward success or failure. Narrative of community, concerned instead with continuity, seeks to represent what gives the community its identity, what enables it to remain itself. The approach is imbued with a concern for process. Writers understood communities to take form through negotiation among diverse, often recalcitrant components—people living at distances from each other; sometimes reluctant individuals; scarce resources; values, practices, and lore that are threatened by time and change; a harsh physical environment—and they foregrounded the specific dynamics through which these elements are continuously reintegrated. Often, these dynamics constitute narrative of community's fundamental structural principle. Narratives proceed episodically; the particular sequence of episodes is generally less important than the episodes' repeated exemplification of the dynamics that maintain the community. Narrative "action" is built around these dynamics and stresses how the elements of community are integrated. The dynamics, then, shape numerous small-scale activities fundamental to the narratives' symbolism: daily tasks, the uses to which objects are put, the exchange of goods, expressions of connection and affection. Mr. Gilfil's presentation of a large piece of bacon to Dame Fripp in "Mr. Gilfil's Love-Story" is typical of the sharing of goods that so often occupies a central position in Eliot's *Scenes of Clerical Life*: the gift reconfigures community relations, as does her subsequent appearance at his funeral. Such apparently minor processes are complemented by the frequent large-scale activities that are also organized by the community's characteristic dynamic—visits, conversations, storytelling, rituals—and reaffirm ongoing collective life in a more formal way. Finally the fundamental dynamic of each narrative often also gives shape to physical movement through the community (strolls, excursions) or narrative movement that radiates out from and back to the community's center. This is a device by which many narratives of community, from *Our Village* to *Country* to Gloria Naylor's *The Women of Brewster Place* (New York, 1982), articulate the boundaries around the community and take stock of how what lies within becomes community.[39]

These process-oriented structures have contributed to critics' unspoken sense of disjunction between their familiar frame of reference, grounded in a drama- and individual-based form, and the communitarian aesthetic of *Lark Rise* and *Country*. No one has ever known what to call *Lark Rise*—Raymond Williams simply terms it an "irreplaceable record"—while discussion of *Country* has often centered on its status and genre. Even Warner Berthoff's 1959 analysis defends it as a fine work of regionalist writing and elucidates a structure he finds effective but idiosyncratic: an alternation between idyllic and anti-idyllic episodes appropriate to its ambivalence about Dunnet's dying way of life.[40] Recently, feminist critics have reversed the terms of past appraisals for *Country* to show that it deliberately refuses linearity in order to achieve an inclusive

[39] Some critical theory suggests that linear structure conflates a number of phenomena, including principles of (Aristotelian) dramatic unity, the bourgeois individualism discussed earlier, the Oedipal quest, which Vladimir Propp and Roland Barthes have both identified as underlying all narrative, and male sexuality itself. See Teresa de Lauretis's chapter "Desire as Narrative" in her *Alice Doesn't: Feminism, Semiotics, Cinema* (Bloomington: Indiana University Press, 1982), for an analysis of the engenderment that can be seen as common to many of these phenomena. It is tempting to wish to see alternative structures as circular, and some feminist thought has implied that the circle is distinctively female. Yet to conceive a nonlinear form only in terms of its opposite, the circular, is not only to run the risk of reproducing the kind of binary in which gender itself is rooted; it does not take into consideration that linearity is so overdetermined that there is room for considerable divergence among forms that are not linear.

[40] Raymond Williams, *The Country and the City* (St. Albans: Palladin, 1975), 313; Warner Berthoff, "The Art of Jewett's *Pointed Firs*," *New England Quarterly* 32, no. 2 (March 1959): 31–53. Despite Berthoff's insistence on the warped nature of the community of women and his valorization of Captain Littlepage's heroic vision, the sensitivity of his discussion is pronounced, e.g., in his observation that storytelling is a major narrative event in *Country;* in her introduction to Jewett (n. 3 above), Pryse also identifies the importance of storytelling, seeing it as a women's act (xiii).

circularity,[41] and close examination of the features on which these critics focus—communication, visits, the Bowden reunion—reveals that all proceed by means of *Country's* essential structural principle: perpetual negotiation. In the visit to Green Island, for example, which Elizabeth Ammons reads as a climactic coming-together of the narrator and Mrs. Todd, such negotiation informs the gestures, physical movements, and conversation that plot the achievement of unity. From an initial unconnectedness exemplified in Mrs. Todd's gruff invitation to the narrator to gather herbs in a pasture, through the narrator's cordial appreciation of the family daguerreotypes (which encourages Mrs. Todd to proceed to her "sainted" place, the pennyroyal grove) to the interplay of speech and silence during their greatest intimacy (the narrator asks no questions, Mrs. Todd never mentions her lover's name), subtle maneuverings organize narrative movement.[42]

---

[41] Critics used to feel forced either to concede that *Country* is not a novel, allowing for its deficiencies in plot and action, or to prove that, despite appearances, it really *is* a novel. Among the former are F. O. Matthiesson, who termed it a series of loosely connected sketches held together simply by the force of Jewett's "unity of vision" (*Sarah Orne Jewett* [New York: Houghton Mifflin, 1929], 101); and Richard Cary, who called it a "paranovel," a form he praised as appropriate to Jewett's subject and accommodation of the details of life, and found restorative for readers but delineated largely in terms of its lack of plot and action, the "big issues," and "the grand passion" (*Sarah Orne Jewett* [New York: Twayne, 1962], 130–31). Many who read *Country* as a novel have resorted to finding a hidden dramatic action, as did Paul D. Volker in his tracing of the story of the narrator (the protagonist) as she becomes one with the community ("The Country of the Pointed Firs: A Novel by Sarah Orne Jewett," *Colby Library Quarterly* 9, no. 4 [December 1970]: 201–43). Though some feminist rereadings have accepted the generic category of novel, they tend to be highly sensitive to the book's nonlinear, undramatic structure (see Pryse, ed. [n. 3 above]; and Elizabeth Ammons, "Going in Circles: The Female Geography of Jewett's *Country of the Pointed Firs*," *Studies in the Literary Imagination* 16, no. 2 [Fall 1983]: 83–92). Feminist discussions that are also ground-breaking about style and form and do not assume the narrator as central protagonist include Folsom (n. 33 above); and Boone (n. 16 above). In the little commentary that exists on *Lark Rise* and its companion volumes, the novel has been a silent standard of measure. Not being a novel, *Lark Rise* has been excluded from the ranks of fiction, labeled, variously, neither novel nor autobiography but "social history" with an unusually "alive . . . personal element"; an "impressive study" and "minor classic"; a "chronicle"; and "rural . . . portraiture engagingly blended with autobiography" (Lane [n. 32 above], 3; Kodish [n. 31 above], 94; Massingham [n. 3 above], 7, respectively).

[42] The persuasiveness of Elizabeth Ammons's very fine reading of this as *Country's* climactic moment reflects the fact that *Country* participates in the novel as well as the narrative of community, and to the extent that it is a protagonist's tale— the story of the narrator's integration into a community of women—Ammons's reading illuminates brilliantly how that story rejects linearity. Significantly, the linear is dominant in the one episode in which community is not achieved, Captain Littlepage's narrative.

The constant sharing of scant resources to maintain the common life also organizes much of the activity in *Country*, and here negotiation takes the form of generosity maneuvering within well-recognized limits (the dealings with food that undergird the Green Island visit [*Country*, 31–54] and Bowden reunion [*Country*, 83–113] are good examples). On the larger scale, negotiation structures the main activity that shapes and unites all the episodes except the reunion, the storytelling through which Dunnet members constantly reestablish the community network. The retelling of the story of the recluse, Joanna Todd, which has been seen primarily as the depiction of a tormented individual, exemplifies and proceeds by this sort of negotiation. The actual recounting is itself an act of negotiation between the community's standing version of an unaccountably recalcitrant woman and a new interpretation of the relationship between recluse and community. Maneuvering between Joanna's insistent, painful individualism and the need to see her in relation to community life, Mrs. Todd and Mrs. Fosdick accept Joanna's own version of herself as someone who has "committed the unpardonable sin" of cursing God (*Country*, 76), yet surround it with an interpretation of her as one afflicted with spiritual "bad eyesight" (*Country*, 77) who could survive on her island only because of the community's tolerant, encircling protectiveness. In the process of jointly fashioning this story, the two also renegotiate their own friendship, in which the issue of Joanna had been a fault line. The narrative inscribes the physical process of their becoming, for the duration of their talk, a single entity (drawing closer, becoming "quite unconscious of a listener"). It also represents their storytelling as a positioning and repositioning of reciprocal voices. Through speech tags and syntactical echoing, the collaborative storytelling charts the process of reunification. When Mrs. Fosdick's question "interrupts" her friend, for instance, Mrs. Todd takes up her mode, posing another question; when Joanna's isolation disturbs Mrs. Todd, Mrs. Fosdick responds to her "sorrowful" lamentation with "kindly" reassurance (*Country*, 69). Finally, storytelling as a process of negotiation with past tellings extends to the narrator, who makes a pilgrimage to Shell Heap Island to establish her own understanding of Joanna. In embracing these successive, inconclusive versions of Joanna's story, the narrative makes central the process of storytelling and conversation. Through the retelling of stories, the community incorporates change and assimilates new members; it thus maintains its own continuity.

The structure of *Lark Rise* foregrounds the kind of social and historical changes that make such long-term cultural continuity, in Thompson's eyes, impossible. Although Lark Rise has been seen as a remnant of traditional peasant life,[43] the community in fact exists only for a brief period and is founded at the intersection between the old peasant life, which for Thompson was self-reproducing and possessed of cultural depth and integrity, and the industrial age, which she sees as fractured by contractual socioeconomic relations and commodification. The dynamic by means of which Lark Rise maintains itself is one of continual adjustment: it draws on peasant traditions, skills, and customs to achieve its unique identity, thus rendering briefly endurable the modernization that will eventually destroy it. Appropriately, *Lark Rise*'s essential structural dynamic is constant contextualization. The narrative proceeds by immersion, establishing the momentary vitality and long-term precariousness of virtually every facet of community life, from the children's games and the women's culinary practices to country language and the condition of agricultural labor. It presents them as they exist in Lark Rise in the 1880s, reconstructs their earlier state, and, often, depicts them as altered beyond recognition in the twentieth century. At the same time it circles out from the hamlet of thirty cottages on a rise and returns to depict men in the fields, women at home, daughters away in domestic service. It then portrays the more modern dimensions of community life such as the children's attendance at the recently founded national school.

The first two-thirds of *Lark Rise* stress the resonance with which community life maintains itself in the 1880s. In a section that situates community life with reference to pre- and post-Enclosure rights and the skills those rights nurtured, the sturdy decades-old cottage of Old Sally, described in terms of size and function, becomes the reference point for all the homes and living practices. In this large house with walls two feet thick, one downstairs room "was used as a kind of kitchen-storeroom, with pots and pans and a big red crockery water vessel. ... In one corner stood the big brewing copper in which Sally still brewed with good malt and hops once a quarter" (*Lark Rise*, 77). From this central description, with its emphatic "still," the narrative considers first the other cottages that also stood on the green before Enclosure, then the "newer, meaner dwellings that had sprung up around and between them" (*Lark Rise*, 79). Circling out to the future, it then recontextualizes Sally's mode of life in the reader's present of 1939: "Today, all has gone, and only the limy whiteness of the soil in a corner of a ploughed field is left to show that a cottage once stood there" (*Lark Rise*, 81). Then it registers the adjustments members of the generation after Sally's have to make as a step toward integration into the "modern"

[43] See Massingham (n. 3 above), "Introduction."

world. Furnished with the "cheap and ugly products of the early machine age" (*Lark Rise*, 98), the homes of this "besieged" generation cannot accommodate brewing beer or baking bread. Yet the old traditions of stretching resources and putting everything to use allow this generation, too, to maintain its community identity. Supplementing bitterly meager wages with such practices as cultivating kitchen gardens and making home tonics, its members can still participate in the ethos of the older life that the section's closing sentences evoke: "You don't want to be poor and look poor, too. . . . We've got our pride" (*Lark Rise*, 118).

If *Lark Rise* presents the viewpoint of the community, invoking historical change as the community adjusts to it, the narrative's overarching structure turns this process inside out to show how adjustment ultimately facilitates the community's destruction by the very forces it sought to accommodate. Increasingly emphasizing the present and future, the later chapters loop farther and farther beyond the hamlet. Although the final one, "Harvest Home"—which portrays rituals by which Lark Rise solidifies its existence—again contextualizes community practice in the past, it does so only to register the community's capitulation to the present. And in the book's final loop, entering the modern era is identical with Lark Rise's full destruction. *Lark Rise* ends:

And all [during the nineties] boys were being born or growing up in the parish, expecting to follow the plough all their lives, or, at most, to do a little mild soldiering or go to work in a town. Gallipoli? Kut? Vimy Ridge? Ypres? What did they know of such places? But they were to know them, and when the time came they did not flinch. Eleven out of that tiny community never came back again. A brass plate on the wall of the church immediately over the old end house seat is engraved with their names. A double column, five names long, then, last and alone the name of Edmund. [*Lark Rise*, 247]

Lark Rise's demise is thus facilitated by that long-standing ethos that, for a brief time, gave it life. "Not flinching" is a favorite community virtue—men in the fields describe their unflagging work during harvest in these terms, as do women in labor—and it has urged the young men into the war that would cause their deaths. This ending interrupts *Lark Rise*'s radial structure physically, returning only to the "mother village" of Fordlow, and chronologically, settling in the present. It insists that for Thompson the structural principle of immersing all aspects of the present in past and future is appropriate only as long as Lark Rise exists as a community.

* * *

In the twentieth century, urban capitalism, whose endangerment of traditional life initially spurred the development of narrative of community, has further eroded that life. For white middle-class women the life of a community such as Dunnet Landing is more often a matter of historical record than a lived memory or experience. Yet narrative of community has continued to flourish. As the example of the working-class Thompson suggests, community is being portrayed by a much more diverse group of writers in this century. This is probably because although community life, and in some cases the ideal of a collective life, has receded for the middle classes, they have remained part of the experience or become an articulated goal of members of many other groups. Not surprisingly, narrative of community has diversified.[44] It appears in Afro-American works like Jean Toomer's *Cane* (New York, 1923), *Their Eyes Were Watching God,* Toni Morrison's *Song of Solomon* (New York, 1977), Alice Walker's *The Color Purple* (New York, 1982), and Gloria Naylor's *The Women of Brewster Place.* Its greater class diversity is also evinced by its presence in narratives like Meridel LeSueur's *The Girl* (Boston, 1978) and Harriette Arnow's *The Dollmaker* (New York, 1954); its ethnic and regional variation is registered as well by its appearance in the Scottish writer Lewis Grassic Gibbon's (James Leslie Mitchell) nationalistic *A Scot's Quair* (London, 1932–34), Bruce Chatwin's *On the Black Hill* (London, 1982), which is about Welsh border country, Canadian writer Alice Munro's *Lives of Girls and Women* (Toronto, 1971), and Joan Chase's *During the Reign of the Queen of Persia* (New York, 1983), which portrays an extended family in rural Ohio. It can even be detected in ethnographic studies like Ronald Blythe's *Akenfield* (London, 1969). These titles suggest that there have been changes in the general model I have identified in this essay. First, linear plotting is much more pronounced in almost all the works I mention than in *Lark Rise* or *Country,* and individual, if not individualized, protagonists more frequent. Second, perhaps because of the particular cultural traditions on which writers like Gibbons, Hurston, and Walker draw, the communities they depict often seem invented or fabulous, and folk-

---

[44] I wish to emphasize that Afro-American literature, like some of the other literatures I mention here, clearly constitutes its own literary traditions and that I am suggesting, not that the genre is the literature's generating principle, but that narrative of community is present in such literature.

loric, mythical, occasionally magical elements are sometimes prominent, as they are in *Song of Solomon*. Third, the fashioning of
community, whether political or cultural, is one explicit objective
of some writers' work. *The Girl* urges readers to construct or take
part in the kind of political community its women characters achieve
at the end, while *Song of Solomon* presents as exemplary Milkman's
quest for a racial community, anchored in history and culture.

While the greater diversity of narrative of community in the
twentieth century attests to the genre's continuing vitality, these
changes need to be explored in depth. Other matters must also be
addressed, including the extent to which twentieth-century narratives of community may be inspired most strongly by writers' own
racial, ethnic, class, and or cultural traditions, and the changing
roles of gender. The question of whether any direct lines of descent
exist between earlier and more contemporary writers of narrative
of community should also be pursued. Finally, we need, on the one
hand, to study the genre's complicated interactions with plots structured around individualized protagonists and, on the other, to investigate structural variations resulting from writers' representation
of a wider range of communities. Even at this point, however, it is
clear that narrative of community continues to flourish in our own
decade. Though the genre may be nostalgically trivialized in Helen
Hooven Santmyer's racist, elitist . . . *And Ladies of the Club* (Co-
lumbus, Ohio, 1982), it is extended by *The Color Purple*'s depiction
of personal empowerment as the foundation for the creation of a
community that endures racism and dismantles patriarchy. It is drawn
on by Pat Barker's *Union Street* (London, 1982), a grim narrative
that uses the device of remaining in one neighborhood, among a
group of women whose lives intersect, to underscore the isolation
of urban working-class life in northern England, and by *On the
Black Hill*, an evocation of a rural community that endures well
into the twentieth century despite modernization as well as personal privation and idiosyncrasy. During the same period when the
most widely recognized strain of English-language literature has
detailed massive cultural loss and despair, emphasizing individual
anomie, fragmented states of consciousness, and the courage of an
often solitary determination to survive, this tradition has followed
another path. Embracing increasingly heterogeneous visions of the
collective life, narrative of community is expanding the story of
human connection and continuity.

Department of English
Oberlin College

About the Contributors

LOURDES ARIZPE is an anthropologist teaching in the department of history at the National University of Mexico in Mexico City. She is the author of several books and numerous articles on women workers and migration in Mexico. Among her works in English are "Cultural Change and Ethnicity in Rural Mexico" (in *Environment, Society, and Rural Change in Latin America,* ed. David Preston [London: Wylie, 1981]); "The Rural Exodus in Mexico and Mexican Migration to the United States" (reprinted in *The Border That Joins: Mexican Migrants and U.S. Responsibility,* ed. Peter G. Brown and Henry Shue [Totowa, N.J.: Rowman & Littlefield, 1983]); "Anthropology in Latin America: Old Boundaries, New Contexts" (in *Changing Perspectives in Latin American Studies: Insights from Six Disciplines,* ed. Christopher Mitchell [Stanford, Calif.: Stanford University Press, 1988]); and, with Josefina Aranda, the much-reprinted "The 'Comparative Advantages' of Women's Disadvantages: Women Workers in the Strawberry Agrobusiness in Mexico" (*Signs* 7, no. 2 [1981]: 453–73).

SIMONE DE BEAUVOIR (1908–86) is the author of the controversial *The Second Sex* (Paris: Gallimard, 1949; first American edition, New York: Vintage, 1952), one of the earliest and best-known feminist works of this century. A highly influential intellectual, activist, and writer, Beauvoir is also the author of other works in existentialist philosophy, several novels, and four volumes of autobiography. Several volumes of her journals and letters have been published posthumously, and she has been the subject of several notable biographies.

PAULA BENNETT is assistant professor of English at Southern Illinois University, Carbondale. She is the author of *My Life a Loaded Gun: Dickinson, Plath, Rich, and Female Creativity* (Urbana: University of Illinois Press, 1990). With support from a Southern Illinois research grant, she currently is working on a critical text titled "Dissenting Angels: American Women's Poetry, 1850–1900" and on an edition of the poetry of Sarah Morgan Bryan Piatt.

VÈVÈ A. CLARK is associate professor of African and Caribbean literatures in the African-American studies department at the University of California, Berkeley. She is a specialist in African diaspora literatures, theater, folklore, and African-American dance theater. She is coeditor of *The Legend of Maya Deren, a Documentary Biography* (New York:

Anthology Film Archives/Film Culture, 1984), an account of the life and work of the independent filmmaker.

JANE DESMOND is an associate professor of women's studies and American studies at the University of Iowa. Formerly a professional modern dancer and choreographer, she is currently editing a collection of post-structural dance criticism for Duke University Press, tentatively titled "Meaning in Motion: New Scholarship in Dance." Among her publications are "Ethnography, Orientalism, and the Avant-Garde Film," *Visual Anthropology* 4 (Summer 1991): 147–60; "How I Met Miss Tootie: The Home Shopping Club," *Cultural Studies* 3, no. 3 (1989): 340–47; and "Mapping Identity onto the Body," *Women and Performance* (in press).

JANE FLAX is professor of political science at Howard University and a psychotherapist in private practice. A new book of her essays, *Disputed Subjects,* will be published by Routledge in 1993. These essays respond to some of the questions raised by readers of her previous book, *Thinking Fragments* (Berkeley and Los Angeles: University of California Press, 1990). Currently she is thinking about ways to reconceptualize race, gender, and justice.

EVELYN BROOKS HIGGINBOTHAM is associate professor in the department of history at the University of Pennsylvania. She has written several articles on the history of African-American women and is the author of *Righteous Discontent: The Women's Movement in the Black Baptist Church, 1880–1920* (Cambridge, Mass.: Harvard University Press, 1993).

ALICE JARDINE is professor of romance languages and literatures at Harvard University and the author of *Gynesis: Configurations of Woman and Modernity* (Ithaca, N.Y.: Cornell University Press, 1985). She has edited *The Future of Difference* (Boston: Hall; New York: Barnard College Women's Center, 1980) with Hester Eisenstein; *Men in Feminism* (New York: Methuen, 1987) with Paul Smith; and *Shifting Scenes: Interviews on Women, Writing, and Politics in Post-68 France* (New York: Columbia University Press, 1991) with Anne Menke. She is also cotranslator of Julia Kristeva's *Desire in Language* (New York: Columbia University Press, 1980) with Thomas Gora and Leon F. Roudiez. She is currently working on a book-length manuscript titled "Of Bodies and Technologies: Woman and the Machine."

RUTH-ELLEN BOETCHER JOERES   is professor of German at the University of Minnesota where she works in the social and literary history of German women in the eighteenth to twentieth centuries and in comparative feminist theories. She is coeditor of *Signs* and the author or editor of eight books, including *German Women in the Eighteenth and Nineteenth Centuries: A Social and Literary History* with Mary Jo Maynes (1986), *Interpreting Women's Lives: Feminist Theory and Personal Narratives* as part of the Personal Narratives Group (1989), and, most recently, *The Politics of the Essay: Feminist Perspectives* (in press), all from Indiana University Press (Bloomington).

TERRI BRINT JOSEPH   is an associate professor of English and comparative literature at Chapman University, where she teaches criticism, literature, and creative writing. She is coauthor with Roger Joseph of *The Rose and the Thorn: Semiotic Structures of Marriage in Morocco* (Tucson: University of Arizona Press, 1987), which presents in more detail some aspects of "Poetry as a Strategy of Power." Her study *Ezra Pound's Epic Variations* is to be published by the National Poetry Foundation at the University of Maine Press in 1993, and *"The Dancer" and Ballet Studio Poems* is scheduled for publication in 1993 by Inevitable Press.

AUDRE LORDE   (1934–92) was a professor of English at Hunter College, where she held the Thomas Hunter Chair. Teacher, poet, and activist, Lorde was a founder of Kitchen Table Women of Color Press and of SISA (Sisterhood in Support of Sisters in South Africa) and lectured widely throughout the United States and abroad. She was the author of ten volumes of poetry, a novel she called a biomythology, and three collections of essays. Among the best known of her works are *The Black Unicorn* (New York: Norton, 1978), *Zami: A New Spelling of My Name* (Trumansburg, N.Y.: Crossing Press, 1983), *The Cancer Journals* (Argyle, N.Y.: Spinsters, Ink, 1980), and the essays "Poetry Is Not a Luxury," "Uses of the Erotic: The Erotic as Power," and "The Uses of Anger: Women Responding to Racism," reprinted in *Sister Outsider* (Trumansburg, N.Y.: Crossing Press, 1984).

CARMEN NARANJO   is the Costa Rican author of more than twenty volumes of poetry and fiction. Her technically innovative novels and short stories have received Costa Rica's and Central America's most prestigious awards. (Three of her short stories are available in English translation: "The Flowery Trick," "The Journey of Journeys," and "Inventory of a Recluse" are included in *Five Women Writers of Costa Rica*, ed. Victoria Urbano [Beaumont, Tex.: Asociación de Literatura

Femina Hispanica, 1978].) She also has had a notable career in public administration, becoming the first woman to hold important administrative positions in several national and international organizations. She has headed the Central American University Publishing House (EDUCA) since 1984.

CHIKWENYE OKONJO OGUNYEMI is a member of the Sarah Lawrence College faculty, where she teaches courses in womanist fiction and in African and African-American literatures. She has just completed a book-length manuscript titled "Africa Wo/Man Palava: The Nigerian Novel by Women." She is currently writing a work titled "Ectomy: A Treasury of African Women's Writing."

LESLIE W. RABINE is professor of French and director of women's studies at the University of California, Irvine. She is author of *Reading the Romantic Heroine: Text, History, Ideology* (Ann Arbor: University of Michigan Press, 1985); coauthor with Claire Moses of *Feminists and French Romanticism* (Indiana University Press, in press); and coeditor with Sara Melzer of *Rebel Daughters: Women and the French Revolution* (New York: Oxford University Press, 1992). She is presently working on a project concerning figures of historical impasse in contemporary women's culture.

ADRIENNE RICH lives in California. She is a founding member of the collective editing *Bridges: A Journal for Jewish Feminists and Our Friends.* Her most recent volume of poems, *An Atlas of the Difficult World* (New York: Norton, 1991), received the Lenore Marshall/*Nation* prize, the *Los Angeles Times* Book Award in Poetry, the Lambda Literary Award in poetry, and the Poets' Prize. Her *Collected Early Poems, 1950–1970* will be published by Norton in 1993.

MADELON SPRENGNETHER is professor of English at the University of Minnesota, where she teaches critical and creative writing. She has published numerous articles on Renaissance literature and is a coeditor of *The (M)other Tongue: Essays in Feminist Psychoanalytic Interpretation* (Ithaca, N.Y.: Cornell University Press, 1987) with Shirley Nelson Garner and Clare Kohane. She is also the author of a collection of poems titled *The Normal Heart* (St. Paul, Minn.: New Rivers Press, 1981); a collection of personal essays titled *Rivers, Stories, Houses, Dreams* (St. Paul, Minn.: New Rivers Press, 1983); and a critical study titled *The Spectral Mother: Freud, Feminism, and Psychoanalysis* (Ithaca, N.Y.: Cornell University Press, 1990).

SANDRA A. ZAGARELL is professor of English at Oberlin College, where she teaches nineteenth-century American literature and feminist literary theory/criticism and has been an active member of the women studies program since 1979. She is coeditor with Lawrence Buell of *"The Morgesons" and Other Writings, Published and Unpublished, by Elizabeth Stoddard* (Philadelphia: University of Pennsylvania Press, 1984) and editor of *A New Home—Who'll Follow?* (New Brunswick, N.J.: Rutgers University Press, 1990) by Caroline Kirkland. She has published essays on nineteenth-century British and American literature and is writing a book-length study of the cultural work to which representations of community in nineteenth-century American literature laid claim.

JOYCE ZONANA is assistant professor of English and women's studies at the University of New Orleans. Her published articles include "'They Will Prove the Truth of My Tale': Letters as the Feminist Core of Mary Shelley's *Frankenstein,*" *Journal of Narrative Technique* 28, no. 2 (Spring 1991): 170–84; "Swinburne's Sappho: The Muse as Sister-Goddess," *Victorian Poetry* 28, no. 1 (Spring 1990): 39–50; "The Embodied Muse: Elizabeth Barrett Browning's 'Aurora Leigh' and Feminist Poetics," *Tulsa Studies in Women's Literature* 8, no. 2 (Fall 1989): 241–62; and "Matthew Arnold and the Muse: The Limits of the Olympian Ideal," *Victorian Poetry* 23, no. 1 (Spring 1985): 59–74. She is completing a book-length study of Victorian aesthetics, "The Earthly Muses," and her current interests are in feminist literary history, with emphasis on uses of classical and biblical motifs.

Index

Abortion: Simone de Beauvoir on, 38–39
African Diaspora: problems of women writers in, 235, 237; U.S. blacks' connections to, 108
African-American women. *See* Black women
Aidoo, Ama Ata, 232; on African women writers, 237; *Our Sister Killjoy,* 238, 241, 243, 245–46
AIDS: and racial/sexual stereotyping, 112
Althusser, Louis: on "ideological state apparatuses," 94
American Delsarte movement, 196–98; influence of on Ruth St. Denis, 199; Ted Shawn on, 198
Anatomy: and gender relations, 82–83; and sexuality, 82–83; *See also* Biology; Sex
Arizpe, Lourdes: interview with Carmen Naranjo, 51–63; *See also* Naranjo, Carmen, interviewed by Lourdes Arizpe
Art. *See* "High" art; "Exotic," the; Popular culture
Autobiography. *See* Personal narrative
Avant-garde, the: Carmen Naranjo and, 57; sexist views of, 57; Simone de Beauvoir on, 44–45

Bâ, Mariamba, 232; *So Long a Letter,* 241, 242, 243, 245

Bakhtin, M. M.: on power of language, 96
Baldwin, James: *The Fire Next Time,* 246
Barnett, Ida Wells: *See* Wells, Ida B.
Barthes, Roland: on race as myth, 94–95
Beauvoir, Simone de, interviewed by Alice Jardine, 37–49; on abortion, 38–39; on autobiography, 47; on the avant-garde, 44–45; on battering, 38–39; on capitalism, 40; on Cixous, 42, 44; on class and language, 43, 44; on class struggle, 40, 48; on Colette, 46; on essentialism, 43; on ethnology, 47; on existentialism, 37, 45; on the family, 42, 48; on fascism and women, 45–46; on feminine vs. feminist, 46; on "feminine" writing style, 42, 44; on feminism, 39, 40–41, 42, 48; on Freud, 41; on Friedan, 39; on Goldman, 47; on her books, 46, 49; on human universality, 44; on ideological domination, 44; on Irigaray, 41, 45; on Kristeva, 45; on Lacan, 41; on R. D. Laing and Mary Barnes, 42; on language, 42, 43–44; on Marxism, 39, 40; on men writing about women, 46; on Millett, 47; on Nin, 47; on oppression, 44, 45–46; on politics, 39, 40; on